TOLSTOY ON THE COUCH

Tolstoy on the Couch

Misogyny, Masochism and the Absent Mother

Daniel Rancour-Laferriere

NEW YORK UNIVERSITY PRESS
Washington Square, New York

© Daniel Rancour-Laferriere 1998

First published in the U.S.A. in 1998 by
NEW YORK UNIVERSITY PRESS
Washington Square
New York, N.Y. 10003

This book is printed on paper suitable for recycling and
made from fully managed and sustained forest sources.

Library of Congress Cataloging-in-Publication Data
Rancour-Laferriere, Daniel.
Tolstoy on the couch : misogyny, masochism, and the absent mother
/ Daniel Rancour-Laferriere.
p. cm.
Includes bibliographical references and index.
ISBN 0-8147-7509-8
1. Tolstoy, Leo, graf, 1828-1910—Mental health. 2. Tolstoy, Leo,
graf, 1828-1910—Psychology. 3. Tolstoy, Leo, graf, 1828-1910-
-Relations with women. 4. Misogyny in literature. 5. Masochism in
literature. 6. Psychoanalysis and literature. I. Title.
PG3415.M45R36 1998
891.73'3—dc21
                                                        98-6757
                                                        CIP

Printed in Great Britain

Contents

Acknowledgements and Abbreviations

I am indebted to many people who have commented in a constructive way on ideas raised in successive drafts of this book. Most influential was my wife, Barbara Milman, who encouraged me to look long and hard at the dark, misogynistic side of Tolstoy's psyche. Yuri Druzhnikov, my Russian colleague at the University of California in Davis, provided extensive consultations on Tolstoy's often tricky use of the Russian language. Other scholars who have been helpful include: Joe Aimone, Kay Blacker, Catherine Chvany, Jackie Dello-Russo, Joanne Diehl, Carl Eby, Alan Elms, Aleksandr Etkind, Jim Gallant, Assya Humeska, Charles Isenberg, Kathryn Jaeger, Gary Jahn, Andrew Jones, Lola Komarova, Ronald LeBlanc, Hugh McLean, Karl Menges, Robert A. Nemiroff, Thomas Newlin, David L. Ransel, James L. Rice, Mikhail Romashkevich, Lev Tokarev and Alexander Zholkovsky. I am particularly grateful to the members of the UC Davis Humanities Research Cluster in Psychoanalysis for their attentive comments on a presentation I made in November of 1995. Timothy Bartlett of New York University Press provided extremely valuable editorial advice. For technical assistance I want to thank Nina Anderson, Jackie DiClementine, Tamara Grivicic and Shidan Lotfi. Opritsa Popa and the personnel of the Interlibrary Loan Office of Shields Library at UC Davis were unfailingly helpful. Finally, I want to thank UC Davis for providing a series of Faculty Research Grants as well as a Publication Grant for this book.

As a basic working text for *The Kreutzer Sonata* I am using the version published in volume 27 of the Jubilee Edition of Tolstoy's works (here indicated as 27: 5–92). All references to Tolstoy's works in the original Russian are from the Jubilee Edition. In some cases I have made slight emendations in the cited translations of Tolstoy, including the excellent translation of *The Kreutzer Sonata* by David McDuff (= Tolstoy 1983). When translating diaries and drafts I have not fixed them up, but deliberately left them in a semblance of their rough, often stylistically imperfect condition. Many of the draft and diary materials are here translated into English for the first time. Translations of Russian texts are mine when not otherwise indicated. Quotations of Freud will be from the Standard Edition, here abbreviated *SE*.

Dates of events in Tolstoy's lifetime are given according to the Old Style or Julian calendar, in use in Russia until 1918 (12 days behind the New Style or Gregorian calendar in the nineteenth century, 13 days behind in the twentieth century).

1

Introduction

1. THE PARADOXICAL TOLSTOY

In the year 1888 Lev Tolstoy decided that human sexual intercourse *should no longer exist*. Tolstoy was, as he later admitted, 'horrified' by this conclusion. Yet for the rest of his life he honestly believed that total sexual abstinence was best. Frequenter of brothels in his youth, father of 13 children by his wife, and at least two children by peasant women before he was married,[1] Tolstoy now had the arrogance to suggest that it would be a good idea if people stopped having children. This 'tireless fucker', as he referred to his younger self in conversation with Maksim Gorky,[2] was repudiating an essential part of himself, and of humanity generally.

How can such a repudiation be explained? It was not merely a literary fact – although it was first revealed to the world in a literary work, entitled *The Kreutzer Sonata* (1889). It was not a religious belief either, although Tolstoy did marshal quotations from the bible to support his thesis. Tolstoy's repudiation of sex was, rather, a fact of his particular biography, a strikingly personal declaration reflecting the state of his psyche at the time he made it.

Tolstoy's rejection of sex was a personal matter, and personal matters are an appropriate subject for psychoanalytic study. In this case, moreover, the personal concern arose within a specific time frame, and was developed in a particular literary work of moderate length. It thus constitutes a well-defined and feasible topic for psychoanalytic study.

Some years ago I suggested that someone, someday, ought to write a psychobiography of Lev Nikolaevich Tolstoy.[3] That someone is not me, however. A true psychobiography of Tolstoy would be a lifetime project (like Leon Edel on Henry James), and I have neither the lifetime nor the desire to produce a full psychobiography of Tolstoy. Even an ordinary scholarly biography of Tolstoy, lacking the depth a psychobiography is supposed to achieve, seems impossibly huge. One thinks of Nikolai Nikolaevich Gusev who, by the time of his death at the age of 86, had only reached the year 1885 in his monumental four-volume work *Lev Nikolaevich Tolstoi. Materials for*

1

a Biography (Moscow, 1954–70). If Tolstoy was too big for Gusev, then who will ever truly encompass him?

Tolstoy's (still incomplete) works come to an impressive total of 91 volumes. Everything contained in these volumes (minus the commentary and the index volume) is a part of Tolstoy's biography. The real, live Lev Nikolaevich wrote what is printed there. For example, every single messy page of every single draft of *The Kreutzer Sonata* has to be a part of Tolstoy's biography, for Tolstoy went to the trouble of writing each page within the bounds of his real lifetime, not within some postmodern, intertextual pseudo-time concocted by late twentieth-century academics. It may be possible to read, appreciate, and even psychoanalyse Tolstoy's literary works without knowing much about Tolstoy 'the man', and here Tolstoy does live beyond the bounds of his literal lifetime. But it is impossible to study the live Tolstoy without an intimate knowledge of the works he produced while he was in the business of living. This is as true of the great novels *War and Peace* and *Anna Karenina* as of the autobiographical *Confession*. Works are always part of a writer's biography, even if the biography does not always take part in the works.

A major problem faced by Tolstoy's would-be biographer is his profound contradictoriness. Tolstoy is a riddle (*zagadka*), as Mark Aldanov said, or a rebus (*ogromnyi moral'nyi rebus*), as N. Timkovskii put it.[4] Tolstoy is a bundle of dualisms, ambivalences, and paradoxes, a 'man of extremes' as E. J. Dillon called him.[5]

The renunciation of sex by a highly sexual man is only one of the contradictions. Born into a wealthy family of Russian nobility, Tolstoy later renounced his property and spent much of his time performing activities appropriate for a lowly peasant, such as ploughing fields, bootmaking, chopping wood, dressing in peasant garb, and so on. Author of two universally acclaimed novels, he later rejected these and various other great works of literary art as immoral. Yet even after he renounced his property and rejected literature, he continued to live off his property and write literary works.

Although educated in the tradition of eighteenth-century rationalism and reason, Tolstoy eventually rejected rationalism, and became an advocate of such arguably irrational views as nonresistance to evil, vegetarianism, pacifism, and total abstinence from sex. Tolstoy's hostility to developments in contemporary science and philosophy was particularly strong – and contagious: to this day there are Tolstoy scholars who are only too eager to follow the master in his anti-intellectualism.

As for Tolstoy's attitude toward the course of history, he knew much more than he thought he knew, or was willing to admit that he knew. Isaiah Berlin characterizes Tolstoy as a savvy 'fox' who convinced himself and others that he had the plodding, single vision of a 'hedgehog'.[6] In his art Tolstoy saw and understood so much, yet, as Aldanov observes, he was always trying to reduce his own field of vision with an almost bureaucratic dogmatism.[7]

If, on the one hand, Tolstoy felt a strong urge to belong, to even 'merge with' the large human (especially Russian) collective, on the other hand he was equally a loner, a 'stranger' within that collective, as Richard F. Gustafson convincingly argues.[8]

Having brooded over the problem of death for most of his life, and having written masterpieces on this theme (*The Death of Ivan Ilyich, Khadzhi Murat*), Tolstoy died an unpeaceful, unseemly death in a train station while on the run from his wife.

When writing *The Kreutzer Sonata* Tolstoy was convinced of the need for total sexual abstinence, yet at the same time he was unable to desist from having sexual intercourse with his wife. While preaching at this time to his public and to himself about the importance of spiritual love, unmistakable signs of hatred for his wife and for women generally keep cropping up.

I cannot begin to classify or otherwise make sense of *all* the contradictions and paradoxes of Tolstoy's life and works. This is not my task, although perhaps it will be someone's task in the future. My goal here is rather more limited. Tolstoy's contradictory feelings about women and sexuality – more prominently paraded in *The Kreutzer Sonata* than in any other of his works – will be the primary concern of this book. Tolstoy's repudiation of sex is embedded within a complex of polarized feelings about women and sexuality. Tolstoy both desired women and punished himself for his desire. He both needed to damage a woman with his sexuality, and to refrain from damaging her. He both idealized women in their maternal role and hated mothers. These and other personal ambivalences spawned the many and fascinating ambiguities of his novella on human sexuality.

2. WHY PSYCHOANALYSIS APPLIES

Tolstoy's attitude toward women was highly ambivalent, as Ruth Crego Benson showed in her forthright study of ideal versus erotic images of women in Tolstoy. For example, while Natasha Rostova is up on the narrator's pedestal for most of the duration of *War and Peace*, the sexually attractive Stepanida comes from the depths of hell, she is the very 'devil' in a late story of that name.[9] If woman is 'stupid' and an 'agent of the devil' in a diary entry of 3 August 1898, in the same entry she is also a saviour: 'Oh, how I would love to show woman all the significance of the virgin woman! The virgin woman (the legend of Maria is no accident) will save the world.'[10]

Taking Tolstoy's mature ambivalence toward women as a given, I wish to look into its early ontogenetic background, to connect it with the mood disorder which afflicted Tolstoy, and most importantly, to investigate the negative pole of the ambivalence expressed in *The Kreutzer Sonata*. Tolstoy's novella is, after all, about the murder of a woman. Bluntly stated, the novella is about Tolstoy's misogyny.

Often, and in a variety of contexts, Tolstoy expressed hostility toward women. In all-male company he was inclined to refer to women with obscene terms.[11] Mere mention of 'the woman question' would invariably make him angry. At a gathering of Petersburg literati in 1856 the young Tolstoy expressed his hatred for Georges Sand, declaring that the heroines of her novels ought to be tied to a wagon and paraded in disgrace about the streets of Petersburg.[12] On numerous occasions and at various periods in his life, from adolescence to old age, Tolstoy would vent his animosity toward women in a straightforward manner:

To marry a young lady means dumping on yourself the whole poison of civilization [*ves' iad tsivilizatsii*].[13]

... women are generally so bad that the difference between a good and a bad woman scarcely exists.[14]

Regard the society of women as an inevitable nuisance of social life, and avoid them as much as possible. Because from whom do we actually learn voluptuousness, effeminacy, frivolity in everything and a multitude of other vices, if not from women? Who is responsible for the fact that we lose such feelings inherent in us as courage, firmness, prudence, fairness, and so on, if not women? Women are more receptive than men, and during the age of virtue were better than we were; but now in this age of corruption and vice they are worse than we are.[15]

Everything would be fine if only they (women) would be in their place, i.e., submissive [*smirenny*].[16]

For seventy years my opinion about women has fallen lower and lower, and it's still falling even lower. The woman question! How can there not be a woman question? But it should have nothing to do with how women should begin to direct life, but how they should stop ruining it.[17]

When I read a letter and see a woman's signature on it, it no longer interests me.[18]

. . . If men knew all women the way a husband knows his wife, then they would never enter into serious conversation with them about anything.[19]

I will hunt for a friend among men. For me no woman can substitute for a friend. Why do we lie to our wives, saying that we consider them our true friends?[20]

One cannot expect a woman to evaluate her feeling of exclusive love on the basis of moral feeling. She cannot do this because she has no true moral feeling, that is, feeling which stands above everything.[21]

Yes, give a woman only a beautiful exterior, and she will be happy. . . .[22]

For a woman it is very important whether there is more or less sugar, or more or less money, but she is sincerely convinced that it makes no difference whether there is more or less truth.[23]

Maksim Gorky's intuition that Tolstoy was 'implacably hostile'[24] toward women is borne out by this sampling. So also is Tolstoy's friend Andrei Rusanov's conclusion that Tolstoy 'did not like women', or pianist Alexander Goldenweiser's observation that 'Lev Nikolaevich rather often, especially in half-joking conversations, displayed features of misogyny [*cherty zhenofobstva*]. . . '.[25]

Examples of Tolstoy's misogyny could be multiplied – and will indeed be multiplied in due course. When it comes to sexuality, especially sexuality in the context of marriage and motherhood, the hostility toward women is even more graphic and intense. *The Kreutzer Sonata*, in all of its drafts and variants, will demonstrate this. All his adult life Tolstoy felt a hatred for woman in her bodily, sexual aspect, but because this particular masterpiece goes to such extremes, the deep psychological structure of the hatred becomes visible.

The object of Tolstoy's hatred, as it turns out, is as much himself as it is women. There is masochistic aggression directed at the self as well as sadistic impulses toward women. Not only women, but men such as Tolstoy himself should remain virgin. Not only women, but men too should be punished for their sexuality. I hope to establish that Tolstoy's misogyny cannot be understood without reference to his moral masochism. Anna Karenina's suicide, for example, is as much a representation of Tolstoy's own wish to punish or kill himself for his sexuality as it is a representation of his hostility toward unfaithful women.[26] Part of this necessary linkage stems from the onto-genetically archaic confusion between mother and child typically experienced in early development, and exacerbated in Tolstoy's particular case by early maternal loss. Punishment of the other and punishment of the self are easily confused when self is confused with (m)other.

There is a narcissistic disturbance in Tolstoy's advocacy of complete chastity: everyone should aim to abstain from sex, in effect, because Lev Nikolaevich Tolstoy so aimed. Tolstoy was blind to the idiosyncrasy of his guilt feelings about marital sex, his odd need to punish himself (and his wife) with attempted sexual abstinence. To Gorky he spoke darkly of 'the tragedy of the bedroom' – as if this idea were somehow self-evident, as if marital sexuality were indeed a misfortune worse than 'earthquakes, epidemics, the horrors of disease, and all kinds of spiritual torments'.[27]

The focus here is on Tolstoy, not his reading public. True, to a large extent it was Tolstoy himself who legitimized wide discussion of the so-called 'sex question' (*polovoi vopros*) in Russia toward the end of the last century. He managed to break a taboo that other writers had not broken. But little can be added to Peter Ulf Møller's marvellous book on the sexual debate which erupted in Russia and abroad after the publication of *The Kreutzer Sonata*, or to Laura Engelstein's more wide-ranging volume on sex and modernity in *fin-de-siècle* Russia.[28] Much can be learned about the history and sociology of attitudes toward sexuality from the public discussions which took place about a century ago. But surprisingly little of psychological depth has been written about the individual who, in large measure, provoked them.

Perhaps this is because what is hidden in the private psyche of a great man can be even more disturbing than what is out in the public domain. In any case, a close psychological reading of the Russian original of Tolstoy's novella (in all its drafts and variants) has never been performed before, nor have the personal diaries and correspondence from the period of writing the novella ever been psychoanalysed in conjunction with the novella. At the very least Tolstoy *invites* psychological study because he took the trouble to write detailed and self-avowedly frank diaries about himself (and declined to make any arrangements for the diaries to be destroyed).

This book will often make reference to psychoanalytic categories to characterize Tolstoy's activities and attitudes, for example 'depressive', 'anxious', 'manic', 'paranoid', 'masochistic', 'narcissistic', 'pre-Oedipal', 'selfobject', and so on. Such terms will be used in a technical sense, but they are also readily understandable to any intelligent reader, and in any case I will explain each one as it is introduced. This procedure is preferable to avoiding the terms altogether (and thereby avoiding Tolstoy's psyche in large measure), or to using inappropriate terms (for example, terms popular in Tolstoy's day when psychological knowledge was less sophisticated than it is today). This procedure is also preferable to utilizing exclusively literary terms, such as 'psychologism', 'realism', 'prosaics', 'monologic', 'homophonic', 'chronotope', 'unmasking', and so on – all of which can be interesting in their own right, but which in the past have had the effect of glossing over inconvenient psychological issues. In any case the concern here is broadly biographical, not exclusively literary.

Although my approach to the living Tolstoy is psychoanalytic, it is not narrowly 'Freudian'. In addition to some of Freud's classical concepts I will be making use of the so-called object relations theories of Melanie Klein and D. W. Winnicott, the self psychology of Heinz Kohut, the separation-individuation theory of Margaret Mahler, and John Bowlby's attachment theory. These ideas and theories will be explained at those points in my account where they become relevant to Tolstoy's psyche. They may at first seem a little obscure to Slavic specialists, but they are commonly applied in current psychoanalytic literary scholarship in the West,[29] and they are becoming staples of the recently reborn psychoanalysis in Russia as well.[30]

In applying psychoanalytic concepts to Tolstoy I will, in a sense, be diagnosing him. But this book is not wholly clinical. It contains

no therapeutic recommendations. Even if Tolstoy were still alive I
would have no interest in 'curing' him, for I suspect his various
psychical ailments were essential to his great art (even if, toward the
end of his life, they started to interfere with it). In addition, there was
much about Tolstoy that was ordinary and normal – yet also
psychoanalyzable, because psychoanalytic concepts apply not only
to mental disturbances. Clinical psychoanalysis is not the only kind
of psychoanalysis.

What I am aiming for is psychoanalytic understanding of the
genesis of a particular work. I wish to explain how and why Tolstoy
arrived at the controversial meanings and images of *The Kreutzer
Sonata*. This book is an exercise in applied, not clinical psychoanalysis.

Some might object that, since Tolstoy is dead, he is no longer available to lie down on the couch and free-associate in the fashion practised in strictly clinical analysis. Quite frankly, however, no clinician
ever had a patient about whom so much detailed and *intimate* information is available as we have about Lev Tolstoy. Not only did
the introspective Tolstoy strive for maximal explicitness and honesty
in his diaries, he had a wife, children, and other relatives, as well
as many friends and colleagues who left behind detailed memoirs
about their relationships with him. Many of these memoirs are included in the bibliography at the end of this book. No single one of
the memoirs is itself adequate to Tolstoy's complexity,[31] and I have
excluded items definitely known to be untrustworthy.[32] But taken
together, the reliable memoirs form a rich psychological trove. Ordinarily a clinician merely works with a patient one-on-one, bringing in
family members and friends for consultation only occasionally, if
ever. In Tolstoy's case the 'patient' has been described by so many
witnesses, and from so many different perspectives, that it is possible to gain deep insight into his psyche – if one is actually willing,
that is, to scrutinize the many volumes of available information.

I have heard some of my Slavist colleagues complain that Tolstoy's
life is 'overdocumented'. This is no doubt true for Slavists who
would rather not have to read the available documents – especially
those intimate, revealing documents which do not always show the
great man in the best light. In my opinion, anyone who suggests that
there is too much to know should automatically be suspected of not
wanting to know too much. But for the scholar who is willing to
plunge into the immense sea of published detail that we have about
Tolstoy's everyday life, who is willing to consider the potential
meanings of trivia – the petty outburst at the wife, the temporary

stomach pain, the slip of the pen, the rejected line or paragraph, the joke told on the sly, and so on – it becomes possible actually to synthesize something new concerning the great and 'overdocumented' Tolstoy. In any serious psychobiographical enterprise, as psychologist Alan Elms says, 'the phrase "Too much data" is an oxymoron'.[33]

Because mundane events in the everyday life of the author of *The Kreutzer Sonata* are as important to psychoanalyzing the author as is the novella itself, much of the present study will be concerned with what was going on in Tolstoy's life during the late 1880s. I will be particularly interested in the year 1889, when most of the composition of the novella actually took place, and when Tolstoy's relations with his wife Sofia Andreevna Tolstaia were strained – to put it mildly.

As a kind of clinical prelude to all of this I am also going to psychoanalyse a brief but famous psychical disturbance which Tolstoy experienced 20 years earlier, in 1869, and which is known in the critical literature as 'the Arzamas horror' (Chapter 2). This analysis, will highlight Tolstoy's vulnerability to separation anxiety and depression, and will lead to a consideration of the immensely important role which Tolstoy's dead mother played in his life and works (Chapter 3). Once the significance of the mother is established, it will be possible to perform the main tasks of this book: to lay bare the argument Tolstoy makes for sexual abstinence in *The Kreutzer Sonata* (Chapter 4), and to psychoanalyse the matricidal psyche which generated this argument (Chapter 5). In other words, I will attempt to show that Tolstoy's ideal of sexual abstinence derives from guilt over uncontrollable rage at the mother who died on him in early childhood. Along the way it will become increasingly clear that Tolstoy suffered an overall disturbance of the self as a result of this loss, with symptoms ranging from grandiosity, paradoxically low self-esteem, and an unclear sense of personal boundaries (Chapter 6). Finally, I will switch my perspective from Tolstoy to the wife whom he victimized with his problems (Chapter 7), and I will close by lamenting the failure of the Russians to publish the full and uncensored autobiography of this most important woman in Tolstoy's life.

2

The Arzamas Horror: a Sample of Tolstoy's Psychopathology

In early September of 1869 Lev Tolstoy had a very disturbing psychical experience which has come to be known in the scholarly literature as the Arzamas horror (*arzamasskii uzhas*) – after the town in central Russia where it took place. The biographical circumstances leading up to this experience are known in some detail, and there is a psychologically revealing fictional representation of the experience as well, entitled 'Notes of a Madman' (*Zapiski sumashedshego*), written in 1884).[34] My purpose here is to psychoanalyse the Arzamas horror in both its non-fictional and fictional variants, and to expose the basic mechanisms whereby Tolstoy came to deal with anxiety and depression.

1. SEPARATING FROM HIS WIFE, HIS FAMILY, HIS NOVEL

In August of 1869, shortly after completing *War and Peace*,[35] Tolstoy read in a newspaper that there was an estate for sale in the village of Il'mino in distant Penza province. Since Tolstoy needed a diversion after his enormous labours, and since he had some extra money received for earlier instalments of the novel, he decided to travel the 1600 kilometres (round trip) to have a look at the estate.[36]

The summer of 1869 had not been a good one for Tolstoy. Bringing his great novel to completion left him in a foul, somewhat depressed mood. According to his wife he spoke frequently of death: '. . . often he said that his brain hurt [*mozg bolit*], that some terrible work was going on inside him, that everything was over for him, that it was time to die and so on'.[37] Given this situation, a change of scene might have seemed attractive. But Tolstoy had not yet made plans about how to occupy himself in the future. And, for someone preoccupied with thoughts of death, a *long* journey *alone* was certainly ill-advised: *Partir, c'est mourir un peu.*

On 31 August, just three days after his birthday, Tolstoy and a young servant named Sergei Petrovich Arbuzov set off from Tula by rail.[38] Once in Moscow, Tolstoy became very concerned about which route to take from there. On 1 September he wrote to his wife from Moscow, saying: 'I spent all day asking questions and in a state of indecision, what route should I take, through Morshansk or through Nizhnii [Novgorod]?' From all of his inquiries the route through Morshansk seemed 'indeterminate, and one might make mistakes', so he opted to travel through Nizhnii. This meant that his wife should write to him in Nizhnii and in Saransk, according to the instructions in the letter. Tolstoy was not going to do without Sonia entirely for the two weeks of their time apart. Her letters were so important to him, in fact, that he added toward the end of his letter: 'In any case I shall be returning in order to receive your letters.' And just in case the letters might miss him, he later made arrangements for them to be returned to Tula where he could be sure to have them, even after his trip was over.[39] In all of this Tolstoy seems overly anxious about maintaining contact with his wife. That is, there is some degree of separation anxiety (and to judge from letters written to Sonia on other occasions when he travelled away from her, this was not the first time Tolstoy had experienced such anxiety).[40]

Having passed through Moscow, Tolstoy and his manservant arrived in Nizhnii Novgorod on the morning of 2 September. There new difficulties arose. It was not easy to obtain an adequate carriage and horses. Tolstoy was afraid that the available carriages would break down, or get stuck in the mud. Because the local fair season was coming to an end, there would be no fresh horses available at nearby transit points. But he wanted a carriage in which he would not have to travel continuously day and night, either. He wrote home to Sonia about these anxieties in some detail that very day.[41] Eventually he hired a post-chaise drawn by a troika of horses, and set off for Il'mino with his servant.[42]

That night the two stopped at a hotel in Arzamas. What happened next is related in a letter to Sonia of 4 September from Saransk:

How are you and the children? Has anything happened? For two days I have been tortured with anxiety. On the night [of the second of September] I stayed overnight in Arzamas, and something unusual happened to me. It was two in the morning, I was terribly tired, I wanted to sleep and nothing hurt. But suddenly such utter anguish, fear, and horror came over me [*na menia nashla toska, strakh, uzhas takie*], as I had never experienced. I'll tell you the details of this feeling later, but I've never experienced such an agonizing feeling before, and God forbid anyone else should experience it. I jumped up and ordered the horses harnessed. While they were being harnessed I dozed off, and woke up feeling fine. Yesterday the feeling returned to a much lesser extent while travelling, but I was prepared and did not yield to it, especially since it was weak. Today I feel healthy and jolly – as much as I can be when apart from the family.[43]

The awful feeling which hits Tolstoy in this passage is clearly in the clinical realm. The 'fear' and 'horror' come on 'suddenly', as Tolstoy says, and they are intense, although *there is nothing concrete to be afraid of, nothing objectively threatening*. As for the 'anguish' – whereby I attempt to translate the untranslatable Russian *toska* – it suggests both the clinical categories of anxiety and depression. Tolstoy is describing what would be recognized today as an anxiety attack (or panic attack) with associated depressive features,[44] or what might more broadly be called depressive anxiety.[45] This idea is supported linguistically by the fact that the standard Ozhegov dictionary defines *toska* as *Dushevnaia trevoga, soedinennaia s grust'iu i skukoi.*[46] That is, both anxiety (*trevoga*) and depressive feelings (*grust'* and *skuka*) are united in the one Russian notion of *toska*. There are also overtones of separation and death in the word. Writing to Sonia in 1871, Tolstoy described *toska* as 'a feeling . . . that the soul is parting from the body'.[47] Death is of course a thought which preoccupies anyone suffering from depression.

Since no one word in English can capture the polysemy of *toska*, and since the word will keep coming up, especially when Tolstoy fictionalizes the Arzamas experience, I will simplify matters by leaving the word untranslated for the duration.[48] But I will speak of depressive anxiety when I am not specifically translating the word.

So, Tolstoy has a severe attack of *toska* or depressive anxiety in Arzamas. The attack is severe enough that it will not go away 'for two days'. Tolstoy had experienced some depression before (for example, when his brother Nikolai died in 1860, or the sporadic low moods when he was writing *War and Peace*),[49] but apparently never anything like this. The Arzamas attack was special, as evidenced by the fact that later attacks of a similar nature were termed the 'Arzamas *toska*' by Tolstoy.[50]

Looking again at the passage quoted from the letter to Sonia, we can see that Tolstoy relates his attack to the continuing separation from his wife and family. The two opening questions suggest not only that Tolstoy has not yet received any word from his wife, but that the attack itself might have something to do with the lack of word from her. There is a slightly superstitious overtone to the questions. *His* attack might be related to something imagined to have happened to *her* (*Ne sluchilos' li chto?*).[51] Objectively, however, anything that might have happened to Sonia is irrelevant. Tolstoy is simply overly aware of the connection between himself and his family at this particular moment of being separated from them ('apart from the family [*vne sem'i*]'). He says so himself right after the passage just quoted: 'On this trip I have for the first time begun to feel how extensively I have become fused with you and the children [*do kakoi stepeni ia srossia s toboi i s det'mi*].' This echoes a statement from two letters back: 'I am always with you . . .'.[52]

To feel this close to wife and family is to indicate how painful it is to be separated from them. But separation does more than make Tolstoy's heart grow fonder, as we have seen. It makes him actually anxious and depressed.

Separation from the recently completed novel is also important. As Richard Gustafson says, the Arzamas horror represents 'a crisis of vocation experienced upon the completion of a major work'.[53] Completion of the novel is, moreover, related to separation from the wife and family. The writing of the novel, with its abundant family thematics, had up until now served as the *occasion* to remain 'fused' with the wife and family. But with the novel done, Tolstoy is very much at loose ends. He has undergone what in current psychological parlance would be termed a 'major life event', which normally increases the risk of anxiety and depression.[54]

The lack of a novel to work on makes Tolstoy incapable of simply being alone:

> I can remain alone while constantly busy, such as when I visit Moscow, but now, when there is nothing to do, I definitely feel that I cannot be alone.[55]

The letter concludes with a declaration: 'The one *good* thing is that thoughts about the novel and about philosophy are completely gone.'[56] But this is precisely the problem. Having finished his novel (with its final 'philosophical' chapter) once and for all, there is now 'nothing to do', so Tolstoy feels lonely and depressed. The fact of having finished *War and Peace* is not at all a 'good thing' for Tolstoy's mental health.

In English one might say that Tolstoy feels left out in the cold by his own act of closure. He is literally cold as he travels further away from his novel in time, and further away from his wife and family in space. He mentions that he forgot to bring his leather coat (*kozhan*), and says: 'The most terrible thing is the foul weather. Just the thought of travelling back those 300 versts through the mud makes my skin creep [*moroz podiraet po kozhe*].'[57]

Although he is not literally alone (the servant Arbuzov is with him), Tolstoy nonetheless insists that he has been utterly alone on the road: 'I travelled the whole time alone, as in a desert, not encountering a single civilized human being.' He must have encountered some peasants, at least, along the way, but apparently they were not 'civilized', and do not count. He encounters some 'wonderful peasant buildings', but does not like them for some reason. The most important thing is the feeling of loneliness, despite the presence of human beings in the form of peasants. Three times within the space of a few lines the word 'alone' (*odin*) occurs.[58] In the previous letter to his wife, too, he had described himself as alone, regardless of his servant's presence: 'I rode from Moscow to Nizhnii [Novgorod] absolutely alone [*reshitel'no odin*], except that as far as Pavlov, 60 versts from Moscow, there travelled with me a merchant, the rich man Labzin, with whom I had an extremely interesting conversation about the divine.'[59] With a rich stranger Tolstoy is not 'alone', but with his social inferior Arbuzov he is 'absolutely alone'. This is obviously not still the attitude of the older Tolstoy, who valued the peasants and arranged to spend as much time with them as possible.

2. ALONE AND ANXIOUS

In 1958 British psychoanalyst D. W. Winnicott published an interesting essay entitled 'The Capacity to Be Alone'. This work is primarily about children, but its conclusions are relevant to a disturbed adult such as the journeying Tolstoy, who is temporarily unable to be alone.

According to Winnicott, in normal development the child acquires an ability to be alone at an early age, in the presence of a mother who is available but not demanding. The 'good-enough' mother provides what Winnicott calls an 'ego-supportive environment' for the child:

> Gradually, the ego-supportive environment is introjected and built into the individual's personality, so that there comes about a capacity actually to be alone. Even so, theoreticaly, there is always someone present, someone who is equated ultimately and unconsciously with the mother, the person who, in the early days and weeks, was temporarily identified with her infant, and for the time being was interested in nothing else but the care of her own infant.[60]

Paradoxically, learning to be alone without anxiety occurs when the child is not literally alone, but is with the mother (or primary caretaker) while at the same time apparently disregarding her. Having unconsciously 'introjected' the mother's supportive presence, the child eventually is able to be alone literally, and not experience anxiety or depression except under unusual circumstances. This ability is one of the key signs of emotional maturity.

Before the child learns to be alone it is especially vulnerable to something called separation anxiety. Freud describes this in his 1926 essay *Inhibitions, Symptoms and Anxiety*:

> As soon as it [the child] loses sight of its mother it behaves as if it were never going to see her again; and repeated consoling experiences to the contrary are necessary before it learns that her disappearance is usually followed by her re-appearance. Its mother encourages this piece of knowledge which is so vital to it by playing the familiar game of hiding her face from it with her hands and then, to its joy, uncovering it again. In these circumstances it can, as it were, feel longing unaccompanied by despair.[61]

Since Freud's time the behavioural and emotional components of separation anxiety (or, when chronic, 'separation anxiety disorder') have been studied in considerable detail.[62] Separation anxiety typically occurs in children aged eight months to four years, and its most notable manifestations are crying, following, and clinging to the primary caregiver, normally the mother. With time such anxiety may be directed toward other trusted adults.

In the psychological literature separation anxiety is said to occur not only in children separated from caretaking figures, but also in adults separated from persons (or places) of psychological significance. Any psychologically healthy adult is capable of experiencing separation anxiety. For example, an individual going through a divorce may experience anxiety of separation from the spouse (even when there is intense conflict with the spouse). There is often a highly ambivalent attachment to the person whom one is anxious about being separated from. Neurotic individuals tend to experience separation anxiety intensely and frequently. For some analysts (especially Bowlby), most forms of adult anxiety have their ontogenetic prototype in anxiety of separation from the mother. Adults with multiple anxiety disorders are more likely to have experienced separation anxiety in childhood than other adults. Agoraphobia itself may be difficult to distinguish from severe separation anxiety, and may be interpreted as an adult form of separation anxiety.[63]

To judge from the psychoanalytic and psychiatric literature, one aspect of Tolstoy's horrible experience in Arzamas must have been separation anxiety. There was more to the experience than separation anxiety, of course; in particular there was depression. But Tolstoy's repeated references to maintaining written contact with Sonia, to being extremely close to her and the children in the past, and to feeling utterly alone as he travels – all point to a core of separation anxiety in the panic attack which took place in the Arzamas hotel room.

Also to judge from the psychoanalytic literature, as we have seen, Tolstoy's mother must somehow have been involved in the attack. This is hardly clear from the letters to Sonia, however (unless Sonia herself is understood to be a mother figure or maternal icon, as I will argue later). But fortunately there is also a fictional representation of the Arzamas horror. Tolstoy's 'Notes of a Madman' provide a rich psychological narrative through which we can explore the depressive dimension of the Arzamas horror, as well as catch a glimpse of Tolstoy's dead mother.

3. DABBLING IN MADNESS

'The Notes of a Madman' is a work of fiction which Tolstoy started in 1884 and never finished. It was only published posthumously in 1912. Tolstoy scholars generally agree that the work refers in part to the Arzamas experience.[64] Why Tolstoy neither finished the work nor published it during his lifetime is not known. But *because* the work is unfinished it has to be relatively close to the Arzamas experience, that is, it must be more revealing, biographically, than a polished literary representation of the experience would have been. As Lev Shestov commented: 'A sketch, a few words, a half-formed thought, can often tell us more than a finished work; the man has not yet had time to adapt his visions to the demands of society.'[65]

Scholars agree that 'Notes of a Madman' is unusual, even pathological. What the work offers, according to Shestov, is 'the brutal, naked truth' about Tolstoy the man. It is a truthful representation of the older Tolstoy's real 'madness', a mental state which is 'a challenge to all normal, human consciousness'.[66] According to G. W. Spence, in the work Tolstoy confronts his own mortality 'with pathological intensity'.[67]

A major consequence of what the 'madman' goes through is an affirmation of the existence of God. If in *Confession* (1879–80) Tolstoy's rediscovery of God is offered to the reader as a consequence of certain reasoned arguments (or at least an attempt at being logical and coherent), in 'Notes of a Madman' it is the spontaneous result of raw anxiety, depression, and guilt. If *Confession* was suitable for public consumption (even though the tsarist censors banned it), 'Notes of a Madman' was most unsuitable because it exposed all too clearly the psychopathology at the heart of Tolstoy's religion.

Although Tolstoy scholars explicitly or implicitly recognize that the narrator of 'Notes of a Madman' is suffering from a mental disorder, they generally are quite vague about the nature of the disorder, and thus they add little to what Tolstoy himself says in the very title of his work. After all, the narrator admits that he has 'attacks' (*pripadki*) and that he is a 'madman' (*sumashedshii*).

The narrator of the work must to a large degree be Tolstoy himself, who admitted to his wife the year following the Arzamas event that he was actually afraid of going mad:

> Sometimes it seems to him – *and this always comes over him away from home and the family* – that he will go out of his mind. His fear of madness [*strakh sumasshestviia*] grows so strong that, after being told this, a horror came over me.[68]

I have inserted italics here to remind the reader of the potential role of separation anxiety in precipitating 'madness'.

In 1884, when 'Notes of a Madman' was written, Tolstoy thought often about the subject of madness. In a diary entry for 26 March, for example, he refers ironically to 'Notes of a Man Not Mad' and adds: 'How vividly I lived through them. . . '. Curiously, in the same diary entry he characterizes his daughter Tania as 'mentally ill', and next day he describes his wife as 'very seriously mentally ill'. On subsequent days he repeatedly writes of 'madness'. He takes to reading psychiatric journals where, among other things, he discovers that prayer is 'an ordinary madness'. It is clear that in this period Tolstoy is preoccupied with the very idea of mental illness,[69] and he seems more than a little worried that he might be deranged himself. By August, however, he relaxes a bit on this subject, composing a humorous *Sorrowful Register of the Mentally Ill in the Yasnaya Polyana Hospital*. The work includes himself as a patient who is suffering from what imaginary German psychiatrists term *Weltverbesserungswahn* ('illusion of improving the world').[70]

Later in the 1880s, as Tolstoy's anxiety attacks and depressive episodes became more frequent and disturbing, he would reject psychiatry altogether: 'Yes, the only people who are hopelessly, unquestionably mad are the psychiatrists, those who declare others to be mad.'[71] Here Tolstoy is not joking. It doesn't take a psychoanalyst to see that his attitude might be just a little defensive. Until the end of his life Tolstoy maintained a low opinion of psychiatry, calling it 'one of the most comical sciences' in an unfinished article of 1910.[72] Such an opinion may be viewed as another aspect of Tolstoy's famous disdain for doctors and the medical profession generally.[73]

The narrator of 'Notes of a Madman', like Tolstoy, is a landowner. He begins by characterizing himself as insane (*sumashedshii*), even though a court has just ruled that he is legally sane. What then follows is an extended flashback[74] to events leading up to the legal judgement.

The insanity, says the narrator, came on only after the age of 35. Before that he had lived 'like everybody' – except for certain episodes before the age of ten, which he then proceeds to describe in revealing detail. In so doing he demonstrates an intuitive understanding of the organic connection between adult psychopathology and childhood psychopathology. He also alludes to many known features of Tolstoy's biography.

The narrator remembers once being put to bed as a child of five or six years old by his dear nanny (*niania*) Evpraksiia who, as Boris Eikhenbaum points out in his commentary in the Jubilee edition is the real-life nanny Evpraksiia whom Tolstoy describes in a memoir.[75] As is so often the case with children at bedtime, there is some expression of separation anxiety (in one variant the narrator says that he as a child tended to get anxious around bedtime).[76] Here the boy proudly steps over the railing by himself and jumps onto the bed, but still *keeps hold of the nanny's hand* (*vse derzha ee ruku*). Only then does he let go of her hand and crawl under the blanket. As for the nanny Evpraksiia, she keeps her distance by addressing the little nobleman with a respectful plural (*lozhites'*), yet also uses the familiar diminutive 'Fedin'ka', which expresses affection. Originally Tolstoy even had her feeling sorry at having to *part* with little Fedin'ka for the night: 'But I see that she herself is sorry to have to part with me [*ei samoi zhalko rasstat'sia so mnoi*] and wants to caress me a bit more.' These words are crossed out in the manuscript,[77] but they point to an oddly contagious feature of the boy's separation anxiety (a similar contagion occurs in Tolstoy's description of his childhood separation from auntie Tat'iana Aleksandrovna: 'I saw that she felt the same as I did, sorry, terribly sorry, but it had to be.')[78]

As Fedin'ka is curling up contentedly in his blanket and thinking of how much everyone in the family loves one another, the housekeeper suddenly bursts into the room and accuses the nanny of taking a sugar dish, that is, either stealing or misplacing it. The nanny denies this vehemently (*ne brala ee*). Poor Fedin'ka is terribly frightened. The morality or competence of someone very important to him is thrown into question. People do *not* love one another. Furthermore, the boy might *lose* his nanny, for she could be dismissed for the alleged misbehaviour. In addition to the usual bedtime separation anxiety, then, an anxiety of long-term separation lurks just below the surface.[79] Horrified, the little boy hides his head under the blanket, but this brings no relief.

Then, without reporting the outcome of this incident, and in the middle of a paragraph, the narrator switches to another unpleasant scene. This time a child is being beaten. Someone named Foka (probably a footman) keeps hitting a child (perhaps a serf-child) in the presence of Fedin'ka while saying: 'You will not.' Although the child says 'I won't', Foka keeps on beating the child and saying 'You will not.' Fedin'ka bursts into tears. He sobs inconsolably, no one can stop him. The grown-up narrator then observes that these desperate sobbing attacks constitute the first 'fits' leading up to his current insanity (*Vot eti-to rydaniia, eto otchaianie byli pervymi pripadkami moego tepereshnego sumashestviia*).[80]

A final childhood incident – again introduced without a paragraph break – brings God into the picture. 'Auntie', who is of course

Tolstoy's beloved aunt Tat'iana Aleksandrovna Ergol'skaia,[81] tells the story of Christ's crucifixion:

> I remember another time how it came over me after Auntie had told us about Christ. She had finished talking and wanted to leave, but we said: 'Tell us more about Jesus Christ.'
>
> 'No there is no time now.'
>
> 'No, tell us', and Mitinka begged her to tell us. So Auntie started telling us all over again the same thing she had told us before. She related how they crucified him, beat him, tormented him, while he just prayed the whole time and did not judge them.
>
> 'Auntie, why on earth did they torture him?'
>
> 'They were evil people.'
>
> 'But he was a good man.'
>
> 'It's already past eight. Listen.'
>
> 'Why did they beat him? He forgave them, so why did they beat him? It hurt. Auntie, didn't it hurt?'
>
> 'It's time now. I'm going to have tea.'
>
> 'Maybe it's not true, they didn't beat him.'
>
> 'Now, now, enough.'
>
> 'No, no, don't go.'
>
> And again it came over me, I sobbed and sobbed, then I began beating my head against the wall.[82]

The reaction here is intensely emotional, and is Tolstoy's own. As a child Tolstoy would easily become upset and was subject to fits of crying (*Leva-reva*, that is, 'cry-baby Lev' was a nickname he earned from his brothers).[83] The child's interest in Christ's willingness to undergo suffering in this passage is also quite in keeping with Tolstoy's own childhood interest in Christ's voluntary suffering. In *What I Believe* (1884) Tolstoy says: '. . . from the earliest period of childhood, when I started reading the Gospel for myself, the thing which most touched and moved me was Christ's preaching of love, submission, humility, self-sacrifice, and answering evil with good'.[84]

The narrative sequence of three incidents is unified by a common theme: guilt versus innocence. In the first incident it is not clear whether the nanny is guilty or innocent of stealing the sugar bowl (or of misplacing it). In the second the boy who is being beaten is apparently guilty of something – of what, it is not clear – and the punishment seems excessive. The third incident, the crucifixion of Christ as depicted by Auntie, features a completely innocent victim of unjust punishment. In all three incidents the narrator-as-child is made anxious by having to witness some form of punishment. The anxiety is so great as to provoke crying fits in the second and third incidents.[85]

In each of the incidents the child feels sympathy for the one who is suffering (this is in line with Tolstoy's well-known revulsion against corporal punishment). The sympathy is particularly intense in the third incident, going over to outright identification: they beat *Christ*, so little *Fedin'ka* beats his own head against the wall (in a variant the identification is unmistakable: 'What did they beat him for? Why are they tormenting *me*?').[86]

The thought of Christ's voluntary suffering elicits head-beating, that is, voluntary suffering by the child. This self-imposed suffering is essential to the 'insanity' of both the child and, as we will see, the grown-up narrator. Psychoanalytically speaking, identification with a sufferer leads to a bout of moral masochism.

4. MASOCHISM AS AN ANTIDEPRESSANT

The term masochism originally referred to a sexual perversion, but in current psychoanalytic thought it has a broader meaning. It is defined by analyst Anita Katz as follows: 'any behavioural act, verbalization, or fantasy that – by unconscious design – is physically or psychically injurious to oneself, self-defeating, humiliating, or unduly self-sacrificing'.[87] This is very roughly what Freud meant by his term 'moral masochism'.[88]

Tolstoy's masochism has received precious little attention in the vast literature on Tolstoy. All of Tolstoy's biographers of course recognize their subject's great concern with human suffering, and to a greater or lesser extent they even deal with Tolstoy's self-sacrificing attitudes. But the psychoanalytic meaning and implications of Tolstoy's willingness to suffer and to humiliate himself are rarely explored, and the term 'masochism' is rarely applied.

The most notable exception to this rule is the chapter on Tolstoy in William H. Blanchard's 1984 book *Revolutionary Morality*.[89] There Blanchard observes that the young Tolstoy was drawn to 'self-inflicted suffering', as in the passage in the second draft of *Boyhood* where the hero holds a heavy dictionary out from his body for a long period of time to test his endurance, or whips his own naked shoulders until bloody welts appear.[90] As an older man Tolstoy continued to welcome suffering. Blanchard discusses the aging Tolstoy's 'long-ing to suffer' primarily in terms of guilt resulting from the privileged social position he continued to occupy despite his teachings. As Blanchard shows, Tolstoy even gained a certain degree of pleasure in despising himself for not always practising what he preached (be-low I will have more to say about the mature adult masochism of Tolstoy in 1889, when he was working on *The Kreutzer Sonata*).

Having finished an account of his childhood fits, the narrator of 'Notes of a Madman' then, rather suddenly and inexplicably, brings sexuality into the picture. He briefly describes his adolescent sexual awakening and young adult life. 'Like all boys', he says, he yielded to a 'vice' which other boys his age 'taught' him. This clear reference to masturbation (possibly in all-male groups) is followed by a reference to his second 'vice', namely, women: 'I began to know women and thus, seeking pleasure and finding it, I lived to age 35.' Like all 'men-tally healthy' boys of his circle, he went to high school and university, then got married, raised children, and ran his estate in the country. Such a developmental sequence, including the reference to adoles-cent masturbation, will be repeated by Pozdnyshev, hero of *The Kreutzer Sonata*.

It is emphasized that the narrator was 'completely healthy' in this period, there being 'no signs of my insanity'. In retrospect, however, the narrator remembers these 20 years of 'healthy' life only 'with diffi-culty and loathing'. Here it becomes clear that he is using the term 'healthy' in an ironic sense, and that he values his current 'insanity' above all.[91] In his current 'insane' period he is at least cancelling guilt by punishing himself, whereas in his 'healthy' period he was feeling an (unacknowledged) guilt for both his autoerotic and heteroerotic activities – otherwise he would not now be terming them 'vices'.

The sudden transition from the childhood incidents to the 'vices' of adolescent sexuality is odd, and raises some retrospective ques-tions about those incidents. Was there a sexual element implicit in the earlier incidents which would have motivated Tolstoy explicitly to bring up sexuality in the midst of his narration? For example, was the little boy in the first incident dealing with bedtime separation anxiety by masturbating? Or, did the nanny who was putting little Fedin'ka to bed masturbate him (as was commonly believed to be the practice among nurses hired by the gentry)?[92] The narrator says, after all, that she wants to 'fondle' him some more (*eshche polaskat'*) before allowing him to go to sleep. Did Tolstoy cross out this phrase because it sounded improper?

The second incident, the boy being beaten by an adult male for some unspecified offence has a vaguely homoerotic overtone, especially in view of the later reference to learning how to masturbate from other boys. The incident is bound to remind the psychoanalytic scholar of Freud's famous 1919 essay 'A Child Is Being Beaten'. There Freud describes a childhood fantasy frequently reported by his patients being treated for hysteria or obsessional neurosis, namely, a fantasy of some child being punished for naughty behaviour. Typically the fantasy is pleasurable, and culminates in masturbation. Analyst Otto Fenichel describes the phenomenon in the following terms: 'On the deepest level the fantasy conserves a memory of the autoerotic period, the beaten child having the significance of penis or clitoris, the beating the significance of masturbatory stimulation.'[93] Considering that one of the slang meanings of 'boy' (*mal'chik*) in Russian is 'penis',[94] then Tolstoy's idea of a 'boy' being repeatedly beaten is suggestive. Tolstoy could well have had masturbatory beating fantasies as a child, especially since autoerotic gratification was a persisting issue in his adult life, including the period when he was working on *The Kreutzer Sonata*. Here, in 'Notes of a Madman', masturbation is not explicitly alluded to until the adolescent phase of the narrator, but its appearance would not seem so unmotivated if we understood that the previous incident of a boy being beaten had autoerotic overtones for the narrator.

Indeed the *subsequent* 'madness' of the narrator might be understood, in part, as a fantasized consequence of masturbation. As Laura Engelstein has pointed out, in nineteenth-century Russia it was widely believed that masturbation was harmful to both physical and mental health. The idea that *insanity* could result from masturbation had been propounded by the Swiss physician S.A. Tissot, whose work was available in Russian translation. An anonymous 1865 domestic text on the subject even asserted that 'masturbation is the surest if not the most direct road to death'.[95]

It is of particular interest that Tolstoy's narrator's childhood 'attacks' come to an end (*vse eto proshlo*) with the onset of adolescent sexuality. This suggests that the new opportunities for sexual satisfaction somehow counteract the 'attacks'.[96] Not until the age of 35 do they return and, as we will see, they occur specifically when the narrator is separated from his wife and therefore cannot have sexual intercourse with her or otherwise be comforted by her. That is, they occur when he is *alone*, and possibly in danger of masturbating. However, the adult 'madness' does not include beating fantasies or other signs of preoccupation with masturbation. There is just massive anxiety, depression, guilt, and eventually moral (not erotogenic) masochism.

The adult variant of the 'madness' starts during the tenth year of the narrator's marriage (to a wife who is never once named). The immediate occasion is a long journey to look at an estate in Penza province for possible purchase. Here many of the details are identical to Tolstoy's own journey. The narrator travels with his manservant. First they travel by rail, then by post-chaise. The narrator gets very tired after a while, decides to stop at a hotel in Arzamas, has an attack of depressive anxiety, leaves suddenly, his *toska* weakens the next day, and so on – as we saw from the letters to Sonia.

Parts of this narration differ from the real life events, however. There is also considerably more psychological detail. The narrator begins to feel anxiety already along the way, but it is not expressed in a series of nervous letters to his wife, as it was in Tolstoy's own case. Rather, it appears in the depiction of interaction with the servant, whose jolly mood contrasts with that of the narrator. At one point the narrator falls asleep while travelling, then wakes up in a state of anxiety and asks himself: 'What am I going for? Where am I going?' The idea of acquiring property now loses its appeal: 'it suddenly seemed to me that there was no point in going off to this distant spot, that I might die here in an alien place, and I became terrified.'[97] There is no hint of this agoraphobic outburst in the letters to Sonia. Conversation with the servant cheers the narrator up only slightly.

The two reach Arzamas at last. The whole town is asleep. Naturally the narrator is very tired and looking forward to sleep and to abatement of his lingering fear. But for some reason his mood gets only worse. The sound of bells ringing, the pleasant little white house he is to stay in, the lively footsteps of the servant unloading his things – all these evoke nothing but sadness, horror, and *toska* in him. A spot on the cheek of the sleepy watchman who shows him to his room also seems horrifying. The room itself is quite unobjectionable, but the narrator's anxiety and growing depression transform it into a chamber of horrors, a tomb even. The mood has changed from agoraphobic to claustrophobic.[98] Some of the sentences are verbless, some of the tense sequences are off, but this clumsy, unfinished quality of Tolstoy's writing actually deepens the depressive effect:

A spotlessly whitewashed, square little room. How it tormented me, I recall, that this little room was specifically square. There was one window with a curtain which was red. A table of Karelian birch and a couch with curved sides. We entered. Sergei set up the samovar and poured tea. I took a pillow and lay down on the couch. I did not sleep but listened as Sergei drank tea and called for me. I was terrified of getting up, the thought of rousing myself and sitting in this room was terrifying. I did not get up and began to doze off. Apparently I fell asleep, because when I woke up there was no one in the room and it was dark. I was again just as aroused as in the carriage. To fall asleep, I felt, was now impossible. Why did I land here? Where am I taking myself to? What am I running from, and where? I am trying to run away from something awful, but I cannot. I am always with myself, and it is I who am agonizing to myself as well. I, there he is, I am all here. No Penza estate or any other estate will either add to me or diminish me. Me, I am sick of myself, I am unbearable, a torment to myself. I want to fall asleep, to sink into oblivion, but I cannot. I cannot get away from myself. I went out into the corridor. Sergei was sleeping on a narrow bench, his arm thrown back, but he was sleeping sweetly, and the night watchman with the spot was asleep as well.[99]

Here, in the fictional account, the depressive aspect of the Arzamas experience comes to the fore, while the anxiety seems less important.[100] The narrator's depression is full blown. His sleeplessness accompanied by a fear of getting up, his sense of the pointlessness of current actions, his self-loathing, and his obsessive thoughts of death – are all clinically familiar.

Because he is so depressed, the narrator has no choice but to confront death as an existential, philosophical issue.[101] Not that an anxiety attack by itself could not have accomplished this. But depression is inherently better suited to a prolonged, meditative confrontation with death than is anxiety by itself. Seriously depressed people cannot avoid thoughts of death, and in fact they sometimes contemplate or even commit suicide. In *Confession*, written a few years earlier, Tolstoy says that he had to hide a rope from himself, and that he would go hunting without a gun in order to avoid the temptation to commit suicide.[102] In the diary for 1884 he repeatedly expresses a wish to die, for example: *Khochetsia smerti nastoiashchei* – this just the day before mentioning that 'Notes of a Man Not Mad' are on his mind.[103]

The 'specifically square' (*imenno kvadratnaia*) little room in white and red is curious. A little later the narrator characterizes his very

horror as 'red, white, square'.[104] And why only one window? The
imagery here seems much too concrete not to have a meaning, yet
scholars have not been able to account for it. I would like to suggest
that the room represents a frightening burial vault for the narrator,
and not just any burial vault. Specifically, it is the Tolstoy family
crypt in the Kochaki cemetery, not far from Yasnaya Polyana, where
Tolstoy's mother, father, and elder brother Dmitrii were buried. That
structure, which I personally examined while visiting the village
of Kochaki in May of 1996, is made of old, smooth brick (which
could account for the *red* colour), it is painted over in *white*wash or
*white*ned sizing, it is roughly *square* at each end, and it has only *one*
window.[105]

What more appropriate place to confront death than in a room that
unconsciously reminds the narrator/Tolstoy of his own anticipated
resting place? Here we should keep in mind that, at the time of the
Arzamas horror, Tolstoy had no reason to assume that he would be
buried anywhere else than in the Kochaki family crypt. Only much
later, in the *Reminiscences* of 1903–06, did Tolstoy express his wish to
be buried at the edge of the ravine where the famous 'little green
stick' inscribed with the secret of happiness was also buried.[106]

But to return to Arzamas. Death first takes the form of something
undefined, then it is personified:

> I went out into the corridor, thinking to get away from what was
> tormenting me. But it [*ono*] went out right behind me, casting
> everything into gloom. I was just as terrified, even more so. 'What
> kind of stupidity is this?', I said to myself. 'What is it that an-
> guishes me [*chego ia toskuiu*], what am I afraid of?' 'Me', inaudibly
> answered the voice of death. 'I am here.' My skin crept. Yes, death.
> It will come. There, there it is, but it ought not to be.[107]

As Kathleen Parthé, has shown, Tolstoy sometimes represents the
idea of death in an indirect way by utilizing the neuter pronoun 'it'
(*ono*) – which is what happens here – or by usage of some other
evocatively indefinite grammatical form (*eto*, *chto-to*, *to*). In this particular case the grammatical parallelism of 'I went out . . .' and 'It
went out . . .' produces a haunting, eery sense, what Parthé, calls an
'effect of nameless, neuter animacy'.[108]

Death is, paradoxically, alive, it goes where the narrator goes. It is
not so surprising, then, when the narrator next says death has a
'voice', that is, when he states that he is being addressed by 'the voice

of death'. Death, an event which brings life to an end, is made to speak. This personification may sound rather trite, but it motivates the subsequent feeling of *personal* offence in the narrator:

> Now I was not afraid, but saw and felt that death was coming, and at the same time I felt that it ought not to be [*ee ne dolzhno byt'*]. My whole being felt the necessity, the right to life – and all the while felt death in action.[109]

To the feelings of depression and anxiety, then, can be added a slight problem of self-esteem, or a feeling of narcissistic injury. The narrator has a 'right to life', as if he somehow were entitled to live forever. His very sense of himself as a worthy object is slighted by the existence of this pushy, aggressive person called death. Fortunately for his narcissism, by the end of the narration he will have convinced himself that this person does not exist any more.

The narrator tries to shake off the horror. He lights a candle, but its red flame seems to speak of death. He tries to think about the purchase of the estate, about his wife. But these are as nothing in relation to death. The horror pushes everything into the background. He tries to sleep, but jumps up in horror. The *toska* is now really getting to him:

> And the *toska*, the *toska*, the same *toska* that occurs before vomiting, only spiritual. It's horrible, terrifying, it seems that death is terrifying, but if you remember and think about life, then a dying life is terrifying. Somehow life and death have blended into one. Something was trying to tear my soul to shreds, but could not. Once again I went to have a look at the others sleeping, once again I tried to fall asleep, but the same horror returned – red, white, square [again the crypt in Kochaki]. Something is straining but does not break. Agonizing, and agonizingly dry and spiteful, I felt not a drop of goodness in myself, but only an even, calm loathing of myself and of that which made me.[110]

That which made me? Here a belief in God is introduced as a potential escape from the awful feeling:

> What made me? God, they say, God. Pray, I remembered. I haven't prayed for a long time, for twenty years, and I haven't believed in anything despite the fact that I have fasted once a year for appear-

ances' sake. I began to pray. God have mercy. Our Father. Mother of
God. I began to make up prayers. I began to cross myself and bow
down to the ground, looking around and afraid that someone
might see me. The fact that someone might have seen me seemed to
distract me, to take away the terror.[111]

It is humiliating for a non-believer to have to pray, but pray he does.
This little masochistic exercise does not work, however. The narrator still cannot sleep.

Finally, he cannot take it any more. He wakens Sergei and the
watchman, orders the horses to be harnessed, and leaves Arzamas in
the middle of the night. This is a highly unusual thing for a tired trav-
eller to be doing. It indicates considerable mental unbalance.

By the next night he at his destination, the estate in Penza province. His visit there is brief and pleasant enough, although in the end
he does not purchase the estate (just as Tolstoy did not buy the estate
in Il'mino). The narrator notes that, on the night of his arrival at the
estate, he manages to fight off *toska* by praying.

The rest of 'Notes of a Madman' focuses on the permanent change
wrought by the night in Arzamas. The narrator prays more and more
often, starts to go to church again, and becomes generally devout
(*nabozhen*). His wife (understandably) nags him about this. He takes
on no new projects, and previously started projects bore him (this to
some extent characterizes Tolstoy's own sense of drift after having
finished *War and Peace*). For the time being the *toska* does not return.
Religiosity plus the presence of a devoted wife function as an adequate antidepressant during this period.

But when the narrator again undertakes to *travel away from home*
there is another attack. This time the narrator has arrived in Moscow
(cf. Tolstoy's trip to Moscow in 1870)[112] and is staying in a small room
in a town house. The 'Arzamas horror' hits him shortly after entering the room, so he decides to go out for the evening in an attempt
to escape it. Dressing quickly, trying not to look at the walls of the
narrow room which for some reason frighten him, he manages to
get away and enjoy a gay evening at the theatre and at a restaurant
with a Khar'kov businessman he has met on the way to Moscow. But
all this is to no avail. As soon as he returns to his room the awful feeling comes back. Another terrible night ensues, 'worse than in
Arzamas'.[113] Thoughts of suicide, not just death, now become explicit and conscious. Again the narrator resorts to prayer and to
bowing down, but this time the prayer is less childish, more like a

conversation with God. There is no reply, however, so the narrator is left all alone with himself: '*I ia ostavalsia odin, sam s soboi.*'[114] To escape this, he makes up lines for God's side of the conversation. Still, God does not actually reveal himself to him. There is still some doubt in the existence of God. But the anxiety and depression abate somewhat. Sleep comes at dawn.

The next evening the narrator arrives home, and fortunately there is no *toska*. A general apathy takes over his life now, however. He has lost interest in his projects, his health weakens. His wife advises medical attention, for she believes that the narrator's ideas about faith and about God result from an illness. There seems to be an increasing psychological distance between wife and husband. A mild depression persists, although the narrator fights it by praying somewhat mechanically and going to church regularly. He reads a lot, plays cards a bit, and hunts. This latter interest provides an occasion for his third, and last nervous attack.

It is winter and the snow is deep. The narrator is hunting in the woods with another hunter (or hunters – the writing is very rough and inconsistent here). Tracking a hare far into the woods by himself, the narrator eventually ends up in a glade (*na poliane*, cf. the name of Tolstoy's estate, 'Yasnaya Polyana', 'Bright Glade'). The hare gets away, then the narrator tries to head back but gets lost in the deep woods. Soon he is exhausted and covered in sweat. He stops. Shouting brings no response. More walking, but he cannot find his way. He becomes frightened, then 'the whole Arzamas and Moscow horror, only a hundred times worse' comes over him. His heart is pounding, his arms and legs are shaking. There is a real possibility of freezing to death:

Death here? I don't want it. Why death? What is death? Once again I wanted to interrogate and to reproach God, but suddenly I felt that I dare not, I must not, that one must not try to make a deal with him, that he has decided what is necessary, that I alone am guilty [*ia odin vinovat*]. I began to pray for his forgiveness, and I became repulsive to myself [*sam sebe stal gadok*].[115]

Then, almost by magic, he walks out of the woods. He is still shaking, but glad. When he gets home and is alone (*odin*) in his study (there is no mention of his wife), he again prays and asks for forgiveness for his sins (*grekhi* – possibly masturbation?), which are few but repulsive (*gadki*) to him.

Now God definitely exists – although not because of a generous, gratuitous leap of faith, but more out of desperation in the face of (imagined) death, that is, out of anxiety and depression. This affirmation of God's existence, moreover, coincides with an open acceptance of guilt ('I alone am guilty') and a feeling of low self-esteem ('I became repulsive to myself'). Now that there is someone before whom the narrator can feel guilty and humiliated, he can go ahead and act on his masochistic inclinations, that is, he can punish and revile himself. He can engage in adult moral masochism, rather than the disgusting erotogenic masochism of the childhood beating fantasies earlier in the narration. The God invented here is really quite convenient, psychologically. The masochistic stance, moreover, seems to lessen the depression. It is therapeutic, it acts as a mild anti-depressant.

The narrator's life changes considerably. Family and household matters no longer interest him. He reads about the Christian saints and they seem more and more worthy as objects for imitation. The sufferings of the peasants gain his attention. At one point he talks to an old peasant woman and realizes what a hard life she must endure, and that landowners essentially live off the poverty and misfortune of such people. When there is another opportunity to buy an estate he declines to do so, because the estate is one where the peasants are forced to harvest the landowner's fields in order to gain access to pasture. This failure to take advantage of a situation enrages the narrator's wife. She scolds him, but he is full of joy, thinking that the peasants are people too – 'brothers, sons of the Father, as it is said in the Gospels'. Simply telling his wife that he does not want to exploit the peasants by buying the estate causes a joyful rending within: 'Suddenly something which had long been aching inside me snapped, as if it had been born.'[116] There is a spiritual rebirth here, but it is not very clearly characterized, except as joy at the abatement of anxiety, guilt, and depression. A deep marital rift is also beginning to form.

Here, the narrator says, is the beginning of his 'madness'. But not quite. To refrain from exploiting the peasants is still not quite the same thing as actively helping them. The work actually ends with the narrator handing out money to the poor and 'conversing with the people' (in a variant he goes so far as to invite three beggars into his house, where he plans to feed and clothe them and let them live.[117] Now he has reached the stage of 'complete madness' (*polnoe sumashestvie*).[118] His wife would no doubt agree.

In the meantime, death and fear are no more (as in *Revelations* 21, 4). Eliminating them was the whole point, after all:

And suddenly it became clear to me that all of this [poverty] should not be [*etogo vsego ne dolzhno byt'*]. And not only that it should not be, but that it was not [*etogo net*], and if it was not, then there was no death and no fear, and there was no more of the former torment, and I was now afraid of nothing.[119]

The narrator's somewhat unconvincing effort at denying the existence of death is now complete. With good reason Osipov characterizes the conclusion of Tolstoy's memoir as a Freudian 'Wunschdelirium'.[120]

What Plekhanov says about *Confession* may be said about 'Notes of a Madman' as well: 'Tolstoy saved himself from death and destruction [*ot pogibeli*] by means of faith'.[121] In fact Tolstoy did no such thing, of course. He died, just as other mortals die. What Plekhanov means to say is that Tolstoy saved himself from the depressing *thoughts* of death and destruction. G. W. Spence is more precise, psychologically, when he says that Tolstoy '. . . had to believe in God in order to save himself from despair and the thought of an inevitable death. . . ', or, more radically, Tolstoy '. . . had to believe in the will of God if only to establish that suicide is wrong'.[122]

A Marxist might say that the narrator of 'Notes of a Madman' makes the oppressive and frightening thoughts of death go away by lowering himself socially. That is, he expresses solidarity with the peasant class, the muzhiks. From a clinical viewpoint, the solidarity is a form of identification, and it encourages, even entails moral masochism. Tolstoy's narrator wards off attacks of depressive anxiety (which includes thoughts of death) by actively identifying with the suffering peasants and by sharing his property with them. He also refuses to get medical help, which his perceptive (yet nameless) wife recommends, and he vigorously abases himself before his God. Within his own social milieu all of this is harmful and humiliating to him, that is, morally masochistic. One pathology, depressive anxiety (with associated guilt), is cured, or at least palliated, by another pathology, moral masochism.[123] This is a kind self-medication or self-therapy.[124] Such a therapy is identical to one the narrator as a little boy had made at the beginning of the story: the depressing (and perhaps guilt-provoking) thought of Christ being tortured to death on the cross led him to torture himself, to beat his head against the wall.

It is well known that the older Tolstoy himself identified intensely with the suffering peasantry (the muzhiks, the *narod*).[125] To Maksim Gorky he bragged: 'I'm more of a muzhik than you are.'[126] Tolstoy went so far as to work with his peasants for days on end in the fields and threshing-barns of Yasnaya Polyana. This made him feel better, although numerous diary entries also attest to how exhausting this work was for him. He would also make his own boots, chop wood, empty his own chamber pot, etc. When dressed in simple peasant clothing Tolstoy was actually taken for a peasant by people not personally acquainted with him.[127] Tolstoy was even willing to go to prison and die, just as peasants were dying as a result of the widespread application of the death penalty to them in late tsarist Russia.[128] In all this the identification and the self-punishment are sometimes difficult to disentangle from one another (not to mention other factors, such as simple generosity, guilt, and exhibitionism), but certainly an *effect* of Tolstoy's active identification with the peasants was that he suffered, and willingly so. And as a result, he felt better, at least temporarily. The masochism was therapeutic.

The masochistic attitudes and behaviours of the 'madman' are unmistakable, yet they are fairly mild and few by comparison to what Tolstoy himself is famous for advocating in some of his later writings, for example, hard manual labour, avoidance of certain kinds of foods such as sugar, white bread, and meat, renunciation of property, love of one's enemies, total abstention from sexual intercourse, and a general 'non-resistance to evil'.[129]

Of these, the sexual abstinence and related ideas advocated in *The Kreutzer Sonata* will be the primary concern of this book. What Tolstoy is saying toward the end of 'Notes of a Madman' is on a collision course with ordinary conceptions of family life, including normal sexual interaction between man and wife. A husband who is searching for the meaning of his life in moral masochism will eventually come upon the masochism of sexual renunciation – and his wife will not be pleased.

Nor will she find it easy to continue to function as the obligatory icon of her husband's idealized, yet hated mother.

3

Tolstoy and His Mother

1. DEATH AND THE MOTHER

'Notes of a Madman', as we have seen, dealt with death by eliminating it outright: 'there was no death'. The chief therapeutic accomplishment which the 'madman' – essentially Tolstoy himself – performs upon himself is to make the depressing thoughts of death go away.

Why the focus on death? As a preliminary hypothesis I would like to suggest this: the first death (and therefore the most important death) Tolstoy ever experienced in his life was the death of his mother when he was still just a toddler. Behind the massive surges of depressive anxiety recorded in 'Notes of a Madman' lurks the most horrible loss of Tolstoy's childhood.

Above I noted the similarity of the room in Arzamas to the crypt in Kochaki where Tolstoy's mother is buried. I also drew attention to the fact that the narrator personifies death by giving it a voice and having it speak to him. According to Diana Lewis Burgin, this voice is maternal. In her fanciful yet insightful study written in verse, Burgin asserts that the person who speaks to the narrator in Arzamas is a derivative of Tolstoy's dead mother, or in Jungian terms an 'anima'. Death personified is the 'Arzamas anima'.[130] Overall, according to Burgin, the idea of death is a return to some form of the mother for Tolstoy.[131] In 'On Life', for example, 'Tolstoy opines that the "exit doors" of death are the same as the "entrance doors" we passed through at birth'.[132] I would add that there is a certain colour parallel in Tolstoy's personal mythology of death and birth: he eventually wished to be buried at the place of the 'little *green* stick', while he was born on the famous *green* couch.

The tomb–womb equation is of course widespread, and not particularly Tolstoyan. It is a commonplace of Russian folklore, as in the image of 'damp mother earth' (*matushka-syra-zemlia*) where all Russians go after dying, or in the quickening of mother Mary's womb as she watches her son die on the cross.[133] The tomb–womb equation is also made in many cultures outside Russia, and has received some attention from psychoanalytic scholars.[134] But Burgin's study of how

33

Tolstoy in particular makes the equation is suggestive, and I would like to pursue her hint by examining the circumstances surrounding the death of Tolstoy's mother, and psychoanalyzing both Tolstoy's long-term response to that death as well as his particularly sharp one-time response known as *The Kreutzer Sonata*.

Another reason for bringing in Tolstoy's mother is the factor of separation anxiety in the Arzamas experience. As we saw, Tolstoy experienced separation anxiety on the road, even before he arrived in Arzamas. As we also saw, however, psychoanalysts such as John Bowlby argue that the archetypal separation anxiety is anxiety of separation from the mother.

The most important reason for looking at early maternal loss in Tolstoy's life is Tolstoy's own belief in the importance of early childhood. In an 1878 fragment entitled 'My Life' Tolstoy complains about how difficult it is to remember the first few years of life, yet he declares that those years are crucial. He asks:

> When did I begin? When did I begin to live? And why is it a joy for me to imagine myself then, when sometimes it was terrifying – just as now many people [*mnogim*] are terrified to imagine themselves entering again [*kogda ia opiat' vstupliu*] into the state of death, which will not be rememberable in words. Surely I lived then, those first years, when I was learning how to look, to listen, to understand, to speak, when I slept, sucked the breast and kissed the breast, laughed, and made my mother happy? I lived, and blissfully so. Surely it was then that I acquired everything that I live by now, acquired so much, so quickly, that I haven't acquired $\frac{1}{100}$ th of that in all the rest of my life.[135]

A psychoanalyst would not only agree with this, but would add that the death of the mother mentioned here was itself an important part of that formative 99/100 of what Tolstoy lived by. For, otherwise, why would Tolstoy suggest that trying to remember early childhood is like trying to imagine *again* entering the state of death?

Years later, in a 1905 quasi-theological tract, Tolstoy is less willing to ascribe any importance to the role of his mother. He speaks as though he were from another world:

> People tell me that I appeared some years ago from the womb of my mother. But what came from my mother's womb is my body – that body which for a long time did not know and does not know

about its existence and which very soon, perhaps tomorrow, will be buried in the earth and will become earth. That which I acknowledge to be my *I* did not appear simultaneously with my body. This *I* of mine began not in the womb of my mother, and not upon exiting from it when they cut the umbilical cord, and not when they weaned me from the breast, and not when *I* began speaking. I know that this *I* began at some time, and yet I know that this *I* has always existed.[136]

In other words, there is a part of Tolstoy that seems to acknowledge that early interaction with his mother was important, yet there is also a part which denies the importance of his mother. The part that originated in the mother is the mere body, the part that is going to die. The part that did not originate in the mother is immortal. It existed before birth, and it will continue to exist after death.

Perhaps it will be possible to forgive Tolstoy for this preposterous doublethink when we consider how terrible the trauma of his mother's early death must have been for him.

2. TOLSTOY SLIPS UP

Lev Tolstoy was separated from his mother for the last time on the day she died, 4 August 1830.[137] Mariia Nikolaevna *née* Volkonskaia was 39 years old, her son was just a few weeks shy of two years old. In his unfinished *Reminiscences* of 1903–06 Tolstoy says he cannot remember his mother, yet he retains a vivid spiritual image of her, and describes his feelings about her at some length. To borrow the phrasing of psychoanalyst Alvin Frank, Tolstoy's mother seems to be both unrememberable and unforgettable.[138] Or, as critic Judith M. Armstrong puts it, Tolstoy's mother is 'simultaneously there and not there'.[139] Here is how she makes her first appearance in the memoir:

I was born and spent my early childhood in the village of Yasnaya Polyana. I do not remember my mother at all. I was 1½ years old when she passed away. By odd happenstance not a single portrait of her remains, thus I am unable to picture her as a real, physical being. I am partly glad of this because in my imagination of her there is only her spiritual aspect [*dukhovnyi oblik*], and everything that I know about her, everything is wonderful, and I think [this is] not only because everybody who has spoken to me about my

mother has tried to say only the good about her, but because there
really was much of this good in her.[140]

Tolstoy's need to idealize his mother is fairly obvious and understandable here. Psychoanalysts find that idealization or glorification of a
lost parent can persist into adulthood,[141] and besides Tolstoy did have
a tendency to idealize people.[142] Tolstoy does have something objective to go on, for his mother was indeed highly educated and cultured
for her time: in addition to Russian she knew French, German, English
and Italian, she played the piano, she was a marvellous storyteller,
and so on. But Tolstoy's mother was more than merely accomplished.
For him she was a lofty ideal who in his mind still really existed, so
lofty and so real that later in life he would even pray to her:

> She seemed to me to be such a lofty, pure, spiritual being that of-
> ten, in the middle period of my life, when struggling with tempta-
> tions which were overwhelming me, I prayed to her soul, asking
> her to help me, and this prayer always helped me.[143]

In old age Tolsoy confessed that he still practically worshipped his
mother. To his children he conveyed a sense that her memory was sacred.[144] In the summer of 1908 he said to the biographer N. G.
Molostvov, holding back tears, 'I only know that I have a *culte* toward
her.'[145] In a diary entry of 13 June of that year he declares that 'I cannot
talk about my mother without tears.'[146] On 10 June he writes: 'This
morning I was walking around the garden and, as always, was reminiscing about my mother [*vspominaiu o materi*], about '*mamen'ka*', whom I do
not remember at all [*sovsem ne pomniu*], but who has remained for me a
sacred ideal. I never heard anything bad about her.'[147]

The sentimentality seems excessive here.[148] With good reason psychoanalyst Nikolai Osipov speaks of '*Tolstois Fixierung an die Mutter-
Imago und seine Sehnsucht nach ihr*'.[149] At some level Tolstoy does not
quite accept the fact that his dear mother has died. Otherwise it
would be difficult to explain the tears – some seventy-eight years
after her death.

When in 1906 the future wife of his son Sergei, Mariia Nikolaevna
Zubova, was introduced to Tolstoy, he responded: 'Now we will
have yet a third Mariia Nikolaevna Tolstaia'[150] – as if the first Mariia
Nikolaevna, his mother, were not yet deceased and continued to occupy the same category as the two living Mariia Nikolaevnas, that is
his sister and his future daughter-in-law.

The fact that Tolstoy prays to his dear mother also indicates that she still exists for him. It does not matter that he follows religious convention, speaking of her 'soul'. The important thing is that she is still somehow with him, still very real for him.

It is true that Tolstoy could be quite emotional, and he cried easily. But his emotionality over his mother was excessive even by his own standards. He did not cry over other long-since deceased family members, such as his father or his beloved elder brother Nikolai. Nor did he pray to their souls. The image of the allegedly unremembered mother is special, she is practically a saint for Tolstoy. But, as I hope to show, this is only a small part of the story. Tolstoy's feelings about his mother were really quite complicated, and idealization of her was only one part of the overall picture. This will become clear if we first pay close attention to the inconsistencies and outright factual errors in Tolstoy's accounts of his mother.

It is not quite true, for example, that Tolstoy 'never heard anything bad about her'. Just before speaking of how highly educated his mother was, he asserts that she was physically unattractive (*nekhorosha soboi*) – this apparently on the basis of reports from his aunts,[151] for Tolstoy has just asserted that he cannot himself remember what his mother looked like. So the claim that 'everything is wonderful' in his imagination about his mother is false, unless that claim is read in some tendentious way, for it is not ordinarily considered 'wonderful' for one's mother to be ugly.

Note also that Tolstoy states that no portrait of his mother remains. This too is not quite true. Although it is true that no full portrait has been authenticated,[152] there does exist a silhouette of Mariia Nikolaevna Volkonskaia as a girl, with an inscription on it in Tolstoy's hand which reads: 'My mother L. T.'[153] The original is on display in the Tolstoy Museum in Moscow.

The inscription 'My mother' is false in a curious way: the person whose shadow cast the silhouette was in fact not yet a mother. Instead, at the time the silhouette was made, she was most probably a sexually inexperienced girl, a virgin. She was what Tolstoy in a draft of *The Kreutzer Sonata* called 'a holy person, the finest representative of the human race in our world'. Or perhaps she was that type of 'chaste girl' who supposedly wants just one thing – children: 'children, yes, but not a husband'.[154]

Finally, it should be noted that Tolstoy incorrectly states his age at the time of his mother's death: he was actually close to two years old, not one and a half when she died on 4 August 1830.[155] Many Tolstoy scholars (whose names I will not mention here) have repeated this error. The mother's death actually occurred in the same month as Tolstoy's birth, that is August. It seems odd that the narcissistic Tolstoy would be ignorant of such an important fact.

On the other hand, back-dating his age at the time of his mother's death *would* make his claim that he did not remember her more credible. Perhaps Tolstoy was trying to convince himself (and his reader) that he really had no memory whatsoever of his mother.

In any case it can be shown that, at some level at least, Tolstoy did know perfectly well when his mother died. In the same *Reminiscences* where he claims to have been one and a half years old when she died, he quotes a note by his auntie Ergol'skaia dated 16 *August* 1836, saying that it was written 'six years after my mother's death'.[156] The Russian phrasing here is '6 let', not 'let 6', which is to say that Tolstoy is being exact rather than approximate.

These inaccuracies and inconsistencies – there will be more of them – may seem trivial. Most of Tolstoy's biographers gloss over them or are unaware of them, and indeed they are not of much consequence either to conventional descriptive biography, or to literary scholarship. For psychoanalytic study, however, they are important. They are the slight cracks in the slick Tolstoyan surface where one can at least *begin* to peer at deep motivation.

3. MATERNAL SEXUALITY AND MATERNAL LOVE

For Tolstoy, his mother's most important trait was her humility. It was a reactive humility, however. In one of the manuscripts of the *Reminiscences* 'very humble' is crossed out, and there follows a discussion of the mother's great self-control: '. . . although she was hot-tempered [*vspyl'chiva*], according to her maid, she was also reserved. "She would turn all red, even start to cry", her housemaid used to say, "but would never utter a coarse word [*ne skazhet grubogo slovo*]." She didn't even know them.'[157] Ignorance of crude words, however, would have been unlikely in the highly intelligent and educated mother Tolstoy is portraying.

It would be interesting to know what Mariia Nikolaevna got so emotional about. Whatever it was, Tolstoy seems proud of the fact that she did keep her emotions under control. This would include her emotions concerning sexual matters. Mariia Nikolaevna was a rather prudish woman, as can be seen from her reading preferences.

In a letter to a friend she declares that a book she had been reading was so full of indecencies (*'si rempli d'indéscences'*) that she had to stop reading it.[158] This sort of thing pleased Tolstoy no end. His wife, in dinnertime conversation with family and friends on a day in June, 1908, told the story of how Tolstoy's mother would avoid reading 'dirty books' (*merzkikh knig ne chitala*). Tolstoy chimed in with a remark about Mikhail Artsybashev's recently published risqué novel about free love: 'My mother read books which were much better than *Sanin*.'[159] The mother – thank goodness – kept a safe distance from sexual thoughts. Tolstoy's own hypermoral attitude toward sexuality was no doubt based, in part, on identification with the mother and her attitude toward sexuality.

According to Tolstoy, his mother was originally betrothed to one of the sons of a Moscow prince. Here too the mother's sexuality – or lack thereof – comes into view:

> This union was not fated to take place, however. My mother's fiancé, Lev Golitsyn – whose name was given to me, the fourth son, in memory of this Lev – died of fever before the wedding. They used to say to me that Mama loved me very much and called me *'mon petit Benjamin'*.
> I think that her love for her deceased fiancé, precisely because it ended in death, was that poetic love which girls experience only once. Her marriage to my father was arranged by her relatives and my father's. She was rich, no longer young, an orphan; my father was a merry, brilliant young man with a name and connections, but ruined financially because of my grandfather Tolstoy (he even was obliged to refuse his inheritance). I think that my mother loved my father, but more as a husband, and primarily as the father of her children, for she was not in love with him.[160]

So, the mother *might* have enjoyed sex with Lev Golitsyn, but then he died, leaving only Tolstoy's father, with whom sexual intercourse was apparently more a duty than a pleasure.

This story does not exactly ring false, but there seems to be an element of wishful thinking in it. Maybe the mother was not 'in love' with the father, but Tolstoy's parents were, by all accounts, happy together. For example, Tolstoy's mother wrote two somewhat sentimental, yet sincere love poems to Nikolai *père*, one in French, and one in Russian.[161] In their correspondence the parents seem quite devoted to one another.[162]

More interesting, however, is Tolstoy's statement that he was named after the man his mother *really* loved. Here Tolstoy seems retrospectively to win an Oedipal battle with his father, who was not his mother's first choice after all, and who was morally weak, the male equivalent of a gold digger. As the all-knowing N. N. Gusev points out, however, there was no such person as Lev Golitsyn in the love life of Tolstoy's mother. Instead, the fiancé was most probably *Nikolai* Golitsyn,[163] that is, a man who bore precisely the name of both Tolstoy's father and elder brother.

If Tolstoy's father Nikolai was not one of the great loves of his mother's life, he, Lev Tolstoy, was. Tolstoy includes himself, although somewhat tentatively, in the chronological list of his mother's four 'real loves', i.e.: 1) her dead fiancé 'Lev', in fact probably Nikolai, 2) her French companion Mlle Hénissienne,[164] 3) her eldest son Nikolai, and finally 4) her fourth son Lev:

> The fourth strong feeling which, perhaps, my aunties used to say to me, existed, and which I so wished to exist, was her love for me, replacing her love for Koko [Nikolai] who, at the time of my birth had already become unstuck from his mother [*otlepivshegosia ot materi*] and had passed over into male hands.[165]

Tolstoy admits that his thinking is somewhat wishful here (*ia tak zhelal, chtoby bylo*), and even implies that his mother did not actually love him (not to mention the two middle sons) while she was busy with her close supervision of Nikolai: 'It was imperative for her not to love herself, and one love was succeeded by another.'[166] Thus at the same time that Tolstoy is praising his mother for her selflessness, he seems to be covertly rebuking her for not spreading the love around more. She could love in series, as it were, but not in parallel.

This rebuke could be understood as a disguised expression of ordinary sibling rivalry, for mothers are normally quite capable of loving more than one child at a time. On the other hand, Tolstoy's mother may in fact have been incapable of more than one serious love at a time (in her letters she talks much more about her eldest, Koko, than about the other children).[167] In either case Tolstoy is covertly expressing a very important subjective feeling: he did not get enough love from his mother. The hearsay evidence that 'Mama loved me very much' is thrown into serious question.

Tolstoy says he greatly admires his mother's indifference to the judgement of others as well as her modesty (*skromnost'*) – such extreme modesty that she even seemed ashamed of revealing her mental and moral advantages to others. These features Tolstoy divined, again, not from direct experience of his mother, but from reading her letters and the 'Journal of Conduct' she kept describing her beloved eldest son Nikolai. Tolstoy also knew these aspects of his mother from this self-effacing Nikolai himself, who, he believes, was very much like the mother.

At this point in the memoir Tolstoy interjects a quip that the writer Ivan Turgenev had supposedly once made about Nikolai, that 'he did not have those shortcomings necessary in order to be a great writer'.[168] The 'great writer' Tolstoy, it is understood, did have these shortcomings. Certainly he brags about his shortcomings incessantly in his memoir (and elsewhere), saying he is 'morally obtuse' and 'filled with vanity', speaking of the 'shameful' lines of his life's story, the 'loathsomeness of my prior life', 'all the filth and crimes of my life', and so on.[169] Tolstoy's description of himself as 'filled with vanity [*polon tshcheslaviia*]' contrasts especially sharply with the characterization of Nikolai: 'he had no vanity [*u nego ne bylo tshcheslaviia*]'.[170] Nikolai had the *other* qualities necessary to be a good writer, such as an ability to make up stories on the spot, an inexhaustible imagination, a good sense of humour, a subtle artistic sense, and so on.[171] He lacked only vanity. Psychoanalytically speaking, his narcissism was healthy, he needed no extra narcissistic supplies, such as those that might be provided by literary fame.[172]

There is considerable psychological insight into the nature of creativity here. But there is also a hidden commentary on the mother. When one considers the quotation from Turgenev in context, it appears that Tolstoy would never have had his many admitted shortcomings *if* he, like his eldest brother Nikolai, had received enough love and attention from his perfectionist mother (he was about to be put through the same maternal regimen Nikolai had experienced when the mother suddenly died). Tolstoy thus seems to be blaming his mother for his imperfections, including his disturbed narcissism.

By bringing in the remark by Turgenev, Tolstoy also casts a whole new light on his stated admiration for both his mother and his brother Nikolai. The compliment has suddenly become backhanded, in effect: 'I was excluded from their realm of virtuous love by her early death, but I am, with all my shortcomings, at least a great writer.' Or to be more explicit: 'I did not get enough love from my mother, but at least the world loves me for my writing.'

As a young man, and in middle age Tolstoy very much liked the admiration he received for his literary accomplishments. For example, when his brother-in-law Stepan Bers told him that some law school friends were reading and enjoying *War and Peace* Tolstoy admitted that he was flattered, and there were tears of joy in his eyes.[173] Even in old age, when struggling to attain humility, Tolstoy knew and recognized that he was a great writer. To Maksim Gorky he said of *War and Peace*: 'Without false modesty – this is comparable to *The Iliad*.'[174]

True, just as often the older Tolstoy would attempt to repudiate his own greatness. In an 1887 letter to Strakhov he refers to his writing as vomit (*blevotina*).[175] Speaking to a couple of his admirers in 1886 he referred to *Anna Karenina* as 'filth' (*gadost'*) and called himself something like a 'bad person' (most likely 'a shit') for having written it.[176] Yet at the time he said this he was actually reading and correcting proofs for a new edition of the novel.

To Gusev, Tolstoy said in 1908: 'I'm just a human being like any other, I didn't write anything special.'[177] Toward the beginning of the *Reminiscences* he also speaks of 'the artistic chatter which fills my twelve volume works to which people of our time attach undeserved significance'.[178] Yet the fact that people revere Tolstoy's work is not denied here, for it is mentioned, perhaps unnecessarily so. What is denied, instead, is the pleasure that would normally come from knowing that one is revered as a great literary artist.[179] This is a curious combination of overt humility, covert grandiosity, and overt masochism. As we will see from the diaries written during the period of creating *The Kreutzer Sonata*, Tolstoy in similar fashion often tempers his grandiosity (or outright megalomania) with moral masochism. But he never reaches the stage of true humility because he is always exhibiting himself (always *telling* people how bad or insignificant he is, always keeping a diary, always publishing religious pamphlets and even literary works). At times Tolstoy dreams of 'abstaining' from writing altogether,[180] but he never succeeds. He cannot do without an audience. He may succeed at self-humiliation, but he never achieves true humility.

4. THE PSYCHOLOGY OF EARLY MATERNAL LOSS

All of Tolstoy's equivocations about whether his mother loved him ultimately result from a simple fact: she died on him. *Could* she even have loved him enough, given that she died so early in his life? *Could* her death have been experienced by Tolstoy the toddler as anything other than an abandonment, proving to him that he was unlovable and inferior?[181]

For an 80-year-old man to cry at the very thought of his mother is unusual. She is still *hurting* Tolstoy by what she did, as if he were still the easily hurt 'cry-baby' child his siblings said he was.[182] The narcissistic injury is still there, unhealed. It would not be surprising if Tolstoy were to feel angry or hateful toward his mother in response to such hurt. Psychiatrist Karl Stern speculates that Tolstoy must have felt as follows: 'I have loved you, you have abandoned me, and therefore I hate you.'[183]

No one has ever produced evidence for such hatred. But I believe it exists. On one of the summer days in 1908 when he is thinking a lot about his mother, he writes in his diary:

> I cannot emphasize enough that anyone who wants to live the true life must first of all make an effort at the true life when alone with his thoughts. It's surprising how few people know this. When you think about someone *with malevolence*, stop, search for the good in him, let him be the most dear creature for you, *as is my mother for me*.[184]

The sequence of affects is interesting here. Positive feelings toward someone can be cultivated specifically as a reaction to negative feelings (*nedobrozhelatel'stvo*). But the fact that these positive feelings are compared to Tolstoy's own feelings toward his mother raises a question: do his positive feelings toward his mother *also* result from initial malevolence toward her? Technically speaking, is Tolstoy's sentimentalization or idealization of his mother a reaction formation?

I think that the answer to these questions has to be yes.[185] Toddlers who temporarily lose their mothers are known to express anger at them when they return.[186] Tolstoy's mother never returned. As we already saw above, Tolstoy seems to blame his mother for his own imperfections, and to rebuke her for being able to love only one person at a time. As we will see later, Tolstoy was also not too happy about being farmed out to substitute mothers. But he never could express his rage toward his mother directly.

Tolstoy once expressed mild envy toward his friend Vladimir Grigorevich Chertkov for the latter's good relationship with *his* mother. But rather than lament the absence of his mother during most of his childhood, Tolstoy criticizes himself for not loving his mother: 'I was very glad to hear about your relationship with your mother. How nice! It would be the same with me too if there were love on my part, and I would overcome; but there is none at all that's real, and often because of this I am hateful to myself'.[187] This blametaking is characteristic of Tolstoy. Why should he feel responsible for having 'real' love for a mother he supposedly cannot remember? Since blame is inappropriate here, it must be defensive. He seems to be shifting blame from his mother onto himself.

Another indirect piece of evidence for Tolstoy's hostile feeling toward the mother who died on him is his attitude toward his birthplace. As is well known, Tolstoy was born and spent the greater part of his childhood on his mother's estate of Yasnaya Polyana.[188] No place on earth was more important to Tolstoy than Yasnaya Polyana. He was esconced there for much of his adult life. Once when some peasant women asked Tolstoy whether he preferred living abroad to living in Yasnaya Polyana, he replied: 'No, no place is better than one's birthplace. For me the best place is Yasnaya Polyana'.[189] Here Tolstoy's word for 'birthplace' is '*rodina*' (cognate with '*rodit'sia*', 'to give birth'). The word is not only the generic term for the larger 'motherland' in Russian, but is also the traditional term peasants use to refer to their native village.

Tolstoy clearly idealizes his birthplace, just as he idealizes his mother.[190] Yet in 1854 the house in which he was born was sold, dismantled, and re-erected by a new owner in the village of Dolgoye, about 20 kilometres from Yasnaya Polyana. Tolstoy himself was responsible for this act of destruction, for he needed the money to pay off gambling debts. Later he was uncomfortable whenever asked to talk about what had happened to the house, and was clearly sorry for what he had done.[191] Indeed he should have been sorry. His youthful compulsive gambling had destroyed his mother's property, in effect her domestic metonym. Only the two wings of the 'big house' remained in Yasnaya Polyana, and it was in one of these that Tolstoy later lived with his wife and raised a family.

In December of 1897 the aging Tolstoy dropped by the village of Dolgoye to have a look at the old place: 'A very moving impression of the tumbledown house. A swarm of recollections.'[192] Clearly he was still attached to his mother's home, the home in which he was born, and the home he had ruined. In 1913 the building was again torn down, this time for wood and bricks.[193]

Tolstoy's son Ilya reports on the way his father referred to his birthplace:

> Whenever anyone asked my father where he was born, he pointed to the tall larch growing at the site of the old foundation.
>
> 'Over there, where the top of that larch tree is now, was Mamen'ka's room. That's where I was born, on the leather couch', he used to say.[194]

A photograph in Ilya's book shows the place where the old house used to stand. It is overgrown with tall trees. One of them is identifiably a larch (*listvennitsa*) with its scraggly coniferous top, and on the photo, about a quarter of the way up the trunk, is a small white cross labelled 'larch at the top of which L. N. was born'.[195] This important photograph is missing from the 1969 Soviet edition of Ilya's book.[196]

In May of 1996 I visited the huge empty spot between the two wings of the the Yasnaya Polyana complex and discovered that the larch tree still grows there, larger than ever. To me this space signified the large, problematical place in Tolstoy's heart occupied by his mother.

As noted above, Tolstoy was 23 months old when his mother died.[197] He would have been in a phase of development termed rapprochement by psychoanalyst Margaret Mahler and her colleagues. This phase lasts roughly from 14 to 24 months of age:

> It is characterized by a rediscovery of mother, now a separate individual, and a returning to her after the obligatory forays of the practicing period. The toddler loves to share his experiences and possessions with mother, who is now more clearly perceived as separate and outside. The narcissistic inflation of the practicing subphase is slowly replaced by a growing realization of separateness and, with it, vulnerability. Adverse reactions to brief separations are common, and mother can no longer be easily substituted for, even by familiar adults.

During this phase, as Mahler notes, there is 'a seeming constant concern with the mother's whereabouts'. Tolstoy the toddler had in all likelihood reached the so-called rapprochement crisis, that is, the point where the sense of separateness from the mother is acute, and ambivalence toward her intense: '. . . the toddler wants to be united with, and at the same time separate from, mother. Temper tantrums, whining, sad moods, and intense separation reactions are at their height.'[198]

We have no way of knowing *precisely* where Tolstoy was in the developmental process when his mother died. But it does seem likely that the 23 month-old Tolstoy was already thinking of his mother as a single, continuously existing individual person different from other persons ('Mamen'ka', as he sometimes called her later in life),[199] and that he felt strong emotions, including love and hatred, about this person. The ambivalent feelings could not but have affected Tolstoy's later thinking about his mother and about mother-figures generally.

There are no direct reports of how Tolstoy, as a young child, responded to his mother's death (although it is known that he behaved rather cantankerously when brought to his mother's deathbed for her final, tearful blessing – see later). However, clinical studies of the responses of young children to the death of a parent do demonstrate that even very young children are capable of grieving.[200] Bowlby furnishes examples of children in their second year (Tolstoy's age) who, although they have not yet acquired language, nonetheless show signs of yearning for an absent mother (not merely separation anxiety), and of sometimes expressing anger toward her if she should happen to return.[201]

Child analyst Erna Furman reports on her group's clinical findings:

With toddlers from fifteen to twenty-four months of age [Tolstoy's category precisely] . . . we observed several instances of a new need-fulfilling person having to take over, or an already loved person having to extend his or her care after the loss of a parent. In each case the young child accepted the newly offered care and related in time to the need-fulfilling person, but *his longing for the lost loved one did not cease*. On the contrary, it appeared that, once his need fulfillment was assured, he could devote more energy to the efforts of dealing with the loss of the love object.[202]

In Tolstoy's case there is one particularly eloquent piece of evidence that longing for the lost mother *never* ceased. On 10 March 1906 the aging Tolstoy wrote the following note to himself on a stray piece of paper:

A dull melancholic state [*tosklivoe sostoianie*] all day. Toward evening this state changed into a tender feeling, a desire for affection, for love. As in childhood I longed to cling to a being who loved me, who took pity on me, and to weep tenderly and be consoled. But who is that being to whom I would cling so? I go over all the people whom I love, and none will do. To whom can I cling? I'd like to make myself small and cling to mother as I imagine her to myself.

Yes, yes, mommy [*mamen'ka*], whom I had not even yet called by that name since I couldn't speak. Yes, she, my most exalted concept of pure love, not that cold, divine type, but a warm, earthy, motherly love. That's what my better but tired soul yearns for. Yes, mommy, come cuddle me [*Ty, mamen'ka, ty prilaskai menia*].

All this is insane [*bezumno*], but it is all true.[203]

Insane indeed. Tolstoy recognizes his psychopathology here, specifying it as his usual depressive *toska* ('*tosk*livoe sostoianie', or outright '*toska*' in the next day's retrospective diary entry).[204] But what is unusual about this particular episode is the direct reference to the mother – 'Mamen'ka', the real, biological mother, not the lofty ideal he prayed to in his youth. He calls her by the name he must have used with her, despite his claim to the contrary, for it is highly unlikely that a 23 month-old Tolstoy did not have rudimentary language skills.[205] Only she, the warm cuddly 'Mamen'ka', can soothe his psychological pain. Many decades have passed, yet he longs for her still.

All his life Tolstoy lived in the shadow of his mother's death. The fact that he longs for his mother in old age indicates that he has never truly mourned her passing, that he has not really reconciled himself to his early loss and still feels a need for the lost object. Even some non-psychoanalytic scholars have suspected this to be the case. As Janko Lavrin observes: 'The image of the mother remained an object of his conscious and unconscious longing.'[206] Marie Sémon says that early maternal loss gave rise in Tolstoy to '*une faim d'amour impossible à rassasier*'.[207] Martin Malia says that early maternal deprivation is plausibly related to Tolstoy's 'later obsession with defining the ideal woman'.[208] Or, to quote another non-psychoanalytic critic, Martine de Courcel: '. . . it is certain that Tolstoy's mother's ghost never stopped roaming within his unconscious thought and begot in it that nostalgia for pure love which was to obsess him during his youth in his periods of debauchery, and still more in his maturity, as is shown by the violence with which he reviled bodily love in *The Kreutzer Sonata*'.[209] As we will see, however, the latter work is more an expression of outright hatred of the 'abandoning' mother than nostalgia for her.

Tolstoy's Mamen'ka note is like those episodes of longing for the
mother which are sometimes met with in psychoanalytic practice.
Karl Abraham gives a couple of examples in a 1924 paper:

> [A] melancholic patient I had said that during his deepest fits of
> depression he had the feeling that a woman might free him from
> his suffering if she expended on him a special maternal love and
> solicitude.

> A young man suffering from depression . . . used to feel himself
> almost miraculously soothed by drinking a glass of milk which his
> mother handed to him. The milk gave him a sensation of some-
> thing warm, soft, and sweet, and reminded him of something he
> had known long ago. In this instance the patient's longing for the
> breast was unmistakable.[210]

These patients, like Tolstoy in his Mamen'ka note, feel that a maternal figure can soothe the pain of depression. The soothing is never
more than temporary, however. One's mother may be a powerful
comforter in childhood, but depression in adulthood requires a
stronger antidepressant than memory of the mother.

5. AMBIVALENCE AND MULTIPLE MOTHERING

Tolstoy's lingering *toska* for his mother suggests that we ought to
consider what that *toska* might derive from ontogenetically, that is,
what it was when Tolstoy's mother was still alive.

Psychoanalyst Melanie Klein believes that all infants experience
depressive feelings, especially around the time of weaning. She
speaks of the 'depressive position' a child occupies when it is still
trying to be reconciled with the unavoidable periodic losses of attention from the mother. The child 'pines' for the absent mother, as Klein
puts it. In this situation the child may feel that loss of the mother and
of the goodness of her bountiful breasts is a result of the child's own
greediness and destructiveness aimed at the mother's breasts. At the
same time the mother herself may be blamed, and the child is inclined to hate the 'bad' mother for not granting all wishes, for not
always being available, for punishing and depriving the child by (in

effect) dying temporarily. This reproachful hatred, however, can be very upsetting. Feelings of guilt come into play, for the hatred threatens the 'good' mother whom the child is also in the process of internalizing. The hatred might also provoke retaliation. Persecutory feelings may develop. According to Klein, a counteractive *idealization* of the mother might then (temporarily, periodically) occur: 'With the young child, the idealized mother is the safeguard against a retaliating or a dead mother and against all bad objects, and therefore represents security and life itself.'[211]

In Tolstoy's case, as we have seen, the mother was idealized well into adulthood and old age (his*culte*). The idealization of her is associated specifically with feeling low and depressed (for example when he prayed to her), which is to say Tolstoy may still have been operating from the infantile Kleinian 'depressive position' where he both 'pined' for his mother and felt bad about himself for hating her because she periodically abandoned him. Unfortunately, his mother abandoned him permanently when he was still in that vulnerable position, so he may have become stuck in it in some sense, not worked his way out of it despite the good substitute mothering he got.

Here it should be observed that the child Tolstoy was cared for by other women in addition to his mother. Even before his mother died other women were involved in his care, most notably his peasant wet nurse, Avdot'ia Ziabreva. Tolstoy's wealthy gentry family was in a position to to bring in all sorts of hired child-care assistants, as well as other servant help. In old age Tolstoy once remarked on how unnatural this was, comparing his mother to those aimless young people who study law out of nothing better to do: 'In thirty years people will be just as surprised at the fact that young men go to law school as we today are surprised at the serfdom of my mother, who was good, sensitive, deep, but who permitted herself to be waited upon by many servants, as was the custom then.'[212] Tolstoy's obligatory reference to his mother's goodness cannot hide the hint of his disapproval of her in this particular case. Very likely he had read one of his mother's letters in which she expresses concern about the temporary illness of the wet nurse she had employed for her eldest son Nikolai, and hopes her doctor will soon permit the wet nurse to breast-feed little Koko again: 'I want this very badly because she has become so attached to the child, and is so well-behaved that I would be sorry to be separated from her.'[213] Tolstoy's mother then goes on to talk about the weather, about her lovely English garden, Italian lessons, and so on. Not a word about poor Koko, the one who is actually deprived.

As an adult Tolstoy disapproved of substitute mothering, especially in the early stages of a child's life. For example, in a letter of
23 June 1889 to one of his followers – and while he was in the throes
of rewriting *The Kreutzer Sonata* – he states that 'collective upbringing of children' on communes is 'bad', and that one should not tolerate a situation where 'there is not upbringing of children by their
own mother'.[214] As we will see below, Tolstoy repeatedly expressed
outright hostility toward women who did not breast-feed their own
children. These attitudes could not but reflect his underlying attitude toward his mother, who did not breast-feed him.

In addition to a wet-nurse, nannies, and other servants, various women relatives lavished love and attention upon the child
Tolstoy. Most important among these was Tat'iana Aleksandrovna
Ergol'skaia, a distant aunt on the father's side, who lived with the
family and was heavily involved with caring for all five of the children
after Tolstoy's mother died. Tolstoy was very close to this self-
sacrificing woman, as is clear from the long passage about her in the
Reminiscences, the touching description of being separated from her
care in 'My Life', and from her fictionalized appearance in *War and
Peace* (the character Sonia). It was Ergol'skaia, Tolstoy believes, who
taught him how to love.[215] And it was in large part fond memories of
this Ergol'skaia that helped and encouraged Tolstoy to concoct
what Andrew Wachtel terms 'the myth of happy childhood' in Russian gentry autobiography.[216]

A particularly revealing passage in the *Reminiscences* indicates sexual and Oedipal elements in Tolstoy's relationship with
Ergol'skaia. Sometimes late at night he (already grown up) would
drop in on her, even after he had already once said good night to
her:

'Come in, come in', she would say. 'I was just telling Natalia
Petrovna [her roommate] that *Nicolas* would come by again.' She
often called me by my father's name, and this was especially
pleasing to me because it showed that her idea of me and of father
was united in her love for both. On these late evenings she was
already undressed [*razdeta*], in a nightshirt with a shawl, with her
chicken-like feet in slippers, and Natalia Petrovna was in the same
négligée.[217]

Tolstoy believes that Ergol'skaia and his father, whom she called
Nicolas, had been in love, but that she had generously given him up

so that he could marry the rich woman who was to become Tolstoy's mother. This story seems a little hard to believe, especially when Tolstoy tells us that Ergol'skaia later refused an offer to marry his father even after he had become a widower (perhaps she was more interested in the mysterious roommate?).[218]

What is also odd is that *Lev* Tolstoy does not mind the fact that Ergol'skaia mistakenly addresses him as *Nicolas* – an error that is just the reverse of an earlier error in the same memoir, where Tolstoy says he was named after his mother's beloved *Lev* who was really *Nikolai* however. In both cases the son, Lev Tolstoy, gets (mis)named after an adult male. In the first instance he receives from his mother the name of the man who might have been his father. In the second instance he is named after his real father by the woman who might have been his mother. This is a curious symmetry, but the important thing is that Tolstoy takes pleasure in the misnaming, especially in the second instance. In a context that is sexually suggestive (it is late at night, Ergol'skaia is 'undressed') Tolstoy momentarily takes on the name of the father, takes the place of his father *Nicolas* in Ergol'skaia's loving imagination, thereby winning an Oedipal round, figuratively speaking. What is more, he wins it without blemishing the memory of his mother, who is absent here, and who was already dead and gone before Tolstoy entered his Oedipal phase (normally occurring from two to five years of age).[219]

All of the substitute mothering Tolstoy got, both before and after his mother died, was important to him, including for Oedipal purposes. None of the substitutes, however, *were* the mother. That, indeed, was a large part of the problem Tolstoy had whenever he tried to think about his mother. The persistent feeling of not having been loved enough by his real mother has to be connected with his experience of substitute mothering. Winning a few figurative Oedipal rounds via Ergol'skaia hardly sufficed to compensate for the massive pre-Oedipal loss. In particular, Tolstoy's awareness of having been nursed at the breast by a peasant woman instead of by his mother left him with feelings of resentment, as will become clear below when we explore the matricidal mind of Pozdnyshev.

Although Tolstoy's mother was not as involved in his care as he would have liked, when she was still alive she was nonetheless in charge of the care of her children, and was often in physical contact with them. There may have been some 'diffusion' of mothering, as Erik Erikson said of Gorky's childhood,[220] and Tolstoy may have resented this, but he did know who his real mother was.

True, that knowledge may have come only later, and when he was still an infant at the breast such knowledge may have been impossible. Tolstoy's primary attachment figure might even have been the wet nurse, not the mother herself. Later conflicting feelings about the mother may have derived in part from feelings initially experienced at the breast of Avdot'ia Ziabreva. Also, Tolstoy's Mahlerian rapprochement crisis, which would have occurred after he had already been weaned from Ziabreva, might have involved a nanny named Annushka, or this nanny and the mother jointly. In the *Reminiscences* Tolstoy speaks of an Annushka 'whom I almost do not remember precisely because I was not conscious in any way other than with Annushka. And just as I did not look at myself and do not remember myself as I was, so too I do not remember Annushka'. Apparently it was quite a revelation to the young Tolstoy to discover that another child living with the family had another nurse, and that therefore 'nurse Annushka was not the general property of everybody'.[221]

Nonetheless, the adult Tolstoy expressed strong feelings about his mother, not about Ziabreva, and not about Annushka. There is not the slightest sign of any reaction to Ziabreva's death in 1868, for example. Also, there are only 16 pages in the 90-volume Jubilee edition where Ziabreva is mentioned (and usually only very much in passing), while there are 50 pages for the mother. Nor are there any overly affectionate literary representations of hired wet nurses in Tolstoy's works (while there are some very positive characterizations of mothers who nurse their own children, and condemnations of mothers who do not, as we will see).

I am going to proceed, therefore, on the assumption that Tolstoy's stated feelings about his mother are about his mother. Mariia Nikolaevna stood out from the crowd of caregivers surrounding Tolstoy in his childhood, however little she was actually involved in caring for him. This idea is supported by a curious but little-known autobiographical fragment entitled 'The Dream' (1857), which Tolstoy never managed to publish. In this work the dreamer is surrounded by a worshipful crowd of people. He is telling them everything that he feels in a strong and firm voice, he is ecstatic, crazed even, and the crowd is ecstatic and crazed with him. Suddenly he senses someone or some 'force' behind him, and he stops speaking. Looking around, he sees a woman standing out in the crowd. Now he feels ashamed. She is indifferent to what he is saying, she needs nothing from him, but she smiles and for a moment gazes at him with pity.

Then she simply vanishes. He is upset, he starts to cry over 'impossible happiness'. In one variant of 'The Dream' the identity of this woman is revealed:

> It was a woman. Without thinking or moving I stopped and looked at her. I became ashamed of what I was doing. The dense crowd did not part, but by some miracle the woman moved slowly and peacefully amidst the crowd, not joining it. I do not remember whether this woman was young and beautiful, I do not remember her clothing or the color of her hair, I do not know whether she was the lost first dream of love or *a later reminiscence of a mother's love*. I only know that in her was everything, and that an irresistible force sweetly and painfully drew me to her.[222]

The negations pile up here ('I do not remember', 'I do not know'), just as they do in those passages in the *Reminiscences* where Tolstoy speaks of his mother. The dreamer barely catches a glimpse of the woman, just as Tolstoy barely knew his mother in early childhood. But the glimpse has been enough for the dreamer to know that the woman in his dream is the most important woman in the world, and her sudden departure from the scene is painful. Meantime, the adulating crowd (= the numerous servants and devoted relatives who cared for Tolstoy) recede in importance as the dreamer harps on the happiness he might have had with this mysterious woman.

Even though Tolstoy (says he) cannot remember his mother, he repeatedly refers to her in various writings as a whole, autonomous individual, as '*Mamen'ka*'. She is not some metonymic part-object left over from before the weaning stage, nor is she some screen eclipsing another primary attachment figure. She is herself, she stands out as an important individual toward whom Tolstoy is 'sweetly and painfully' drawn. Here we may compare some relevant theoretical observations made by Margaret Mahler:

> The primitive ego seems to possess an amazing ability to absorb and synthesize complex object images without adverse effect, and on occasion even with benefit. Thus, the Gestalt of the nurse, who may be relegated to the function of providing immediate need satisfaction, is synthesized with the Gestalt of the mother, who may be available only as an additional or transient external ego. However, it is truly impressive that *although the mother may be less involved in the actual care of the infant, her image seems to attract so much*

54 *Tolstoy on the Couch*

cathexis that it often, though not always, becomes the cardinal object representation.[223]

It is clear that the image of the mother, however blank, did attract enormous cathexis for Tolstoy, and could indeed be considered to be the cardinal object representation in his mind. This is only to restate in psychoanalytic terms what Tolstoy himself said when he spoke tearfully of his *'culte'* of his mother.

Since Tolstoy's longing for his mother in adulthood tended to occur when he was depressed, it would be tempting to make the (essentially Kleinian) assumption that the depressive episodes themselves resulted from unmourned loss of the mother in childhood. However, Tolstoy got depressed about other things besides his mother. Also, there were plenty of depressed adults in Tolstoy's Russia who had not lost their mothers at a tender age. As for statistical clinical studies in our time, they are inconclusive. Some studies demonstrate a correlation between loss of the mother in childhood and development of depressive disorder in adulthood.[224] Other studies show no such correlation, however.[225]

Although the cause of Tolstoy's depressive episodes *per se* is unknown (just as the root cause of depression generally is still unknown in the medical profession), the cause of his yearning or 'pining' (Klein) for his mother in adulthood is obvious: he lost her when he was still a child. The fact that he continued to pine for her in adulthood indicates that he never really came to terms with her loss. The disturbed narcissism also seems pretty solidly tied to the maternal loss, as we have seen.

If longing for the absent mother can persist into adulthood, then anger at her for her absence should theoretically also persist, although it might be more threatening and difficult to deal with consciously. A child who longs for its mother is capable of expressing great anger at her when she returns a few hours or a few days later, as Bowlby, Mahler, and others observe. There is also the factor of idealization, which Klein interprets as a restorative reaction to feelings of anger and hatred toward the 'bad' mother (above). Certainly Tolstoy idealized his mother.

As we have seen, Tolstoy indirectly questions his own idea that his mother 'loved him very much'. In various written documents he conveys an impression of not having been mothered quite enough. But he does not convey *direct* expressions of anger or hatred toward his mother. Yet, to judge from the psychoanalytic literature, those feelings must have been there.

I would like to suggest (with Karl Stern) that Tolstoy did indeed feel a great rage toward his 'abandoning' mother (along with the love), but that he expressed this rage indirectly, displaced it onto other persons who in his unconscious mind bore some resemblance to his mother. Already in childhood, in fact, he was encouraged by the very multiple mothering he received to displace his feelings from one object to another. The objects of his displaced rage included his downtrodden wife and mother of his own children (below I will adduce evidence that Sofia Andreevna was an icon of the mother), some of his fictional mothers (for example the unfortunate Anna Karenina), and even women as a class. Maksim Gorky came closer to the truth than he perhaps realized when he characterized Tolstoy's misogyny as follows: 'It is as if, once upon a time, he had been insulted, and he could neither forgive nor forget.'[226]

My primary concern will be the extreme misogyny of *The Kreutzer Sonata*. The hostility expressed toward women in the diachronic depths of this work – despite its sometimes feminist-looking surface – exceeds even traditional Russian sexism. In particular, the hostility expressed toward *mothers* in this work reflects the devastating, unmourned maternal loss Tolstoy experienced at the age of 23 months.

6. SEXUALITY AND THE DEATH OF THE MOTHER

As we saw above, Tolstoy plays down his mother's sexuality. The fact that she is dead early on in his life makes her particularly pure. She is on a higher pedestal than even most Russian men place their mothers. At the same time, however, there is evidence that Tolstoy reproached her specifically for her sexual behaviour.

Tolstoy was under the false impression that his mother died as the result of complications from childbirth. When he comes to the name Mashenka while listing his siblings in the *Reminiscences*, he appends the clause 'in consequence of whose birth my mother also died'.[227] As Gusev demonstrates, this claim cannot be true. Masha was born on 2 March 1830, while the mother died on 4 August of that year. Five months separate the two events. The official church record indicates a 'fever', but an eyewitness says the fever was of only a few days' duration. Yet another eyewitness speaks of a head injury resulting from being pushed too high on a swing. Apparently, toward the end Tolstoy's mother had headaches and became easily confused, for example she would hold a book upside down when trying to read it.

But whatever the precise medical cause of death, it is clear that Tolstoy was mistaken in believing that his mother died from complications of childbirth.[228] Technically speaking, the death could not have been connected with the puerperium.

Why Tolstoy should make such a mistake is another question, one which a descriptive biographer such as Gusev wisely does not address. The question is most appropriate for psychoanalytic study, however.

We may recall that Tolstoy was also under the mistaken impression that his mother died when he was one and a half years old. That, indeed, *would* have been his approximate age *if* his mother had died as a result of childbirth. Thus we now have two errors that jibe with one another rather well – but not with reality. The larger question becomes: what psychological purpose might have been served by this double lapse?

To phrase the question a bit more directly: why does Tolstoy need to blame the loss of his dear mother on the one time she gave birth after he was born?

This question, in turn, leads to the main theme of *The Kreutzer Sonata*, that is, to sexuality. In order for Tolstoy's mother to have given birth to Maria in August of 1830, she has to have had sexual intercourse with Tolstoy's father nine months earlier, late in 1829 (I think no one would suggest that she had sex with anyone else). At that time, however, the infant Tolstoy was probably still nursing at the breast of his wet nurse, rather than at his mother's breast. Or, if Tolstoy's false assertion that his mother died from birth complications when he was one and a half years old were true, then nine months before that time he would definitely still have been at the breast.[229] The question now becomes: why, by his lapses, does Tolstoy need to blame the loss of his dear mother on the fact of her sexual interaction with her husband at a time when he, the infant Tolstoy, might have been nursing at her breast?

Tolstoy created several fictional characters who question the morality of sexual intercourse. Only Vasilii Pozdnyshev in *The Kreutzer Sonata*, however, elaborates on how utterly disgusted he feels about having sexual intercourse with his wife specifically during the nursing period. That is, only Pozdnyshev advocates and attempts to live in accordance with a postpartum sex taboo. And only Pozdnyshev actually murders his own wife. Whereas Tolstoy's 'madman' merely has thoughts of death in the middle of the night after his long journey to Arzamas, Tolstoy's Pozdnyshev actually kills a fellow human being – also in the middle of the night, and also after a long journey. The richly pathological mind of Pozdnyshev deserves a full psychoanalysis, and such an analysis will, I think, finally answer the questions I have been raising here.[230]

4

Tolstoy's Case for Sexual Abstinence

Tolstoy began working on what was to become *The Kreutzer Sonata* in 1887, completing the work late in 1889. Already in the late 1870s Tolstoy had drafted a short piece entitled 'The Wife Murderer'.[231] But then the idea for such a work was abandoned for quite a while, perhaps because Tolstoy had trouble finding an appropriate narrative form, or perhaps because of the inherent distastefulness of the idea. In any case, work on a story about a man who killed his wife began anew after the actor and storyteller V. N. Andreev-Burlak visited Yasnaya Polyana in July of 1887. Sonia reports: 'He related to [Tolstoy] how once, on a train, a gentleman told him about his misfortune caused by an unfaithful wife, and it was this story that Levochka made use of.'[232] By the autumn of 1887 Tolstoy had arrived at a third, but not yet very substantial draft of his story. After that not much progress was made for some time. Not until the spring of 1889 did Tolstoy set to working wholeheartedly on the novella. The bulk of the writing and rewriting was done in that year. The final version is the ninth draft, completed in December, and is the one published in the Soviet Jubilee Edition (Volume 27, 1933) and now generally available in many languages. The eighth (lithographed) draft, however, was in wide circulation in Russia and abroad from the early 1890s.

I will not give a detailed history of the production of the various drafts and variants, as that task has already been accomplished.[233] The focus here is psychoanalytic, not textological. But I will freely quote from all available published drafts and variants in developing psychoanalytic arguments about the novella and its relationship to Tolstoy the man.

1. ENTER A MADMAN

The scene is a passenger compartment of a train moving somewhere across late nineteenth-century Russia. For anyone who knows

Tolstoy, this already is ominous. Anna Karenina's sexual infidelity is associated with railway travel, and she eventually commits suicide by throwing herself under the wheels of a train. Katia Maslova also threatens to kill herself this way in *Resurrection*. In the present work a murder will occur right after a train ride.

Tolstoy himself did not like riding on trains. In 1857 he wrote to Turgenev: 'The railway is to travel what the whore is to love. It is just as convenient, but it is also just as inhumanly machinelike and mur- derously monotonous.'[234] Trains are for travel, of course, not for sex. But, as Charles Isenberg has argued in a recent book, the relentless, banging motion of a moving train suggests sexuality. The atmo- sphere of Tolstoy's novella is permeated with the clatter of a moving train, which is like 'the clatter of concupiscence'.[235] If this sound in the novella does keep reminding us of sex, then it is a loveless and mechanical kind of sex – the only kind Tolstoy's hero knows, as we will see.

In the train compartment are several people, including the unnamed narrator of Tolstoy's novella. They are having a lively discussion on the subject of marriage and divorce. The two main antagonists are an educated, middle-aged woman in a masculine-looking coat, and an old merchant. The woman believes that if there is no love in marriage, divorce should be permitted (at that time divorce was difficult to obtain among the Orthodox in Russia). In particular, a woman should not have to be chained, figuratively speaking, to a man. But the merchant seems to believe marriages should be ar- ranged, as in the old days, regardless of whether the bride and groom love one another, and divorce is out of the question. A woman should never be given the freedom to leave, and a man who tolerates a woman's sexual waywardness is an 'idiot' (while it is perfectly all right for a man to go on a spree). Women should even live in *fear* (*pervoe delo strakh*):

'What sort of fear?' asked the lady.
'Fear of her *hu-u-u*sband, of course. That kind of fear'.
'Well, my dear man, those days have gone, I'm afraid', said the lady, with an edge of malice in her voice.
'No, missus, those days can never be gone. Eve, the woman, was created from the rib of man, and so she will remain until the end of time', said the old man, with . . . a stern and triumphant shake of his head. . . .[236]

The 'edge of malice' in the educated woman's voice pales by comparison with the threatening tone of the old man. As the woman later observes to the other passengers, his crude hostility seems to come right out of the *Domostroi*.[237] The old man's view of the relations between the sexes is indeed, as Eve Levin has pointed out, 'the medieval position'.[238] In one variant the old patriarch denies that he is referring to the traditional Russian practice of wife-beating, in another he admits that he 'beat her [his wife] a little.'[239] In the final version it is clear that he is referring to this abuse, which was advocated as a disciplinary measure in the*Domostroi*.

After the old merchant leaves the compartment, a new conversation begins. A man by the name of Pozdnyshev (Poznyshev in some variants) who had been following the previous conversation closely but had refrained from participating, now steps in to offer his own brand of misogyny. It will be more subtle – more Tolstoyan – than that of the old merchant.[240]

When the educated lady asserts that 'marriage without love is not marriage at all', Pozdnyshev challenges her to define what love is. She responds by saying that 'Love is the exclusive preference for one man or one woman above all others.' But Pozdnyshev (deliberately?) misinterprets this to mean sexual attraction, and asserts that it can never last very long:

'Every man experiences what you call love each time he meets a pretty woman.'

'Oh, but what you're saying is dreadful! Surely there's an emotion that exists between people called love, a feeling that lasts not just months or years, but for the whole of their lives?'

'Definitely not. Even if one admits that a man may prefer a certain woman all his life, it's more than probable that the woman will prefer someone else. That's the way it's always been and that's the way it still is', he said, taking a cigarette from his cigarette case and lighting it.[241]

When the lady explains that Pozdnyshev is confusing sexual attraction (*plotskaia liubov'*) with real, spiritual love, he cleverly changes the subject: '"Spiritual affinity? Shared ideals?" he repeated . . . . "There's not much point in going to bed together if that's what you're after (excuse the plain language). Do people go to bed with one another because of shared ideals?" he said, laughing nervously.'[242]

For a woman restricted by sexist mores that do not permit her to discuss sexuality openly, Pozdnyshev's response is an effective put-down. It would not be lady-like for her to respond, she now has no choice but to be silent.[243] But the fact is that Pozdnyshev has changed the subject, and this reflects *his* problem. He cannot countenance the coexistence of love with sexual desire or lust (*pokhot'*). He cannot tolerate the juxtaposition of the 'affectionate' and the 'sensual', that is, 'two currents whose union is necessary to ensure a completely normal attitude in love' – as Freud wrote in a 1912 essay on the psychology of love.[244] Quite naturally, Pozdnyshev's interlocutors have trouble understanding what he is trying to say. They are simply normal.

If at one moment Pozdnyshev is equating love with physical desire, the next he goes further, denying the existence of love altogether ('Definitely not'). He seriously doubts 'the existence of any love apart from the physical kind' (in a draft variant he calls love a 'lie' and a 'deception').[245] Here Tolstoy's character is sounding a lot like Olenin in *The Cossacks* (1862), and is stating a view Tolstoy himself had asserted in his younger years. In a diary entry for 19 October 1852 we find the stark declaration: 'There is no love. There is a carnal need for intercourse and a practical need for a companion in life.'[246]

Tolstoy's wife rightly sensed a similarity between *The Kreutzer Sonata* and the youthful diaries of her husband which she happened to be copying in 1890. Of the passage just quoted she writes in her own diary: 'I only wish I had read that remark 29 years ago, then I would never have married him.'[247] On the other hand, she might have married him anyway, understanding that the remark represented only the surface of Tolstoy's true feelings, or his temporary inability to love at the time he wrote the remark.

Particularly interesting is Pozdnyshev's belief that it is 'more than probable' (*po vsem veroiatiiam*) that, should a man actually develop a preference for one woman, she would come to prefer a different man anyway. That is, a woman will emotionally abandon a man if he starts to get involved with her (including sexually). This assumption, like the denial of love's existence, is unfounded for normal people, who are willing to take a chance at love (or at least admit to taking a chance). But the assumption must have some foundation in Pozdnyshev's unique personal experience (or in his creator Tolstoy's). Another man in the compartment, a lawyer travelling with the educated woman, makes the sensible observation that 'there can be mutual affection'. But Pozdnyshev is adamant: 'No there can't....'.[248]

Apparently the impossibility of *mutual* love in a sexual relationship is of paramount concern for Pozdnyshev, although this idea is dropped for the time being. The reader may sense that Pozdnyshev has somehow been hurt in the past (he had taken a chance and been hurt). Psychoanalytically speaking, his narcissism has been seriously injured. In a variant he says: 'Menelaus, perhaps, preferred Helen his whole life, but Helen preferred Paris, and that's the way it always has been and always is in this world.'[249] Pozdnyshev is thus a Menelaus betrayed by his Helen. Or, to use the more strictly Tolstoyan imagery of *War and Peace*, he is a Pierre betrayed by his Hélène (and we know what an ugly death Tolstoy subjected Hélène to).[250]

In conversation with Maksim Gorky Tolstoy once admitted that 'it's not the woman who holds you by your [prick] who is dangerous, but the one who holds on to your soul'.[251] Tolstoy, like his Pozdnyshev, understood deep down that the primary issue in the relations between the sexes was emotional attachment, not sex.

In the same variant Pozdnyshev goes on to say: 'Only in stupid novels is it written that they loved each other for their whole life. Only children can believe that.'[252] Perhaps as a child Pozdnyshev did indeed believe that, and perhaps his narcissistic injury occurred when he was attached to someone important to him specifically in childhood. As Freud says of the 'affectionate' and 'sensual' currents in the same 1912 essay mentioned above: 'The affectionate current is the older of the two. It springs from the earliest years of childhood. . . '.[253]

Pozdnyshev's belief that his own sad experience (whatever it might have been) should somehow apply to the majority of people is rather self-oriented, that is, narcissistic.[254] Contrary to what Peter Ulf Møller says, Pozdnyshev does not offer 'a devastating criticism of modern marriage', nor does Tolstoy's story implement 'a drastic unmasking of modern marriage and the miserable sensuality of the upper classes'.[255] Rather, *The Kreutzer Sonata* offers an 'unmasking' of Pozdnyshev's own injured, sick psyche, as well as of Tolstoy's disturbed thinking about the relations between the sexes. Pozdnyshev's assertions seem 'hair-raising', as Møller rightly terms them, because most of Tolstoy's listeners and readers are ordinary, normal.

As the conversation proceeds it becomes more and more evident that Pozdnyshev is mentally disturbed. Many scholars and other readers have noticed this disturbance. Pozdnyshev's discourse becomes increasingly shrill, distraught, and 'Dostoevskian', as Robert

Louis Jackson has shown. H. Beck, a German psychiatrist and contemporary of Tolstoy's, characterizes Pozdnyshev as 'psychically degenerate', with a 'neuropathic disposition'. Jungian critic Bettina Knapp speaks of 'Pozdnyshev's psychosis' and calls Tolstoy's hero a 'psychopath'. Françoise Flamant argues that Pozdnyshev is suffering from paranoia, as does Vladimir Golstein. Angus Calder terms Pozdnyshev 'a very neurotic man'. Johannes Holthusen says Tolstoy depicts Pozdnyshev as 'a scatter-brained neurotic' and 'a psychopathological case'. Marie Sémon calls Pozdnyshev a 'madman', even a 'holy fool' (*iurodivyi*) in the Russian tradition. Pozdnyshev later himself admits that he is a 'wreck', a 'cripple', even 'a sort of madman'. In a draft of his afterword Tolstoy speaks of critics who believe Pozdnyshev is a 'psychopath', and who call Tolstoy himself a 'madman' (*sumasshedshii*). In a diary entry from early 1890 Tolstoy says he has heard that people are referring to his Pozdnyshev as a 'sexual maniac'.[256]

This sampling of diverse (not necessarily technically correct) diagnoses ought to make it clear that Pozdnyshev's disturbance, whatever it is, is real. And still other diagnoses will be brought up in the course of this book. For now it is sufficient to note that signs of a mental disturbance are apparent early on in the novella. Concrete physical symptoms do not escape the attention of the people seated in the train compartment with Pozdnyshev. His face becomes red with agitation, a muscle of his cheek twitches, he periodically emits a peculiar half-sobbing, half-laughing sound from his throat.[257] Pozdnyshev's companions become embarrassed and uncomfortable in his presence, especially after he informs them that he is *that* Pozdnyshev they may have heard about, the one who *murdered his wife.*

There is a stunned silence. At this point there can hardly be any more discussion about the question of love in marriage.

Later on we learn that Pozdnyshev was kept in prison for only 11 months after his crime, and then acquitted and released by the court: 'At my trial they decided I was a wronged husband who'd killed his wife in order to defend his outraged honour (that's the way they put it in their language).'[258] Iakov Botkin, a forensic psychiatrist and contemporary of Tolstoy's, argues that Pozdnyshev killed his wife in an uncontrollable burst of 'criminal affect'.[259] Botkin appears to be suggesting a form of temporary insanity defence.

After a time, Pozdnyshev and the unnamed man who is narrating Tolstoy's novella are left alone in the train compartment (the others have left, apparently embarrassed by Pozdnyshev's momentary exhibitionistic burst).[260] This is an opportunity for Pozdnyshev to tell his story, and the narrator expresses a willingness to hear him out. Tolstoy is going to give us a story framed within a story, that is, his novella is an example of the so-called frame narrative.[261] From this point on the narrator will sit quietly for the most part, and attention will be focused on Pozdnyshev. The narrator himself is a kind of blank whose primary function is to absorb Pozdnyshev's sad tale and sick theory. He is 'Pozdnyshev's dummy', as Isenberg puts it.[262] This narrator transmits what he has heard to us, the readers, documenting Pozdnyshev's considerable emotional agitation along the way.[263] In so doing he no doubt also absorbs some of the distasteful emotional intensity of the spoken tale for us, thereby making us more willing addressees. It is unlikely that most people, especially women, would be willing actually to hear out a person as disturbed as Pozdnyshev obviously is.

The absence of the educated lady is particularly important, for it would be difficult for Pozdnyshev to tell his misogynistic tale in her presence (early in the eighth – lithographed – draft Pozdnyshev is so agitated that 'it is as if he were angry and wanted to say something unpleasant to the lady').[264] In the first draft Pozdnyshev tries to pretend the lady is not there in order to avoid getting angry at her directly. For example:

> *Crossed-out.* 'But that isn't love', said the lady.
> The dark-haired one [Pozdnyshev] winced with vexation, but he didn't even turn to look at her, and continued addressing himself only to the gentleman with the nice things.

Or:

> 'She was a woman without an education', said the lady.
> Again he got angry at the lady and, not looking at her, continued answering the gentleman with the nice things.
> 'She had the same education as women who say of themselves that they are educated.'[265]

What Tolstoy has done by removing these unpleasant little scenes at an early stage is to give Pozdnyshev room to elaborate on his hostility to sexuality and to women. A man-to-man misogyny is not possible in mixed company. By the third draft Pozdnyshev (for the time being called Leonid Stepanov) is alone with a young male narrator.

Most of the rest of (the final version of) *The Kreutzer Sonata* is a monologue [266] spoken in Pozdnyshev's words, with relatively few substantive interruptions by the narrator. Pozdnyshev's discourse will be long, even rambling in places. His lengthy moral sermon will sometimes seem incompatible with his own narration of his crime. [267] His story is inappropriately intimate for strangers who have met for the first time on a train, [268] and who are not even consuming alcohol. [269] But at least the speaker and the (later narrating) listener are of the same sex.

What Pozdnyshev says will repel many readers, and what he does to his wife is unforgivable. Yet his story is hard to put down, and many readers even feel sympathy for the murderer. All this, as Mark Aldanov observes, is testimony to Tolstoy's considerable artistic powers. [270] Or, as Aylmer Maude says, 'Tolstoy's craftmanship did not fail him.' [271] Pozdnyshev himself demonstrates considerable Tolstoyan talent in the way he tells his story to the narrator. [272] As T. G. S. Cain puts it, the narration is 'magnificently handled', even if it is 'introduced by, and partly interwoven with, an obsessively unintelligent, simplistic series of generalisations on the nature (and sources) of sexual passion'. [273]

Much of what Pozdnyshev has to say reflects Tolstoy's own attitudes at the time of the work's composition (in the third variant Pozdnyshev is even *Leo*nid). Late in 1890 Tolstoy said to Dr E. J. Dillon that he regarded the work as 'the text of his doctrine'. [274] The similarity between what Pozdnyshev says and what Tolstoy thinks is especially evident from the afterword Tolstoy wrote in late 1889 and early 1890 in response to the urgings of his friend Vladimir Grigorevich Chertkov, as well as to the many letters he had received from inquisitive readers. [275] There may have been a factor of personal dissatisfaction with the literary work by itself. Ruth Crego Benson says: 'His need to write an Epilogue [afterword] suggests that, in this case, the act of writing led Tolstoy to inadequate catharsis and failed to free him from his preoccupation with sexuality'. [276]

In the new piece Tolstoy sets out to explain precisely what he was 'trying to say' in his story. The afterword may be 'weak' artistically, as Aldanov says, but it is as biographically revealing as the novella itself, and besides, it is not intended as art. In any case, even without the afterword and various other personal documents, Tolstoy's Russian public understood that he was expressing his own views through Pozdnyshev. Early in 1890 Konstantin Pobedonostsev, Procurator of the Russian Orthodox Church Synod, stated: 'It's true that the author speaks on behalf of a sick, agitated character who is full of hatred for what has caused him suffering, but everybody feels that the idea belongs to the author.'[277] This statement is true to this day among readers, critics, and scholars of Tolstoy's novella.

2. WIVES AS PROSTITUTES

In the first place, Tolstoy says in his afterword, he wanted to impress the reader with how immoral he thinks extramarital sexual intercourse is. For example, he strongly disapproves of prostitution, which he characterizes as 'institutionalized debauchery'. If in the main text Pozdnyshev describes his loss of virginity in a brothel as a 'fall', and wants to cry afterwards, so too Tolstoy himself experienced his first 'fall' in a Kazan' brothel at the age of 14, and cried beside the bed of the prostitute afterwards.[278]

Tolstoy was not consistent in his disapproval of prostitution. He continued visiting prostitutes even after he 'fell', for example. He even wrote a long (but unsent) letter to Nikolai Strakhov in 1870 defending prostitution as a kind of safety valve for preserving the institution of the family.[279] But here, in the afterword of his novella, Tolstoy comes down hard on what he calls the 'mendacious science' which recommends 'institutionalized debauchery' for the health of young men before they are married.

The trouble is, as Laura Engelstein had shown, 'science' recommended no such thing. Tolstoy proves to be out of touch with late nineteenth-century medical science, which advised male sexual continence for the most part.[280] This discrepancy is already a sign that Tolstoy's tract on sexuality will be more in the realm of personal fantasy than responsible social commentary.

Tolstoy's opposition to young men visiting prostitutes was not just an abstract idea, but also a concrete feeling which he hoped those near and dear to him would follow. For example, he wanted his sons to avoid prostitutes and to remain sexually pure before marrying. In a 1914 memoir Il'ia L'vovich demonstrates what an emotional issue this was for his father in the late 1880s:

> I will never forget how, one time in Moscow, he was sitting and writing in my room at my desk, when by chance I ran in to change my clothes.

My bed stood behind a screen, and from there I could not see my father. Hearing my steps, and without turning around, he asked:

'Il'ia, is that you?'

'Yes'.

'Are you alone? Close the door. Now nobody will hear us, and we can't see each other, so we won't be embarrassed. Tell me, have you ever had anything to do with women?'

When I said no, suddenly I heard him start sobbing and crying like a little child.

I started howling too, and for a long time the two of us cried some good tears. . . .[281]

Il'ia terms this moment 'one of the happiest in my entire life'. He was glad he was behaving in a way that his father wanted him to behave. And the intrusive Tolstoy was obviously enormously gratified to have a son who avoided women sexually.

In *The Kreutzer Sonata* Tolstoy disapproves of prostitution not only for the sake of male morality, but also because it involves the exploitation of women. There is an almost feminist flavour to some passages of the afterword:

. . . it cannot be right that for the sake of the health of some the bodies and souls of others should be caused to perish, just as it cannot be right for the sake of the health of some it should be necessary to drink the blood of others.[282]

As if this Vampiric metaphor were not enough, Tolstoy compares prostitution to incest. In his opinion young men must '. . . exclude from their thoughts the possibility of having intercourse with chance women [*s chuzhimi zhenshchinami*], just as every man excludes such a possibility between himself and his mother, his sisters, his relations and the wives of his friends'.[283]

Tolstoy is clearly disgusted at the very existence of prostitution. In the main text of the story Pozdnyshev expresses similar disgust at what young men do with hired women. There, however, the supposed connivance of the family and medical authorities is more strongly emphasized. Young men are as much pushed toward prostitutes as they are drawn to them by physical need:

The danger of infection? But that, too, is taken care of. Our solicitous government takes pains to see to it. It supervises the orderly running of the licensed brothels and ensures the depravation [*razvrat*] of grammar-school boys. Even our doctors keep an eye on this problem, for a fee of course. That is only proper. They assert that debauchery is good for the health, for it's they who have instituted this form of tidy, legalized debauchery. I even know mothers who take an active concern for this aspect of their son's health.[284]

The maternal image is curious. Tolstoy wants us to be particularly disgusted by what mothers supposedly do to their sons. There will be many more attacks on mothers in the course of this novella (and its drafts). There will be no attacks on fathers (in their role as fathers), however.

Images of prostitution are utilized in the early part of the novella to convey a certain sense of disgust – both Pozdnyshev's and Tolstoy's disgust. But the disgust is aimed at something broader than prostitution. It is not just prostitutes who should be avoided. It is heterosexual intercourse generally. In his afterword Tolstoy asserts that '. . . abstinence [*vozderzhanie*], which forms the essential condition of human dignity outside marriage, is even more necessary in marriage itself'. Man and wife should '. . . replace carnal love with the pure relations that exist between a brother and a sister'. In a draft of the afterword he says: 'Lust [*pokhot'*] for a woman is an unchristian feeling with which true Christianity struggles and has always struggled.'[285]

Scholars have correctly understood Tolstoy to be categorically opposed to sexual intercourse. Ernest J. Simmons says Tolstoy calls for 'absolute chastity', Amy Mandelker refers to the 'radical chastity' advocated by Tolstoy, Laura Engelstein speaks of Tolstoy's 'radical antisex position', Richard Stites jokes about Tolstoy's 'lugubrious asceticism', Edward Greenwood condemns Tolstoy's 'twisted attack on sexuality', and so on.[286] According to the early Russian psychoanalyst Nikolai Osipov, although 'Tolstoy the artist shows the full power of sexuality' in *The Kreutzer Sonata*, 'Tolstoy the moralist negates, hates, and represses sexuality'.[287]

Although Tolstoy's novella was widely read, discussed, and even admired both in Russia and abroad, its moral thesis was rejected by many, if not most readers.[288] Tolstoy admitted to Petr Ganzen in April of 1890 that he was writing (and repeatedly rewriting) the afterword to fend off 'all the objections and attacks'.[289] Typical readers held the normal, healthy view that sex was basically a good thing, particularly in marriage, and that the human race should not be brought to extinction (certainly no one has ever claimed that there was a decrease in the birth rate among Tolstoy's readers). The great artistic quality of the work could not make up for its underlying negative idea. Tolstoy recognized this implicitly in statements he made to Aleksandr Zhirkevich after the work became widely known. In 1890 he told him: 'People talk and shout so much about the artistry of my *Kreutzer Sonata*. But I have only given this artistry just enough room for the terrible truth to become visible. Generally, many in Russia do not understand me.' Two years later he declared to Zhirkevich that the public 'did not understand' the novella, 'not because it is unclearly written, but because the viewpoint of the author is too distant from generally accepted views'.[290] Here Tolstoy was entirely correct. He was even willing (in an 1891 letter to Chertkov) to admit that there might have been 'something bad' in his motivation for writing the novella, since it had provoked such hostility (*Takuiu zlobu ona vyzvala*).[291] However, he never was able consciously to put his finger on the 'something bad' (*chto-nibud' skvernoe*) which lay at the heart of his masterpiece on psychosexual pathology.

When it first dawned on Tolstoy that most people were not agreeing with Pozdnyshev, he seemed surprised. On 15 January 1890 he names some specific readers in his diary and characterizes their reaction: 'Samarin, Storozhenko, and many others, Lopatin. They think this [Pozdnyshev] is some special kind of person [*eto nechto osobennyi chelovek*], that there's nothing like that in themselves. Can they really not find anything?' For some reason people were not experiencing the 'repentance' he thought they would.[292]

To utilize a famous image from *What is Art?*,[293] Tolstoy had failed to 'infect' most of his readers with his own guilt and disgust about sexual intercourse. But perhaps he did 'infect' them all too well with an idea of what it feels like to be a psychopathic wife-murderer, with what Mahoko Eguchi calls a feeling of 'extremism' or what Vladimir Golstein calls 'nasty feelings'.[294]

Tolstoy had maintained a more moderate, if ambivalent view of sexuality in various earlier works, for example, in his 1884 tract *What I Believe*:

> I . . . understand that monogamy is the natural law of humanity which must not be infringed. . . . I cannot approve of a celibate life for those who are ripe for marriage. I cannot promote the separation of husbands and wives. I cannot make a distinction between unions called marriages and unions not so named, nor can I fail to

consider a union a man has once entered into as being holy and obligatory.[295]

Here sexual intercourse is practically a basic human right. When Tolstoy was visiting Egor Lazarev in Butyrki prison in the winter of 1884–85 and noticed a cooing young couple nearby in the visiting room, he inquired about them from Lazarev and learned that they had been married in prison: 'You mean they are still in the situation of bride and groom?' Without lowering his voice, he repeated, 'You mean they don't allow them to remain alone, to sleep together?' Lazarev smiled in embarrassment. Tolstoy frowned and pondered. After an awkward silence he declared, tears in his eyes, 'What barbarity!'[296]

As late as March of 1888 Tolstoy was telling Chertkov in a letter that sexual intercourse in marriage for the purpose of giving birth to children was 'God's will'.[297] But by 9 October of that year he was saying that men and women should 'strive for complete virginity', and on 6 November he recommended to Chertkov and his wife that the 'safety valve' (*spasitel'nyi klapan*) of sex should remain permanently shut, adding: 'let everyone aim never to get married, but once having gotten married, to live with one's wife as brother and sister'.[298]

The change of heart was categorical and definitive. In the afterword to *The Kreutzer Sonata* Tolstoy says that he himself was surprised: 'I never expected that the train of my thoughts would lead me where it did. I was horrified at my conclusions.'[299] He was not horrified enough to relinquish them, however. Tolstoy's biographer Aylmer Maude gently chides the master of Yasnaya Polyana:

> It is quite right that a man's mind should grow and change, and we should be grateful to a writer who is frank enough to tell us that he no longer holds his former views; yet we have to ask ourselves whether it is certain that one whose opinion yesterday and the day before yesterday was erroneous or incomplete, is altogether infallible to-day.[300]

On the 'sex question' Tolstoy was as fallible as on any other. It is a premise of this book that Tolstoy's fallibility can be understood – to some extent even explained – in psychoanalytic terms.

Tolstoy is quite emotional in stating his disapproval of sex. In his afterword he characterizes heterosexual relations as 'a condition of animality that is degrading [*unizitel'noe*] to human beings'.[301] In the eighth (lithographed) version Pozdnyshev declares: 'Of the passions the strongest and the most evil is sexual, carnal love. . .'.[302] No matter how 'lofty' or 'poetic' the portrayal of the relations between the sexes may be in popular opinion, art, and literature, carnal desire nonetheless constitutes the essence of these relations, say both Tolstoy and Pozdnyshev. What goes on in the marriage bed is essentially the same as what goes on in brothels, says Tolstoy in one of the notebooks for his afterword: 'Set up brothels, and set up marriages, institutions of the flesh, but be aware of the fact that, just as there cannot be Christian brothels, there also cannot be Christian marriages.'[303]

Carnal desire is generally bad, and women who stir up such desire in men are particularly bad. For example, a woman who connives with 'the doctor bastards' to arrange for contraception is a 'complete prostitute'.[304] Or, the elegant and attractive clothing women wear is just 'borrowed from prostitutes'.[305] Indeed, from a male viewpoint, most women essentially *are* 'prostitutes', simply by virtue of the clothing they wear. Pozdnyshev declares:

That's the reason for those insufferable jerseys, those fake posteriors, those bare shoulders, arms – breasts, almost. Women, especially women who've undergone the 'education' provided by men, know very well that all talk about higher things is just talk, that all a man really wants is her body, and all the things that show it off in the most enticing fashion possible. And that's what they give him. You know, if only one is able to kick the habit of all this squalor that's become second nature to us and takes a look at the life of our upper classes as it really is in all its shamelessness, one can see that what we live in is a sort of licensed brothel [*sploshnoi dom terpimosti*].

. . . Look at those poor despised wretches [prostitutes], and then cast a glance at our society ladies; the same exposure of arms, shoulders, breasts, the same flaunted, tightly-clad posteriors, the same passion for precious stones and shiny, expensive objects, the same diversions – music, dancing, singing. Just as the former seek to entice men by all the means at their disposal, so do the latter. There's no difference. As a rule, we may say that short-term prostitutes are generally looked down upon, long-term prostitutes [wives] are treated with respect.[306]

Following this line of reasoning, however, one could just as well say that most men are sex fiends as to say that most women are prostitutes. Or, the author (or his surrogate) could have focused on an assertion to the effect that a prostitute is a short-term wife, rather than the idea that a wife is a long-term prostitute. But Pozdny-shev/Tolstoy is more interested in the female than the male body, and he wants the reader to be as repulsed as possible by sexual interaction with that body, so he chooses the most derogatory (yet still printable)[307] image applicable to women: women are 'prostit-utes'.[308]

The idea that the women with whom one has sex are 'prostitutes' comes up in the letter of 6 November 1888 to Chertkov. There Tolstoy makes a little list of sexual acts which he feels are repulsive:

> ...an old man indulges in sexual intercourse with a prostitute – this is terribly offensive [*protivno*]; a young man does the same thing, and this is less offensive. An old man flirts sensuously [*chuvstvenno liubeznichaet*] with his wife – this is fairly offensive, but less offen-sive than if a young man does it with a prostitute. A young man indulges in sensuality [*chuvstvenno otnositsia k*] with his wife – this is still less offensive, but still offensive.[309]

The comparisons are interesting. The female in each one is either a wife or a prostitute (as if there were no other kinds of women!). Wives and prostitutes thus form a kind of equivalence class. They are the same thing.[310] And sexual interaction with either of them is al-ways 'offensive', even if there are differing degrees of offensiveness. In the same letter Tolstoy argues for complete abstinence. The best thing is to love and help one's wife, but never to open the 'safety valve'. Tolstoy's shame, guilt, and disgust at the idea of sexual inter-action with a woman is all too evident.

Viewed objectively, prostitution is merely a means of exchanging sexual services for resources. It is possible to study prostitution from an economic perspective, or even to incorporate its heavy emotional baggage into a larger sociobiological picture.[311] For Tolstoy, however – and probably for most of his readers, even today's feminists – pros-titution is a degrading, exploitative practice. Tolstoy takes advan-tage of this general distaste for prostitution in an attempt to convey his own distaste for *any* sexual interaction with women. His attempt at moralizing fails for most readers, however, and *The Kreutzer So-nata* succeeds only as art.[312]

3. SOME INTERTEXTS

Before considering the psychoanalytic implications of Tolstoy's hostility to sexuality in the novella, I want to remind the reader that his approach is not altogether original. Elements of Tolstoy's thinking about sexuality may be discerned in sources as different from one another as Marxism, feminism, the writings of Dumas *fils* and de Maupassant, Platonic ethics, New Testament Christianity, American sectarianism, and Schopenhauer's metaphysics of sex.

To begin with, Marxist thinkers like Friedrich Engels and August Bebel had denounced bourgeois marriage as essentially a form of prostitution some years before *The Kreutzer Sonata* was written.[313] In *The Origin of the Family, Private Property and the State* (1884), for example, Engels characterized the typical bourgeois marriage in France and Germany as essentially a 'marriage of convenience' in which the wife 'only differs from the ordinary courtesan in that she does not let out her body on piecework as a wage worker, but sells it once and for all into slavery'.[314] By the early twentieth century such comparisons of marriage with prostitution had become a commonplace among both Marxists and feminists.[315] In Russia, the leading feminist Aleksandra Kollontai believed that *both* prostitution and the contemporary family ought to be eliminated under communism:

> Woman is on the one hand placed in an economically vulnerable position, and on the other hand has been conditioned by centuries of education to expect material favours from a man in return for sexual favours – whether these are given within or outside the marriage tie. This is the root of the problem. Here is the reason for prostitution.[316]

Tolstoy's view of the analogy between marriage and prostitution is different from this of course. While the Marxists and the Russian feminists focused on economic and power issues in the relations between the sexes, Tolstoy zeroed in on sexuality. The seeming feminism of some passages of *The Kreutzer Sonata* – sometimes mistaken for real feminism[317] – is massively cancelled by an abnormal disgust and hostility toward women and toward women's bodies, as will become clear when Tolstoy's sexual imagery is closely scrutinized. In addition, both Pozdnyshev and Tolstoy disapprove of contraception and abortion, as we will see, and an anti-choice position can hardly be considered feminist.

Outside the political realm connections were also being made between marriage and prostitution. In literature of the nineteenth and early twentieth centuries, for example, there existed what Alexander Zholkovsky terms a 'family complex' in works on the theme of prostitution. Writers like Alexandre Dumas *fils*, Guy de Maupassant, Émile Zola, Feodor Dostoevsky, Aleksandr Kuprin, Maksim Gorky, and others sometimes equated what goes on in respectable families with what takes place in brothels. Zholkovsky includes Tolstoy's tirade against the way women dress in *The Kreutzer Sonata* as an example of this tendency.[318]

Alexandre Dumas *fils*, whose conservative theories about marital relations Tolstoy admired, published a novel in 1866 about a man who kills his unfaithful wife. It is entitled *Affaire Clémenceau*, and is narrated as a 'memoir of the accused'.[319] Unlike Pozdnyshev, Clémenceau is still in jail. But Pozdnyshev kills his wife the same way Pierre Clémenceau kills his wife, that is, he stabs her under the left breast. If Pozdnyshev believes there is no real difference between wives and prostitutes, Pierre Clémenceau's wife *is* a prostitute, selling herself to various men in the course of her unhappy marriage.

The analogy of marriage to prostitution was explored in depth by Tolstoy's contemporary, Guy de Maupassant.[320] A striking example is the story 'In the Bedroom' (*Au bord du lit*), first printed in 1883.[321] A husband who has been ignoring his wife sexually and visiting 'cocottes' suddenly becomes jealous when another man starts paying attention to her. He complains to her, saying he is in love with her again. She responds by asking him how much he pays per month for his most attractive cocotte. He tells her, but is puzzled by the question. She explains that he can again have sexual access to her (his wife) by paying her the amount he has just named. He relents, pays her, and the marriage is saved for the time being. In effect the man's wife becomes his prostitute.

The 1881 story 'Paul's Wife' (*La Femme de Paul*) is set in an establishment frequented both by prostitutes and proper wives. The title itself is ironic, for the 'wife' (or 'woman') in question is actually a prostitute Paul has fallen in love with, and people laugh at his inappropriate attachment to her. When Paul tries to interfere in a conversation the prostitute is having with some lesbian friends, she retorts: 'I am not your wife, am I?'[322] Eventually the distraught Paul drowns himself in the Seine.

de Maupassant's 1888 novella *Pierre et Jean* revolves around two brothers who discover they do not have the same father. Tolstoy was very touched by the scene where the mother tearfully confesses to her son Jean that she had been unfaithful to the man he previously believed was his father.[323] As for the other son, Pierre, he starts to despise his mother when he realizes what she had done. At one point he imagines a local prostitute sneering at him: 'Ah, but you see, dear, I know these married women, they're a nice lot! They've got more lovers than us [prostitutes], only they keep them hidden because they are hypocrites. Oh yes! A nice lot they are!'[324] Again, wives are like prostitutes. A little later in the novella Pierre is wandering about a beach populated with seductively dressed women, 'an immense flowering of female perversity'.

> So this great sea-front was nothing but a market for love in which some [women] sold themselves and others gave themselves, the first set a price on their favours, the second merely promised them. All these women thought only of one thing, offering and making desirable their flesh *which was already given, sold or promised to other men*. And he realized that all over the world it was the same.[325]

Obviously, wives who go to the beach can no more be trusted than the prostitutes who are there. All women are reduced to their commodifiable sexuality in this misogynist spectacle. For Pierre, the misogyny is easily traceable to hatred of the mother, since the very next sentence reads: 'His mother had done the same as the rest, that was all!' (later Pierre has a fantasy of beating his mother for her adultery). For Pozdnyshev (Tolstoy), too, the hatred of women is derived from a hatred of the mother, but there is a much greater resistance to making this derivation conscious, as we will see.

In various other works by de Maupassant the analogy between wives and prostitutes is made. Tolstoy may or may not have been consciously aware of what de Maupassant was doing with the analogy, and he may not have read all the works I have mentioned before 1889 (although he had certainly read 'Paul's Wife' by then).[326] In any case, he does seem to have been infected by the analogy of wives to prostitutes at some point, and continued to work with the analogy after *The Kreutzer Sonata*, for example, the character Mariette in *Resurrection*.[327]

Of course the infection could not have occurred if Tolstoy had not been predisposed to it in the first place, that is, if he had not felt some deep need to compare marriage with prostitution – a need which, understandably, offended Sonia and caused her to delete the reference to wives as 'long-term prostitutes' in one of the editions of *The Kreutzer Sonata*.[328]

Other sex-thematic intertexts with (or outright subtexts of) the novella can be demonstrated. Liza Knapp has shown the existence of some interesting parallels between Plato's *Republic* and Tolstoy's novella. Socrates says to Glaucon at one point, for example, that real love 'can . . . have no contact with this sexual pleasure and lovers whose mutual love is true must neither of them indulge in it'.[329] Like Pozdnyshev, Plato's Socrates also expresses hostility toward the arts. Knapp points out that Tolstoy was reading Plato in the summer of 1889, that is, at a late stage of composing his novella.[330]

The antisexual doctrine of Jesus Christ makes for yet another interesting point of comparison with Tolstoy's view. In fact Tolstoy explicitly states that he is following the teachings of Christ in recommending universal chastity as an ideal. He may or may not be right (see Matthew 5:28, where looking at a woman with desire is already despicable 'adultery', vs. Matthew 19:12, where being a 'eunuch for the sake of the kingdom of heaven' is entirely optional). But apart from the issue of whether Tolstoy is correctly representing Christ's view of sexuality, he is not *primarily* concerned with Christ's view, or even with religious matters generally. Tolstoy's chief goal in both the main text and the afterword of *The Kreutzer Sonata* is not to propagandize Christianity, but to express moral views that are deeply his own.[331]

If Tolstoy can explicitly refer to the Gospels to support his opinion, so much the better. Indeed, toward the end of the afterword he begins to beat his reader over the head with the club of religiosity, as if to say: 'If you will not understand how repulsive sexual relations are, I will show you that your own Jesus Christ disapproved of them.' As he sounds increasingly more-Christian-than-thou, Tolstoy's arrogance begins to show. He counts on his reader being a conventional, church-going Christian, but claims to be teaching 'Christ's authentic doctrine of the ideal', as opposed to a merely 'ecclesiastical Christian doctrine'.[332]

The idea that there could be something wrong with being Christian is of course out of the question: 'The Christian doctrine of the ideal is the *only* doctrine that is capable of guiding mankind.'[333] Anything else is mere 'external rules' – as if other people did not have *internal* rules to guide them, or for that matter needed any 'guidance' at all regarding their sexual attitudes and behaviour, whether from

Jesus Christ or from Lev Tolstoy (the parallel between Christ and Tolstoy will not seem so surprising when we consider passages in Tolstoy's diary where he suggests that he *is* Christ (see later)).

Two other influences on Tolstoy's thinking about sexuality were specifically American in origin. In 1889 Tolstoy became acquainted with the ascetic beliefs held by the American Shakers, which included advocacy of complete sexual abstinence.[334] By this time, however, Tolstoy too was already urging complete abstinence. In November of 1888 Tolstoy was also pleasantly surprised to receive Dr Alice B. Stockham's treatise *Tokology: A Book for Every Woman,* which urged sexual restraint (although not complete abstinence) in marriage.[335] As Robert Edwards has shown, there are some substantial similarities between the Stockham book and Tolstoy's novella, including the comparison of marriage with prostitution.[336] But, as with the Platonic and Christian ideals of abstinence, the 'tokological' ideal served more to reinforce views that Tolstoy already held than to give him profoundly new ideas. As Tolstoy himself stated in a letter written in English to Stockham on 30 November 1888: 'It is strange, that last week I have written a long letter to one of my friends on the same subject.'[337] This is a reference to the letter of 6 November 1888 to Chertkov (quoted above), in which Tolstoy had already expressed in some detail his views on both marriage and prostitution. And in any case, while Stockham encouraged intercourse within marriage when there was an intent to have children, Tolstoy rejected sexual intercourse altogether.

Sigrid McLaughlin has discerned yet another influence on Tolstoy's thinking about sexuality, namely, Arthur Schopenhauer's metaphysics of sex. Tolstoy had already started reading Schopenhauer in the late 1860s. Both Pozdnyshev and Schopenhauer (in *The World as Will and Representation,* 1819) characterize the sexual act as something unfortunate, shameful, even a 'crime'. Both view love as an illusion which must sooner or later disappear, once sexual intercourse has occurred. The end of human life is welcomed by both Pozdnyshev and Schopenhauer as a beneficial result of sexual abstinence.[338]

Tolstoy himself, in a diary entry dictated to Sonia in early May of 1890, refers to a Czech woman who had written him a letter in 1886, and who had later visited him and made a 'strong impression' on him. Although this woman is not named, Tolstoy claims that the 'basic idea' or 'feeling' of his novella originates with this woman, who had railed against the sexual oppression of women by men in her letter. In the same diary entry Tolstoy also asserts that his idea that the biblical injunction against looking on another woman with lust includes one's own wife belongs to a certain 'Englishman'.[339] The 'Englishman', like the Czech woman, is not named.

I am convinced of the reality of these various influences upon Tolstoy, and no doubt still other historical sources will be detected by the subtext sleuths in future studies of *The Kreutzer Sonata*. A writer is only influenced, however, by the texts he or she is predisposed to be influenced by, and my concern here is with the psychological basis of Tolstoy's predispositions. Intertexual connections, however real and interesting in themselves, are the stuff of literary and intellectual history. The reader does not have to be aware of them in order to appreciate the aesthetic and ideological qualities of Tolstoy's novella, nor was Tolstoy himself (necessarily) consciously constructing them as he wrote. His task was deeper: to lift repression, to write the unwritable, to enunciate his highly personal, unspeakable feeling of revulsion toward what a man and a woman do together in the sexual act.

4. HARM TO WOMEN

Let us now return to the issue of Tolstoy's actual hostility toward sexuality. Why should sexual relations with women be 'degrading', even in marriage? The metaphorical usage of the term 'prostitute' for most women, even proper bourgeois wives, indicates Tolstoy's shame, guilt and disgust, but not yet the deep personal sources of these feelings.

One possible source is the assumption that sexual interaction damages or harms the female body. For example, it can be painful for a woman to lose her virginity (Tolstoy's Pozdnyshev characterizes his wedding night as a horror). Women also get pregnant. The idea of sex with a pregnant woman is repellant to Tolstoy. Women also nurse their children. This too is reason to avoid one's wife sexually: 'Non-abstinence during pregnancy and nursing is . . . undesirable, because it damages the physical, and more importantly, the emotional strength of the woman.'[340] One does not have to believe this is true in order to believe that Pozdnyshev believes (or Tolstoy believes) it is true.

Pozdnyshev, like Tolstoy, entertains the idea that sex is somehow damaging for a woman, but he is more graphic and more emotional than the Tolstoy of the afterword:

What other word can there be for it but crime, when she, poor creature, became pregnant in the very first month, and yet our piglike
relationship [that is, sexual intercourse] continued? Perhaps you
think I'm losing the thread of my thought? Not a bit of it! I'm still
telling you the story of how I murdered my wife. They asked me in
court how I killed her, what I used to do it with. Imbeciles! They
thought I killed her that day, the fifth of October, with a knife. It
wasn't that day I killed her, it was much earlier. Exactly in the same
way as they're killing their wives now, all of them....[341]

Here the sexual act itself is 'murder' of the pregnant wife (would that
Pozdnyshev had understood this truth about himself before he committed a real murder, but alas, he learned too late, 'pozdno', as his
name *Pozdny*shev suggests).[342] In the next-to-last (lithographed) draft
this 'murder' is extended even to women with whom Pozdnyshev
had had sexual intercourse before his marriage: 'I murdered her before I knew her, I murdered a woman the first time I came to know her
without loving her, that's when I murdered my wife.'[343]

As for the phrase about 'all of them' killing their wives,
Pozdnyshev is again projecting his own unfortunate personal experience onto the world in his usual narcissistic fashion. What is surprising is that some critics actually accept this projection at face
value, for example, Peter Ulf Møller: 'As there is only a difference of
degree, but not of essence, between Pozdnyshev's stabs and what is
taking place everywhere in respectable homes, the Pozdnyshevs'
marriage can stand as a typical marriage.'[344]

The connection Pozdnyshev makes between sexuality and murderous hostility is Tolstoy's own. Even the inclination to project
this connection onto other people is Tolstoy's. Gavriil Andreevich
Rusanov reports on a conversation he had with Tolstoy in February
of 1888:

> 'Marriages are for the most part unhappy', said Tolstoy, 'because
> they are based on sensuality [*chuvstvennost'*].'
> According to Lev Nikolaevich, in most cases husband and wife
> desire each other's death. If only now and then, in passing, the
> idea pops into one's mind: 'If only she would die!' Where such an
> idea comes up, if only once, you have an unhappy marriage.
> 'Have you ever had such an idea?', asked Lev Nikolaevich.
> I answered in the negative.
> 'Then your marriage is an exception', he said.[345]

Below I will bring in more evidence for the connection Tolstoy makes between sexuality and death wishes against a woman. Here it suffices to establish the remarkable coincidence between Tolstoy's and Pozdnyshev's views on the matter, and to draw the obvious conclusion that Tolstoy at times felt an impulse to murder his dear Sonia. Tolstoy, like Pozdnyshev, is convinced that most marriages are unhappy because of sexuality, and that death wishes against the spouse are the norm. Rusanov's negative reply does nothing to shake Tolstoy in his belief.

Since the explicit equation of sex with murder may seem a little extreme, Pozdnyshev shifts to a tamer metaphor a couple of paragraphs later. He asserts that sexual intercourse during pregnancy and/or nursing causes the illness of hysteria, whether the traditional *klikushestvo*[346] of the Russian folk or the clinical hysteria of Charcot's patients:

> In other words, the woman has to go against her nature and be expectant mother, wet-nurse and mistress all at the same time; she has to be what no animal would ever lower itself to be. And she doesn't have the strength for it, either. That's where all the hysteria and 'nerves' come from, and it's also the origin of the *klikushi*, the 'possessed women' that are found among the common people. You don't need great powers of observation to see that these *klikushi* are never pure young girls, but always grown women, women who have husbands. It's the same in our class of society. It's equally the case in Europe. All those nerve clinics are full of women who've broken the laws of nature. But after all, the *klikushi*, like the patients of Charcot, are out-and-out cripples; the world's full of women who are only semi-crippled.'[347]

In the eighth (lithographed) version Pozdnyshev simply declares: 'Charcot would certainly have said that my wife was hysterical...'.[348]

From hysteria Pozdnyshev then jumps to the image of cannibalism, thus defining the kind of 'murder' oversexed husbands perpetrate on their pregnant or nursing wives: 'And we carry on with our talk of freedom and women's rights. It's just as if a tribe of cannibals were to fatten up its captives before eating them, all the while assuring them of its concern for their rights and freedom.'[349]

At first glance it is not clear how Pozdnyshev can move so rapidly from one overcharged image to another – first murder, then hysteria, then cannibalism. But at least it is clear that, in Pozdnyshev's mind, a man does something really quite terrible and cruel to a woman by having sex with her, particularly if she is pregnant or nursing. As psychoanalyst Nikolai Osipov observes, Pozdnyshev's idea of male sexuality has distinctly sadistic overtones.[350]

It would not be surprising, by Pozdnyshev's reasoning, that a woman might want to be *rid of* a man who harmed her so (recall Pozdnyshev's irrational belief that a man's involvement with a woman would lead to her emotional *abandonment* of him). A woman might of course also want to be free of a man like Pozdnyshev for reasons of her own, for example, because of his disregard for whether *she* might want sexual intercourse when she is pregnant or nursing.

According to Pozdnyshev's thinking in this part of the novella, sexual intercourse would normally occur at the beginning of a marriage, and then would occur again only for a brief period after the weaning of each successive child produced in the marriage.[351] As the sensible narrator puts it, any husband who followed Pozdnyshev's line of thinking would be able to 'love' his wife only once every two years or so, which would obviously be intolerable for most men (not to mention most women). Pozdnyshev is not most men, however, and he brushes off the objection. Yet his unusual attitude cries out for an explanation. For, by today's medical standards, there is normally no reason to avoid sexual intercourse during pregnancy and breast-feeding,[352] although in Tolstoy's time some medical authorities held somewhat more restrictive attitudes (for example, Alice B. Stockham, as already mentioned; and Egor Pokrovskii, see below). Nor does marital intercourse cause hysteria, nor was it thought to cause hysteria in Tolstoy's day. And as for the image of cannibalism, it is truly bizarre, and can only be the product of a deranged mind fixated on the 'murderous' oral issues of infancy, as we will see later. Indeed, as will become clear when we explore what else was going on in Tolstoy's life in 1889 besides the writing of his novella, Pozdnyshev's peculiar views derive from personally archaic issues that Tolstoy was trying to deal with in his own life.

5. HARM TO CHILDREN: THE PRIMAL SCENE

Even if Tolstoy were correct in believing that intercourse is harmful to a pregnant or a nursing woman, he still offers no rational reason why spouses should abstain from sexual relations *all* of the time. That is, he cannot logically explain why man and wife should

> . . . strive together to free themselves from temptation, to make
> themselves pure, abstain from sin, and replace conjugal relations,
> which are opposed to the general and the particular service of God
> and men, replace carnal love with the pure relations that exist be-
> tween a brother and a sister.[353]

To label normal conjugal relations a 'temptation' and a 'sin' is, again, only to condemn them, not to explain what is wrong with them. It should be noted, however, that Tolstoy does make some allowance for failure to live up to his posited 'ideal'. He says couples should 'strive' (*stremit'sia*) to free themselves from the 'temptation' of sexual intercourse – which suggests that it would not be the end of the world occasionally to fall into this 'sin'. Sexual intercourse gener- ally might function as a temporary 'safety valve', although it is pre- ferable that the valve remain shut off (Tolstoy was already using this kind of imagery to advocate sexual abstinence in marriage in letters written to Chertkov in 1888).[354]

Certainly Tolstoy himself released his 'safety valve' and 'sinned' even after he was well into writing *The Kreutzer Sonata*, and continued 'sinning' for years after completing the work. Fortunately for his repu- tation and his narcissism, however, Sonia did not actually get preg- nant again after the existence of the work became generally known.

Still, why should one even have to 'strive' to avoid marital inter- course, why should complete chastity be the 'ideal?' What is *wrong* with sex in marriage? Tolstoy simply does not provide an answer, although there must be an answer. The man who was so famous for seeking answers cannot be offering his advice gratuitously. There has to be a reason for his hostility to sex in marriage (and to sex in general), even if he is not capable of stating it openly and explicitly. It would be out of character for Tolstoy to be devious, so the fact that he fails to state his reason suggests that he is not conscious of it. Psycho- analytically speaking, it must be lodged in his unconscious. Cer- tainly if he were conscious of it he would state it forthwith. It is that important.

If the wife is pregnant or nursing, Tolstoy believes she will be dam- aged physically and emotionally, as we have seen. That would be one avenue into Tolstoy's unconscious motivation. Another avenue runs parallel to the first. If a husband has intercourse with a pregnant or nursing wife, harm might come to the foetus or to the nursing child. J. M. Coetzee believes that Pozdnyshev '. . . imagines sexual intercourse as a probing by the vengeful phallus after the life of the unborn child, with whom he identifies, within the mother'.[355] A child may even be harmed by the use of contraceptives:

> It is a bad thing for people to use contraceptive devices, in the first place because it frees them from the care and hard work which children bring and which serve as an expiation of carnal love [*iskupleniem plotskoi liubvi*], and in the second place because this is something very close to the act which is more repugnant to the human conscience than any other: the act of murder.[356]

In effect, children are a punishment for the very sin of sexual intercourse which produced them.[357] But if one attempts to avoid this punishment by means of contraception, then one has almost committed 'murder', that is, 'murder' of the child which might have been conceived.

Of course, by abstaining from sexual relations altogether one similarly 'murders' the children which might have been conceived. But Tolstoy is not too concerned with logic. His goal is to infect the reader with his own abhorrence of marital intercourse. A child is *harmed*, or a mother is *harmed* by sex in marriage. This brings us closer to the unconscious source of Tolstoy's preaching.

It goes without saying that, if Tolstoy is opposed to contraception, he also abhors abortion and infanticide – which come closer to real 'murder'. Here, however, he lets Pozdnyshev speak for him: '. . . I know of dozens of cases – there's a vast number of them – where they've murdered the child while it was still in its mother's womb, claiming she was unable to give birth to it, and where the mother has subsequently given birth to other children without difficulty. . .'.[358] What the upper classes accomplish with their contraception, according to Pozdnyshev, is really the same as infanticide:

> It's only whores and soldiers' wives who drown their children in ponds or throw them down wells; they, of course, should be locked up in prison, *but we do it all in our own good time and without any mess.*[359]

Children are as important an element in Tolstoy's repugnance for sex as are women. Children live in the womb, they nurse at the breast, they are 'murdered' by contraception, abortion, and infanticide. Most importantly, children could be saved if people would just re- frain from getting married in the first place: 'It would make much more sense if . . . people, instead of entering into marriage in order to produce children, were to sustain and rescue those millions of chil- dren who are perishing all around us because of a lack not of spiritual, but of material food' (again, Tolstoy does not mind 'murdering' the children who are not produced as a result). Indeed, it is on the issue of children that Tolstoy is willing to explicitly deviate from his posited ideal of abstinence: 'A Christian could *only* enter into a marriage [which entails carnal love] without any consciousness of having fallen or sinned if he could be absolutely certain that the lives of all existing children were assured.'[360]

This is a most admirable altruism, but quite as impossible as sexual abstinence. What we may infer from it is this: to enter into marriage is to harm not only one's own resulting (real or potential) children, but to neglect the children of others. Children seem to take a terrible beating from the very existence of marriage and sexuality. Tolstoy seems very concerned with the overall idea that children become victims because adults get married and have sex. Tolstoy's is a practically infanticidal theory of marriage and sexuality.

While writing and rewriting *The Kreutzer Sonata* in 1889 Tolstoy had occasion to think about how peasant children react to their par- ents' sexuality. On 15 June he writes in his diary: 'The same vain at- tempts at writing [the novella]. So I stop trying. I dropped in on Konstantin [Ziabrev].[361] He is lying down and trying to sleep on a bed, and his wife on the stove. Now here is where the ruin of life is, and where I ought to help.' Just what 'ruin' (*pogibel'*) Tolstoy has in mind is not immediately evident, perhaps. But a little later in the entry there can be no doubt as to Tolstoy's meaning: 'Does not the bad attitude of children toward their parents depend on the children's contempt for their parents' sensuality? Somehow they feel this. Verochka K. hates her parents.' On the same day, in another notebook, Tolstoy writes: 'The bad relationship between children and parents is from the depravity [*ot razvrata*] of the parents.'[362]

The Verochka K. in question is Konstantin's child (that is, Konstantinovna). Tolstoy has the idea that her 'bad' attitude toward her parents is determined by what she, like most Russian peasant children, experiences on a regular basis: she witnesses (sees and/ or hears) her parents engaging in sexual intercourse. True, in this case her father Konstantin (probably under Tolstoy's influence) is making an effort to sleep separately from the mother, for he sleeps on a bed rather than above the stove. That is unusual, however, and obviously he has not managed to do so in the past, or else there would be no children. The traditional peasant practice was for the whole family to sleep *together* on the *polati*, a large raised platform which usually extended over the stove. In such a crowded situation it was unavoidable for children to be aware of the sexual behaviour of their parents.[363]

There is an extensive psychoanalytic literature on what Freud termed the *primal scene*, that is, the 'scene of sexual intercourse between the parents which the child observes, or infers on the basis of certain indications, and phantasies'.[364] Curiously, Freud invented this notion as a result of a mistaken interpretation of a dream reported to him by his Russian patient Sergei Pankeev, the famous 'Wolf Man'.[365] Pankeev, like Tolstoy, was a nobleman who grew up in a spacious mansion with separate bedrooms, not a crowded peasant hut.

In any case, the primal scene was a commonplace fact of life for every peasant child, even if not necessarily for Freud's Russian aristocrat or for Tolstoy during childhood. The adult Tolstoy does make it clear that he knows what goes on in the peasant hut and, moreover, *he declares his knowledge specifically from the viewpoint of a child*. The child's 'bad attitude' toward the parents derives from the supposedly disgusting thing parents do together. Tolstoy is not merely reporting an ethnographic fact, but is expressing his concern for children who have to grow up in the surroundings of what he feels is sexual barbarity. The adult in him also sympathizes with Konstantin, who, like Tolstoy himself, is striving to avoid sex with his wife. But *the child in Tolstoy* feels that young Verochka, and children generally, are victimized by what their parents do.

In old age Tolstoy once solemnly declared to his secretary Nikolai Gusev: 'The fact that a person emerges from the womb of the mother, that I would tell a child if the child were to ask, but the fact that a person results from copulation – that I would not tell.'[366] Here again Tolstoy is concerned that adult sexual relations might harm children – only in this case it is mere information about sexuality that he wants to protect the child from.

Generally speaking, in Tolstoy's view the very existence of human heterosexuality is bad for children. One may agree with Tolstoy's idea that children need to be shielded from certain things. But Tolstoy goes to such an extreme – adults should stop having sex altogether – that we have to suspect that some personal trauma is involved, some experience from his own childhood that would make him focus specifically on how children feel. He passionately wants us to believe that children would no longer be victimized if adults would just cease their pernicious practice of sexual intercourse. The fact that children would also no longer exist as a result – suits him just fine.

6. AN END TO CHILDBIRTHING

By now it should be clear that Pozdnyshev is as concerned with reproduction generally as with the sexual act itself. Indeed, he is not matched in this aspect anywhere else in Tolstoy. John M. Kopper observes that, 'of all Tolstoy's characters, Pozdnyshev is concerned most with the reproductive side of sex; his speeches on bearing and raising children take up nearly half his discourse'.[367]

In conversation with his friend Vladimir Chertkov in May of 1886 Tolstoy remarked: 'My brother [Sergei] was telling me that in some article on *The Death of Ivan Ilych* was expressed a strange idea which came down to this: 'Tolstoy has revealed the truth that people die.' So now I would like to reveal yet another truth – that women give birth. But still I won't manage. People do not want to admit this.'[368]

Tolstoy is joking, but he is also serious. Having declared at the end of 'Notes of a Madman' that 'there is no death', and at the end of *The Death of Ivan Ilych* that 'there was no death', he was now ready to advocate that there be no birth as well. Human reproduction should come to a halt.

What sexual abstinence does is put an end to giving birth (artificial insemination and in-vitro fertilization had not yet been invented). At one point in the afterword Tolstoy is discussing the fact that universal abstinence would mean the end of the 'human race'. The Russian phrasing here (and in both the 1888 correspondence with Chertkov and in Pozdnyshev's treatment of the same topic) is *rod chelovecheskii*,[369] which occurs three times within four lines. The expression might better be translated, however, as 'human birthing', since *-rod-* is itself the Russian root morpheme meaning 'birth', and because Tolstoy keeps referring to birthing processes (for example, *unichtozhat' detorozhdeniia*, 'to destroy the births of children' a few lines earlier). Sexual abstinence would put an end to women giving birth before it would put an end to the human race.

In a diary entry of 7 August, as he is approaching the end of writing his novella, Tolstoy notes: 'Read about suffering and the antiseptic method for dressing stations and birthing houses. They arrange battles and birthing houses, then they arrange methods to make them harmless.' Here Tolstoy is expressing his ironic attitude toward two forms of physical violence – war and giving birth. In another notebook from the same period, the message is more direct: 'The antiseptic method is good chiefly for war and for birthing houses, that is, for *what should not exist.*'[370] Just as there should be no war, there should also be no birth. The comparison is interesting, and would lead to a consideration of Tolstoy's famous pacifism and his theory of non-resistance. But the negation of birth is what is relevant here. The 'birthing houses' stand as a metonymy for the process of birth itself. To say they 'should not exist' is to assert that birth should not exist.

In Tolstoy's fiction there are some stark examples of the potentially terrible consequences of childbirth. Lise Bolkonskaia dies shortly after giving birth in *War and Peace*. Anna Karenina goes into a depression and is convinced she will die in childbirth (in fact she dies later in a scene rife with birth imagery).[371] Kitty's prolonged delivery of her first child is absolutely agonizing, and is accompanied by an intense couvade on the part of her husband. Levin is desperately afraid of losing Kitty. Katiusha Maslova almost dies after giving birth to her illegitimate child (the child itself dies shortly after arriving at a foundling home).

Here we should recall that Tolstoy falsely believed that he lost his mother as a result of complications from childbirth. The hostility to childbirth must be connected to his archaic narcissistic wound. If Tolstoy's mother had not given birth that one time after he was born, he would not have lost her. If Tolstoy's mother had stopped having sexual intercourse after he was born, he would not have lost her. If people stopped having intercourse and giving birth – Tolstoy would not have lost his mother? Of course not, but Tolstoy's evident narcissism suggests he was thinking this way (more on this later).

With birthing and intercourse brought to a halt, the 'human race' would eventually – within the span of one lifetime – come to an end. In the meantime, however, people would have an opportunity to love one another in a non-sexual way. Instead of uniting sexually, according to Tolstoy, people would be 'united by love' (*soedineny liubov'iu*). This is a somewhat unclear concept, yet it is not unimportant. Apparently it means that swords would be beaten into ploughshares, spears would be converted to pruning-hooks, lions would lie down with lambs, and so on – as prophesied in the Old Testament. The general idea seems to be peace, concord, lack of competition. Men and women would theoretically be at peace when Tolstoy's ideal of a universal, loving chastity is attained. Everyone would be 'united' in a sort of desexed spirit of loving cooperation. Yet everyone would also still be struggling against sexual temptation (see below on mandatory masochism), and it is difficult to see how this persistent misery would promote a peaceful, loving 'uniting' process.

At a philosophical level, Tolstoy is operating here, as elsewhere, in what Richard Gustafson calls 'the Russian tradition of metaphysical total unity'.[372] Other Russian thinkers in this tradition, such as Aleksei Khomiakov, Vladimir Soloviev, and Nikolai Fedorov are famous for their inclination to 'unite' people in some fashion or other. This tradition, in turn, is part of the general tendency toward collectivism or communitarianism (as opposed to individualism) in Russian culture.[373] It should be said, however, that although there is a trace of this kind of thinking in Tolstoy's afterword, it is hardly his main point (and for Pozdnyshev it is irrelevant, being mentioned only once in passing in the main text).[374] Overall, the thrust of Tolstoy's novella is much too negative and depressive to accommodate so positive and manic a thesis as 'uniting' humankind, except as an unrealized side-effect of sexual abstinence. If there is any real 'uniting' in the novella, it comes during the performance of Beethoven's 'Kreutzer Sonata', when Pozdnyshev feels a momentary symbiosis with the maternal figure of his wife, or it takes a pathological form in which Pozdnyshev feels his wife's body is part of his own.

Tolstoy seems almost to wish for the end of humankind. He is no more concerned about the survival of humans than about other animals which have already become extinct. In a letter to Chertkov of 6 November 1888 he declares: 'I feel no more sorry for this two-legged animal than for the Ichthyosaurus...'.[375] Tolstoy's Pozdnyshev asserts that there will be no more *need* for humans to live, once the ideal union is achieved (*emu nezachem budet zhit'*).[376] This almost sounds like a death wish, although not the suicidal kind that the depressed Tolstoy entertained in Arzamas, but the intellectual kind which owes its origins to Tolstoy's readings in Schopenhauer, Hartmann, and the Buddhists (all of whom are mentioned by Pozdnyshev), and which is in profound agreement with Tolstoy's overall theology.[377] Pozdnyshev goes on to say:

The human race disappear? Is there anyone, no matter how he views the world, who can doubt this? I mean, it's just as little in dispute as death is. All the churches teach the end of the world, and all the sciences do the same. So what's so strange about morality pointing to the same conclusion?

As N. K. Gudzii observes, the wording here is similar to what Tolstoy himself says in a diary entry for 23 September.[378]

The story continues, and the narrator makes one of his rare appearances:

> He said nothing for a long time after this. He drank some more tea, put his cigarette out, and transferred some fresh ones from his bag to his old, stained cigarette case.
> 'I follow your meaning', I said. 'It's a bit like what the Shakers preach.'
> 'Yes, and they're right', he said. 'The sex instinct, no matter how it's dressed up, is an evil, a horrible evil that must be fought, not encouraged as it is among us. The words of the New Testament, that whosoever looks on a woman to lust after her has already committed adultery with her in his heart, don't just apply to the wives of other men, but expressly and above all to one's own wife.'[379]

Biologically speaking, precisely one's chief reproductive resource, the one who gives birth, one's wife, should be avoided.[380]

If, on the one hand, Tolstoy seems to wish for the end of humankind, on the other hand in his afterword he seems to take back the implication that the human race must come to an end. He says his ideal is only that – an ideal, which is an infinite distance away. Not to be concerned: 'An ideal is only genuine . . . when its realization is only possible in idea, in thought, when it is only attainable in the infinite and when, consequently, the possibility of approaching it is an infinite one [*vozmozhnost' priblizheniia k nemu – beskonechna*].' The thinking here is very similar to that inherent in Tolstoy's self-perfectionism. Anything an infinite distance away, however precious, will, by the very definition of infinity, never be reached. Life will – indeed should – go on after all:

> The entire meaning of human existence is contained in the movement towards this ideal, and thus not only does the striving

towards the Christian ideal in its totality and towards chastity as
one of the preconditions of that ideal not exclude the possibility of
life; on the contrary, it is the absence of this Christian ideal that
would put an end to that forward movement and consequently to
the possibility of life.[381]

The waffling is understandable. When pinned down on the logical
consequence of his proscription against sex, Tolstoy does not want to
appear to be a complete madman to his readers (he leaves that to
Pozdnyshev, who does not waffle). Yet, even as a mere ideal, the
wished-for universal abstinence from sex struck – and still strikes –
many readers as mad. And besides, the mad Pozdnyshev is more
eloquent than the Tolstoy of the afterword, as various critics have
noted.[382]

7. MUTUAL ENSLAVEMENT OF THE SEXES

Tolstoy represents the age-old battle of the sexes as a kind of mutual
enslavement. Men lord it over women, but women enslave men as
well.

   On the latter subject Pozdnyshev is quite interesting, although not
altogether original. He admits that men have rights and privileges
which women do not, but insists that women too exercise power by
means of their sexual attractiveness: '"Aha, you just want us to be
the objects of your sensuality [*predmet chuvstvennosti*], do you? All
right, then, it's as objects of your sensuality that we'll enslave you,"
say women.' As Barbara Heldt says of this: '. . . women are rhetor-
ically pushed into a corner, and then seen to dominate from that corner'.[383] Or, as Reshma Aquil puts it, the relationship between the
sexes is 'a vicious circle in which both men and women are helpless
victims'.[384]

   But do women truly dominate, and is there really a vicious circle?
When the narrator asks Pozdnyshev to produce evidence for his
seemingly odd view, Pozdnyshev comes up with a marvellously
paranoid fantasy about women and consumer goods:

   All life's luxury articles are made in order to meet the demands
   of women, and be consumed by them. Just look at all those factories. By far the majority of them produce useless ornaments, carriages, furniture, playthings for women. Millions of human beings,

generations of slaves perish in factories doing this convict labour merely in order to satisfy the caprice of women. Women are like empresses, keeping nine tenths of the human race in servitude, doing hard labour. And all because they feel they've been humiliated, because they've been denied the same rights men have. And so they take their revenge by acting on our sensuality and ensnaring us in their nets.[385]

There is a sort of grudging feminism in Pozdnyshev's admission that women are denied the rights men have, but this is hardly noticeable or consequential in the swamp of sexist paranoia that he concocts here. Can anyone but a paranoid sexist truly believe that women as a class 'keep nine tenths of the human race in servitude, doing hard labour?'

I use the term paranoia in a clinical sense, for Pozdnyshev is sincerely and humourlessly afraid of something that does not, objectively, call for fear:

> . . . I always used to get an uneasy sensation whenever I set eyes on a woman dressed in a ball-gown, but now that sight inspires me with genuine terror [*priamo strashno*]: I really do see in her something that's dangerous to men, something that's against all law, and I feel like calling for the police and appealing to them for protection against this danger, demanding that the hazardous object be confiscated and taken away.[386]

The narrator laughs, but Pozdnyshev insists he is not joking (*Eto vovse ne shutka*). Some readers were appalled. Robert Ingersoll, writing in an 1890 issue of the *North American Review*, captures the misogyny of the passage:

> The story of 'The Kreutzer Sonata' seems to have been written for the purpose of showing that woman is at fault; that she has no right to be attractive, no right to be beautiful; and that she is morally responsible for the contour of her throat, for the pose of her body, for the symmetry of her limbs, for the red of her lips, and for the dimples in her cheeks.[387]

With considerable Darwinian insight, Ingersoll observes that women cannot be blamed for the way natural selection has designed their bodies.

Adelaide Comstock, in her bracing 1906 review, says of (a variant of) the passage: 'At this point I begin to look on it as a confused jumble of ideas blown off by explosion of the brain of some pitiful licentious crank; and wonder how Tolstoi could ever bring himself to put such stuff in print.'[388]

The idea of 'calling the police' here is even more extreme than the stereotypically sexist idea that a victim of rape is 'asking for it' just because of the way she dresses. Pozdnyshev actually wants the police to exercise control over women who dare to be sexually attractive.

If not before this point, then certainly by now the reader has to understand that Pozdnyshev is not merely upset about some misfortune that has befallen him, but that he is truly a madman. And no madman (or madwoman for that matter) can be a genuine feminist. Feminism, unlike sexism, is a rational view.

The other side of Pozdnyshev's theory of the mutual enslavement of the sexes, that is, that men enslave women, is equally important. Men enslave women not because they beat them, confine them, or otherwise abuse them (all of which, especially in Russia, they do), but mainly because, according to Pozdnyshev, they enjoy them sexually. What's more, they enjoy them sexually only when they choose to do so: '. . . in sexual relations she's not the man's equal. She doesn't have the right to avail herself of the man or abstain from him, according to her desire. . . '.[389] In other words, a man's control over a woman is precisely his control in the sexual realm (it is implied that a wife cannot refuse a husband, but a husband can refuse a wife; still deeper there is the suggestion that intercourse can take place without female orgasm, but cannot take place without male orgasm).

Because a woman is capable of functioning as an instrument of a man's pleasure, *at* his pleasure, she is somehow *therefore* a slave. However educated and 'emancipated' she may become, she is still a sexual being subordinated to another sexual being: 'And there she is, still the same humiliated and debauched slave [*raba*], while men continue to be the same debauched slave-masters.'[390] In the eighth (lithographed) version Pozdnyshev calls for 'the emancipation of the woman – not in the universities [*ne na kursakh*], not in the legislative assemblies, but in the bedroom'.[391] The very sexuality of the relationship between the sexes is what enslaves women. This is yet another way (in addition to those discussed above) of bringing harm to her. As we will see later (especially from some of the drafts), Pozdnyshev gets anatomically specific about how he believes male sexuality harms a woman: the erect male organ itself damages a woman's body during sexual intercourse.

Pozdnyshev's theory of marriage as mutual enslavement might be summarized thus: women enslave men by means of their sexual attractiveness, men enslave women by enjoying them sexually whenever they please. In other words, the enslavement is primarily dependent on sexuality. Economics is a peripheral issue (as Heldt eventually also grants).[392] Here Pozdnyshev has found yet another way to express his disgust or guilt concerning heterosexual interaction. The only way to put a stop to the mutual enslavement is for people to cease having sex altogether. Such a position is neither rational nor feminist.

According to Pozdnyshev, his own marriage was chiefly characterized by mutual hostility, with intervening periods of reconciliation which he contemptuously refers to as 'love'. Curiously, the reconciliations were facilitated by sexuality. Pozdnyshev is upset by the idea that he often fought with his wife: 'We were like two prisoners in stocks, hating each other, yet fettered to each other by the same chain, poisoning each other's lives and trying not to be aware of it.'[393] Yet Tolstoy's hero seems even more upset that he continued to have sex with his wife despite the antagonism, or that the hostilities themselves were often patched up by means of sexual intercourse: '. . . ugh, how vile it is to remember it even now – sometimes, after we had both said the cruellest things to one another, suddenly, without a word, there would be looks, smiles, kisses, embraces . . . Ugh! What loathsomeness!'[394]

To kiss and make up is a perfectly normal phenomenon of marital psychodynamics. Pozdnyshev cannot resist yet another opportunity to castigate himself for being a sexual creature. If he thought that he was a character in a famous work by Lev Tolstoy, his repetitious self-flagellation would be highly exhibitionistic.[395] As it is, however, he is only addressing an anonymous, lone interlocutor in a dark train compartment. The mildly masochistic self-flagellation is contained. It is Tolstoy who is exhibiting himself.

But it is both Pozdnyshev and Tolstoy who feel inappropriately guilty, for self-flagellation is a sure sign of guilt feeling. Marital intercourse does not normally provoke guilt, nor is there any evidence that it did in Tolstoy's sociocultural milieu. The unconscious cause of such guilt thus remains to be explained.

5

Sexual Abstinence: The Hidden Agenda

Thus far I have only scratched the surface of Tolstoy's case for sexual abstinence. Buried in the depths of *The Kreutzer Sonata* is a much more disturbed and disturbing motivation for the ideal of chastity. Yet what is hidden in the novella, when brought to light, will help us understand much more about Tolstoy than we might have anticipated from a glance at the quirky surface of this work.

1. NARCISSISM, JEALOUSY, AND THE MATERNAL ICON

The focus on the sexual aspect of the quarrelling is evident from the very first quarrel, which occurs on the honeymoon. When his wife unaccountably bursts into tears Pozdnyshev assumes that '. . . her worn-out nerves had given her an insight into the truth about the vileness of our relationship . . .'. In fact, however, the wife declares that she is missing her mother (*grustno bez materi*). Pozdnyshev refuses to believe her, he is so fixated on the sexuality of the situation. But his wife is actually behaving quite normally for a young woman who has just been torn away from the bosom of her family (Tolstoy's own Sonia missed her mother terribly for some time after her wedding).[396] Pozdnyshev's wife insists that she really does miss her mother, and it is appropriate for her to reproach her husband for being insensitive to this feeling, for not really loving her.

But it is doubtful that Pozdnyshev is capable of loving anyone. We may recall that, at the very beginning of the story, he had declared to the educated lady that a woman will emotionally abandon a man if he starts to develop a preference for her. He seems to have been armoured against love from the start. Not once in *The Kreutzer Sonata* is there any indication that Pozdnyshev risks actually loving another person. He says that his wife receives from him at most 'a bit of that love she'd been told about [*koe-chto iz etoi liubvi*]'.[397] Even this is doubtful, however, for none of the imagery surrounding the

94

courtship and early stages of the marriage suggest real love on Pozdnyshev's side (whereas Tolstoy – to judge from his diaries, or from the famous depiction of Levin in love with Kitti in *Anna Karenina* – was madly in love with Sonia in the early stages of their relationship). Pozdnyshev does not once even name his wife (as various critics have observed),[398] and this serves to emphasize his emotional distance from her. Tolstoy's Pozdnyshev seems incapable of loving either his wife or his mistresses from before his marriage. It is also unlikely that he loves his children (as opposed to wanting to get custody of them after killing their mother).[399] Pozdnyshev's only *amour* – to paraphrase La Rochefoucauld – seems to be an easily wounded *amour propre*. Or, to speak in more properly psychoanalytic terms: 'The man . . . is so profoundly narcissistic, that he cannot love anyone but himself.'[400]

Although Pozdnyshev's wife cannot make him really love her, she is able to make him intensely jealous.[401] Jealousy, as Harold K. Schefski has shown in a recent article, was a very important emotion for Tolstoy:

> . . . Tolstoy was jealous of every man who spoke to Sonya in anything but a formal way. Thus, he was jealous of the local teacher Erlenwein, with whom Sonya enjoyed exchanging views on his profession and of the casual visitor Pisarev, who sat down next to Sonya at tea time and (in Tolstoy's view) was too willing to help her with serving. Tolstoy invited this guest to leave the next morning and personally saw to it that his horses were harnessed at the crack of dawn.[402]

Readers of *Anna Karenina* will recognize this last incident (Levin sends Veslovsky packing after he appeared to be flirting with Kitti). In the same novel other episodes of jealousy play an important role, such as Kitti's angry outburst at Levin for having allowed Anna to flirt with him, or Karenin's pretence at *not* being jealous when his wife is unfaithful to him. In *War and Peace* there are also some important episodes which result from jealousy, such as Pierre's duel with Dolokhov over Hélène, or Dolokhov's vengeful beating of Nikolai Rostov at cards.

The Kreutzer Sonata, as Schefski observes, is 'Tolstoy's most concentrated work on jealousy'.[403] Pozdnyshev's jealousy in this work is inseparable from his narcissism. Pozdnyshev just assumes (narcissistically) that, since he chased after other men's wives when he was

single, then men will always be trying to seduce *his* wife. Tolstoy
tended to make this same assumption regarding his own wife.
Indeed the name of the supposed rival in the first draft of the novella
is *Leonid Nikolaevich*[404] – as if this character were originally a personification of the womanizing tendencies of *Lev Nikolaevich*'s bachelor
days.

In Pozdnyshev's view, jealousy is inevitable in marriage. In the
eighth (lithographed) draft he imagines that any man who speaks
with his wife is saying to him: 'What can I do? Now it's my turn.'[405]
That is, it is his 'turn' to be cuckolded. As the fights with his wife in-
crease in frequency (in part because of the jealousy), life becomes
'hell'. Pozdnyshev concludes (again narcissistically) that most other
marriages must *also* be 'hell'. Igor Kon is certainly correct in characterizing this level of jealousy as 'pathological'.[406]

The attacks of jealousy start after the first child is born. The children
are a crucial factor in the jealousy. In the final version the jealous feelings are not actually directed at the children, however. On the advice
of doctors, Pozdnyshev's wife does not breast-feed her first child,
but hires a wet nurse instead. In Pozdnyshev's view, this frees his wife
to engage in the 'female coquetry' (*zhenskoe koketstvo*) which supposedly causes his jealousy:

> . . . when I saw with what ease she threw aside the moral ob-
> ligations of a mother, I correctly, though unconsciously, drew the
> conclusion that she would find it just as easy to throw aside her ob-
> ligations as a wife, especially since she was in perfect health and, in
> spite of what the dear doctors told her, subsequently breast-fed all
> our other children herself, and did it excellently.[407]

It is difficult to see any 'coquetry' here, however, and Lady Asquith is
quite right in referring to the 'preposterously unfair inference' drawn
in the passage.[408] If there is any 'coquetry' in Pozdnyshev's wife, it
comes much later, if at all. Pozdnyshev is being paranoid again (in
one of the notebooks of 1889 he is so 'jealous' he even attempts to
murder his wife when she does not breast-feed the child).[409]

Pozdnyshev is also being narcissistic, interpreting his wife's perfectly reasonable wish to follow her physician's advice to avoid
painful breast-feeding as a sign of potential unfaithfulness to *him*. He
is putting himself at the centre of attention, in the position of a child,
rather than in the position of a normal husband who would be primarily concerned about the health and comfort of his wife. It is as if

he were the child who is supposedly being harmed because of an irresponsible mother.

Even when the wife does become heavily involved in the care of her child, and therefore does not have time to engage in 'coquetry' with another man, Pozdnyshev is offended. This is especially evident in some of the drafts. In the eighth (lithographed) version Pozdnyshev refers with disgust to the 'sensuality' (*chuvstvennost'*) of the mother's attitude toward her little child. In the first draft Pozdnyshev is clearly jealous of what goes on between mother and child:

There was a child. Well then, the child was also very beautiful: there was a cradle, a little bath, children's clothes – they all kept her occupied, but even in the children's room she flirted very well [*no i v detskoi koketnichala ochen' khorosho*]. So you couldn't figure out whether she was washing the child in order to clean the child or in order to show her white arms, whether she was caressing the child in order to comfort it or in order to get her head close to the child's little head.[410]

The verb 'to flirt' (*koketnichat'*) is bizarre in this context. It is not bizarre in the sense that Pozdnyshev is making an accusation of sexual child abuse against his wife (he is not). Rather, he is being jealous of his own child in a way that is inappropriate for a mature adult, that is, he is himself acting childishly. His jealousy is a primal, sibling jealousy. In another variant he says that, because of the typical mother's 'sensuality' (*chuvstvennost'*, not *chuvstvitel'nost'*) in dealing with her child's 'tender, beautiful little body', there arises 'hatred, mutual rivalry of all kinds between growing children and parents'. A mother who actually enjoys her child (as opposed to sacrificing herself to it) is indulging in a 'weakness' for the child, is plunging into 'a kind of drunkenness', and 'the further she plunges, the more tangled up her family life becomes for her'.[411] Or rather, the more offended Pozdnyshev becomes.

Children are no blessing for Pozdnyshev: 'Children are a torment, nothing more'.[412] There are some passages in the novella where Pozdnyshev goes into considerable detail about all the attention required by his five children, especially from their mother. These are too long to be quoted here, but they give the double impression that the wife is being overprotective and that Pozdnyshev is offended that the children are getting so much care at his expense:

That was no life we led. It was a kind of perpetual state of danger,
escape from it, then fresh danger, again followed by desperate efforts at escape, and then – another escape; constantly the sort of
situation there is on board a ship that's in the process of sinking. It
sometimes used to seem to me that it was all an act she was putting
on, that she was just pretending to be worried about the children in
order to score points over me.[413]

In other words, he was feeling a bit guilty for not caring enough about
the children, for being the selfish man he obviously was.[414] *She*, meantime, cared too much: '. . . she herself suffered terribly, and constantly
punished herself with guilt about the state of her children's health,
about their illnesses'.[415] She was just too devoted to her children's
health, she was 'the maternal type, and she was easily gulled [*cha-
doliubiva i legkoverna*]'.[416] If she were not so worried about the possibility of her children dying, if she had the old-fashioned faith in God
rather than in doctors, she would be better off:

> For if they [women] had faith, like in the old days, that what the
> Lord giveth the Lord taketh away, that an angelic soul is going to
> God, that it's better for the dead child to have died in innocence
> than to have died in sin, and so forth – as people really used to
> believe; if they had something like this faith, then they would be
> able to bear the sicknesses of their children more peacefully. . . .[417]

– And of course Pozdnyshev would be able to bear their sicknesses
more peacefully too, and would get more attention from his wife.
Meantime, Pozdnyshev's death-wish against his children is rather
thinly disguised here.
    If Pozdnyshev felt his own mother had loved him enough, he would
not be condemning mothers this way, nor would he be so hard on the
mother of his own children. He clearly feels something is wrong when
his wife throws herself into the multifarious activities of mothering. He
cannot stand to see his own children being mothered because *he* wants
some mothering, *he* has evidently not received adequate mothering in the
past. Narcissistically damaged by the early experience of his mother, he
treats the currently most important woman in his life as if she *were* his
mother. In context Pozdnyshev's wife temporarily represents his mother.[418]
    Or, to utilize the (Peircean) semiotic term I applied to Tolstoy's
Pierre Bezukhov in Pierre's more infantile moments, Pozdnyshev's
wife functions as an *icon* of the mother.[419]

That a wife can signify one's mother is a commonplace of psycho-analysis.[420] Well before the invention of psychoanalysis, however, Tolstoy understood quite well what a mother-icon was, as in the following passage from *Anna Karenina*: 'Levin scarcely remembered his mother. The thought of her was sacred to him and in his imagination his future wife was to be a repetition of that enchanting and sacred ideal of womanhood which his mother had been.'[421]

Or, to take an example from Tolstoy's relationship to his own wife, there is the famous green couch on which Sonia usually gave birth. For Tolstoy the couch was special because it was precisely the one on which his mother used to give birth as well. When asked once where he was born, Tolstoy replied: 'In Yasnaya Polyana on the leather couch.'[422] When Nikolai Gusev came into his study to wish him a happy birthday in 1908, Tolstoy, with tears in his eyes, pointed to the couch near the wall and said: 'Right there on that couch. . . ' .[423]

Speaking of Sonia's first delivery in 1863, Tolstoy writes in his diary: 'In the intervals [between Sonia's contractions] I ran about and saw to arranging in [Sonia's] room the couch on which I had been born. . . '. [424] In addition, Tolstoy on that important occasion begged his wife not to hurry: 'Sweetheart, wait until midnight.'[425] This special request was made so that the birth would take place not on that day, the 27th of June, but on the next, the 28th, which Tolstoy considered a lucky number because his mother had given birth to *him* on 28 August 1828.[426] Clearly, Tolstoy's wife represented his mother for him, was his mother-icon at these intense moments.[427]

Even before he married, Tolstoy envisaged his future wife as occupying the position his supposedly unremembered mother had once held. Writing to his auntie Ergol'skaia from a military post in 1852, the homesick Tolstoy tries to picture his future happiness back in Yasnaya Polyana. His *'beau rêve'*, among other things, includes this:

> I am married – my wife is a sweet, good, affectionate person; she loves you in the same way as I do. We have children who call you 'grandmama'; you live in the big house, upstairs – the same room that grandmama used to live in; the whole house is as it was in papa's time, and we begin the same life again, only changing roles; you take the role of grandmama, but you are even better; I take the role of papa, but I despair of ever deserving it; my wife, that of mama [*ma femme celui de maman*]; the children – our own. . . .[428]

This regressive fantasy would essentially be fulfilled in due time, with Sonia playing the *'rôle . . . de maman'* – but not knowing herself

how extensively Tolstoy would 'act out' with her, to use an appropriately theatrical psychoanalytic term.

With his children Tolstoy often referred to his wife as 'Mama'.
Here of course he was assuming their viewpoint, but his own regressive viewpoint was always lurking not far in the background.
For example, in a note to his daughter Tania in April of 1889 he
writes:

> Just now I received some letters and I am sending the notices.
> Mama's letter [*Mamà pis'mo*] pleased me very, very much. This is
> the best medicine for my stomach. By the way, it doesn't even hurt.
> Kiss Mama and everybody – not figuratively, but take them and
> kiss them.[429]

Here Tolstoy is emphatically asking his child to represent *him* with
respect to his wife, as if he too were a child. In a postscript to
the note Tolstoy asks: 'How are Mama's breasts?' (*Kak grudi
mama?*). Again he is asking his child to represent him, this time to check
up on a specifically maternal function of his wife (she had been suffering from mastitis). One can imagine how put upon poor Tania
must have felt.

'Mama's breasts' were often on Tolstoy's mind, as will become
clear when we examine Tolstoy's strong antipathy to wet-nursing
(see next section). Here it suffices to indicate that Tolstoy was inclined
to take a child's view of Sonia's breasts, to shape Sonia into the
mother he wished had nursed him. In an 1870 notebook he writes:
'The connection of the mother and her nursing child is still evident.
When the child is hungry the milk starts to flow.' This reference to
Sonia's nursing of her fourth son Lev is followed by a remarkable
assertion: 'The very same connection exists between a wife and a
husband.'[430] That is, the husband (Tolstoy, later Pozdnyshev) is like a
child at the mother's breast (or the wife is like a mother, that is, a
mother-icon nursing a child). When the husband (Tolstoy, Pozdnyshev) is hungry for sex, he does something like what the child
does in nursing at the mother's breast.

In Pozdnyshev's case, there is one striking resemblance between
his wife and his mother which suggests that the former is functioning as an icon of the latter: both women are nameless.

First, the wife. For the entire duration of his sad story Pozdnyshev
does not once name the woman he desires, hates, and eventually
murders. He is willing to name her supposed lover, Trukhachevsky, and

several of her children are named as well. But it is remarkable that the woman around whom all his emotions appear to revolve remains nameless. True, the wife is not very interesting as a character; she is no Anna Karenina or Natasha Rostova. Also, as R. F. Christian points out, all attention is focused on Pozdnyshev's monologue, which by its nature 'is unable to actualise the character of [the] wife'. John Kopper also refers to the wife's 'inertness', and reminds us that the focus is on Pozdnyshev's 'own discourse, the self-exposure of confession'.[431] Yet, even if Pozdnyshev is only fantasizing his wife's adultery in a self-centred discourse, she is still a main participant in his fantasy.

Second, the mother. It is curious that nowhere in the final version of *The Kreutzer Sonata* is Pozdnyshev's mother ever named, or even mentioned. Yet his father, his sister, his older brother, his wife, his children, his sister-in-law, and various other more remote relatives all receive some attention. Pozdnyshev is thus another of the many characters in Tolstoy's fiction who are in one fashion or another deprived of a mother, such as Nikolai Irten'ev, Prince Andrei, Pierre Bezukhov, Konstantin Levin, and Anna Karenina.[432] In Pozdnyshev's case it is not clear whether the mother has died and Pozdnyshev is a maternal orphan, or she is just absent from the narration for no particular reason. The latter would seem unlikely, for a mother is normally the most important person early in one's life, and there ought to be a reason if she is absent later when other family members are present. In any case, she is not absent in the final version simply because Tolstoy had never included her at the start, for she *is* present in some drafts. For example, at one stage Tolstoy has Pozdnyshev referring to himself as 'his mother's only son', and arranges for the mother still to be alive when Pozdnyshev marries. The mother is even mentioned in the next-to-last (eighth lithographed) version as being faithful to his father, as his father was faithful to her.[433] So the absence of the mother in the final draft represents an actual deletion, an omission. The same thing happened in *War and Peace*, when Pierre's mother, whose maiden name was Ofrosimova, vanished in the final version of the novel, as did Prince Andrei's unnamed mother.[434]

Since, among the important people in Pozdnyshev's life, only the wife and the mother go unnamed, there must be some special psychological relationship between the two in Pozdnyshev's mind. It is reasonable to suggest that this relationship is the same as elsewhere in Tolstoy (and elsewhere in the real world), that is, the one signifies the other. The unnamed wife is an icon of the unnamed and unmentioned mother.

The namelessness of these two women will take on added significance when we come to consider the unnameability of the emotions Pozdnyshev experiences as he listens to a Beethoven sonata.

2. TOLSTOY AT THE BREAST

Breast-feeding is so important in Pozdnyshev's mind, as we saw earlier, that he (irrationally) thinks it is necessary to avoid sexual intercourse with a woman during the period when she is performing this function. Pozdnyshev may feel jealous of his children in some contexts, but when it comes to breast-feeding he takes sides with, not against his children. This is a more profound feeling, for it simultaneously gives him an opportunity to identify with children and to express hatred of the mother-icon (whereas the jealousy of the children offered only the former).

For Pozdnyshev, a mother who breast-feeds her child truly cares for that child. Mothers who avoid breast-feeding supposedly do so precisely because of the problem of becoming too emotionally attached to the child: 'Most mothers in our well-off section of society will tell you they're so scared their children are going to fall ill and die, they don't want to have any, and even if they do have children, they don't want to breast-feed them in case they grow too attached to them and suffer as a result.' These mothers '. . . don't sacrifice themselves for a being they love, what they do is sacrifice to themselves a being that's intended to be loved'.[435] In Pozdnyshev's opinion, this deplorable attitude is a manifestation of the 'selfishness' (*egoizm*)[436] of mothers. Indeed, a mother who does not breast-feed her child is a 'monster' (*urod*).[437] A profound hatred of mothers is now coming to the fore.

Pozdnyshev may demonstrate some insight into the psychology of mothers who are preoccupied with themselves, and who have difficulty directing their attention to the actual needs of their children. But his feelings on the subject are so extreme (especially on the subject of breast-feeding) that they must be grounded in some unfortunate personal experience. It is difficult to avoid the impression that Pozdnyshev is unconsciously thinking of his own (never once mentioned) mother, who probably did not or could not breast-feed him, as he contemplates the morality of women whose low-cut dresses partially expose their breasts, and in particular as he obsessively ruminates on the behaviour of his (never once named) wife.

Meantime, Pozdnyshev is quite blind to his own selfishness, narcissism, and general inability to love. What he is aware of instead is his incessant jealousy: 'Never once, throughout all my married life, did I cease to experience the tortures of jealousy.'[438] He is willing to modify this extreme statement only when he thinks of his wife in a nurturing, maternal role: '. . . it was only her pregnancies and breast-feeding that saved me from the tortures of jealousy. If it hadn't been for that, everything would have happened sooner than it did.'[439] The jealousy (that is, the reaction to narcissistic pain) thus subsides somewhat when his mother-icon is performing what he deems to be her proper maternal functions (as long as she does not enjoy them too much). This is especially true of nursing, for Pozdnyshev gets quite upset when his wife has difficulty breast-feeding her first child and hires a wet nurse, but is quite pleased when she is able to breast-feed subsequent children.

Pozdnyshev is not alone among Tolstoy characters in this respect. For example, Jane Costlow discusses 'the idealization of the maternal breast, the injunctions against wet nurses, [and] the unproblematic conflation of woman, nature, and nourishment' in *Anna Karenina*. One of the major character contrasts in this great novel is between Kitti, who breast-feeds her newborn child, and Anna, who does not: 'Kitti feels the flow of milk that binds her to her son; she *knows* her son with a knowledge grounded in physiology (the synchrony of hunger and fluid) that moves toward moral and spiritual intuition . . . '. Anna, on the other hand, hires a wet nurse, and ends up rather ignorant about the progress in her child's development. She has other things to do, such as keeping herself attractive to Vronsky and helping him manage an estate: 'Anna's refusal to nurse, her use of birth control, her preoccupation with 'masculine' activities on the estate are but evidence of the depths of her estrangement from the self constructed of women's traditional roles as mothers.' Costlow makes a convincing case that 'Kitty and Anna represent opposite poles of good and bad mothering, the nurturing and absent breast . . . '.[440]

Elsewhere in Tolstoy's literary works there is also a noticeable amount of attention given to breast-feeding and breast-imagery generally. For example, the famous 'marble' bust of Hélène in *War and Peace* is an object of Pierre's libidinal desire, and the narrator goes to considerable lengths in describing the attractions of Hélène's upper torso early in the novel. Yet Hélène's breasts are never put to their proper maternal use, that is, she never nurses a child. In contrast, one of Natasha's great virtues at the end of the novel (according to the narrator) is that she nurses her children herself.[441]

Tolstoy's last novel *Resurrection* is rife with breast imagery. At one point, for example, the novel's main protagonist Dmitri Nekhliudov is contemplating his mother's breasts as they are represented in a large portrait of her. Nekhliudov tries to repress his disgust at this sight, but hostility oozes from the free indirect discourse of the narrator:

> She was wearing a low-cut gown [*s obnazhennoi grud'iu*] of black velvet. The artist had evidently taken great pains over the modelling of the bosom [*grud'*], and the shadow between the breasts [*mezhdu dvumia grudiami*], and the dazzlingly beautiful shoulders and neck. This was absolutely disgraceful and disgusting. There was something revolting and profane in this representation of his mother as a half-naked beauty.[442]

Breast imagery figures prominently in the depictions of the two other important women in Nekhliudov's life, Missy Korchagina with her low-cut ball dress, and Katiusha Maslova whose prominent breasts are mentioned repeatedly. Maslova herself is the daughter of an unwed mother who had failed to breast-feed five of her babies in succession, with all of them dying as a result.

Khadzhi Murat, in the late novella that bears his name, expresses a distaste for Russian women who wear low-cut dresses. Apparently this feeling derives from a childhood trauma, for Khadzhi's mother used to sing to him: 'Your damask blade slashed open my white breast, but I pressed it to my darling boy, and washed him in my hot blood, and the wound healed without help of herbs and roots.' This gruesome song refers to an attempt by Khadzhi's father to kill his wife after she had refused to serve as another woman's wet nurse. As a boy Khadzhi Murat would ask his mother 'to show him her side where the scar was'.[443] Unlike Pozdnyshev's wife – who is stabbed in the same area – Murat's mother survives the knife attack.

Tolstoy's stories written for the peasantry sometimes feature nursing mothers or wet nurses. In 'Where Love Is, God Is', for example, the hero feeds a woman who is so emaciated she cannot nurse her infant. In 'What People Live By' a healthy young woman rescues twin infants from their recently dead mother, and then proceeds to breast-feed them both, along with her own infant: 'Sometimes I'd feed two at a time, with the third waiting, and when one had had its fill, I'd put the third to my breast.'[444]

Tolstoy's numerous and often highly charged literary representations of the maternal breast have to be connected to extraliterary reality. We are not dealing here with just a chance, mundane image from *The Kreutzer Sonata*, but with a recurring cluster of striking images which define the early mother–child relationship. It only makes sense to look into the relevant biographical background to this imagery, starting with Tolstoy's own experience of his mother.

In the autobiographical fragment *My Life* Tolstoy imagines his supposedly blissful early life: 'Surely I lived then, those first years, when I was learning how to look, to listen, to understand, to speak, when I slept, *sucked the breast and kissed the breast, laughed, and made my mother happy?*'[445] From this one might assume that it was his mother's breast that the infant Tolstoy 'sucked' and even 'kissed'. But Tolstoy is deceiving himself and/or his reader. The ever sober Nikolai Gusev informs us that the Tolstoy family hired the peasant woman Avdot'ia Nikiforovna Ziabreva (18??–1868) as a wet nurse when Lev was born. At the time this woman was nursing her own daughter Avdot'ia (Dunia), born in the same year as Tolstoy. Later Tolstoy maintained a friendly relationship with the Ziabrev family, and referred to Dunia as his 'milk sister' (*molochnaia sestra*).[446]

In taking on her duties as a wet nurse Avdot'ia Ziabreva was moving up in the world. For a time she lived in the Tolstoy household. Her husband was permanently released from his obligations as a serf, that is, he and his immediate family no longer had to labour in the fields for the benefit of the landowner. Anything they earned now belonged to them, not to the landowner.

In *A Landowner's Morning* (1856) Tolstoy's wet nurse makes a brief appearance as the lively, middle-aged peasant woman who is on friendly terms with the autobiographical hero, Nekhliudov: 'In her facial features, and especially in her large, dark eyes there was a great similarity to the face of the landowner.'[447] Nekhiudov does not refer to her by name, but keeps addressing her as 'wet nurse' (*kormilitsa*). Levin's wet nurse in *Anna Karenina* also goes unnamed, despite the fact that his famous affection for the peasantry was 'imbibed probably, as he said himself, with the milk of his peasant nurse'.[448]

Curiously, Tolstoy also does not name Avdot'ia Ziabreva in either the *Reminiscences* or *My Life*, nor does he refer to a Dunia, a Dusia, or the other normal nicknames for this Avdot'ia. The most archaic personal object he can bring to mind in these works, as we saw earlier, is an old nurse named Annushka.[449] Only in 'The Posthumous Notes of Elder Fedor Kuzmich' (1905) do we get a wet nurse with a name. She is Avdot'ia (Duniasha) Petrova, who breast-feeds Tsar Alexander I for the first eleven months of his life, and later receives a visit from him in her humble home when he has become a young man. The visit is depicted as a welcome respite from the palace intrigues, envy, and quarrels which Alexander normally has to put up with. Everyone in Avdot'ia's family smiles warmly upon the emperor, including the beautiful daughter, his 'milk sister'. The emperor's mother, on the other hand, is sad and distant. He confesses that he never felt any love for her.[450] This is similar to Tolstoy's own admission to Chertkov that he never felt real love for his mother.

Apparently it was the general practice among the Russian gentry to utilize wet nurses,[451] so it may seem unnecessary to be paying so much attention to what was an integral part of Russian gentry culture. A strictly cultural approach in Tolstoy's particular case, however, would be unsatisfactory. Tolstoy may never have consciously reproached the memory of his mother specifically for failing to nurse him at the breast. But we do know that he questioned his mother's supposed love for him in other ways, and that he repeatedly reproached his wife (his mother-icon) when she felt unable to breast-feed her own children.

Many Tolstoy scholars have noted the bizarre response Sonia's recurring mastitis elicited from her husband,[452] but none have considered its ontogenetic background. Concerning her first child Sergei, Sonia writes in her diary on 3 August 1863: '*I was not able* to nurse Serezha, and this made him [Tolstoy] angry.'[453] Sonia's sister Tania confirms this in her memoir, and elaborates on the form Tolstoy's anger took: 'Lev Nikolaevich went about looking downcast.' When the doctor then examined Sonia and forbade her to breast-feed her child, 'Lev Nikolaevich was very dissatisfied with his advice and got into an even worse mood'. He refused to go into the children's room any more.[454] In his diary he complained that his wife did not love him (even that she had not loved him in the past), and that she was unjustifiably representing herself as 'the unhappy victim of my changeable fantasies about breast-feeding and looking after the child'.[455] In a later diary entry he admitted he was wrong,[456] but it is curious that he should ever have interpreted Sonia's inability to breast-feed her child as a failure to love *him*. This was a narcissistic interpretation of her mastitis, to say the least.

Sonia, attempting to please her husband, tried desperately for weeks to breast-feed her child. Tolstoy's father-in-law, a physician, wrote to scold everyone involved, and said to Tania: '. . . just hit

Levochka with whatever comes to hand, so that he smartens up. He is a great master at speaking and writing, but when it comes to doing, things are different. Let him write some story about how a husband torments his sick wife and wants her to keep breast-feeding her child. All the womenfolk will start throwing stones at him.'[457] Eventually Tolstoy gave in, and a wet-nurse was hired. But then the wet-nurse herself developed mastitis, and the baby had to be bottle-fed. Tolstoy's sister-in-law Tat'iana Kuzminskaia describes how Tolstoy himself participated: 'I remember, once I came upon Lev Nikolaevich alone in the children's room. In order to calm the child, with a trembling hand he was putting the feeding bottle [*rozhok*] into the child's mouth, while with the other he was pouring milk.'[458]

When child number two came along Sonia was apparently able to nurse, and her husband was quite satisfied, as he indicates in a letter to his sister-in-law: 'Sonia is very beautiful and nice with her nestlings, and bears her labours easily and gaily.'[459] But the problem recurred with the third child, Il'ia, and Tolstoy again withdrew emotionally: 'He is cold in the extreme toward me. My breasts hurt, I nurse with terrible pain and sufferings. Today I called in Mavrusha to do some nursing, in order to give my breasts a chance to heal up. My pain always has a bad effect on him in the relationship with me. He becomes cold. . . '.[460] At about this time Tolstoy referred to his wife's preoccupation with nursing in the following terms: she is 'immersed in tits and nipples and pacifiers [*pogruzhena v siski, soski i soski*]'.[461] This little joke found its way into *The Kreutzer Sonata*, where Pozdnyshev says the same thing about his wife.[462]

After the birth of the fifth child, Mariia, in February of 1871, Sonia developed a life-threatening puerperal infection. She stopped breast-feeding her child within weeks, turning her over to a wet-nurse.[463] This time there is no record of Tolstoy complaining, probably because Sonia was so seriously ill and he was so depressed (see below, on the 1871 crisis).

Tolstoy's daughter Aleksandra was born in 1884, at a time when Tolstoy's relationship with his wife was very strained. Apparently Sonia felt no obligation whatsoever to nurse this particular child, who was turned over to a wet nurse right away.[464] In a letter to Chertkov Tolstoy complains about what Sonia has done, 'despite my clearly expressed opinion that hiring a wet nurse away from her own child to feed someone else's is the most inhuman, unreasonable, and unchristian act'.[465] In his whimsical *Sorrowful Register of the Mentally Ill in the Yasnaya Polyana Hospital*, written after some improvement in the relationship with his wife, Tolstoy comments on his new daughter: 'Currently with a wet nurse. Completely healthy and may be safely discharged [from the imaginary mental hospital]. But in case of residence in Yasnaya Polyana she is also certainly subject to contagion, since she would soon find out that the milk consumed by her is bought from a child born to her wet nurse.'[466]

As late as 1888, after the birth of her thirteenth and last child Ivan, Sonia's mastitis still plagued her. Writing from Moscow to her husband (who had abandoned her three weeks after the birth and gone back to Yasnaya Polyana), she complained: 'One breast has become so sore that after each feeding I am all in a sweat and ready to break out into hysterics, and I can't refrain from tears. What hellish pains!'[467] There are several letters in this vein. Tolstoy responds, as Zhdanov observes, 'with restraint'.[468] A better word would be ambivalence. For example, on 5 May he writes:

> Yesterday, dear friend, I received your letter about your pains. This is terribly sad and a pity. As for the question of how much you can and should endure, only you can decide. We have to hope that, as on previous occasions, this will not continue very long, and will heal with the help of a wet nurse. But you have to decide for yourself, nobody can advise you. My only advice: don't despair, and in everything, including these sufferings, find what is good and necessary.[469]

This is the best Tolstoy can come up with in response to his wife's terrible cries of distress. He cannot bring himself simply to tell her to stop breast-feeding, to get a wet nurse immediately. He dilutes his sympathy with an admonishment to masochism ('find what is good and necessary' in the 'sufferings'), that is, he would like her, as usual, to be like him and welcome suffering. On the other hand, since he is not right there in Moscow with her, but has run away from her and from his husbandly responsibilities to her, he cannot very well advise masochism categorically. So he backs off: 'only you can decide' – counting on her devotion and guilt feelings toward him (and toward the child) to keep her breast-feeding the child.

Tolstoy was perfectly capable of sympathizing with a woman suffering from mastitis. There are some curious diary entries from the summer of 1881, when he is spending a lot of time with peasants:

> 28 June. [Konstantin's] woman has mastitis [*grudnitsa*], there are three girls, but there is no bread. By four they still hadn't eaten. The girls went out looking for berries, ate some.

5 July. With Tania I dropped in on Konstantin. Nadezhda has terrible mastitis, she wants to die.

6 July. Konstantin's Nadezhda came with her mastitis, terribly pitiful.[470]

In about the same time period Tolstoy makes several references to his own wet nurse:

29 May. The daughter of my milk sister, so sweet, small. No bread, no hut.

5 July. Today the grandson of my wet nurse came asking for help with taxes. He is skinny, with cheek bones sticking out, a bass voice. His hand hurts, blistered from the mowing.

7 July. The granddaughter of my wet nurse. She has to be weaned. There is no bread. The fallow field is unplowed, the taxes –

8 July. My milk sister Avdot'ia is afraid to enter. She doesn't want anything.[471]

These peasants are suffering, and Tolstoy is obviously suffering along with them.

In his 1915 compendium of anecdotes about Tolstoy's involvement with the peasants of Yasnaya Polyana, Aleksei Ziabrev relates an incident concerning one of the poorest peasants, Aleksei Zhidkov. It is harvest time, and Tolstoy has been helping Zhidkov, who is ill. At one point Tolstoy comes into Zhidkov's hut to ask about his health and finds him in bed, unable even to get up and rock the nearby cradle which contains a crying, hungry infant. Tolstoy himself tries rocking the cradle, but the infant only cries louder. Zhidkov says the baby's mother is working in the threshing-barn, and that only she can soothe the baby by breast-feeding it. Upon hearing this, Tolstoy stops rocking the cradle and, 'almost at a trot', heads off to fetch the mother. When he finds her he sends her back to the hut to nurse her child, himself remaining in the barn and doing her work for her.[472]

There is another curious incident where Tolstoy unites a peasant mother with her infant. Toward the end of 1887 Tolstoy, who was living in Moscow at the time, received a desperate letter from Chertkov, who was living at Krekshino, an estate of his relatives outside

Moscow. Chertkov explained that his wife, unable to adequately breast-feed their ailing newborn daughter, had obtained the assistance of a wet nurse. This destitute peasant woman had recently abandoned her own newborn child to a foundling hospital, and was producing abundant milk. But she wanted to get her child back, and Chertkov was writing to enlist the influential Tolstoy's help in locating the child and returning it to its mother. The idea was for the woman to keep her own child while continuing to serve as a wet nurse for the Chertkovs' child.

Tolstoy was delighted to help. 'I am very, very happy about all this', he wrote to Chertkov.[473] He dropped everything and set to work finding the infant. Within 24 hours the job was done, and Tolstoy wrote in a note accompanying the infant which was being taken to the Chertkovs: 'I am sending you the child, dear friend. Everything worked out easily. I am afraid of the cold, but I am also afraid to keep the child without its mother.'[474] Thus did Tolstoy return another child to its mother's breast.[475]

Approximately two weeks later Tolstoy was at Krekshino to visit the Chertkovs. There he told Chertkov's wife about his plans to write a work 'How a Husband Killed His Wife'.[476] This was of course a reference to *The Kreutzer Sonata*.

Perhaps the most impressive evidence of Tolstoy's concern for breast-feeding among the peasantry is his 1889 polemic about the traditional Russian baby pacifier known as the *soska* (from the verb *sosat'*, *'to suck'*).

The *soska* was a piece of wet rag placed in the mouth of the infant. It contained grain or other bits of food that had been partially chewed by some family member. This bacteria-infested device was typically put into use soon after an infant was born. It was especially relied on during the summer months, when mothers were called upon to work all day away from the peasant hut. Gastrointestinal disease was unavoidable in such a situation, and was often deadly. Historian David Ransel has demonstrated that the *soska* contributed significantly to the high infant mortality rates in Russia during the second half of the nineteenth century (nearly half the peasant children born died before the age of five). The extent of some of the summer disease outbreaks among infants was appalling. For example, during one summer in the Vereia district of Moscow province, 67 out of 100 children born died within a month.[477]

Physicians and others concerned with peasant children's health were aware of what was happening. In 1890 a doctor by the name of

Egor Pokrovskii (1835–95), head of the Moscow Children's Hospital published a popular booklet on child care which dealt with the problem (among others). Tolstoy was personally acquainted with Pokrovskii, who had helped him find a wet nurse for the Chertkovs. Tolstoy even had a hand in the writing of Pokrovskii's booklet, for he had seen the manuscript and thought that it was very important, but that it was also 'very poorly written' and needed extensive revision.[478]

In the process of helping Pokrovskii to revise the booklet, Tolstoy (anonymously) wrote into it his own polemical insert about the *soska*, about a page and a half long, which has since been published as well in the Jubilee Edition.[479] This insert was finished in early February of 1889.[480] Tolstoy planned later to develop this passage into a separate work. As it turns out, however, he never got around to writing the separate piece, and indeed he had great difficulty writing what he did write, as can be seen from some diary entries of late 1888 and early 1889: 'About the *soska* I really have to, I have to. I didn't write' (16 December); 'I wanted to write about the *soska*, but fell asleep, and all day there was weakness' (28 December); 'I wanted to write about the *soska*, but didn't succeed' (1 January).[481] In psychoanalytic parlance, Tolstoy was experiencing some resistance to this subject. The narcolepsy of 28 December is characteristic.

In any case, by April of 1889, after several conversations with Pokrovskii in Moscow, and after some correspondence with Chertkov, the manuscript was finished and sent to Posrednik for publication. (At this time, of course, Tolstoy was beginning serious work on *The Kreutzer Sonata* as well). Tolstoy's insert about the *soska* opened as follows:

> Abroad in England and in other countries, where a mother feeds her infant only at the breast and knows nothing about the *soska* and does not use it, in these countries only 9, 10, 12 out of 100 newborns do not live to the age of one, while with us in Russia 33 out of 100 newborns, in places even 60, do not live to the age of one. What is it that destroys these 20 or more children who die out of every hundred? It's awful, but that's the way it is. What has destroyed millions of children, and what continues to destroy them by the thousands and thousands is none other than the *soska*, that idiotic custom of giving children the *soska*. And not only do fewer children die abroad than with us, but even our Tatar children in Russia die at half or even a third the rate our Russian children do. And why? Only because with the Tatars, according to the law of

Mohammed, every mother is obliged to feed her child exclusively at the breast. It's time to get rid of this idiotic and cruel custom which is destroying millions of children. It's no use citing our grandfathers and great-grandfathers, our grandmothers and great-grandmothers, saying that they were no stupider than us and that that's the way things have been for centuries, so why should we change. It's time we stopped talking that way. The people's wisdom was, and is, not to do what our ancestors did. If that were so, then we would still be eating people the way our ancestors did.[482]

The writing here is loose, repetitious, even clumsy, and very polemical. There is no mistaking Tolstoy's categorical disapproval of the *soska*. Or rather, there is no mistaking Tolstoy's hostility to any mother who would deprive her child of the breast, and instead give the child the 'cruel', 'idiotic' *soska*. The culminating cannibalistic image is particularly striking: mothers who use the *soska* seem to be 'eating people' – when of course it ought to be children who are 'eating' their mothers, that is, nursing at the breast. Here we may recall that the imagery of cannibalism would later in 1889 find its way into *The Kreutzer Sonata*, where Pozdnyshev says of sexual intercourse during pregnancy or nursing: 'It's just as if a tribe of cannibals were to fatten up its captives before eating them, all the while assuring them of its concern for their rights and freedom.'[483]

Tolstoy rightly feels that his polemical position is supported by statistics. In an early variant of *The Kreutzer Sonata* there is also a reference to statistics when (the future) Pozdnyshev says: 'I know that a child taken from the breast loses one half of its chances for life, statistics proves this to me.'[484] Here mention of the *soska* is altogether absent, and we see that Tolstoy is primarily concerned with loss of the breast.

Some other items that Tolstoy inserted into Dr Pokrovskii's text will also sound familiar to readers of *The Kreutzer Sonata*. For example: 'Sexual relations are legitimate [*zakonny*] only when children can result from them, consequently they are illegitimate during pregnancy and nursing.'[485] Here the word 'consequently' reveals either Tolstoy's medical ignorance or his wilful illogic, for conception can perfectly well take place when a woman is nursing. When he does come across Dr Pokrovskii's statement that 'no amount of nursing can prevent a woman from conceiving', he inserts: 'Only abstinence of the spouses can prevent [conception] when a child is in need of a woman for nursing.'[486] The point is to avoid bringing (alleged) harm to a child, not to be logical.

But the worst thing a peasant mother can do to her child, according to yet another insertion which goes beyond Dr Pokrovskii's text, is for her to hire herself out as a wet nurse:

> Let such mothers understand that they are guilty of the *deaths* of their children and that, in abandoning their children and becoming wet nurses, they commit the greatest sin that a woman can commit, deviating from the law given to them by God.[487]

These are strong words. The 'greatest sin' (*samyi velikii grekh*) is not even the sex act, but the (alleged) deprivation of the child of its own mother's breast and the child's (alleged) death. Whereas Pozdnyshev had merely complained that wet-nursing 'exploited' peasant women,[488] Tolstoy attacks the peasant women themselves. Never mind that Tolstoy's own 'milk sister' did just fine sharing her mother's milk with him, and that peasants who become wet nurses often improve their economic situation. It's just that the *idea* of wet nursing is so horrible and hateful to Tolstoy that it *must* somehow be connected to death.

Even if a wet nurse is already childless (for example, her infant has died during birth or shortly after birth), and therefore is not depriving her child by hiring herself out as a wet nurse, Tolstoy still disapproves. In a letter to the Chertkovs of 20 April 1889 (they are expecting), Tolstoy declares that it is better to bottle-feed a baby than to find a wet nurse whose child has died. The very idea of a wet nurse 'with a dead child' is 'unpleasant', he says. As evidence for his position, he mentions several people he knows who survived bottle-feeding, including his own wife and his eldest child. He states his belief that bottle-fed children have as good or better a chance of surviving than children fed by wet nurses, 'especially wet nurses with a dead child. The cause of death could just as well be in the wet nurse.'[489] This totally unfounded medical opinion again indicates how difficult it is for Tolstoy to extricate the idea of death from the idea of wet nursing.

In all of this Tolstoy is primarily concerned about the child, not the mother or the wet nurse. For example, there is not the slightest indication of any sympathy for a wet nurse 'with a dead child', that is, who has just lost her child and who would naturally be upset and depressed about this. Or, when Sonia suffers with her mastitis, Tolstoy feels more concern for the deprived child (and himself) than for

Sonia. When he condemns the *soska*, he focuses exclusively on infant mortality, and does not consider the horrendous living conditions and enormous social pressures on peasant mothers who resort to the *soska*.

The overall psychoanalytic meaning of Tolstoy's preoccupation with breast-feeding may now be stated as follows: 'children should be fed at the mother's breast, not deprived of the mother's breast, as I was. You are not going to treat that child the way my mother treated me!' With this formulation I hope I have captured the covertly narcissistic concern behind Tolstoy's overtly altruistic attitude toward children who are not breast-fed by their own mothers.[490]

3. THE ORAL HANG-UP

> Love and hunger, I reflected, meet at a woman's breasts.
>> Sigmund Freud

One of the things that is disgusting about sexual intercourse, according to Pozdnyshev, is that it is associated with inappropriate *oral gratification*.[491] A woman who gives sexual pleasure, whether a prostitute or a lady of the court, is referred to as 'sweet morsel' (*sladkii kusok*),[492] that is, something to put into the mouth. Pozdnyshev remembers his honeymoon (in Russian, *medovyi mesiats*, literally 'honey moon', something edible) as revolting, as making him want to vomit:

> A honeymoon is an embarrassing, shameful, loathsome, pathetic business, and most of all it is tedious, unbearably tedious! It's something similar to what I experienced when I was learning how to smoke: I felt like vomiting [*rvat'*], my saliva flowed, but I swallowed it and pretended I was enjoying myself.[493]

In an early variant Pozdnyshev says his loss of virginity ('I fell') took place not because a woman seduced him, but because he simply 'wanted to fall', much the same way that he 'began to drink, to smoke' – that is, two specifically oral activities. As N. K. Gudzii has noted, this passage is very similar to a passage in Tolstoy's diary for 29 March: 'At dinner I was talking with Urusov, and it occurred to me how I and the majority of people ruin their innocence – not from seductions, not because a woman was enticing, but simply because they coldly decide that right there in front of them is yet another pleasure, fornication [*blud*], *like smoking and drinking*, and they go and fornicate.'[494]

In another instance too the parallel between genital sex and oral gratification is reinforced by a parallel between Pozdnyshev and Tolstoy (the latter again noted by Gudzii). Thus in a variant Pozdnyshev says: 'I became what is called a lecher [*bludnikom*]. To be a lecher is a physical condition similar to being a drunkard.'[495] Tolstoy himself writes in his diary for 19 August: 'Like a drunkard, [a lecher] can abstain, but a drunkard – a drunkard and a lecher – a lecher [*bludnik*], at the first weakening of his attention, will fall. I am a lecher.'[496] This last passage is somewhat ungrammatical in the original, but the parallel between *sexual activity and drinking* is clear, and the parallel applies to both Tolstoy and his Pozdnyshev.

If sexual activity is like oral activity, then abstinence from the one is like abstinence from the other. On 7 April Tolstoy writes (somewhat incoherently) in his diary: 'Still earlier [than yesterday I got up]. You don't have to sleep much at all when you don't overeat. For four days now I haven't been eating sugar or white bread, and I feel great. It's the same as what I discovered about sexual depravity and about the lawfulness and joy of abstinence, it's the same with food – fasting. One is tied to the other.'[497]

Sometimes the oral activity can be indirectly tied to breast imagery. In a variant Pozdnyshev, intending to kill his wife, quickly smokes *two* cigarettes, then walks into the bedroom where his wife is sitting topless (*bez koftochki*) before a mirror.[498] In another he shoots her *twice* in the chest.[499]

Sexual desire itself can be stimulated by putting too much into the mouth. Pozdnyshev says: 'Yes, the stimulating, superabundant food we eat, together with our complete physical idleness, amounts to nothing but a systematic arousal of lust [*razzhiganie pokhoti*].'[500] In the eighth (lithographed) draft the formulation is even more narrowly oral, and, to use a technical term, more crazy: 'All our loves and marriages, all are for the most part caused by food [*obuslovleny pishchei*]. You are surprised? But you should be surprised that we do not see this.'[501]

Pozdnyshev's oral theory of sex derives from Tolstoy's, but in his afterword Tolstoy is satisfied to express it merely in the form of a simile: '. . . the achievement of union either in marriage or outside it, with the object of one's love, no matter how poeticized, is not a goal that is worthy of human beings, any more than is the goal, considered by many as the highest good imaginable, of procuring large quantities of delectable food for oneself'.[502]

In the case of prostitution, as we saw earlier, sex is like 'drink[ing] the blood of others'. Or, as Pozdnyshev said, people who have sexual intercourse during pregnancy or lactation are like 'a tribe of cannibals' who 'fatten up its captives before eating them'.

In all of these images the orality is excessive, greedy, immoral, even sadistic. It is just as wrong to have sex as to put (too much of) certain things into one's mouth. Conversely, it is just as good to abstain from sex as to limit oneself to consuming only the minimum amount of food necessary to work.

The analogy of food to sex in *The Kreutzer Sonata* is of course not something new for Tolstoy. Indeed, it pervades Tolstoy's life and works, as has been shown in revealing detail by the investigations of Ronald LeBlanc. In the Epilogue to *War and Peace*, for example, Tolstoy declares: 'If the purpose of food is nourishment and the purpose of marriage is the family, then the whole question resolves itself into not eating more than one can digest and not having more wives or husbands than are needed for the family – that is, one wife or one husband.'[503] In the famous restaurant scene early in *Anna Karenina*, where Levin and Oblonskii dine while discussing women, Tolstoy 'conflates . . . gastronomic and sexual discourses', as LeBlanc says. 'Why a married man would commit adultery is just as incomprehensible to the puritanical Levin as why one would ever go to a baker's shop and steal a roll after having eaten one's fill in a restaurant.'[504] Anna herself, as LeBlanc points out, represents objects of sexual desire as 'dirty ice cream' toward the end of the novel.

Part of Tolstoy's gastronomic asceticism was his vegetarianism, which intensified in the second half of the 1880s, that is, precisely when *The Kreutzer Sonata* was being composed. As LeBlanc observes, Tolstoy's writings on vegetarianism maintain the fantasy about a connection between food and sex. In his 1891 vegetarianist essay 'The First Step' Tolstoy writes, for example:

> The gluttonous person is not equipped to struggle against laziness, nor will the gluttonous and idle person ever be strong enough to struggle against sexual lust. Therefore, according to all moral teachings, the striving for [sexual] abstinence commences with the struggle against the lust of gluttony; it commences with fasting.[505]

With good reason LeBlanc terms Tolstoy's vegetarianism 'the way of no flesh', that is, it is a vegetarianism with a built-in anti-erotic slant. LeBlanc argues convincingly that Tolstoy was less concerned about cruelty to animals than about 'ascetic discipline and moral self-perfection'.[506] From a psychoanalytic viewpoint, the vegetarianism (and associated sporadic abstinence from white bread, sugar, milk, eggs, and so on) was yet another expression of the conjoined moral masochism and narcissism in the overall clinical picture.

Etiologically, Tolstoy's vegetarianism probably served to counter-act archaic cannibalistic wishes to consume the once unavailable maternal breast. Tolstoy was so 'hungry' for the breast his mother never proffered that he very likely feared he might destroy it, and avoidance of flesh – in both senses of the word – would have served as (one) defence against this fear. Psychoanalyst Stanley Friedman describes a vegetarian patient who feared that 'the act of eating meat would make him lose control and transform him into a rapist and killer'.[507] Tolstoy's character Pozdnyshev does indeed lose control, killing his wife, his maternal icon, by stabbing her in the vicinity of the breast, as we will see below when we consider the drafts of the murder scene. Tolstoy himself does not go this far, of course, although he repeatedly admits how angry he is with Sonia in his diaries, and he actively identifies with his infant children when they damage Sonia's breasts and cause her great pain during nursing.

Drinking and smoking, as much oral activities as eating meat, also became repulsive to Tolstoy in the late 1880s. He started asking people to sign a sobriety pledge ('an agreement against drunkenness') in late 1887, that is, around the time he finished the third draft of *The Kreutzer Sonata*. Various letters in volume 64 (1888–89) of the Jubilee Edition solicit friends to sign the sobriety pledge. In April of 1888 Tolstoy advises his son Ilya to stop smoking and drinking.[508] On 4 June of that year he criticizes his son Lev for having enjoyed a dinner with wine.[509] On 18 March 1889 Tolstoy boasts that 'we now have around 1,200 members'.[510] He also talked with various of the peasants in Yasnaya Polyana, and got many of them to sign the pledge. Tolstoy himself managed to quit smoking completely by February of 1888.[511]

Sonia, sensing the *oral and masochistic* bases of her husband's rejection of meat, alcohol, and tobacco in the late 1880s, introduces her own oral-masochistic image in a letter complaining to her sister after Tolstoy has again set off on foot for Yasnaya Polyana: 'I was very disappointed about this and I resisted, but he, as I say about him, *has taken the bit between his teeth [zakusil udila]*, he doesn't eat meat, he hasn't smoked for two months, he doesn't drink wine.'[512]

The older Tolstoy particularly frowned on anyone drinking alcohol, and anyone who became drunk elicited his disapproval. But for him the worst kind of drunkard was a drunken *mother* – as in this depressing scene Tolstoy once depicted as he was out walking with Maksim Gorky:

> 'In Moscow, in the fall on a back street near the Sukharev Tower, I saw a drunken woman. She was lying right by the pavement. From the courtyard a stream of dirty water flowed straight under the woman's head and back. She lay there in this cold soup, muttering, floundering about in the wetness with her body, but she could not get up.'
>
> He flinched, squinted his eyes, shook his head, and quietly continued:
>
> 'Here, let's sit down. A drunken woman [*p'ianaia baba*] – this is the most horrible, most repulsive thing. I wanted to help her get up, but I couldn't, I got squeamish: she was all slippery, slimy, if you were to touch her it would take a month to wash your hands off. It was awful. And on the curbstone was sitting a fair, grey-eyed boy, tears flowing down his cheeks. He was sniffling and reaching out hopelessly, tiredly:
>
> 'Ma-ma, oh Maaa-maaa, get up. . . '.
>
> 'She shifted about with her arms, snorted, lifted her head, and again – plop goes her head into the mud.'[513]

Tolstoy himself is moved to tears as he paints this heartrending picture for his friend. It is not difficult to spot the grey-eyed Tolstoy's identification with the 'grey-eyed boy' whose mother is so neglectful.

Nursing lies at the centre of Pozdnyshev's oral concerns. A child nursing at the mother's breast takes milk into its mouth. This is what, ideally, Pozdnyshev wants his children to be doing, and probably what he wishes he himself had been able to do. According to Pozdnyshev, a mother who refuses to provide this oral gratification to her children is guilty of 'selfishness'. It is as if the mother were *taking* rather than *giving* milk (recall from the Pokrovskii booklet that mothers who give the child a *soska* rather than the breast are cannibals). Hence Pozdnyshev's intense disgust, even hatred (*nenavist'* . . . *strashnaia*) when his wife slurps what she is drinking: 'Sometimes I'd watch the way she poured her tea, the way she swung her leg or brought her spoon to her mouth; I'd listen to the little slurping noises [*shliupala*] she made as she sucked the liquid in, and I used to hate her for that as for the most heinous act.'[514] Apparently Tolstoy is referring to his wife here. Daughter Aleksandra reports that Sonia had a nervous habit of swinging her leg in the fashion Tolstoy attributes to Pozdnyshev's wife, and that she would slurp loudly with her lips while taking in food (*vbirat' v sebia pishchu gubami, gromko khliupaia*).[515]

Pozdnyshev's animosity toward his wife's personal habits, especially the 'slurping', is utterly irrational. Such hatred can only have been generated from within, from a personal past which has nothing to do with the wife's objective 'slurping'. I would like to suggest that, because Pozdnyshev himself most likely never had an opportunity to 'slurp' in his mother's milk, he becomes intensely angry at his mother-icon when she 'slurps' her tea. Later, when this woman runs away from home for a whole day during one of their worst fights, Pozdnyshev sits around occupying *himself* with oral activities – smoking incessantly, and drinking (tea, then vodka and wine). Pigott quite rightly says this behaviour is an expression of 'oral frustration'.[516] But perhaps the most horrifyingly oral image of Pozdnyshev in the novella comes in the third and eighth drafts, where he is about to tell the narrator how he came to kill his wife:

> His [Pozdnyshev's] face changed completely, his eyes became pitiful, completely different, his nose practically disappeared, his moustache and beard moved up to his very eyes, while *his mouth became huge and terrifying*.[517]

At this point Pozdnyshev appears to be one great big, pre-Oedipal baby with wide open mouth, imploring some mother for milk, begging the world for love.

4. THE HOMOSEXUAL ELEMENT

In Pozdnyshev's opinion, the turning point in his relationship with his wife is her decision, on the strong advice of doctors, to stop having children. Here Pozdnyshev is behaving in accord with Tolstoy's plan. In a diary entry of 2 July he writes: 'Forbidding her to give birth has to be made the central passage. Without children she is driven to fall.'[518]

In retrospect, ceasing to give birth should have suited Pozdnyshev just fine. But before he killed his wife Pozdnyshev had not yet developed his theory of sexual abstinence, and besides, he and his wife practised birth control not by complete sexual abstinence, but by other means.[519]

In any case, as a result of ceasing to have children, the wife is soon no longer occupied with nursing and otherwise caring for an infant much of the time. She is free to take better care of her personal appearance, she fills out and becomes more attractive than ever (in a draft she turns into a 'beautiful little beast' at this point).[520] From Pozdnyshev's disturbed viewpoint, she becomes sexually available (to someone else besides Pozdnyshev), and she is tempted to engage in 'coquetry', to 'fall'. Objectively, she is free to pursue new amusements and to take up old interests again, including the piano.

Enter Trukhachevsky, the semiprofessional violinist who shares musical interests with Pozdnyshev's wife (he is a painter in some of the drafts). He seems a decent enough fellow from the reader's viewpoint, but is 'mediocre' and 'rubbishy' in Pozdnyshev's opinion, he is just a 'dirty lecher' in the eighth (lithographed) version.[521] In the third draft he comes from a disreputable family, has 'something Jewish' in his appearance, and there is something greasy and unclean about him.[522] He is the third party in a triangle which eventually forms with Mr and Mrs Pozdnyshev, and appears to be the cause of Pozdnyshev's becoming jealous of his wife.

I say that Trukhachevsky *appears* to be the cause because, when the narration is examined closely, it is clear that Pozdnyshev himself is the cause, as almost all the critics and scholars of the novella have noticed. Pozdnyshev actually invites Trukhachevsky to meet his wife, when no such invitation is necessary:

> I didn't like the look of him from the very outset. But it was a strange thing: some peculiar, fatal energy led me not to repulse him, get rid of him, but, on the contrary, to bring him closer. After all, what could have been simpler than to speak to him coldly for a couple of minutes and then bid him farewell without introducing him to my wife? But no, of all things, and as if on purpose, I started to talk about his playing. . . .[523]

Pozdnyshev (believes he) sees that his wife and Trukhachevsky are sexually attracted to one another, yet he fails to send Trukhachevsky away when the opportunity arises, and instead invites him over again to play duos with his wife. He seems to have unconsciously *arranged* the fatal triangle, when he could perfectly well have avoided it.

One motive for this behaviour becomes apparent when we consider how much Pozdnyshev hates the idea of sexual intercourse with a woman, and how fascinated he is with the very sexuality of the man he has invited into his home:

> He had moist eyes, like almonds, smiling red lips, and a little moustache that was smeared with fixative; his hair was styled in the latest fashion; his face was handsome in a vulgar sort of way, and he was what women call 'not bad-looking'. He was slight of physique, but not in any way malformed, and he had a particularly well-developed posterior [*s osobenno razvitym zadom*], as women have, or as Hottentots are said to have. I believe they're also said to be musical.[524]

Two psychoanalytic studies from the 1930s by Immanuel Velikovsky and Benjamin Karpman deal with the homosexual implications of Pozdnyshev's hatred of women and his jealous fascination with Trukhachevsky (in a 1922 paper Freud had already argued that 'delusional jealousy' is based on latent homosexuality).[525] Velikovsky observes, for example: 'The homosexual, unaware of his inclination, arranges to have his wife meet the man to whom he himself is attracted.'[526] The attraction is hard to miss. Pozdnyshev is fascinated with every detail of Trukhachevsky's physical appearance and behaviour. He is of course just as fascinated with his wife's sexual attributes. But homosexual interest does not exclude heterosexual interest. Beneath his heterosexual exterior Pozdnyshev is bisexual. Karpman terms him 'an unadjusted bisexual'.[527]

At a conscious level, Pozdnyshev tells himself that he tolerates Trukhachevsky's presence to prove to others (and to himself) that he is not giving in to jealousy. Yet all the while he *is* intensely jealous, imagining to himself in lurid detail how passionately his wife and Trukhachevsky must desire one another. Paradoxically, the more jealous he becomes, the more affectionately he behaves toward Trukhachevsky (*laskat' ego*). He is unable to formulate his feelings in a way that would be logically consistent with an exclusively heterosexual orientation. For example, at one point he says 'He [Trukhachevsky] and his music were the cause of it all', while in the very next paragraph he insists that 'Whatever her relationship with that musician was, it wasn't important to me. . . '.[528]

Beethoven's *Kreutzer Sonata*, when performed by Trukhachevsky and Pozdnyshev's wife, provokes strange, unaccountable emotions in Pozdnyshev. He feels that his soul momentarily 'merges' with the soul of the male composer. He is enraptured, he enters a new 'state of consciousness' which is not his own, but which is nonetheless irresistible for him. The music is so grand it should be reserved only for special ceremonial occasions where 'certain solemn actions' are to be performed along with the music. Certainly the music has no place in a heterosexually suggestive environment: '. . . take its first movement, the presto: can one really allow it to be played in a drawing-room full of women in low-cut dresses?'[529]

Can one indeed? Perhaps the piece would be better played in a room full of *men* in low-cut dresses, men precisely of the type Pozdnyshev encountered on his honeymoon in decadent Paris: there the 'bearded lady' he saw in a show turned out to be 'nothing but a man in a woman's low-cut dress', that is, a cross-dresser.[530] Perhaps also the sense of 'merging' with Beethoven is as much sexual as spiritual, and the unspecified 'actions' (*postupki*) called for by the music are homoerotic rather than heteroerotic in nature.

On the other hand, the sonata is being performed by two individuals of different sex who, in Pozdnyshev's inflamed imagination, are having an illicit affair. The immediate and obvious charge of the situation is heteroerotic, as many critics and scholars have noted. Also heteroerotic is Pozdnyshev's ludicrous generalization: '. . . everyone knows that it's precisely these pursuits, music in particular, that cause most of the adulteries in our class of society'.[531] This idea is apparently grounded in Tolstoy's personal experience from his younger days, when he witnessed sexual intrigues at the various musical evenings he used to attend with his friends. A diary entry of 27 February 1858 reads, in part: 'With Vasin'ka I went to Chikhacheva's. A man, a girl, and a piano with Beethoven and Mozart. Three times now I've seen this. Good.'[532] Clearly Tolstoy had something to go on in making the association between music and sexuality. But the association is unlikely for the majority of readers – either in his day or in our time.

Pozdnyshev just assumes that people who play duos become so close that sex is practically unavoidable: 'between them they have the bond of music, the most refined form of sensual lust [*sviaz' muzyki, samoi utonchennoi pokhoti chuvstv*]'.[533] Yet the very lunacy of this suggestion tells us that it cannot be taken at face value. Pozdnyshev does not assert that music causes heterosexual intercourse, but rather that it causes adultery, that is, a form of heterosexual interaction which for Pozdnyshev has homosexual overtones as well.[534]

5. REGRESS ALONG WITH BEETHOVEN

Que me veut cette musique?
(Tolstoy to son Sergei)[535]

At the centre of *The Kreutzer Sonata* is a musical composition of the same name by Ludwig van Beethoven. Tolstoy's feelings about Beethoven's music were ambivalent. The attack on Beethoven in *What is Art?* is famous, but Tolstoy's love of Beethoven is just as important. When he actually heard Beethoven's music being played well, Tolstoy usually could not resist enjoying it. He would be carried away by it and admire it. After his friend Aleksandr Gol'denveizer would play some Beethoven sonata, for example, Tolstoy would come up to the pianist and say: 'You have just now reconciled me with Beethoven.'[536]

Tolstoy himself was a musician. According to various family members and friends, Tolstoy played the piano reasonably well, and sometimes would play for hours on end. According to his brother-in-law Stepan Andreevich Bers, for example, he would often sit down to play for a while before starting to write, 'most likely for inspiration'.[537] During the 1870s Tolstoy and his wife often used to sit down and play piano four hands after dinner.[538] When Tolstoy's sister Mar'ia Nikolaevna visited he would play piano four hands with her as well.[539]

All his life Tolstoy 'loved all music passionately', says son Lev.[540] 'Music penetrated the deepest recesses of his soul, it stirred his whole being, it released in him embryonic thoughts and emotions of which he himself was not cognizant', reports daughter Alexandra.[541] Those who knew Tolstoy agree in asserting that music produced a strong emotional effect on him, elicited in him what Caryl Emerson has called 'the anxiety of music'.[542] Nikolai Gusev says: 'I never saw a person upon whom music acted as strongly as it did on Lev Tolstoy.' Gusev adds: 'His face would go pale and would assume a special expression, his eyes would gaze into the distance, and very often, when listening to good music, he could not keep back the tears.'[543] Stepan Bers, describing a younger Tolstoy than the one Gusev knew, registers a similar impression: 'I noticed that the sensations aroused in him by music were accompanied by a slight pallor in his face and a barely noticeable grimace expressing something akin to horror.'[544]

Tolstoy's son Sergei says that his father heard him (and violinist Iulii Liasotta) play Beethoven's *Kreutzer Sonata* in the 1880s.[545] The Tolstoys' family governess Anna Seuron describes Tolstoy sitting in tears as he listened to performances of the work during the winter of 1884.[546] Tolstoy was again moved by a performance (or performances) in the summer of 1887.[547] Here is how Tolstoy's son Lev describes the musical evenings in Yasnaya Polyana during the summer of 1889, when Tolstoy was working hard on *The Kreutzer Sonata*:

> Imagine . . . a summer evening in Yasnaya Polyana. Everyone is gathered in the drawing room. On the table a huge samovar is boiling. Lev Nikolaevich has already seated himself in his large armchair near the end of the piano, the performers are ready, and the first tragically sorrowful notes of the violin ring out.
>
> Immediately these notes rivet our attention. I understood perfectly what was going on in my father's soul and mind. In those days I lived his life and felt for him.
>
> Occasionally glancing now at his moist, inspired gray eyes as they looked straight ahead, I saw that he was not only listening, but that he was thinking with tense concentration, that he was feeling and creating. For in those days he was in the midst of discovering one of the greatest truths, one of the most powerful truths: the filth and falsehood of contemporary marriage.

After a brief rehearsal of Pozdnyshev's beliefs and criminal behaviour, the devoted son returns to a description of his father:

> . . . he listened to the sonata, from start to finish not moving from his armchair.
>
> Only once he could not contain himself, he jumped up, went over to the window opening on to the garden, and breathed a deep sigh, as though panting.
>
> The music came to an end and Lev Nikolaevich, unable to utter a word, could only blow his nose. His eyes were full of tears.[548]

Tolstoy obviously experienced very strong emotions when listening to the sonata after which his novella is named.

Pozdnyshev, like Tolstoy, is moved by Beethoven's *Kreutzer Sonata*, although not to tears. The passage describing Pozdnyshev's reaction to the music is very revealing, more so than Tolstoy's own mere tears. The passage is the one occasion where Pozdnyshev is able to experience a few moments of freedom from his intense ambivalence about his wife. True, his emotions are strong, but they are curiously positive and even non-sexual. They are also very difficult to capture in words:

Ah! It's a fearful thing, that sonata. Especially that [first] movement. And music in general's a fearful thing. What is it? I don't
know. What is music? What does it do to us? And why does it do to
us what it does? People say that music has an uplifting effect on the
soul: what rot! It isn't true. It's true that it has an effect, it has a terrible effect on me, at any rate, but it has nothing to do with any uplifting of the soul. Its effect on the soul is neither uplifting nor
degrading – it merely irritates me. How can I put it? Music makes
me forget myself, my true condition, it carries me off into another
state of being, one that isn't my own: under the influence of music
I have the illusion of feeling things I don't really feel, of understanding things I don't understand, being able to do things I'm not
able to do.

On me, at any rate, that piece had the most shattering effect; I
had the illusion that I was discovering entirely new emotions, new
possibilities I'd known nothing of before then. 'Yes, that's it, it's
got absolutely nothing to do with the way I've been used to living
and seeing the world, that's how it ought to be', I seemed to hear a
voice saying inside me. What this new reality I'd discovered was,
I really didn't know, but my awareness of this new state of consciousness filled me with joy. Everyone in the room, including him
and my wife, appeared to me in an entirely new light.[549]

This is an overwhelming, if only temporary change in Pozdnyshev's
feelings. The semi-reconciliations with his wife and the attractions of
Trukhachevsky were never like this, for they were merely sexual for
him. For the time being jealousy is an irrelevant trifle (as is explicitly
stated in the eighth, lithographed version),[550] and the idea of music
as 'sensual lust' is contradicted.[551] The demonic and bestial forces in
Pozdnyshev have faded, his psyche is here transformed, he reaches
a 'new state of consciousness' which, within the frame of the story,
has never occurred, and never again will occur.

Gorky's memoir has Tolstoy characterizing music as 'the mute
prayer of the soul' (*nemaia molitva dushi*). When asked to explain the
epithet 'mute', Tolstoy replied: 'Because it is without words. In
sound there is more soul than in thought. Thought is a purse with
coins in it, but sound is not dirtied with anything, it is inwardly
pure.'[552] Pozdnyshev's experience of Beethoven is pure in this sense.

Tolstoy eventually named his story after the musical piece which
provokes Pozdnyshev's most positive and meaningful experience

(although his *view* of this positive experience is itself not altogether positive, i.e., is ambivalent).[553] But what exactly *is* the experience? It is powerful, joyful, yet vague and seemingly devoid of content. It is induced by music, but the very wordlessness of the music makes it difficult for Pozdnyshev to put the experience into words.

Tolstoy himself had the same problem. His statements on music are often phrased in the interrogative. To his children's tutor V. I. Alekseev he asked: 'I don't understand, why does music move me so, agitate me, upset me?' (cf. also the epigraph above).[554] Responding once to an acquaintance's assertion that music produces pleasure, Tolstoy said: 'Pleasure – this is not the right word. Music produces a strong effect, but not pleasure. How to express this? In no way should you pick such a word.'[555] But what word should one pick? The great Tolstoy is speechless.

To Gusev Tolstoy said that 'music cannot be expressed in words'.[556] Similarly, to Chertkov he said: 'I think that musical impressions can never be described.'[557] Even music with words left Tolstoy at a loss for words. Once, after listening to a gramophone recording of a woman singing a Russian folk song, the aging Tolstoy said that the song made him aware of 'God knows what ancientness [*drevnost'*]'.[558] God knows, indeed, but Tolstoy did not know, or could not know consciously what he was remembering.

At one point Pozdnyshev expresses a curious paradox about knowing yet not knowing what emotions are elicited by music: '... she had experienced the same feelings as I had, and ... she, like myself, had discovered or perhaps had remembered new and unfamiliar emotions'. There is a catch here, an oxymoron right at the moment Tolstoy is about to change the subject and move on to the murder: how is it possible to *remember* something *new* and *unfamiliar* (*kak budto vspomnilis' novye, neispytannye chuvstva*)?[559]

To answer in psychoanalytic terms: Pozdnyshev undergoes a regression ('it carries me off') to a very early, preambivalent psychical state, and this movement is experienced as remembering. But since Pozdnyshev ordinarily *cannot* remember this state, it is perceived as new and unfamiliar. Because the unique condition for remembering this state is music, Pozdnyshev can honestly say he is 'remembering' something at the same time that he characterizes it as 'unfamiliar' (cf. also the paradox of 'feeling things I don't really feel'). Some kind of barrier is overcome as a result of listening to Beethoven's opening movement, and a previously inaccessible, unremembered – yet once upon a time familiar – emotion is tapped. Moreover, since the remembered emotion in this case is basically indescribable or non-verbalizable, there is reason to suspect that the regression is extreme, going all the way back to Pozdnyshev's pre-verbal origins.

In Tolstoy's enchanting early novella *Childhood* music is also characterized in terms of its power to evoke distant, non-verbalizable memories:

Mamma was playing the second concerto of Field, her music-master. I sat day-dreaming, and airy luminous transparent recollections appeared in my imagination. She started playing Beethoven's *Sonate pathétique* and my memories became sad, oppressive and gloomy. Mamma often played those two pieces and so I well remember the feelings they aroused in me. They resembled memories – but memories of what? It almost seemed as if I were remembering something that had never been.[560]

The ten-year-old child here has the same difficulty 'remembering' what Beethoven's music reminds him of as does the grown-up Pozdnyshev. His 'remembering something that had never been' is like Pozdnyshev's 'feeling things I don't really feel', and 'understanding things I don't understand'.[561]

In a diary entry for 29 November 1851 Tolstoy asks: 'Why does music act on us as recollection?'[562] Again, to answer psychoanalytically: music facilitates a regression to early emotional states which are non-verbalizable. Thus, according to Heinz Kohut, '. . . the extraverbal nature of music lends itself particularly well [to regression] by offering a subtle transition to preverbal modes of psychological functioning'. Kohut's characterization of the emotional effects of music fits Pozdnyshev's (and Tolstoy's) experience:

The significance of musical activity for earlier psychological organizations is derived from its capacity to allow subtle regression via extraverbal modes of psychic function. It appears to contribute to the relief of primitive, preverbal tensions that have found little psychological representation and it may provide for the maintenance of archaic object cathexes by virtue of its relationship to an archaic, emotional mode of communication.[563]

In other words, music is capable of eliciting the pre-Oedipal, preverbal child's unspeakable emotions. It functions to bring the adult back to what Margaret Mahler terms the 'symbiotic phase' of development, a very early phase when the child is truly at one with the mother insofar as it is not yet even aware of its separateness from the mother. Music, for Pozdnyshev/Tolstoy, re-elicits what Mahler calls the 'preverbal phenomena of symbiosis'.[564]

Two literary scholars have arrived at essentially these psychoanalytic insights in their own way. Ruth Rischin says that the sounds of the mother playing Beethoven in *Childhood* 'express the child's connectedness at this very young age to the central figure in his world', that is, to the mother.[565] Anne Pigott, writing specifically about *The Kreutzer Sonata*, says that the pleasure of music represents '*l'état fusionnel dans lequel baigne la mère et le nourrisson*'.[566] Rischin's 'connectedness' and Pigott's '*l'état fusionnel*' sound very much like Margaret Mahler's psychoanalytic notion of pre-Oedipal 'symbiosis'.

Pigott's assertion would suggest that the child (*nourrisson*) is actually at the mother's breast. Right before attempting to describe the blissful emotion music elicits in him, Pozdnyshev asks: 'Can one really allow it [the presto] to be played in a drawing-room full of women in low-cut dresses?' Or: 'To be played, and then followed by . . . the eating of ice cream. . . ?'[567] That is, can the music which brings Pozdnyshev to a state of momentary bliss be juxtaposed with women whose *breasts* are partially exposed, and with people who are consuming a frozen form of *milk*?

As Kohut says: 'One may sit with closed eyes and open mouth and drink in music, in regressive enjoyment, as he once sucked his mother's breast.'[568] Pozdnyshev does just that, but first he has to deny that he is doing it by stating his disapproval of exposed breasts and ice cream.

Above I drew attention to the fact that Pozdnyshev fails to name either his wife (mother-icon) or his mother. But a child at the breast also cannot name its mother (or wet nurse), for the child is pre-verbal, it cannot yet speak. This also fits well with the problem of not being able to name the emotions elicited by Beethoven's music. The namelessness of the two most important women in Pozdnyshev's life would appear to be further evidence that Pozdnyshev is operating at a very archaic, pre-verbal, pre-Oedipal level in relating to them.

Pozdnyshev's profoundly pre-Oedipal feelings about music are Tolstoy's own. Mariia Nikolaevna Tolstaia played the piano. The infant Tolstoy would certainly have heard her practising the piano before he learned to speak. She herself mentions practising the piano in her letters. For example, while she was pregnant with Tolstoy's brother Dmitrii, and while a wet nurse was probably still breast-feeding little Sergei, Tolstoy's mother played 'every day, seriously, for about an hour'.[569]

In August of 1908 Tolstoy characterized music as an essentially incorporeal, spiritual phenomenon: 'In the other arts there is an admixture of the bodily, while in music the bodily is absent [*net telesnogo*].'[570] But Tolstoy conceived of his mother in just this way. He retained not a bodily, but a spiritual image of her (*dukhovnyi oblik*), as we saw earlier. In a diary entry for 10 June 1908, where Tolstoy is thinking about his mother, the image of her incorporeality is graphic:

> I never heard anything bad about her. And as I was walking along the birch path, and coming to the walnut path, I noticed a woman's little footprints in the mud, and I thought about her, about her body [*ob ee tele*]. And the idea of her body did not penetrate me. The bodily [*telesnoe*] would just defile her. What a good feeling toward her![571]

Thus, in the summer of 1908, the same image of incorporeality is applied both to the experience of music and to the experience of trying to remember the mother.

Tolstoy says he cannot remember his mother's body. Its mental representation does not penetrate (*ne vkhodilo v*) him. But the trace of it is there, in the mud. The mother's body is disembodied, as it were. It is there, but it is not there. He is remembering, but he is not remembering. In the same diary entry for 10 June, a few lines earlier, Tolstoy says: 'This morning I was walking around the garden and, as always, was reminiscing about my mother [*vspominaiu o materi*], about '*mamen'ka*', whom I do not remember at all [*sovsem ne pomniu*], but who has remained for me a sacred ideal.'[572] Strictly speaking, this is an oxymoron. One cannot reminisce about something one does not remember.

But again, the same oxymoron came up in Tolstoy's characterization of music, as we saw above. Both Irten'ev and Pozdnyshev assert that they remember something they do not remember.

For Tolstoy, then, the musical and the maternal are linked in a profound association. Through his experience of certain kinds of music Tolstoy was able to remember – or not remember – his mother. Through music Tolstoy was able temporarily to regress to the pre-Oedipal, largely pre-verbal stage of his existence – the only stage where he ever had any real experience of his mother. For, by the time he entered fully into the realm of language and gained an opportunity to pass through the usual Oedipal trials and tribulations, Mariia Nikolaevna Tolstaia's body was already rotting in the crypt of Kochaki.

6. MURDERING THE BREAST-MOTHER

Latent homosexuality is hardly the only reason why Pozdnyshev arranges a triangle with his wife and Trukhachevsky. Karpman argues that Pozdnyshev is also unconsciously acting with 'the goal of killing his wife'.[573] Pozdnyshev himself states his wish clearly enough when, in the midst of a horrible argument in front of the children, he shouts: 'Oh, I wish you were dead! [*O, khot' by ty izdokhla!*].'[574] This is before the attractive Trukhachevsky appears on the scene. In another variant the death-wish is stated even earlier, right after we are informed that the wife will no longer be able to give birth.[575] During one of the fights, after the triangle has already formed, Pozdnyshev yells at his wife: 'Go, or I'll kill you!'[576] This last outburst, accompanied by throwing and smashing objects, is very similar to a temper tantrum thrown by the jealous Pierre Bezukhov early in *War and Peace*.[577] It is also similar to a tantrum Tolstoy himself threw (minus the death threat) when once he found his pregnant wife sitting on the floor and going through some bundles.[578]

It is rather striking that, once Pozdnyshev finally does murder his wife, he loses all interest in Trukhachevsky, who simply disappears from the scene. Trukhachevsky was just dust ('*trukha*' means 'dust'),[579] he was merely a convenient, disposable excuse for committing murder, an 'unwitting accomplice' as Charles Isenberg puts it.[580] Pozdnyshev states explicitly: 'If it hadn't been him, it would have been some other man. If jealousy hadn't been the pretext, some other one would have been found [*Esli by ne predlog revnosti, to drugoi*].'[581] In other words, Pozdnyshev would have found some other reason to kill his wife if a third party and the resultant homosexually-tinged jealousy had not been found. The jealousy and the homosexuality *per se* were not the main issues. The problematical relationship with the wife was, or more distally, the lingering hatred for an abandoning mother was the issue. At the deepest level the murder will be a matricide.

The murder comes all in a rush toward the end of the novella. Less than a page after his experience of musical, pre-Oedipal bliss at the breast, Tolstoy's hero is jealous again. Away from home on government business, he receives a letter from his wife, his mother-icon, who casually mentions that Trukhachevsky has brought by some music. This sends Pozdnyshev spinning into such a fit of jealousy that he cannot sleep that night. He imagines that his wife and Trukhachevsky have by now already had sexual intercourse (*mezhdu neiu i im vse koncheno* – the phrasing *vse koncheno* is already present in the first draft).[582] They *must* have, he argues, again narcissistically: '. . . it was for the sake of that simple, straightforward thing that I married her, for the sake of it that I've lived with her, it's the only thing about her which I actually want and which other men, including the musician, therefore also wants'. His wife could not have resisted any sexual advance by Trukhachevsky, he tells himself: 'Would she be able to hold him back? I don't even know who she is. She's a mystery [*taina*], just as she's always been, just as she'll always be. I don't know her. I only know her as an animal. And nothing can or should hold an animal back.'[583]

Pozdnyshev is completely convinced of his wife's guilt, he obsessively imagines scenes of sexual interaction between his wife and Trukhachevsky, he even revels in the masochistic feelings of humiliation her fantasized unfaithfulness affords him: 'I was consumed with rage, indignation and a kind of strange, drunken enjoyment of my own hurt pride as I contemplated these pictures, and I couldn't tear myself away from them.'[584]

Such obsessive thinking not only lays bare Pozdnyshev's intensely narcissistic and masochistic concerns, but also reminds us that he has never really dared to love his wife. He is so wrapped up in *himself* that he has never come to know *her*, except 'as an animal', that is, except sexually. He admits that his own wife is a 'mystery' to him, yet presumes to know that she has been unfaithful to him only on the basis of her previous sexual interaction with *him*. Meantime, to an outside observer (including the majority of scholars who have studied the story), there is no solid evidence that Pozdnyshev's wife has actually been unfaithful to him. Artistically, this is an improvement over early drafts, where the wife's unfaithfulness is (explicitly or implicitly) an objective fact.[585] Tolstoy very effectively foregrounds Pozdnyshev's fantastical narcissism by backgrounding reality.

Pozdnyshev is consistent in his ongoing lack of contact with the reality of other people. The artificiality and concoctedness of his jealousy is like his previous gratuitous declaration that, if you were to fall in love with a woman, she would automatically abandon you. It makes no more objective sense for Pozdnyshev to be jealous of his wife (in the final version) than to entertain the theory that all women are abandoners.

Of course the very existence of the jealousy means that Pozdnyshev thinks that his wife *has* abandoned him. But the abandonment is primarily fantasized, not real. His wife is no Hélène, and Trukhachevsky is no Dolokhov – to name two infamous corners of a love triangle from *War and Peace*. We cannot find objective evidence that Pozdnyshev's wife has actually failed to love him, at least not in the late versions.[586] But there is plenty of evidence that he is unable to love her. What, then, can be the reason for Pozdnyshev's manifestly groundless jealousy?

I would like to suggest that, primed by the pre-Oedipal regression of the musical episode, Pozdnyshev cooks up his final, fatal jealous attack *in order* to (re-)experience the feeling of being abandoned. And Pozdnyshev wants to have this feeling *in order* to have a motive for lashing out at his wife, the iconic signifier of the pre-Oedipal mother whom he lost. In other words, Pozdnyshev is unconsciously looking for an excuse to take revenge for an archaic narcissistic injury, so he sets up a triangle that will provoke the jealous rage required to accomplish this. The apparent Oedipal triangularity of Tolstoy's story conceals a deeper, more disturbing pre-Oedipal, dyadic layer in which a childish Pozdnyshev needs to express his boundless narcissistic rage against his bad/lost mother. This approach is consistent with Heinz Kohut's notion that destructive rage is always motivated by an old injury to the self.[587] This approach also reflects Hildegard Baumgart's notion that pathological jealousy involves a reactualization of the primal mother–child relationship.[588]

By killing his wife, Pozdnyshev finally gets rid of (the icon of) the object which provokes painful and contradictory feelings in him. Of course he could more easily have accomplished this by simply leaving his wife. So the need to express his rage must be primary.

Much of the imagery immediately surrounding the murder has to do with mother–child relations. To get at his wife Pozdnyshev first tries to pass through the two children's rooms (he could have just gone through the drawing room and not risked disturbing the children).[589] He thinks: 'Five children, and she's kissing a musician because he's got red lips! No, she isn't human, she's a bitch, a repulsive bitch! Right next door to a room full of children she's pretended to love all her life.'[590] A most unsatisfactory mother she is, especially to her son Vasya: 'My Vasya! Now he was seeing a musician embracing his mother. What must be taking place in his poor soul? But what did she care?'[591] Here we should recall that Pozdnyshev's first name, too, is Vasya. His sympathetic identification with his son is assisted by the coincidence of names, and makes his wife all that much more a mother (-icon) to him.

On the other hand, it never once occurs to Pozdnyshev that, in killing his wife, he is depriving five children of a mother. As Vladimir Golstein points out: 'Pozdnyshev wants to destroy sex, but in fact he destroys the mother. . . '.[592] Any identification with the children is merely episodic and narcissistic. Even after the foul deed is done and the dying wife declares that she won't let Pozdnyshev have the children, he does not concern himself with how they feel.[593] He is busy trying to comprehend the terrible thing he has done to her.

The murder itself is accomplished with premeditated precision. 'I rushed at her, still keeping the dagger hidden in case he tried to stop me plunging it into her side, under the breast [*v bok pod grud'iu*]. That was the spot I'd chosen right from the outset.'[594] It is ironic that this area of the body was once attractive to Pozdnyshev, back when it was wrapped in a sexy jersey during the courtship.

For a moment Trukhachevsky manages to block Pozdnyshev, but then he runs off in abject terror (never again to appear). This leaves Pozdnyshev free to hit his real target. He strikes his wife in the face with his elbow, then tries to strangle her, and finally he stabs her in the side with the dagger: '. . . I struck her with the dagger as hard as I could in her left side, beneath her ribs'.[595]

Now Pozdnyshev's wife will die (unlike Khadzhi Murat's mother, who survives a knife-wound in the same part of the body). Pozdnyshev has now committed the most heinous crime, he has perpetrated the most extreme act of violence imaginable. But this had to happen, after all. Sexuality must lead to violence by Pozdnyshev's theory, that is, by Tolstoy's theory. From the very beginning of writing his novella Tolstoy had hoped to convey the idea that sexuality tended to result in 'murder'. In the first draft (the future) Pozdnyshev says – referring to himself still in the third person: '. . . he killed his wife because he loved her. And he could not not [sic] do this.'[596] In another variant Pozdnyshev says: 'Yes, sir, if men and women, husbands and wives were to love one another with just this animal love that they write about in novels, they would long since have all slaughtered [*pererezali*] one another. . . '.[597] In another (crossed-out) variant even monogamous love which lasts a lifetime (*vsiu zhizn'*) leads to widespread murder, for Pozdnyshev says in response to a question: 'There is [monogamous love], thank God, rarely, because if this were frequent, then the majority of people would have slaughtered one another.' Or: 'If there were love without debauchery [that is, without promiscuity], then there would be slaughter. We would all butcher one another.'[598] The 'animal' aspect of sexuality fades in these formulations, and we can discern the belief that real, lifelong sexual love – for example, Lev's love for Sonia – is just as murderous as any other kind.

For the most part Tolstoy believes that women, not men, end up being 'slaughtered' by love. In the fragment entitled 'The Wife Murderer', which clearly anticipates *The Kreutzer Sonata*, a (former) wife is disembowelled by her jealous husband: 'They say he ripped out all her innards [*Ves' potrokh vypustil, skazyvaiut*].'[599] In the first draft of the novella itself a crossed-out passage reads: 'with a knife, a dagger, he let out his wife's guts'.[600] In another crossed-out passage in the same draft Pozdnyshev decides to surprise his wife with her lover, gets a revolver, but changes his mind and takes down a dagger from the wall instead. He plans to hold the dagger with its curve turned upward 'in order to rip open the belly from below, so the guts would come out'.[601] Later in the same draft he actually does kill his wife in this fashion after seeing the artist enter her balcony window: 'I ran up to her, stuck the dagger in from below, and pulled it upward. She fell and grabbed me by the arm. I tore out the dagger with my hands. Blood spurted out. I became disgusted from her blood.'[602]

The fury with which Pozdnyshev attacks his wife's body is reminiscent of the rage he must once have felt toward his mother. Melanie Klein depicts the fantasy life of the pre-Oedipal child as highly sadistic with respect to the mother's body: '. . . the subject's dominant aim is to possess himself of the contents of the mother's body and to destroy her by means of every weapon which sadism can command.'[603] This sadism amounts to a death-wish against the mother:

When a baby feels frustrated at the breast, in his phantasies he attacks this breast; but if he is being gratified by the breast, he loves it and has phantasies of a pleasant kind in relation to it. In his aggressive phantasies he wishes to bite up and to tear up his mother and her breasts, and to destroy her also in other ways.

A most important feature of these destructive phantasies, which are tantamount to death-wishes, is that the baby feels that what he desires in his phantasies has really taken place; that is to say he feels that he *has really destroyed* the object of his destructive impulses, and is going on destroying it. . . .[604]

Tolstoy arranges his plot in such a way that Pozdnyshev does 'really destroy' the body of his wife, his maternal icon. Tolstoy's infantile, autobiographical hero thus fulfils a sadistic wish which, for a real infant at the breast, would be no more than a wish. Pozdnyshev even plans, as we saw earlier, to stab his mother-icon 'under the *breast*'.[605] In a variant, instead of stabbing her, Pozdnyshev shoots her *twice in the chest* and, when he comes back to see her on her deathbed, she is lying propped up on a bed in an unbuttoned, open blouse, chest bandaged.[606]

What if Pozdnyshev, like Tolstoy, was breast-fed by a wet nurse rather than his mother? Then, it seems to me, the 'Kleinian' rage against the maternal figure of the wife would be even more under-standable. Whatever hostile impulses may have existed toward the (breast of) the wet nurse during infancy would later have been retro-spectively magnified by the realization that the real mother had withheld her breasts completely. With both the wet nurse and the mother out of the adult framework of the story, however, the target of Pozdnyshev's hostility becomes the (breast of) the maternal wife – a wife who at one point, moreover, refuses to nurse her child.[607]

With Pozdnyshev's destructive aggression being discharged in the vicinity of the breast of the maternal icon, it should not be sur-prising that images of *orality* are abundant. The reader may recall Pozdnyshev's earlier characterization of woman as a 'sweet morsel', or his notion of sex as cannibalism, or his proverbial definition – in the lithographed edition – of one's own wife as something you put into your mouth: 'Someone else's wife is a swan, one's own is bitter wormwood.'[608] Shortly before the murder itself, Pozdnyshev arrives home to find his wife engaging not in sex with Trukhachevsky, but *eating* with him ('in there they ate and laughed'). At this moment he imagines that his wife must be appealing to Trukhachevsky, even if she is 'not quite fresh' (*uzh ne pervoi svezhesti*[609] – an expression the primary meaning of which applies to unfresh edibles such as meat or vegetables).

Earlier, Pozdnyshev seems particularly offended by Trukhach-evsky's oral activities, such as crunching the gristle of a cutlet as he eats, or seizing the rim of a wineglass with his 'red lips'. The 'red lips' come up several times in the narration. They go all the way back to the first draft, when Trukhachevsky does not yet have a name, and is an artist rather than a musician.[610] In the final version they take on a life of their own, they seem even to compete with Pozdnyshev for access to the breast of his maternal icon.[611] They lose their obscene red colour, that is, they turn pale (*poblednel . . . do gub*),[612] only at the moment Pozdnyshev threatens to kill Trukh-achevsky.

Klein says that '. . . in the oral-sadistic stage which follows upon the oral-sucking one, the small child goes through a cannibalistic phase with which are associated a wealth of cannibalistic phantasies. These phantasies, although they are still centred on eating up the mother's breast or her whole person, are not solely concerned with the gratification of a primitive desire for nourishment. They also serve to gratify the child's destructive impulses.'[613] Thus, for Pozdnyshev to characterize his wife's sexual body as 'not quite fresh' suggests not only that this body is 'edible' for him, but also that it is slightly disgusting. That is, the cannibalistic desire for nourishment is sadistically tinged. This is clearer in 'The Wife Murderer', where the precursor of Pozdnyshev rips out the innards of his wife, for innards (*potrokh*) also suggest a Russian culinary delicacy termed *potrokha* or *potroshki*, which are the edible innards of animals ('haslets', 'giblets').[614]

The first draft of the novella makes nearly explicit the idea of adultery as sharing milk from a breast. Pozdnyshev is describing (in the third person) how other men were attracted to the milking station of his beautiful wife:

> . . . he did not consider that there would be lots of people seeking after these pleasures which he had arranged for himself, including intelligent people who not only knew that sometimes it is very pleasant to live with a woman, but that in order to get this you don't have to go through all this fuss and bother of married life. Instead it's much more pleasant to gather cream without any trouble from a milking [*sobirat' slivochki s togo podoia*] arranged by someone else.[615]

The key word here, *podoi*, is an unusual regionalism.[616] It is cognate with such words as the verb *doit'* ('*to milk*') and the noun *doiarka* ('*milkmaid*').

Another passage in the first draft is also very explicit about the oral gratification involved in adultery, although without a specific reference to milk:

> He was in a bad way, poor fellow. Why? Because for him his spouse was only a sweet, tasty morsel [*sladkii, vkusnyi kusok*]

which he was used to eating, and the sweeter was the morsel, the clearer it became to him that others were sure to want to eat and had already in part eaten or sooner or later would eat this sweet morsel.[617]

The repeated and awkward usage of various forms of the verb 'to eat' (*el, khotiat s"est', s"eli, s"ediat*) in this unfinished passage is strikingly oral. A page later in the draft Tolstoy picks up the oral imagery again, after Pozdnyshev is sure his wife is again having an affair with the artist: 'She is mine, [crossed out: my sweet morsel], but I am not the reason for this radiance of hers, he is'. Her tastiness increases with his awareness of her unfaithfulness to him: 'Mine, but not mine, still sweeter [*slashche*] she seemed to him. Not mine, but mine. The more he loved, the more he hated.'[618] The ambivalence here is intense. It is the ambivalence of a child at the tasty breast.

Earlier we saw that the failure of Pozdnyshev's wife to breast-feed her first child was interpreted as 'coquetry' by Pozdnyshev. This was a paranoid idea, but Pozdnyshev is consistent in his paranoia, for now, late in the story, it is in the general area of the offending, orally charged breast that the wife is stabbed in revenge. If the wife had been nursing (or pregnant with) a child, she would not have been engaging in imagined 'coquetry' with Trukhachevsky, that is, if the maternal metonym had been providing nourishment to a child rather than being offered sexually to an interloping adult, then it would not have become the target of Pozdnyshev's rage. In short, if the wife had been able to live up to Pozdnyshev's paranoid, regressively pre-Oedipal expectations, she would not have been murdered by him (but then Tolstoy would not have had a story, either).[619]

The manner in which Pozdnyshev murders his wife suggests not only a regressive destruction of the mother's breast and innards, but also leads to another answer to the question I have repeatedly posed: why is he so opposed to sexual intercourse in the first place? Could it be that sex necessarily entails this very destruction of the mother's breast and innards? Pozdnyshev had felt, after all, that he had 'murdered' his pregnant wife simply by having sexual intercourse with her.[620]

I have in mind the shape and action of the murder weapon. A dagger is a long, pointed object which, in this case, is wielded by a man and is inserted into a woman's body. It appears to be a classic 'phallic symbol' of the type Freud discerned in his *Interpretation of Dreams* and in his subsequent writings on dreams.[621]

However, this 'Freudian' reading would be true only in a certain sense, for it is exactly backwards. Pozdnyshev's problem (and Tolstoy's) is that he views the sexual act as 'murder', not that he views murder as 'the sexual act'. This is a subtle but important difference. As Robert Louis Jackson says, the (admittedly) 'phallic organ' is 'a kind of murder weapon'.[622] We have here the (implicit) erect penis signifying a weapon of destruction, not a weapon of destruction signifying the erect penis. Such an interpretation of the iconic signification of Pozdnyshev's unmentioned penis explains why Pozdnyshev thinks sexual intercourse 'murders' the woman: *sex 'murders' a woman because the penis is not only a penis, but in the context of sexual excitement it is actually experienced by Pozdnyshev as a destructive weapon which harms the interior of a woman's body.* The *actual* murder which occurs at the end of the tale only follows through on what Pozdnyshev believes sexual intercourse with his wife has been accomplishing all along.

Such an interpretation takes us beyond – although it does not contradict – classical Freudian iconicity, and is in agreement with Kleinian theory: 'In the earliest stages of his life the male child looks upon his penis as the executive organ of his sadism. . .'.[623] Normally, according to Klein, this idea of a destructive penis is overcome:

> In the sexual relation to his love partner the man's early aggressive phantasies, which led to a fear of his penis being destructive, come into play to some extent, and . . . the sadistic impulse, when it is in manageable quantity, stimulates phantasies of reparation. The penis is then felt to be a good and curative organ, which shall afford the woman pleasure, cure her injured genital and create babies in her. A happy and sexually gratifying relationship with the woman affords him proofs of the goodness of his penis, and also unconsciously gives him the feeling that his wishes to restore her have succeeded. This not only increases his sexual pleasure and his love and tenderness for the woman, but here again it leads to feelings of gratitude and security.[624]

This, however, is precisely what does *not* happen in Pozdnyshev's case, for his feelings about his wife can hardly be characterized in terms of 'love and tenderness', or 'gratitude and security'. Instead, Pozdnyshev is still thinking like an infant, he still believes he is 'murdering' his wife every time he experiences sexual desire for her, that is, every time he gets an erection.

In two passages of the first draft, for example, Pozdnyshev suggests that murderous excitement is interchangeable with male
sexual excitement. The first describes what Pozdnyshev (speaking
of himself in the third person) does after arming himself with the
dagger in expectation of finding his wife with her lover:

> He entered her room. She was alone and asleep. Upon seeing
> him she exclaimed: 'ah!' For a moment he was sorry that now he
> didn't have to give free rein to the beast in himself, but then some-
> thing else awoke in him. It's all the same thing, just two sides of the
> same coin. Romances and murder. Yes sir![625]

This is crossed out and replaced later by a passage involving a different long, pointed, dangerous object, that is, a *pistol*:

> The first time, grabbing a pistol, he gave full rein to the beastly feel-
> ing, and another beastly feeling grew stronger. It's all the same,
> only the other side of the coin[626]

Whereas the first 'beastly feeling' is the urge to kill the wife, the second
is sexual desire for her, the urge to penetrate her sexually. In a flash
Pozdnyshev moves from one to the other, so one is clearly the semantic and emotional equivalent of the other, is 'all the same' as the other.
This equivalence or interchangeability of emotions is discernible in
another variant, where Pozdnyshev declares: 'Previously it used to be
that, the more I abandoned myself to carnal love, the more I hated her.
Now it came out the other way around: the more I hated her, the more
I desired her.'[627] Yet another variant has: '. . . I never desired her so
passionately, and I never hated her so passionately'.[628] The final variant tones down this equivalence somewhat by making the two opposed emotions non-simultaneous, that is, by making them alternate
with one another: 'A bout of love would be followed by one of animosity; a vigorous bout of love would be followed by a long bout of animosity, while a less intense bout of love would be followed by a
correspondingly shorter bout of animosity.' Yet even here the equivalence of the 'love' (*liubov'*) and the 'animosity' (*zloba*) is emphasized:
'We didn't realize it then, but this love and animosity were just two
sides of the same coin, the same animal feeling.'[629]

So, sexual desire ('what we called "love"') and hatred are the same
thing. This will seem rather peculiar to the normal reader, but it is a
very real sensation for the disturbed Pozdnyshev, and probably was

for Tolstoy as well. Tolstoy would not have been so hostile to sex if he had not perceived (male) sex as so hostile.

Here again Tolstoy looks like a certain kind of feminist. Andrea Dworkin, in her unscholarly and frenzied first chapter of *Intercourse*, does capture Tolstoy's message: 'The radical social change demanded by Tolstoy in this story – the end of intercourse – is a measured repudiation of gynocide: in order not to kill women, he said, we must stop fucking them.'[630] Dworkin, like Tolstoy, believes heterosexual intercourse 'kills' the woman, is 'gynocide'. This idea is the basis of her great resentment: 'Maybe life is tragic and the God who does not exist made women inferior so that men could fuck us. . .'.[631] But whereas Dworkin utilizes the idea of a necessarily hostile male sexuality ('fucking', as she puts it, not mere intercourse) to support her real, militant feminism, Tolstoy has his own – misogynist – agenda. The resemblance of Tolstoy's position to Dworkin's position is an accident due to resemblance of psychopathologies: both the Russian misogynist and the American feminist are obsessed with the idea that sex harms a woman's body.

If love did not have to involve sex, then the problem might be alleviated. In a passage crossed out in the third draft Pozdnyshev says: 'this love, egotistical, and thus sensual, is not love, but malice, hatred'.[632] Love, it seems, becomes its opposite, hatred – if sexual feelings are allowed into the picture.

Why not, then, simply delete sex from marriage? This, as we already know, is precisely what Tolstoy advocates. Only now we also know yet another reason why: sexual abstinence is to be desired because intercourse involves wielding a dangerous, aggressivized phallus against a woman.

The idea that sexual intercourse with a woman somehow harms her, destroys her, 'murders' her – is not something new in Tolstoy's literary art. In the earlier novel *Anna Karenina* Vronsky is imaged as a 'murderer' when he has sex with Anna for the first time, as numerous critics[633] have noticed: 'He felt what a murderer must feel when he sees the body which he has deprived of life.' Extending his metaphor, Tolstoy has Vronsky trying to dispose of the body of his victim, who is obviously Anna: 'And with hostility, as if with passion, the murderer throws himself upon this body, dragging it and cutting it up; in this fashion he too was lavishing kisses upon her face and shoulders.'[634]

Less direct is Tolstoy's 1903 tale 'After the Ball', in which a soldier is forced to run a gauntlet and flogged half to death for desertion. What connects this act of violence to sexuality is the fact that the victim of the beating is escorted through the gauntlet by a colonel who, just the night before, had danced with his own daughter at a ball. The narrator of the tale, an idealistic young man who admires the colonel and is in love with the colonel's daughter, is so upset after witnessing the beating that his love for the girl fades, and he decides not to join the army. Alexander Zholkovsky, drawing on Russian folklore and Christian mythology, has demonstrated the structural equivalence between the beating and the dancing. According to Zholkovsky, 'the soldier's tortured body replaces and lays bare for the hero that of his beloved. . .'.[635] As a particularly strong piece of evidence, Zholkovsky quotes the related 1905 piece entitled 'Posthumous Papers of the Elder Fedor Kuzmich', where Tolstoy writes: 'The thought of the murdered, sensuously beautiful Nastasia and of the bodies of soldiers lashed by rods, blended into one stimulating sensation.'[636]

7. CASTRATION, MASOCHISM, GUILT

The sheer quantity of reasons for a man to avoid sexual intercourse with a woman is remarkable. According to Tolstoy (and his Pozdnyshev) the reasons for sexual abstinence include more than a dozen (somewhat overlapping, not always consistent) categories:

1) To become sexually involved with a woman is to risk emotional abandonment by the woman.
2) Sexual intercourse is degrading and animalistic ('piglike') for both participants.
3) Christ (supposedly) preached abstinence.
4) Sex makes a 'prostitute' of a woman.
5) Sex leads to the mutual enslavement of men and women.
6) Sex damages the health of pregnant and/or nursing women.
7) Sex is like gluttony or cannibalism (especially cannibalism of the maternal breast).
8) Defloration is painful.
9) Sex leads to the horrible experience of childbirth.
10) Sex with contraception is 'murder' of unborn children.
11) Sex can result in other forms of 'murder' of offspring, i.e., abortion and infanticide.
12) Sex causes female hysteria.
13) Sex causes jealousy.

14) Jealousy can result in disturbing homosexual feelings.
15) The erect penis is a dangerous weapon wielded against a
    woman's body.
16) Sex can literally lead to murder of the woman.

Finally, we should not forget Tolstoy's moral masochism:

17) Sex is pleasurable.

– and this is a reason to *avoid* sexual intercourse. In his afterword
Tolstoy says:

> The Christian ideal is . . . the renunciation of self [*otrechenie ot
> sebia*] for the service of God and of one's neighbour. Marriage and
> carnal love are, on the other hand, the service of oneself. . . .[637]

Self-renunciation here clearly includes renunciation of 'marriage
and carnal love', that is, marital intercourse. It is better to suffer.

The importance of the specifically masochistic reason should not
be underestimated. Masochism explains why, in a diary entry for
9 November 1889, Tolstoy asserts that a woman has a greater right to
take the sexual initiative than a man because she at least is going to
have to suffer as a result (that is, give birth, care for the child, and so
on). For a man, on the other hand, sexual intercourse is merely a
pflichtloser Genuss, as Tolstoy puts it.[638]

Masochism also explains Tolstoy's attitude to castration. Even if it
were possible to avoid sexual intercourse by means of the purely
mechanical and temporarily painful procedure of castration, Tolstoy
would disapprove. Again, long-term suffering is essential.

Thus in an 1888 letter to Chertkov, when he is already thinking
aloud about the possibility of complete sexual abstinence, Tolstoy
touches on the question of self-castration. This topic is not nearly as
unlikely as it may seem, for in Russia there existed a well-known religious sect called the *Skoptsy*, or 'eunuchs' (from the verb *skopit'*, 'to
castrate'). Tolstoy was well-informed about their practices, which
included the cutting off of one or both testicles, and sometimes the
penis ('root') as well.[639] According to Tolstoy, lechery and castration
were 'equally bad and sinful':

> But the second, castration, is worse. In lechery [*blud*] there is no
> pride, but there is shame, while in castration people have no shame
> and they are even proud of the fact that they have in one fell swoop

violated the law of God in order not to fall into temptation and not to have to struggle. You have to castrate your own heart [*Serdtse svoe nado oskopit'*], then external castration will not be necessary. . . .[640]

In other words, you have to suffer. One must follow the long, difficult path of renunciation rather than taking the easy way (and besides, as Tolstoy correctly observes, even self-castration does not always remove sexual desire).

During the public debate which followed the publication of *The Kreutzer Sonata* at least one critic compared Tolstoy's position (unfavourably) with that of the *Skoptsy*. I. F. Romanov, writing under the pseudonym 'Rcy', declared that the *Skoptsy* are 'more magnanimous' than Pozdnyshev/Tolstoy 'because they do not use their knives on their innocent wives but on the very root [*sic*] of what they consider sinful'.[641] As Peter Møller observes, Romanov was primarily concerned with criticizing Tolstoy's asceticism,[642] or psychoanalytically speaking, Tolstoy's moral masochism.

Over the years Tolstoy stuck to this position on the *Skoptsy*. Chertkov reports on a conversation Tolstoy held with an old *Skopets*:

L. N. 'You have to make an effort in order to abstain from sexual relations; the task of life is in this struggle with temptations.'
N. (*Skopets*). 'For the ordinary person who is healthy, Your Excellency, this is impossible. Take the Dukhobors, whom we saw a lot of in Siberia. They used to say that they had decided to abstain, to live chastely. We said to them: "That's what you say now, but we'll see what happens when you reach Yakutsk." – And what do you know, a year later we saw them again, and they had lots of cradles and infants!'
L. N. 'You have to try. It's impossible to be perfect, but it is possible to strive for perfection.'
N. 'Your Excellency, may I say something to you?'
L. N. 'Please, speak.'
N. 'Your Excellency, it is necessary to observe chastity, is it not?'
L. N. 'Of course it's necessary, that goes without saying.'
N. (Quietly, with conviction, categorically, as of something completely obvious). 'In that case, tell me, Your Excellency, for what . . .? Why . . . ? Would it not be better to free oneself of . . . ?'
L. N. (smiling). 'Yes, it's hard to answer that one.' (afterwards L. N. remembered this argument of the *Skopets* several times and admitted that it had taken him aback). 'But in that case one may say: what

is life for? Wouldn't suicide be better? For if everybody followed your example, then the human race would destroy itself.'

N. 'No. Suicide is something Christ did not permit. One has to suffer.'

L. N. 'So there, abstain and suffer. For if a drunkard does not get drunk because he has no money, or because there isn't a tavern nearby, then he is not so virtuous. No, you must abstain, when there is a possibility of sinning.'[643]

This should put to rest the idea that Tolstoy (or his Pozdnyshev) was advocating the end of humanity. What Tolstoy really wanted was for people to suffer and to struggle against sexuality, as he did. To castrate oneself as N. did, to take a shortcut, so to speak, which eliminates subsequent sufferings and struggle against temptation, is wrong. In *The Kreutzer Sonata* Tolstoy advocates 'a sort of *psychological* self-castration' at most, as Martine de Courcel has said.[644] The purpose of abstaining from sex is suffering, self-punishment, not chastity. Moral perfection is a worthy goal, a narcissistic ideal looming in the far distance, but never to be touched. The more immediate and palpable goal is moral masochism, endless wished-for suffering – and suffering not only in the sexual realm.

8. TOLSTOY'S MORAL MASOCHISM

One way Tolstoy deals with his almost constant physical and psychical pain in 1889 is to actively welcome it. He is not satisfied merely to complain. He needs to gain some sort of mastery over (not necessarily pleasure in) his suffering, and for this he needs to actually seek out suffering.

Examples of Tolstoy's overall masochistic attitude in 1889 abound. On 17 July, for example, he asserts that 'withstanding hardships, humiliations, and hostility is a necessary condition for spiritual life'. Tolstoy repeatedly reminds himself that sufferings of all kinds are necessary:

Remember that your life is only in the fulfillment of the will of God on earth. You can unquestionably fulfill God's will only by developing your spiritual essence. You can only develop your spiritual essence by observing purity in your animal life, humbleness [*smirenie*] in your human (worldly) life, and love in your divine life. To observe purity you need hardships, for humbleness you need negative publicity and humiliation, for love you need people to be hostile toward you. . . .

If all these bad things come your way, says Tolstoy, do not grieve, but be glad of them (*ne ogorchat'sia, a radovat'sia*).[645]

Similar thinking may be found in correspondence with friends. In a letter of 19 February to the Ges (father and son), Tolstoy writes that one should live 'only in *purity*, i.e., free of all forms of lust – overeating, wine, smoking, sexual lust and fame; in *submissiveness* [*v smirenii*], that is, always ready for people to abuse my work and to shame me; and *in love*, i.e., when this happens, to be free of rage, vexation, or a desire to separate from any human being whatever.'[646] To Chertkov Tolstoy writes on 27 August: '. . . one can do these things [such as plowing and writing] . . . as an observance and purification in the work of that divine instrument which constitutes my life, and then nothing can destroy my interest and joy up to the last day and hour, for this business of my life grows with deprivations, sufferings, sicknesses, and death.'[647]

This is not just empty theorizing. Tolstoy welcomes suffering in specific, concrete instances. For example, on 12 July he characterizes the difficulties of living with a wife who holds moral views opposed to his as a necessary 'cross' which is beneficial: 'this is like sickness, old age, and death – happy conditions of my life'. On 25 September he writes that Sonia's venomous reproaches, however painful, 'have been good for me'.[648] Here it is clear that attempting to avoid his wife sexually was not the only kind of masochism Tolstoy practised in relation to her.

There can be no doubt that masochism kept the aging Tolstoy living with his wife for years longer than would otherwise have been the case. Tolstoy may have had a 'burning wish to be free of being tied to any woman', as Edward Greenwood says.[649] But the masochistic counterwish was greater. Toward the very end, in conversation with M. P. Novikov in 1910, Tolstoy declared: 'For myself alone I did not leave, I carried my cross.'[650] Tolstoy's son Ilya also uses the image of a cross to characterize his father's determination to remain with his mother: 'He courageously took his cross and courageously carried it.'[651] Tolstoy's physician and friend in the late years, Dushan Makovitskii, says: 'To Sofiia Andreevna he constantly turned the other cheek, morally. He patiently endured it when she attacked him, his friends, his teaching'.[652] This is somewhat of an exaggeration, for Tolstoy did sometimes lose his temper with Sonia, as he admits in the diaries. He was also very possessive of her, and for the most part he did not (masochistically) tolerate her flirtatious behaviour toward Sergei Taneev in the mid-1890s.[653] In addition, Tolstoy treated his wife rather sadistically in the sexual sphere (as we will see below). But masochism in no way excludes anger, possessiveness, or sadistic impulses.

One specific instance of masochistic fantasizing concerns *The Kreutzer Sonata* itself. In repeatedly rewriting and improving this work Tolstoy could not avoid thinking about its artistic quality (or lack thereof). If the work were to be too well written, Tolstoy feared, then he would gain too much narcissistic pleasure. In late August he wrote in his diary:

> I was thinking that I busy myself with writing *The Kreutzer Sonata* out of vanity [*iz za tshcheslaviia*]; I don't want to appear before the public without the finishing touches, not well-made, even bad. And this is poor. If there is something there which is useful and ne-cessary for people, then people will get this from what is bad. The novella will not make my conclusions any more convincing by being written to perfection. One should be a holy fool even in writ-ing [*nado byt' iurodivym i v pisanii*].[654]

This, however, is mere fantasy. Not all of Tolstoy's masochistic the-orizing was put into practice. Any artistic weaknesses of the novella result primarily from Pozdnyshev's (Tolstoy's) preposterous and re-pellant sexual theories, not from deliberately bad (even uncon-sciously deliberately bad) writing on Tolstoy's part. The drafts are generally inferior in artistic quality to the final product – which means that Tolstoy actually aimed at improving his novella as he repeatedly wrote and rewrote it over the course of many months. Until near completion, that is, December of 1889 when he was writing the final draft, he was (characteristically) trying to improve it on the artistic level. A diary entry for 5 December reads, in part: 'I looked through it, I crossed out, I corrected, I added things to the whole of *Kreutzer Sonata*. I am terribly sick of it. The main thing is that it is not right, artis-tically, it rings false.'[655] These are not the words of a man who is self-defeating in his art. Tolstoy could never really be a masochist at the artistic level, only in his personal life, or at most in the persons rep-resented in his art. If many of the later works do not measure up to the earlier masterpieces, this is because their author's creative strength was waning (in part because of the increasingly intrusive depression and various specific anxieties and obsessive beliefs), not because the masochism was seeping into the literary activity itself. Tolstoy's *thematics* were becoming increasingly masochistic in orientation – for example, a nobleman follows a prostitute to Siberia, a monk chops off his own finger when sexually aroused, a good-natured peasant accepts all the work piled on him, and so on – but the literary *handling* of these themes was never deliberately or even unconsciously compromised. Tolstoy was a creative artist to his narcissistic core. He could no more stop writing well than he could stop having sex.

Tolstoy's Pozdnyshev is himself masochistically inclined. We may recall his 'strange, drunken enjoyment of my own hurt pride' as he tries to imagine what his wife and Trukhachevsky are doing together.[656] In a variant Pozdnyshev philosophizes in true Tolstoyan fashion: 'It is possible to love in a human way [*liubit' po chelovecheski*] only those who disturb your peace and happiness. Thus it is said, "Love those who hate you".'[657]

Nor should we forget Pozdnyshev's repeated castigation of himself throughout *The Kreutzer Sonata* for experiencing sexual desire. To regard his loss of virginity as a 'fall' or to view normal marital intercourse as 'piglike' is to express inappropriate guilt, that is, to punish oneself to excess. This too is a mild form of masochism.

Tolstoy's moral masochism is Christian to the core, yet it did not jibe with contemporary Russian Orthodoxy. Indeed Tolstoy was curiously ignorant about the native ascetic tradition within Russian Orthodoxy, as Father Aleksandr Men' observes in his introduction to a recent, post-Soviet edition of *Confession*.[658] Instead, Tolstoy's masochistic attitude was based on his own personal predilections and (later) his own reading and understanding of the four Gospels. Thus during the period of writing *The Kreutzer Sonata* he often thinks of those aspects of Christ's teachings which involve pain and suffering. On 31 July he writes: '. . . one can love only one's enemies, those to whom one is not attracted. One can love only in offering [the other] cheek, only those who beat [you], and therefore in order to have the happiness of loving, it is necessary that you be beaten [*nado, chtoby tebia bili*].' For this reason, Tolstoy goes on to say, 'the fact that they beat you or humiliate you is not an annoyance capable of producing irritation, but is a joy, is a fulfillment of what is to be expected, as I have been writing here, namely, when dealing with people, expect an insult as something to be desired'.[659] All of this is of course a reflection of Christ's famous words on the mountain: 'Do not resist one who is evil. But if any one strikes you on the right cheek, turn to him the other also;' 'Love your enemies and pray for those who persecute you' (Matthew 5: 39, 44). Tolstoy takes these words very much to heart, much more so than does the 'official' Russian Orthodox tradition.

The reward for Christian endurance is the endurance itself. One must never boast about (exhibit) what one has endured. In a letter to Chertkov of 18 March 1889 Tolstoy complains about 'false tone' in some religious writing, giving as an example of this a paraphrase of his own of the words of Christ: 'If some evil bad guy should hit you on the cheek, you, good guy [*dobryi molodets*], turn the other cheek without a whimper and so on.'[660] No heroics, no braggadocio should accompany the masochism.[661] (Whether Tolstoy was actually capable of denying himself narcissistic pride for his masochism is another question).

Psychoanalysis holds that masochistic attitudes and practices originally develop from some defect in the early relationship with the mother. For example, Edmund Bergler characterizes the masochistic attitude as: 'I shall repeat the masochistic wish of being deprived by my mother, by creating or misusing situations in which some substitute of my pre-oedipal mother-image shall refuse my wishes.'[662] Kerry Kelly Novick and Jack Novick assert that '. . . the first layer of masochism must be sought in early infancy, in the child's adaptation to a situation where safety resides only in a painful relationship with the mother'.[663]

It is not appropriate here to detail the extensive clinical evidence for such assertions,[664] but it is worth recalling that Tolstoy was deprived of a mother's love and forced to accept maternal surrogates early in life. There was much pain indeed in his early relationship with his mother and/or her substitutes. His problematical pre-Oedipal situation made him an even more likely candidate for later masochism than is usually the case in Russia (with its traditional encouragement of submission to the collective, acceptance of fate, glorification of suffering, and so on). Add to this his guilt about his matricidal impulses, and it becomes difficult to imagine how Tolstoy could ever have avoided masochistic fantasies and behaviour.

One particular Russian cultural practice should be mentioned here, namely, swaddling of infants. Among the peasantry since time immemorial, among the aristocracy who hired peasant help, and even recently among Russian urban dwellers, women customarily wrapped up their infants in narrow strips of cloth (*pelenki*) from birth. These swaddling bands served both to contain the child's excretions and to severely restrict bodily motion. The arms and legs of a swaddled child were rendered immobile. When fully swaddled the entire child (except for its face) was tightly embraced in a kind of womb-substitute. As I have argued elsewhere, this practice contributed to the development of masochistic practices and attitudes in adulthood. The swaddled infant was forced into a kind of submission, was encouraged very early to take an accepting attitude to the bad things which happen in life.[665]

Among the Russian gentry of Tolstoy's day infants were more likely to be swaddled by mother-surrogates than by mothers themselves. In an autobiographical fragment of 1878, Tolstoy himself reports on how he felt about being swaddled:

I am bound [*ia sviazan*], I want to stick my hands out and I cannot. I cry and weep, and my cry is disagreeable even to me, but I cannot stop. Some people are standing bent over me, above me . . . I remember that there are two of them, and [crossed out: they feel sorry for me, but because of some strange misunderstanding they] my cries have an effect on them: they are alarmed by my cries but do not untie me [*ne razviazyvaiut menia*], which I wish they would, and I cry still louder. To them this seems necessary (that is, that I be bound), while I know it is not and I want to prove this to them [crossed out: and it is this misunderstanding that tortures me most of all and forces me] so I let forth a cry repellent to myself but irrepressible. I feel the unfairness and cruelty not of people, because they feel sorry for me, but of fate and I feel sorry for myself.[666]

Tolstoy may not actually be remembering the experience of being swaddled, that is, he may be having what psychoanalysts would term a screen memory.[667] Nonetheless, this description vividly captures how Tolstoy felt about being restricted at some point in his childhood, and eloquently expresses his longing for freedom. Just as important, however, is his budding acceptance of non-freedom in the passage, his submission to that special Russian kind of 'fate' (*sud'ba*),[668] and his reluctance to blame the two women who are restricting him. These women are both mother-substitutes of some kind, or perhaps one of them is even the mother herself. Tolstoy says he is not certain whether the incident took place while he was still nursing and less than a year old, or later when he had an outbreak of sores and was swaddled to prevent scratching. The event is very distant and unclear, but the emotional remnants of the event are intense – as intense as the emotion we know Tolstoy felt for the mother he supposedly could not remember.

Tolstoy seemed to have an intuitive grasp of the maternal element in moral masochism. One of the most astonishing things he writes in the 1889 diary concerns his daughter and fellow-masochist Mar'ia L'vovna: 'For Masha it was a great good fortune that her mother did not love her'.[669] What is 'fortunate' here is the fact that, because of her inadequate mothering (amply documented),[670] Masha is *like* him. Tolstoy's special, masochistic misery loved company. Nothing would have pleased Tolstoy more than for other members of the family to share his self-punishing attitude. During the period of writing *The Kreutzer Sonata* Masha was the one family member who tended to go along with her father's ideas about the need for self-sacrifice, turning the other cheek, loving one's enemy, and so forth. This was not because Tolstoy propagandized her (he propagandized everyone else in the family too, and some, like his daughter Tat'iana, tried valiantly to become Tolstoyan masochists, while Sonia resisted).[671] Rather, Masha went along because 'her mother did not love her'.

Among some family members Masha's masochism was characterized as 'English', perhaps because her English was more fluent than her Russian as a result of her having been cared for by her English governess 'Miss Emily'. Thus she was said to suffer from something called 'mania anglicana – as you like it' (English original) which, according to Tolstoy's grandson Sergei Mikhailovich Tolstoi, consisted of 'not doing what you like to do, but doing what others want you to do'. Masha was always ready to help others. She was utterly devoted to the peasants of Yasnaya Polyana, working with them in the fields, nursing them in their illnesses, teaching them to read and write. With good reason Sergei Mikhailovich says that Tolstoy 'recognized himself' in Masha and calls her 'the most consistent Tolstoyan of all Tolstoy's children'.[672] And again, as Tolstoy says, all because 'her mother did not love her'.

It was during the period of writing *The Kreutzer Sonata* (starting in late 1888) that Tolstoy was first in danger of losing his dear Masha, for she and his devoted disciple Pavel Biriukov fell in love with one another and expressed a perfectly normal desire to get married. But Tolstoy resisted. In a letter to Biriukov himself Tolstoy utilizes very emotional phraseology: 'terrifying' (*zhutko*), 'awful', 'something cruel as it were, unnatural'.[673]

The virgin Masha was precious to Tolstoy, especially at a time when he was vituperating against sexuality in his novella. A diary entry of 25 April 1889 reads: 'Masha arrived. I feel a great tenderness for her, for her alone. She somehow makes up for the others.' On 12 June he writes to Biriukov: 'Masha is a great joy to me at home.' On 22 August he writes to V. I. Alekseev: 'Of my children Masha alone is a kindred spirit [*blizka mne po dukhu odna Masha*].' In the summer of the previous year, when labouring with his Masha in the fields, Tolstoy refers to her as 'my very greatest joy'.[674] And so on.

Tolstoy could not bear to lose Masha, this daughter who bore his mother's name. To lose her to a husband would mean not only that she would be sexually defiled (according to his theory), but that he would also be deprived of his only true family companion in masochism.

9. GUILT AND THE MATRICIDAL IMPULSE

The simplest proximate explanation for Tolstoy's masochistic need to suffer must be guilt, because suffering assuages guilt. Most of the reasons for sexual abstinence listed previously, certainly suggest that Tolstoy/Pozdnyshev does feel guilty (sex is 'piglike', it 'enslaves' or 'murders' a woman, it harms her health when she is nursing, it harms her children, and so on). As I noted earlier, guilt feelings about sexual intercourse would be inappropriate or excessive in the normal marital situation. The question I would like to raise now is: why does Tolstoy feel so guilty about having sexual intercourse in the first place? It is one thing to establish *that* Tolstoy is beating his breast to masochistic excess, it is quite another to discover *why* he should be doing so. And here, of course, I take the liberty of assuming that Pozdnyshev's guilt *is* Tolstoy's guilt, for the 1889 diary is full of guilty statements about his own sexuality, such as 'I am a lecher' (19 August), 'I am very bad' (6 June), and so on, and more of these indications of massive guilt will be cited below in an exploration of Tolstoy's psychiatric symptoms while writing *The Kreutzer Sonata*.[675]

It seems to me that, since the guilt which the adult Tolstoy feels is atypical, that is, since it goes beyond even the ordinary chronic guilt Russians tend to feel, its cause ought to be searched for in Tolstoy's own unique ontogeny. In the course of personal development most people, including Russians, get beyond the idea that a man

somehow hurts a woman by having sexual intercourse with her –
even if that idea is never totally forgotten, and in *some* situations is
retrieved for the purpose of inducing guilt. But if guilt is normally
the result of doing something morally wrong, and if marital sex is
not *normally* thought of as something wrong, then what in Tolstoy's background might have caused him nonetheless to believe
that marital intercourse was wrong? That is, what elements from his
personal past would lead him to *misjudge the moral significance of
sexual intercourse?*

I would like to suggest that Lev Tolstoy felt guilty about the heterosexual act because he felt that it was an expression of hatred toward
the woman. And it was an expression of hatred because he in fact
hated his mother, raged against her for her sexuality and especially
for her perceived abandonment of him in early childhood. Sex for
Tolstoy had matricidal overtones. And conveniently enough for
Tolstoy, his mother herself maintained rather prudish attitudes toward sexuality as already mentioned, so at one level he was only
identifying with the very object he hated.[676]

Tolstoy suffered the loss of his mother at an early age, that is, at a
crucial phase of development when he was ambivalently attached to
her and was bound to experience her loss as an abandonment of him
and to feel matricidal hostility toward her as a result. Perhaps
Tolstoy even felt that the loss of his mother 'killed' him in some sense
(recall Pozdnyshev's harping on infanticide). In an interesting recent
paper by Russian psychoanalyst Mikhail Romashkevich it is argued
that matricidal impulses can derive from chronic infanticidal fantasies in narcissistically disturbed individuals.[677]

Well into old age, as we saw, Tolstoy tended to get very emotional
about his mother whenever he tried to think of her. His idealization
of her was extreme (the *'culte'*), and at the same time he tended consciously to dissociate her from any sexual ideas. Yet, in order for
Tolstoy to have come into existence, his mother has to have had
sexual intercourse with her husband. Ordinarily such a thought
would not be earthshaking, and most people do eventually adjust to
the idea of their own parents having sex. For Tolstoy, however, sex
was not the good thing which brought him into this world, but the
bad thing which took his mother out of his world. Tolstoy was under
the false impression that his mother *died* because of childbirth
complications, which is to say that he (thought he) lost her because
she previously engaged in sexual intercourse. Sexuality took on a
permanent deadliness for Tolstoy, as in a note he wrote to himself

about marital sex many years before creating *The Kreutzer Sonata*: 'In carnal union there is something terrible and blasphemous. It is not blasphemous only when it results in offspring. But still, it is terrible, *just as terrible as a corpse.*'[678]

If only Tolstoy's mother had been nursing him at the breast and otherwise caring for him directly, rather than fobbing him off onto mother-substitutes and having sex with her husband (cf. his advocacy of postpartum sex taboo), she might not have died on him. That is, there might not have been a maternal 'corpse' of the type so graphically depicted, say, in the novella *Childhood*, or in the story 'Three Deaths', or after the heroine's suicide in *Anna Karenina*, or on the final page of *The Kreutzer Sonata*.[679] The stinking corpse of Nekhliudov's mother in the late novel *Resurrection* is especially to the point, for it is described specifically in the context of Nekhliudov's disgust toward the portrait of his highly sexual mother, with her half-exposed breasts.

In order for a mother's 'corpse' to appear, someone's mother has to die. In the early work *Childhood* Tolstoy was not yet prepared to avenge his mother's abandonment of him, so the mother there dies merely of natural causes (at most she is 'killed' by the narrator). Likewise for 'Three Deaths', where the children continue to play in a distant room as their mother's body lies in state. As for the neglectful mother Anna Karenina, she takes her own life (although the puritanically disapproving Tolstoy essentially plays God in arranging for this act of vengeance to happen). In *The Kreutzer Sonata*, however, the character Pozdnyshev – a hateful stand-in for Tolstoy himself – actively kills a maternal figure. *This* is what Tolstoy had been wanting to do to his abandoning, sexually active mother all along. The unconscious idea of matricide motivates the actual uxoricide which takes place in Tolstoy's novella.[680] For this once in Tolstoy's literary life the guilty metaphor of sex as 'murder' of the woman is not enough, and an actual murder occurs as well.

An underlying matricidal impulse, I believe, best explains Tolstoy's guilt feelings. Because Tolstoy unconsciously hated his mother all his life long, he experienced chronic guilt. The guilt tended to surface not only in the context of wanting sexual intercourse with a woman (the mother supposedly died on him because of her sexual activity), but also in the context of wanting oral gratification (the mother would not breast-feed him). Again, it is not surprising that the advocacy of sexual abstinence overlaps with the activism against alcohol, tobacco, meat, and so on. The masochism in these areas was nurtured by a common matricidal guilt.

The fact that Tolstoy's mother was already dead did not lessen his death-wish against her. Indeed, *because* she was dead he never had the opportunity to work through his narcissistic rage and guilt in interaction *with her*. He had to settle for dealing with substitutes for her, that is, with maternal icons in his real and literary life. The original rage remained, it could not be quelled, nor could the resulting guilt be subdued except by incessant self-punishment or moral masochism. All his life Tolstoy found himself, to varying degrees, in the horrible, guilt-ridden position experienced by: the husband after the wife's death in 'Three Deaths' (he had not sent her soon enough to Italy for a cure); Vronsky after Anna's suicide (he had not returned soon enough in response to her telegram); Prince Andrei after Lise's death in childbirth (he had abandoned her when she was pregnant); Pozdnyshev after murdering his wife. All of these men feel guilty. Of them, however, only Pozdnyshev has gone so far as actually to murder a maternal figure.

10. REPETITION OF PAST TRAUMAS

Although Pozdnyshev's murder of his wife represents Tolstoy's vengeful feelings toward his abandoning mother, the murder also represents the very death of the mother as Tolstoy experienced it. That is, the death of Pozdnyshev's wife is not only an act of revenge, but is a re-staging or repetition of the loss for which revenge would have to be taken. This is particularly evident right at the deathbed scene.

Just as Pozdnyshev is brought to his wife's deathbed for a final goodbye, Tolstoy the toddler had been brought to his mother's deathbed to receive her final blessing. The original experience was apparently quite unpleasant for all involved. Gusev quotes a story told to Tolstoy by the wife of Tolstoy's tutor:

> You were just a little tot at the time, two or three years old at most. I remember, Lev Nikolaevich, how your mother, our dear mistress died. I remember, I will never forget how they gathered at the bed-side of the dying woman – the doctor, the husband, the children, relatives, house-serfs, all with sad faces. Quietly, carefully, they crowded in there, pressing against one another, everyone who wanted to could look, could say goodbye to a dear, kind person. The

sick woman was lying there, hardly breathing, pale as death. Her eyes were beginning to grow dim, she seemed dead already. But her memory was still sharp and good. In a quiet, weak voice she was calling over to herself her husband, her children, she was making the sign of the cross, blessing them, saying goodbye to all of them in order. And then, when it came your turn, she quickly cast her eyes about, searching, and asked: 'Where is Levushka?' Everybody rushed searching for you, while you, Lev Nikolaevich – so little, chubby, and with fuzzy rosy cheeks – you were busy running and jumping like a top in the children's room. And your nanny, no matter how much she tried to persuade you and stop your ringing laughter, could not. I remember, Lev Nikolaevich, how they started taking you up to your dying mother, and how much trouble they had with you then. Two of them were holding on to you, but you kept trying to break away, you were screaming, crying and wanting to go back into the children's room. I remember how your mother, as with the others, made the sign of the cross over you and blessed you. And two big tears rolled down her pale, thin cheeks. What you did, Lev Nikolaevich, added to your mother's pain.[681]

Of course Tolstoy the toddler could not know how inappropriate his behaviour at his mother's deathbed was – at the time. But later? Later the mother was no more. The very tantrum described here might have been connected in little Levushka's mind with the fact that he never saw his mother alive again (and the woman telling the story – in her substandard Russian – seems even to be putting some blame on Tolstoy).

I would like to suggest that the experience described here was traumatic for Tolstoy, if only after the fact. The several female death-bed scenes in Tolstoy's fiction, moreover, seem to be attempts at mastering this trauma. As Gusev points out, there are some similarities between what went on at Tolstoy's mother's deathbed and the mother's deathbed scene in the distinctly autobiographical novella *Childhood*.[682] But other deathbed scenes would bear scrutiny in this connection. In 'Three Deaths', for example, the dying wife (named Mar'ia, that is, Tolstoy's mother's name) calls her husband to her deathbed and reproaches him for not adequately looking after her. In *War and Peace* Prince Andrei, having run away from his pregnant wife to fight a war, returns to her bedside just before she dies in childbirth. Aleksei Karenin comes to what he *thinks* is Anna's deathbed in order to forgive her for cuckolding him in *Anna Karenina*. In *Resurrection*

Dmitrii Nekhliudov's mother takes her son's hand as she lies on her deathbed, asking him not to reproach her for her disreputable past.

Only in *The Kreutzer Sonata*, however, is the man at the woman's bedside actually her killer. Tolstoy is attempting to master the trauma of his mother's death by having had Pozdnyshev actively cause death to happen. This once the mother did not merely die on Tolstoy, rather he caused her to die.

When Pozdnyshev's wife dies she leaves *five* children (*vse piatero detei*) – precisely the number left by Tolstoy's mother when she died.[683] In a variant of the novella the eldest of these children is named 'Nikolin'ka', that is, the name Tolstoy used to call his eldest brother, the first of the five children in Tolstoy's family.[684] On his way to his wife's deathbed Pozdnyshev passes by the children's room (*mimo detskoi*) and notices the children inside, while Tolstoy the toddler is discovered in the children's room (*v detskoi*) just before being brought to his dying mother. If in some variants of the novella the dying wife motions Pozdnyshev over to her (*pomanila*), in real life the dying mother calls (*zovet*) her children to her for a final blessing. When the wife speaks to Pozdnyshev her voice is extremely quiet in a couple of variants,[685] as is the mother's in the account quoted above. The wife also sobs (*vskhlipnula*) – just as Tolstoy's mother cried ('two big tears') in blessing him. By the time the wife actually dies, Pozdnyshev has been taken away by the authorities – just as little Levushka had been taken away by those in charge of him before his mother's death.

Some of these parallels are probably accidental, but there seem to be too many of them for the overall similarity between the death of Pozdnyshev's wife and the death of Tolstoy's mother to be a mere accident.

In addition to parallels there are of course differences. The biggest contrast is in the attitudes of the dying women: whereas Pozdnyshev's wife practically curses him, Tolstoy's mother blesses her child. But the horrific 'I hate you!' uttered by Pozdnyshev's wife just before she becomes delirious would capture very well what little Levushka Tolstoy must have *imagined* his mother felt in dying on him, in abandoning him, in ceasing indeed to look upon him any more: 'I hate you!'[686] in the Russian original is *Nenavizhu!*, etymologically 'I do not willingly look upon you.' Here we may note that Pozdnyshev was very concerned about how he *looked* to his wife just before he stabbed her (more on this below), and that his blow to her face gives her a black eye, partially blocking her vision ('She looked up at me with difficulty'). At the same time this blow renders the once beautiful wife ugly. Pozdnyshev speaks of her 'disfigured face' and says 'She had no beauty at all now'[687] – precisely Tolstoy's opinion of his mother's appearance. As for the 'Forgive me' Pozdnyshev's wife utters in some variants,[688] that too would have been appropriate coming from a mother who had offended little Levushka by fobbing him off on to a wet nurse and devoting most of her attention to the two Nikolais in her life.

Tolstoy's dead mother is not, however, the only woman reflected in the image of Pozdnyshev's dying wife. As it turns out, there is another, more recent trauma lurking in the novella's deathbed scene. In 1871 Tolstoy's wife *almost* died after the birth of her *fifth* child. This was a very important event in Tolstoy's married life, in part because the dark past was repeating itself.

On 12 February of that year Sonia gave premature birth to a daughter and named her Mariia (Tolstoy's mother Mariia Nikolaevna had given birth to *her* Mariia Nikolaevna, Tolstoy's sister, some forty-one years earlier). Apparently Sonia's pregnancy had been difficult, and there were complications afterwards. Sonia became seriously ill, and for a while she was actually near death (might this be the source of Tolstoy's false belief that his mother died as a result of the birth of her fifth child, also named Maria?). Gusev speaks of a puerperal fever (*rodil'naia goriachka*),[689] which is a systemic bacterial infection with symptoms such as fever, rapid heartbeat, uterine tenderness, malodorous vaginal discharge, and general abdominal pain. The syndrome, usually the result of unsterile obstetric technique, can lead to prostration, renal failure, bacteremic shock, and death.[690]

In a letter of 3 March to his sister-in-law Tolstoy speaks of 'fever and sweating followed by fever and sweating'.[691] To his friend D'iakov he writes: 'The day after the delivery there was an attack [*paroksizm*] of fever with chills and sweating. On the third day there was another attack, with abdominal pains in the form of spasms.'[692] Fever, abdominal pain, and elevated heart rate continued sporadically even after doctors treated Sonia with quinine and cold compresses. But by early March she was out of danger.

Understandably, Sonia did not want to repeat this horrible experience. In addition, her doctors advised her not to have any more children (by today's medical standards such advice on the occasion of a puerperal infection would be unwarranted, although sexual abstinence would be advised until after the infection cleared up). Tolstoy was quite upset about Sonia's new reluctance to have any more

children, as he indicated in a statement made (in a whisper) to Pavel
Biriukov in 1906:

> After a serious illness my wife, acting on the advice of doctors,
> refused to have children. This situation had such a grave effect on
> me, it was so contrary to my whole idea of family life, that for a
> long time I could not decide in what form this life should continue.
> I even contemplated divorce.

Later, Tolstoy adds, 'our family relations cleared up all by themselves'.[693] In other words, Sonia stopped refusing any sexual ad-
vances her husband was making.

In the meantime, however, Tolstoy felt quite isolated and depressed. Gusev adduces a diary entry under 26 May 1884, where a
despondent Tolstoy writes about 'the absence of a beloved and loving wife', and declares: 'It began from that time, 14 years ago, when
the string snapped, and I became aware of how alone I was.'[694] Sonia
too says that 'some kind of shadow' came between her and her husband during the winter 1870–71, when the two of them were ill, and
that afterwards Tolstoy was 'no longer the person he used to be'.[695]

Sonia's illness was primarily physical, that is, the puerperal infection. Tolstoy's ailments were both physical and mental. At first there
was some kind of fever and joint pains, accompanied by insomnia and
mild depression. Eventually, with the intensification of his wife's illness and her reluctance to bear more children – which for Tolstoy
meant a termination of sexual relations – Tolstoy's depression came to
centre stage. Sometime in April or May Tolstoy wrote to his close
friend, the mathematician S. S. Urusov: 'My health is still terrible. I've
never in my life experienced such *toska*. I don't want to go on living.'[696]
This sounds almost as bad as the *toska* in Arzamas, which we may recall had occurred a year and a half previously. In early June Tolstoy
wrote Afanasii Fet about his 'nervous exhaustion' (*upadok sil*).[697] The
horrible *toska* continued off and on, but abated somewhat after Tolstoy travelled to the Samara steppes to take *kumys* during June and
July. After his return to Yasnaya Polyana in early August he must
have resumed sexual relations with Sonia, however, for she was pregnant by October, and gave birth to Petr in June of 1872.

Sonia's initial refusal to have any more children must have been experienced by Tolstoy as a narcissistic injury, even a trauma, for
otherwise it would be difficult to explain the rapid onset of deep depression in the spring of 1871. Gusev, no psychoanalyst, none-

theless makes a sound psychological observation about this whole affair: 'Tolstoy could not imagine family life without its consequences – children. This 'snapping of the string of family life' was such a torment for him that he became seriously ill. Throughout his life Tolstoy would get ill not so much for physical as for moral reasons [*ot nravstvennykh prichin*]. Such was the case this time around.'[698]

The possibility of avoiding having children by means of birth control is never mentioned in either Lev's or Sonia's accounts of the 1871 crisis. Tolstoy would not permit birth control. He was a much more forceful personality than his Pozdnyshev, who tolerates his wife using birth control after child number five is born,[699] but who comes to hate his wife even more as a result.

The parallel between Pozdnyshev and Tolstoy is clear not only from events which occur after the respective births of their fifth child. Further similarities may be observed by examining the sex and age distributions of Pozdnyshev's children in two of the manuscript variants. In the third draft Pozdnyshev's five children and their ages after 12 years of marriage are as follows:

  boy, age eleven
  girl, age nine
  boy, age seven
  boy, age five
  boy, age three[700]

With this list we may compare Tolstoy's own (living) children after 12 years of his marriage to Sonia, that is, in September of 1874:

  boy, age eleven
  girl, age nine
  boy, age eight
  boy, age five
  girl, age three
  boy, age five months[701]

The first four items in each list match almost perfectly (there is an age discrepancy of one year for the third child). The fifth child in each list is three years old, but the two are of different sexes. The sixth child in the list of Tolstoy's living children is only a kind of appendage, since this child would soon die while still an infant (in February of 1875).

In another variant the similarity is even clearer. Pozdnyshev, having returned home from a dinner with his buddies, finds all his children have been put to bed. He then proceeds to list them by name, and the result is:

boy, age 10
girl, age eight
boy, age unspecified
boy, age unspecified
girl, age two[702]

This age and sex distribution corresponds almost perfectly with the age and sex distribution of Tolstoy's living children late in 1873 (Tolstoy's first daughter was already nine, not eight). Despite the slight differences, then, it is clear that Tolstoy, at least unconsciously, had his own past family situation in mind when he listed Pozdnyshev's five children in drafts of *The Kreutzer Sonata*.

In particular Tolstoy was remembering his wife's refusal to have more children after the birth of their fifth child in the early 1870s. True, Sonia, unlike Pozdnyshev's wife, eventually recanted on the refusal, and 'family relations cleared up', as Tolstoy put it. But the temporary crisis could not be forgotten, the narcissistic wound festered because it so resembled the much deeper wound from the more distant past: Tolstoy's mother had injured Tolstoy by not breast-feeding him and by dying on him after the birth of *her* fifth child, *her* Mariia (Tolstoy's sister bore the same name as his daughter). These two injuries – one by the wife, the other by the mother – seemed to work synergistically in Tolstoy's unconscious, fuelling a tremendous narcissistic rage which led to (among other things) the fictional murder of Pozdnyshev's wife.

11. ATTEMPTED REPARATION

The murderous attack on the wife is followed by an attempt to make amends. Like a Kleinian infant who fantasizes restoration of the mother's breast after destroying it,[703] Pozdnyshev wants somehow to make reparation for having stabbed his maternal icon 'under the breast'.

The attempt may seem rather weak and pathetic to the reader, but it is psychologically very real for Pozdnyshev. He approaches his wife on her deathbed, at first thinking *she* will want to beg *his* forgiveness for her supposed infidelity (in some variants she does ask forgiveness). Instead she is extremely hostile, declaring that she will not let him have the children and that she is giving them to her sister:

> I looked at the children, at her battered face with its bruises, and for the first time I forgot about myself, about my marital rights and my injured pride; for the first time I saw her as a human being. And so insignificant did all that had hurt me and made me jealous appear, and so significant what I'd done, that I wanted to press my face to her hand and say: 'Forgive me!' – but I didn't dare to.
>
> She fell silent, closing her eyes, and obviously without the strength to speak any more. Then her disfigured face began to quiver and was creased with a frown. Feebly, she pushed me away.
>
> 'Why did all this happen? Why?'
>
> 'Forgive me', I said.[704]

She does not forgive him, however. His last-minute attempt to make things right fails. He will be forever thwarted in his act of reparation, in his request for forgiveness.[705]

After this, there is nothing left for Pozdnyshev to do but feel sorry for himself:

> 'I only began to grasp it when I saw her in her coffin . . .'. He gave a sob, but continued hastily, at once: 'It was only when I saw her dead face that I realized what I'd done. I realized that it was I who had killed her, that it was all my doing that from a warm, moving, living creature she'd been transformed into a cold, immobile waxen one, and that there was no way of settling this to rights, not ever, not anywhere, not by any means. If you've never experienced that, you can't possibly understand . . . Oh! Oh! Oh!' he cried several times, and fell silent.[706]

Tolstoy is really quite clever here. He makes us – or at least some of us, his readers – feel sorry for a vicious murderer whose only external punishment turns out to be a very brief prison term. The internal self-punishment, Pozdnyshev's repeated self-lacerations for having had a sex life and having married, distract us, even if they are not quite credible (Vronsky, feeling guilt over the death of Anna, was much more credible when he headed off toward almost certain death in war). It is difficult not to patronize Pozdnyshev, he feels so sorry for himself that we cannot help joining in. We, along with the narrator, reinforce his narcissism by sympathetically hearing him out.

In a sense, Pozdnyshev has no one left *but* us readers to soothe his gaping narcissistic wound. His wife, the mother-figure who might have comforted him, is dead by definition. The mother herself, whose premature absence put the whole deadly plot into motion, is also unavailable by definition. Then there are the children, who have been taken away. Pozdnyshev is truly alone. Even the narrator, who has patiently heard him out, has not become a friend. At the end of the novella the narrator is still the same stranger met by chance on a train. True, the narrator has been moved by Pozdnyshev's tale of woe, but no bond has formed. He gets off the train at his stop, leaving Pozdnyshev forever.

There is nothing uplifting or positive about the ending of *The Kreutzer Sonata*. Pozdnyshev feels regret over his marriage and his sexuality – strikingly so in the eighth (lithographed) version: 'If I had known what I know now, things would have been completely different, I would not have gotten married.'[707] But he only half-heartedly repents of the murder itself. Commenting on this contrast, Mark Aldanov rightly asserts that Pozdnyshev experiences no true remorse.[708] Or the remorse is transformed, the pangs of conscience are misplaced. As Tolstoy's contemporary Dmitrii Ovsianiko-Kulikovskii observes, Pozdnyshev should be repenting of his jealousy and hatred, not his sexuality.[709] Pozdnyshev is no Othello, as Robert Bird observes, for he does not take personal responsibility for his real crime.[710]

Pozdnyshev would certainly not be able to remarry and love a woman.[711] On the contrary, if Pozdnyshev were to marry again, he probably would kill again. He still hates women and their sexuality. In the end he just lies there before the narrator's eyes, preoccupied with himself and showing no signs of movement toward real spiritual renewal. He has achieved convincing insight into the impossibility of sexual relations in *his* life, as Chertkov observed in a letter to Tolstoy in 1889.[712] But he has not convinced the narrator – nor has he convinced the majority of Tolstoy's readers, including even the devoted Chertkov – that sexual abstinence is best.

This failure, indeed, is part of Pozdnyshev's excessive narcissism – as if *his* conclusion could be true for everybody! Thus Pozdnyshev remains in character, as it were, until the very end. Any change in character, such as a spiritual rebirth, would have to have been motivated, and would have required many more pages of written text.

This was not a risk Tolstoy was willing to take, even though Chertkov had advised him to.[713] Pozdnyshev cannot do without 'the cult of himself' (*kul't svoego 'ia'*), as Ovsianiko-Kulikovskii puts it.[714] Narcissus triumphs in the end. Tolstoy fails to make his case for sexual abstinence.

6

Tolstoy's Problematical Self

It might well be suspected from what has been said so far that the author of *The Kreutzer Sonata* was mentally disturbed. I would now like to take a look at some of the specific psychiatric symptoms Tolstoy suffered from while he was writing his novella, and then consider these (and some other symptoms he had experienced at various times in his life) within a larger psychological framework. Overall, the life and works of Tolstoy manifest what may be called a disturbance of the self. Tolstoy's problematical self is the basis of both his psychopathology and his creativity.

1. PSYCHIATRIC SYMPTOMS WHILE WRITING *THE KREUTZER SONATA*

Something was definitely wrong with the mind of Tolstoy as he composed his novella – even if it is difficult to specify a concrete and persisting 'disorder' according to criteria of the current *Diagnostic and Statistical Manual of Mental Disorders,* published by the American Psychiatric Association.[715] During the spring and summer of 1889, when the bulk of the writing was done, numerous symptoms are reported in the diary (and I have pointed to a few of these already). Some of the symptoms are explicitly psychological in nature, others are physical but may be psychosomatic in origin, that is, Tolstoy may be 'somatizing' some of his underlying anxiety and depression. Here I translate some selected diary entries:

> Agoraphobia: 'I left [a factory just visited] at once and became afraid that on the way my stomach would start to hurt, and that I was all alone on the deserted road' (28 March); 'I went to an art exhibition but I got scared of the large number of people and returned' (12 April).

> Depression: 'Dejection [*unylost'*]' (10 April); 'an indefinable gloom' (30 May); 'There is constantly this internal *toska* and dissatisfaction and a desire to escape' (1 June); 'I am very oppressed by life'

(11 June); 'In the evening I felt a *toska* in the pit of my stomach [*pochuvstvoval tosku pod lozhechkoi*] and at night I did not sleep' (28 June); 'I am terribly weak and despondent' (20 July).

Thoughts of death: 'I feel that I don't have long to live' (25 May); 'I feel like dying' (10 June); 'I am ready to die' (29 June).

Sleeplessness: 'I couldn't sleep until five. Insomnia' (27 March); 'Last night I slept hardly at all, and then only very badly' (24 May); 'Went to bed late, slept *badly, badly*' (19 Aug).

Weakness: 'My nerves are a little weak' (9 April); 'I feel weak' (3 May); 'Very weak' (10 June); 'A great physical and spiritual weakness' (25 July).

Abdominal pains: 'My belly started to hurt' (15 March); 'My stomach is upset' (15 April); 'It was hurting in the pit of my stomach' (23 April); 'My belly is hurting' (28 May); 'Very weak and constant heartburn' (18 June); 'I'm very gloomy because of my liver [*mrachen ot pecheni*]' (31 May).[716]

This is just a small sampling of the symptoms reported in the diary. They also turn up occasionally in letters to friends and relatives, for example: 'Sometimes I feel very much like dying' (9 February to daughter Masha); 'an irritable condition which brings on, if not a gloomy, then a depressed state of mind' (1 June to Pavel Biriukov).[717] Overall there is both anxiety and depression as Tolstoy works away on *The Kreutzer Sonata*. These psychological phenomena are difficult to separate from the physiological problems. The various aches and pains appear so frequently in the diary of this period that it is difficult to believe they are all organic in origin.[718] Indeed, the way Tolstoy describes some of them makes it difficult to know whether he is describing a mental state or a physiological symptom (or both). Is it possible to feel 'gloomy from the liver' (cf. English 'liverish')? Can one experience *toska* in the pit of the stomach? Apparently Tolstoy could.

On 25 October he writes: 'Got up very late, my belly hurts, I am struggling against bile. Almost got into a fight with Sonia about arithmetic.'[719] Here the fact that Tolstoy's tummy hurts would suggest that the bile (*zhelch'*) is meant literally, but the next sentence about anger at Sonia suggests it is meant figuratively. In fact, both the literal and figurative meanings are suggested.

An analogous overlap of the physical and the mental may be observed in other categories, too. For example, when Tolstoy says he is

feeling 'weak' it is not always clear whether he means this in a physical or in some psychological sense. The entry from 25 July clearly suggests both senses ('A great physical and spiritual weakness'). There is
especially frequent mention of 'weakness' in early 1890, when Tolstoy is working hard on the afterword, for example: 'I want to write,
but I am weak' (3 February); 'I slept badly. Weakness. I am doing
nothing' (6 February).[720]

As for the references to sleeplessness, they either mean that
Tolstoy literally, physically, cannot sleep, or they suggest that Tolstoy is not sleeping because he is doing something in bed which is
morally reprehensible to him, that is, masturbating, and subsequently feeling guilty. Certainly the expression 'sleep badly' (*durno
spat*') is not meant literally when Tolstoy says, as he often does,
'I wanted to sleep badly' (*Khotel durno spat*').[721] It does not take a
psychoanalyst to see that Tolstoy is referring to masturbation, as
may be seen from the work of some literary scholars and biographers
who have come to the same conclusion.[722] Tolstoy's predecessor
in this kind of honesty was of course Jean-Jacques Rousseau.[723]

Toward the end of 1889 Tolstoy is reading about the differences between matter and spirit in a book entitled *The Divine Law of Cure*, by
W. F. Evans (1884). In late November he writes entries in two different
notebooks which are relevant to the phenomenon of his psychosomatic
symptoms:

> Spirit governs matter: matter is the consequence of the activity of the
> spirit, but only manifesting itself in matter does it [spirit] submit to
> its laws – space and time. An example: the fact that I am ill has an
> influence on my spirit, but *the fact that I am ill is a product of my spirit.*

> . . .the unconscious functions of the organism are directed none-
> theless by the spirit, by unconscious thought. And then about the
> meaning of the imagination and of thought in influencing func-
> tions. This is not as superficial as I thought. I tried to stop my heart-
> burn, having decided that it did not and should not exist. And now
> it's twelve o'clock, and it's gone.[724]

Whether or not Tolstoy actually got rid of his heartburn by a sheer act
of the will is debatable, but certainly he demonstrates here an implicit
openness to the idea that some of his physical symptoms might have
a psychological cause. He grants, in principle, that some of his bodily
functions are determined by *un*conscious thought (*bessoznatel'noi*

mysl'iu). At the same time, however, he believes he can get a conscious handle on these functions, control them, and thereby improve himself. He then feels better about himself not because the pain is gone (he was a masochist after all), but because in controlling a part of himself he was improving himself.

2. THE SELF-IMPROVEMENT KICK: GOD AS IDEAL SELF

Stopping the heartburn was just another manifestation of Tolstoy's narcissistic preoccupation with himself, with self-improvement. Throughout the 1889 diaries Tolstoy repeatedly expresses a desire to improve himself. This is nothing new, of course. Self-improvement is a theme that runs through all of Tolstoy's diaries, from their beginning in 1847 to the end in 1910. Tolstoy also held a perfectionist attitude toward everything he wrote, revising manuscripts many times over, sometimes revising works even after they had been published (see especially N. K. Gudzii's book *How Tolstoy Worked*).[725] As Richard Gustafson says: 'From his earliest days Tolstoy believed the purpose of life was the continual quest for perfection.'[726]

What this quest implies is that, from his earliest days, Tolstoy actually felt imperfect. This may seem terribly obvious, but it is also important. Like all human beings, Tolstoy *was* imperfect. What is psychologically important, however, is that Tolstoy *felt* imperfect, and chronically so. Ordinary people are not preoccupied with their imperfections. But Tolstoy was, and this preoccupation drove him in his quest for perfection (*samosovershenstvovanie*), or what Kohutian psychoanalyst Arnold Rothstein calls 'the narcissistic pursuit of perfection'.[727] To express this in the earlier, more 'Freudian' terminology of Russian psychoanalyst Nikolai Osipov, Tolstoy tended (narcissistically) to love not his 'real ego' but his 'ideal-ego', or; his narcissism was contaminated with 'ambivalence', he tended to hate himself as much as he loved himself.[728]

For a few days in the spring of 1889 Tolstoy becomes preoccupied with the idea of spiritual self-improvement. Curiously, this concern is represented in terms of maternal surrogation: 'Life is given to us, as a child is given to a nanny, in order to rear it [*chtoby vozrastit' ego*].' The important thing is always to be improving oneself, not necessarily hiding one's negative features the way a 'bad nanny' tries to hide the dirtiness or improper behaviour of her charge (29 May). The next day Tolstoy complains in his diary about relatives who are always preparing for life, but not really living: 'They busy themselves with food, sleep, studying, resting, continuing the species, upbringing. But one thing is missing – life, the growth of one's life. Yes, our business is like the job of a nanny, to rear what is entrusted to us, our life.' By 1 June Tolstoy is complaining about his 'internal *toska*', 'frivolity of speech', and other internal imperfections, but he again emphasizes the possibility of improvement: 'This evening I spoke about the single meaning of life, about the growth, not the growth but the growing of one's charge [*ne o roste, a o roshchenii svoego vospitannika*]. To prepare for life, but not to live is the same as when a nanny becomes occupied with herself and not her charge.'[729] This imagery of nanny and child is utilized in a similar way in some of Tolstoy's correspondence in mid-1889 as well.[730]

To translate Tolstoy's self-improvement kick into more contemporary terms, we might say that he is faced with the task of baby-sitting his own life. When he does make progress in perfecting himself his baby-sitter is functioning as she should, but when he does not she is being neglectful.

Tolstoy is rightly aware that others might look on his concern for self-improvement as overly narcissistic: 'People shouldn't utter that old commonplace that improving one's life is selfishness [*rastit' svoiu zhizn' – egoizm*]. To improve one's life is to serve God. Love *your* Lord God with all your heart, all your soul, and with all your thinking; love your neighbor as yourself' (emphasis Tolstoy's). In other words, one has to find one's own personal God, and such a God can only be located within oneself, indeed, *is* oneself: 'I must find and pick out within myself that which is worthy of love – God' (30 May).[731] Certainly this is close to the '*egoizm*' Tolstoy initially denies it is.[732]

To love God is to love oneself. If this startlingly grandiose notion is not clear in May, it was clear on 2 March of the same year:

The goal of my life, and of everyone's life, is the improvement of life [*uluchshenie zhizni*]. There is only one means for this: improvement of oneself. (I can't figure this out – later). But this is very important. That's the way it is, I thought about it while going for a walk, and I came to a conclusion that satisfied me, that one really has to be perfect, like the Father. One has to be like the Father. One should not only not shy away from such pride [*robet' ot takoi gordosti*], but one should shy away from any thought of forgetting it. I am not an instrument but an organ of the Divinity. I am the same as the Father, as Jesus said, but I am his organ, cell, and entire body.

The relationship is similar. It is impertinent to equate yourself with the Father only when you consider yourself and him as personalities. But when it is clear that there exists only my relationship to him, then I cannot but consider myself identical with him. I and the Father are one [*Ia i Otets odno*]. And when you grasp this – I am the same as the Father [*ia to zhe, chto Otets*] – what spiritual strength is gained.[733]

What spiritual strength indeed – some would say arrogance. Tolstoy is appropriating *for himself* the very words Christ spoke in the Gospel according to John (10:30): 'I and the Father are one.' Similarly, in a letter to Chertkov later that year, he says: 'I am one with Him [*ia s Nim odno*].'[734] As G. W. Spence says of Tolstoy's religious writings generally: ' . . . it is hard to see what Tolstoy's distinction is between the self and God, or between the son of God and the Father'.[735]

Here Tolstoy does not want merely to 'approach' God by improving himself (as he had, for example, in a letter to Chertkov in the fall of 1888: 'I am beginning to feel joy in the very act of working on my sins and on approaching the Father [*priblizheniem k Ottsu*]')[736] Nor does Tolstoy here want merely to 'imitate' Christ, as is done in all the Christian traditions of asceticism. Rather, Tolstoy is operating more in the Russian sectarian and theological tradition of *equating* oneself with God, of becoming a 'God-human' (*Bogochelovek*). Tolstoy wants to *be* Christ and to *be* God the Father, and thereby *be* God.[737]

True, at the same time Tolstoy wants to abase himself before his God. The willingness to accept punishment from God, to abnegate himself before God is part of Tolstoy's 'tendency . . . to think of God as Master'.[738] Whether Tolstoy was literally bowing down to the ground before God during his brief Orthodox spurt,[739] or repeatedly telling himself in the later diaries that one had to choose between *serving* God or *serving* Mammon – he maintained a consistently masochistic stance before his God. On the other hand, if we juxtapose this stance with the equally strong tendency of Tolstoy to equate himself with God, we may say of Tolstoy's ideal service, with G. W. Spence, that 'God is obeying Himself.'[740]

Two semantic operations eventually save Tolstoy from the apparent megalomania of his perception of himself as God. First, the perception applies (ought ideally to apply) to everyone else too. All human beings find God within themselves, as in the 1893 title *The Kingdom of God is Within Us*. Tolstoy is just one of the countless other God-Humans among 'us' in the world. Second, the self who is being perceived as God is not merely the lower 'personality' or the 'animal I' (for example, the 'I' of Pozdnyshev when he is physically attracted to his wife), but a higher, more abstract, and (tautologously) 'divine' self. Tolstoy's theology is much more complicated than this dualism would indicate, however, and has been extensively studied by scholars.[741] Yet a detailed psychoanalytic study of Tolstoy's religious views remains to be done.[742]

Tolstoy is quite aware of how narcissistic is his search for God in himself, that is, he knows that all his attention in this search is toward himself. On 12 September he writes not only that everyone should be concerned with searching for the kingdom of God which is within one's own soul, but that being concerned with the external world is rather pointless: 'It would be better if I could move the muscles of other people and animals as I see fit, but I cannot, and for that reason all my attention is on myself. This is very, very important.'[743] Indeed this *is* important. Psychoanalytically speaking, Tolstoy is telling us that his narcissistic preoccupation derives from the inherent failure of omnipotence of thought. Everyone knows that you cannot control the muscles of other people and animals, but it takes a Tolstoy to come away from this fact narcissistically preoccupied, offended even.

The narcissistic supplies offered by grandiose thinking ('I and the Father are one') must have been very comforting to a psyche as fragile as Tolstoy's. They never lasted very long, however, for Tolstoy kept reverting to self-doubt and self-flagellation for his imperfections. A low opinion of himself was the norm, while feelings of grandiosity were merely a temporary reaction against this norm.

3. LOW SELF-ESTEEM AND THE NEED FOR ATTENTION

Every narcissist is plagued with low self-esteem. From early childhood Tolstoy felt that he was physically unattractive, for example, and sought ways to compensate for this defect: 'I was comforted by the fact that I could think – I will be ugly, but I will be smart.'[744] His contemporaries did in fact often take note of his unattractive face.[745] As a young man Tolstoy often spoke to others or wrote in his diary about his awkwardness, unattractive appearance, and general unworthiness.[746] Just before his marriage Tolstoy became particularly conscious of his unattractive appearance and felt unworthy of his bride's love. In a diary entry on his birthday, 28 August 1862, he wrote about himself: 'You ugly mug [*skvernaia rozha*], don't think about marriage . . . '. To his future wife he wrote a few days later that he was 'an old, unusually unattractive devil'. On the very morning of the wedding he barged in on Sonia and expressed his doubts that she loved him (this episode is captured in Levin's famous last-minute visit to Kitti in *Anna Karenina*).[747] Right after the wedding Tolstoy got angry at his new wife because she was crying over having to leave her family. Sonia reports: 'He hinted to me that I must not love him much if it's so hard for me to part from my family.'[748]

Some days after the wedding on 23 September Tolstoy expresses 'doubts about her love' in his diary, and Sonia writes in her own diary on 8 October that her husband has told her that he 'does not believe' her love. Even several months after the wedding both spouses are still writing in their respective diaries that Lev does not believe Sonia loves him. On 8 January 1863 Tolstoy declares (with emphasis) in his diary: '*She will stop loving me [menia razliubit]*. I am almost certain of this.'[749]

Tolstoy was wrong, of course, and Sonia was driven to despair over her husband's obstinate refusal to believe her: 'How sorry I am for him at those moments when he doesn't believe me, and there are tears in his eyes, and his look is so meek and sad. I could smother him with love at those moments, but the thought haunts me: *he doesn't believe, he doesn't believe.*'[750] The problem was that Tolstoy did not believe that Sonia loved him because he felt essentially unlovable (although this feeling was no doubt aggravated by his wife's initial anorgasmia).[751] Even in relation to a woman who obviously loved him and was devoted to him his self-esteem was so shaky that he could not believe that she could love him.

Connected with the problem of low self-esteem was Tolstoy's constant need to have people's attention. As a child he was always doing things deliberately to amaze others, such as: jumping out of a second-storey window and knocking himself unconscious; getting out of a carriage and running ahead of it as fast as he could; diving into a pond fully clothed; and so on.[752] In *Reminiscences* Tolstoy states his admiration for people like his mother and his brothers Dmitrii and Nikolai, who were supposedly completely 'indifferent' to the opinions of others about them. Tolstoy himself, on the other hand, confesses in old age: 'I have always, even most recently, been unable to escape being concerned about what people think.'[753] With considerable insight, Tolstoy states in non-psychoanalytic terms his everlasting narcissistic problem: 'I have always remembered myself, been aware of myself, have always sensed – mistakenly or not – what people think of me and how others feel toward me, and this has spoiled the joys of life for me.'[754] To Maksim Gorky and Anton Chekhov he declared that he had rarely ever been happy for the simple reason that he had always felt obliged to live 'for show, for people' (*napokaz, dlia liudei*).[755]

Tolstoy's narcissistic problem may have 'spoiled' his happiness, but it brought joy into the lives of many of his readers. Precisely because he was continually preoccupied with what people were thinking of him (whether good or bad), Tolstoy's powers of observation became very highly developed. It is no accident that his cousin ('granny') Alexandra called him thin-skinned and observant in the same breath.[756] By observing himself, Tolstoy became a character for himself, or he made a character of himself. As a consequence, he was in a better position to create literary characters. It is difficult to imagine how Tolstoy could have become so skilled at character-portrayal in his fiction without his narcissistically-derived powers of observation. This is true not only for such obviously autobiographical characters as the self-conscious young narrator of the early fragment *The History of Yesterday*, or the self-absorbed Nekhliudov of the late novel *Resurrection*, or the narcissistic characters Pierre and Prince Andrei of *War and Peace*–but also for characters who are less obviously Tolstoy himself, such as Anna, or Natasha, or Karataev. Here I have to agree with Tolstoy's biographer A. N. Wilson, who says: 'Tolstoy was profoundly self-obsessed, and it is this self-obsession which made him a writer.'[757]

A particularly good example of Tolstoy's concern with what people thought of him occurred in connection with *The Kreutzer Sonata*. In late December of 1889 the work was read before a gathering at Yasnaya Polyana by Tolstoy's friend, Mikhail Stakhovich. A. M. Novikov, a teacher of Tolstoy's children, tells what happened next:

After the story and the newly written afterword had been read, silence fell.

'Well, how about it?' asked Tolstoy.

There was general silence, then one by one the guests took their leave of the head of the household, and went downstairs.

Everybody gathered in the library, the doors were closed, and there followed a discussion of the story. It had produced a stunning effect on the listeners. The general opinion was that it was weak, its idea too contrived and pretentious, the development of the plot artificial, and so on. In the middle of the conversation I went out the door, and right there I banged into Tolstoy, who was eavesdropping.[758]

Clearly, as Novikov remarks, Tolstoy desperately wanted to know what people thought of a work that he had put so much of himself into. A diary entry a few days later includes the remark: 'Stakhovich understands nothing.'[759] At this point Tolstoy is still denying that people honestly do not agree with him and with his Pozdnyshev (a couple of weeks later he gets past denial).

In *The Kreutzer Sonata* itself Tolstoy's narcissism is of course most visible in Pozdnyshev's attitudes and behaviour. There are, for example, the outbursts of jealousy. To be jealous is to be overly concerned that some particular person's evaluation of you is low. Ontogenetically, as I observed earlier, to be jealous is to act in a certain way in response to an old, underlying narcissistic injury. Each successive 'scene' thrown by Pozdnyshev brings him closer to the psychological source of his hurt, his low opinion of himself, and his rage.

Apart from the jealousy, Pozdnyshev is worried in general about the impression he makes on people. Toward the beginning he takes great pleasure in the fact that he 'surprises everybody' with his pronouncements about the virtual impossibility of love.[760] The impression he makes on his wife is also important to him. She should focus her attention on him in a certain way, he thinks. When he gets angry at her he becomes very self-conscious:

> I leapt to my feet and moved toward her; I remember that at the very moment I got up I became aware of my animosity and asked myself whether it was a good thing for me to abandon myself to this feeling, and then told myself that it was a good thing, *that it would give her a fright*; then immediately, instead of fighting off my animosity, I began to fan it up in myself even further, rejoicing in its steadily increasing blaze within me.
>
> 'Go, or I'll kill you!' I shouted suddenly, going up to her and seizing her by the arm, *consciously exaggerating the level of animosity in my voice. I must really have appeared terrifying* . . . .[761]

Just before he kills his wife/mother-icon there is a curious passage where Pozdnyshev is even afraid of *looking bad* in her eyes:

> . . . I reflected that it would be ridiculous [*smeshno*] to run after one's wife's lover in one's stockinged feet; I didn't want to look ridiculous, I wanted to look terrifying. In spite of the terrible fury that gripped me, I was constantly aware of the impression I was

making on others, and this consideration even guided my actions to
a certain extent.[762]

Here Pozdnyshev is 'at once actor and audience', as Isenberg says.[763]
The sudden concern with how he looks to his wife, in the midst of an
attack of destructive rage, is yet another indicator of the source of that
rage: a low regard for himself resulting from prior narcissistic injury.
Pozdnyshev would not have become enraged at his wife if he had not
initially felt himself injured. Furthermore, Pozdnyshev has just
struck his wife *in the eye*, as if to punish her for seeing how foolish he
(believes he) *looks*.

In some of the drafts Pozdnyshev is also quite concerned with what
his wife thinks of him even before he marries her, and this makes him
appear more vulnerable than he is in the early parts of the final version. For example: 'I still had not found the ideal of perfection of a
woman worthy to be mine, the more so because I was proud like all
depraved people, and therefore was figuring to get a wife somewhere
where there would be no possibility of a refusal.' In other words, he
was bending over backwards to avoid any narcissistic injury (or any
further narcissistic injury? – the immediately preceding sentence
is: 'My mother was [still] alive'). When Pozdnyshev does find the girl
he is looking for, the question of her worth or value again comes up:
'Yes, I suddenly decided that she was worthy of being mine – not me
worthy of being hers, but her worthy of being mine.'[764]

This is a very interesting distinction. Now that he is an older man
Pozdnyshev sees the faults he had in his youth (especially his promis-
cuity) and realizes that *he* might not have been worthy of the girl of his
choice. He even harps on his faults in retrospect (here he is being
Tolstoy again). But he does not seem to notice how *vulnerable* he had
once been to the judgement of the woman with whom he planned to
spend the rest of his life. Paradoxically, he was insensitive to how sensitive he was.

In another variant Pozdnyshev focuses on a man's continuing unworthiness before a woman even after he has married her:

She is higher than a man both as a girl and after becoming a woman.
She continues to be higher because, as soon as a woman begins to
give birth, there is genuine activity, while a man has none. A
woman, in giving birth and in nursing, is firmly convinced that she
is carrying out God's will, while a man, regardless of whether he
chairs the German Reichstag, or builds a bridge across the

Mississippi, or commands an army of millions, or discovers new bacteria or phonographs [*sic*], cannot have this confidence.[765]

To this list of supposedly questionable male accomplishments we might add: regardless of whether the man writes famous novels like *War and Peace* and *Anna Karenina*. But then Pozdnyshev (in this variant) backs off from his idealization of motherhood, saying that a mother's activities are really neither high nor low, but indifferent. Their value depends only on what purpose a mother has in doing them. This retreat is clearly defensive, for Pozdnyshev's (Tolstoy's) conflicted evaluation of motherhood, as we saw earlier, is really the engine that moves the plot of *The Kreutzer Sonata*.

4. UNCLEAR BOUNDARIES OF THE SELF

For a time Tolstoy cannot decide which question to pose: is Pozdnyshev good enough for his future wife, or is she good enough for him? But this very wavering suggests a question: where does Pozdnyshev leave off and the future wife begin? There is a boundary problem here.

Above, I discussed the joyful experience Pozdnyshev had as he listened to the Beethoven sonata being played by his wife and Trukhachevsky. Part of this experience was the sense that his wife was feeling the same emotions as he, that the boundary between him and his wife – or between him and the composer – was erased. Tolstoy too, as we saw, would sometimes experience an indescribable sense of merger when he listened to music. He also sometimes felt this way about God (for example, his fondness for the biblical 'I and the Father are one'). I argued that this feeling of oneness or merging is archaic, going back to very early, pre-Oedipal experience. Psychoanalysts speak of 'primary identification' or 'symbiosis' or 'merger' with the mother. The child's task is to achieve 'separation-individuation' (Mahler) from the maternal object, but this takes place fitfully, and not without difficulties. For some time, or from time to time, the mother is not distinct from the self, but is experienced as a part of the self. Gradually the mother becomes a 'selfobject' (Kohut) with which the child is still sometimes delusively and narcissistically merged. The identity of the self in this evolving process changes, is unclear and indefinite.[766]

The sense of no boundary between self and other can be pleasant, even ecstatic. It can also facilitate literary creativity, helping Tolstoy temporarily to 'be' the characters he creates, or capture the natural world he depicts. But it can also be horrible. Pozdnyshev resents the possibility that his nameless wife might do with her body as she pleases, for he feels he has 'a complete and inalienable right to her body, *as if it were my own'.*[767] In the first draft the fusion of self and other is more vivid and even more infantile. Pozdnyshev is talking somewhat incoherently about the impossibility of a married couple separating (*razoitis'*), once they have come together (*soitis'*). His language is extremely loose and colloquial, but the message is clear:

> Well, here begin all those questions about how to separate voluntarily and freely. How can you separate freely when they – pointing to the steward – needed this here arm of yours, so, it's that simple. Why be shy, let him take my arm and be off. He will have three arms, I will have one. And I'll just quietly give it away. So this is how it all started, something you seem to think is so easy to settle.[768]

A wife, in other words, is a part of one's own body, like an arm. To voluntarily separate from one's wife is as ridiculous as to freely part from one's own arm. But for a mature individual who has gone through an uneventful separation-individuation from the mother in childhood, this trope will itself seem faintly ridiculous (and Tolstoy did well to remove it in the final version).

If a wife is imaged as part of one's own body, then it should not be surprising that some confusion arises when Pozdnyshev gets angry. Is he angry at himself or at his wife? Does he want to kill himself or kill her? At one point he declares: 'I suddenly got a feeling that at any moment now a terrible quarrel was going to start, the one that would make me either want to kill myself or kill her.'[769] After he has stabbed his wife he considers killing himself.[770] In the third draft there is a passage where the boundary between self and other is questioned in the very syntax of Pozdnyshev's thinking:

> I am sure that she was thinking: wouldn't it be good if he died. And I, so very often in moments of bitterness, recognized in terror that I desired this with all my heart [*soznaval, chto ia vsei dushoi zhelaiu etogo*].[771]

What did he desire – his own or her death? The passage is about as ambiguous in the original as in the translation that I have attempted here.

Here I should note that the question of who to kill is different from the question of why to kill. I have already dealt with the latter (Pozdnyshev's/Tolstoy's rage at an absent, sexually active mother). The former, on the other hand, is a structural question, another manifestation of the problematical self. If Pozdnyshev has trouble deciding who to kill, the boundary between what is self and what is other is defective.[772]

There is a curious passage in *Anna Karenina* describing how Levin feels during one of his first quarrels with his wife Kitti:

> Then it was that he first clearly understood what he did not realize when leading her out of church after the wedding: that she was not only very close to him but that he could not now tell where she ended and he began. He understood this by a tormenting sense of cleavage which he experienced at that moment. For an instant he was offended, but immediately knew he could not be offended with her because she was himself [*ona byla on sam*]. For a moment he felt like a man who, receiving a blow from behind, angrily and revengefully turns round to find his assailant and realizes that he has accidentally knocked himself, that there is no one to be angry with and that he must endure and try to still the pain.[773]

Pozdnyshev's problem precisely – but the outcome, as is well known, is much more favourable: Levin continues to love Kitti in his eccentric way, rather than killing her. Meantime, Tolstoy 'kills' Anna Karenina.

In *War and Peace* it is Pierre Bezukhov who repeatedly experiences a sense of no boundary between himself and another. With Natasha, for example: ' . . . as he looked into her eyes Pierre felt that he was disappearing and that neither he nor she existed any more, but that there was just the one feeling of happiness'.[774] And again in the meantime, Tolstoy 'kills' Hélène Bezukhova.[775]

Pozdnyshev's, Levin's, and Pierre's boundary problems with their wives reflect Tolstoy's boundary problems with *his* wife. From the very beginning of the relationship with Sonia the self–other distinction was interrogated. Thus, madly in love with her shortly before their marriage, he twice writes – on 12 and 13 September 1862 – that he is so worked up that he might 'shoot himself' (*zastrelius'*). Then, when she does accept his proposal of marriage on 16 September, he writes: 'She said yes. She is like a bird that has been shot and wounded [*ptitsa podstrelennaia*].'[776] Instead of 'shooting' himself he has 'shot' her. The element of hostility toward Sonia, even as he loves her, is also evident here.[777]

In conversation with G. A. Rusanov in August of 1883 Tolstoy characterized the difficulty he was having in renouncing his property as follows: '"Two will be united in one flesh"– my wife and I are one [*ia i zhena moia eto odno*]. She is one half of *me*, she is the same as I am, what is mine is also hers, and I cannot give away all of my property as long as she does not want this, and she does not want it.'[778] The same biblical imagery comes up in conversation with A. V. Zhirkevich nine years later, in September of 1892, where Tolstoy describes marriage generally:

> It is a great and terrible thing, marriage. And it is true when they say that here 'two beings are united in one flesh'. If subsequently a husband or wife turns out to be unsuited for the marital union, nonetheless the bond, once established, cannot be broken. It's just as if one half of a person's body were paralyzed. The person is weighed down by it, it is superfluous, it causes sufferings. But tear it away he cannot, and he is forced to endure it until death.[779]

The masochistic component is unmistakable here: one must 'endure', the 'sufferings' are obligatory (divorce is out of the question). The psychological issues of merging and masochism often do occur together in the clinical literature, as I have shown elsewhere.[780]

When the Tolstoys' beloved son Vanichka died in 1895 Sonia went through an especially intense and prolonged mourning. The sympathetic reaction on Tolstoy's part is described in a letter he wrote to his son Ilya: 'Now, when she is suffering, I have felt with my whole being, more than ever before, the truth of the words that husband and wife are not separate beings, but are one . . . '.[781]

In a letter to Sonia of November 1896 Tolstoy tries to express how close he still is to her:

> . . . our differences of opinion are only external, and I am ever certain that they will be annihilated. What ties us is the past, the children, our awareness of our faults, our pity, and irresistible attraction. In a word, [we are] solidly tied and laced up together [*zaviazano i zashnurovano plotno*]. And I'm glad of it.

Later in the letter he writes:

> I want very, very much to be with you as soon as possible and, in all
> modesty, not so much for myself as for you, but since you are I [*ty –
> ia*], then for myself as well.[782]

Here Sonia is functioning pretty clearly as a Kohutian selfobject for
Tolstoy.

Tolstoy also *projects* onto others the idea that husband and wife are
inseparable. For example, shortly after his son Ilya married Sophia
Filosova in 1888, he wrote to the young couple with his usual intru-
siveness:

> You are living through an important period. Everything is import-
> ant now, every step is important, remember this: your life and [the
> life] of your mutual relations is taking shape, it is a new organism of
> *homme–femme*, of one being, and the relationships of this complex
> being to the whole rest of the world are also taking shape – to Marya
> Afanasievna [a nanny living with the Tolstoys], to Kostiushka [a
> Yasnaya Polyana peasant], and so on, and to the inanimate world,
> and to your food and clothing, and so on, everything is new.[783]

If Tolstoy feels he is 'one flesh' with his wife, so should other married
couples. Only here the rhetoric is slightly different, it is the *homme–
femme* metaphor borrowed from conservative writer Alexandre
Dumas *fils*, who believed that a wife is so much the property of the
husband that the husband has a right to kill her if she is unfaithful.[784]

Incidentally, Ilya and Sophia did not survive as *homme–femme*.
They eventually went their separate ways, after having children. Ilya
remarried and lived out his unhappy life in the United States.[785]

Tolstoy's tendency to cancel the boundary between himself and
others (or between other people and their others) carried over into his
relationship (or his characters' relationships) with the wider natural
world. For example, Jacqueline de Proyart has demonstrated that
Tolstoy is inclined to match the 'internal landscape' of his positive
characters with the surrounding 'external landscape'.[786] One thinks
of Anna Karenina's famous train ride in a snowstorm, where the
'storm' in her psyche matches what is going on outside. Sometimes
the matching involves a clearly maternal figure in the external environment. For example, de Proyart views Nikolai Irten'ev's tendency

to commune with nature as a compensation for the maternal loss he suffered.[787] At times the sensation of merging with 'mother nature' is intense. On magical, moonlit summer nights Irten'ev would be contemplating every stirring of nature around him, when suddenly a sad, beautiful and large-breasted woman (s . . . *vysokoi grud'iu*) would appear, and would seem to offer him her voluptuous embrace. But, however attractive this woman was, nature herself was superior, and in the end the hero would fuse with her: 'it seemed to me in these moments that nature, the moon, and I were all one and the same'.[788]

There is a particularly graphic image of fusion with nature in the 1878 memoir 'My Life':

Nature [*Priroda*], up until the age of five, did not exist for me. Everything that I can remember took place in my bed in the top room. Neither grass nor leaves nor the sky nor the sun existed for me. It is impossible that I was not given flowers or leaves to play with, that I did not see some grass, that they did not shade me from the sun. But up until the age of five or six there is not a single memory of what we call nature [*prirodoi*]. Probably one has to go away from it in order to see it, but I was nature [i*a byl priroda*].[789]

To *be* nature is to admit of no boundary with her, with the mother that is. In Russian, as in English, nature is a maternal phenomenon: *priroda-mat'* corresponds exactly to our 'mother nature' (cf. also *ditia prirody*, 'child of nature', and *na lone prirody*, 'in the bosom of nature').[790] The Russian word 'priroda' itself contains the root morpheme -*rod*-, meaning basically 'birth'. In addition to the repeated *priroda*, moreover, the cognate words 'novorozhdennyi' ('newborn') and 'zarodysh' ('embryo') each occur repeatedly in the immediately preceding paragraph. The -*rod*- root thus occurs so frequently in a short interval that it is difficult to escape the impression that Tolstoy is preoccupied with his mother, the one who, after all, gave birth to, *rodila* him.[791]

For Tolstoy to harp on the absence of 'priroda' from his early memories is, it seems to me, to emphasize the absence of his mother, his birther. He cannot consciously remember his mother, so he claims, yet he keeps signifying her covertly through the use of the word for mother nature and through other -rod- words. But then he culminates his little tirade by asserting that he *was priroda*. That is, he *identifies with* his birther, his absent mother. He *was* his mother. We have here, I think, a trace of 'identification with the lost object' which occurs in some kinds of mourning.[792]

Other traces of identification with or incorporation of the lost object may be detected in some characteristics of Tolstoy which were
also characteristics of his mother: the pedagogical interests, the
storytelling ability, the playing of the piano, the interest in collecting
moral maxims, and perhaps some others. I think there is room here
for further psychoanalytic study. In some ways Tolstoy became the
mother with whom he was angry for dying on him. In Freud's famous
formulation: ' . . . the shadow of the object fell upon the ego'.[793]

5. FINISHING OFF THE NOVELLA: INTERACTING SELF-
DISTURBANCES

As we saw earlier, Tolstoy was experiencing a variety of psychiatric
symptoms as he composed *The Kreutzer Sonata* during the spring and
summer of 1889. The symptoms let up somewhat after he finished the
seventh draft of the work on his birthday, 28 August 1889 (with a few
slight changes added on the 29th).[794]

When Tolstoy gives his first public reading of the work to friends
and relatives gathered at Yasnaya Polyana on 31 August the reaction
is narcissistically gratifying: 'This evening I read *The Kreutzer Sonata*
to everyone. It got everyone worked up. This is very necessary.'
Next day, having again read the work aloud to his friend N. N. Ge and
his son Lev, Tolstoy writes: 'On everyone, and most of all on me, it has
made a big impression. All of this is very important and necessary. I
have upset myself. I got very excited, went to bed at two.'[795] The narcissistic jolt is evident here, especially in the phrase 'most of all on *me*'.
Tolstoy's work has literally made a big impression on Tolstoy. Narcissus is captivated by what he sees reflected in the water, and he becomes slightly manic (that is, hypomanic).

The change in attitude is remarkable. Tolstoy is suddenly healthy
and full of energy. On 2 September he is 'like a wild man all day, and
therefore insufficiently attentive to God . . . '.[796] But then, a few days
later he falls ill, apparently with a real intestinal infection (*sil'neishii
grip*). Yet he continues to be in good spirits, and comments: 'an awareness of life and the return of talent has become mine. And I constantly
remember this.' In the same entry he declares that his major concern
in life is the development of his soul (*moe delo – moia dusha*).[797] The 'talent' will continue to bring him attention and fame from without,
while the development of his soul will be an inner growth. There is
no real contradiction here, for both processes involve narcissism,

attention toward the self. The spurt of positive feelings about his literary talent shows that it is possible to be narcissistically preoccupied without *also* being masochistic. With the completion of the seventh draft Tolstoy is at least temporarily released from the grip of moral masochism, and is just an ordinary grandiose narcissist for a while. He wants people to pay attention to his story, telling Chertkov in a letter of 9 September that he intends to bring it out with the newspaper *Nedelia*, where it would not have to be subjected to censorship. He writes to Chertkov: 'I know that people need what is written there.'[798]

The good feelings about himself do not last, however. On 16 September he takes a look at the seventh draft again, and is very disappointed with it (*Ochen' ne ponravilos'*). Apparently he doesn't like the way he has handled the 'action' toward the end of the story. He may have been stung by his daughter Tania's remark that Pozdnyshev's wife didn't really have anything to 'confess'.[799] By that evening he is despondent (*unylo*), and over the next few days, as he renews work on his novella, he grows seriously depressed. The whole process appears to be a temporary manic-depressive downswing. If on 15 September he had written a large, bright paragraph affirming that 'the business of life, its purpose, is joy [*radost'*]', by 20 September he is saying that 'I am despondent, there is no joy [*ne raduius'*]'.[800] Thoughts of death come to the fore. He again takes to writing 'If I'm alive' (*Esli budu zhiv*) after the next day's date in his diary. This was something he was doing sporadically before the recitations of 31 August and 1 September. Such a practice is of course highly narcissistic, for even if Lev Tolstoy were*not* alive the next day, the date would still be the same!

Most interesting is the new idea on 21 September of deleting the murder scene altogether: 'I have conclusively decided to rework [it], the murder is unnecessary.'[801] As the editors of the Jubilee Edition observe, however, there is no variant or draft of *The Kreutzer Sonata* without the murder scene.[802] Tolstoy's notion to eliminate the murder must have been short-lived. Certainly it is difficult to imagine this story without its violent climax. Pozdnyshev piques the reader's interest right from the beginning by admitting he is a murderer, and he maintains that interest by advocating a weird philosophy of the 'murderous' nature of human sexuality (below, I will make a guess as to why Tolstoy temporarily changed his mind).

By 23 September the murder plan has been restored, and it remains in from then on. Meantime, as Tolstoy continues work on the eighth draft, he is back to the business of saving his soul, and he castigates himself for having been briefly happy after his public recitation of the seventh draft: 'Yes, I feel like dying, I am guilty. I was feeling down primarily because I seemed to have forgotten my purpose in life: to save and to watch over my soul.'[803] Two days later he says that the poisonous attacks on him, which are like bees attacking one's eyes, are of 'considerable use', for they help him live in a Godly fashion. That is, they offer an avenue for him to act on his masochistic inclinations. And as for the long letter he writes to Chertkov on the 26th, it is full of exhortations to moral masochism, as we have already seen.

In subsequent weeks Tolstoy works less on the novella than he did during the summer. His mood generally improves, except when he does work on it. For example, on 10 October he writes: 'I was looking over and correcting everything from the beginning. I am experiencing disgust with this whole work. Much depression [*upadok dukha bol'shoi*]'. On 16 October: 'I wrote a lot, correcting *Kreutzer Sonata*. I haven't experienced such a dispirited condition [*takogo podavlennogo sostoianiia*] in a long time.'[804] On 31 October: 'yesterday I received a long letter from Chertkov. He quite validly criticizes *The Kreutzer Sonata*, I would like to follow his advice, but I have no desire to. Apathy, sadness, despondency. But I don't feel bad. Ahead is death, that is, life, so how can I not be joyful?'[805] Such joy does seems a bit contrived, however.

In early November Tolstoy receives news that a public reading of (the eighth draft of) his novella in Saint Petersburg has produced a very strong impression. This brings real joy (*Khorosho i mne radostno; raduius'*).[806] But now he is not thrown off balance the way he was when he himself gave the first readings to family and friends back in late August and early September. Masochism efficiently intervenes, he calmly contradicts himself: 'I received news that *Kreutzer Sonata* is having an effect, and I am joyful. This is not good [*sic*].'[807] As long as Tolstoy can honestly think that renewed fame is 'not good', his grandiosity is kept in check. Meantime the eighth draft, copied down and distributed in lithographed and hectographed editions, was becoming widely known in Russia.

Toward late November Tolstoy's psychological balance is again disturbed – so disturbed that for two days he fails to make any diary entries and has to reconstruct events of those days in the third day's entry.

The problem begins on 28 November when he experiences one of those slightly manic (hypomanic) moods of diffuse love for every-

one. Life is love, he says, and there ought to be some way of expressing love for fellow human beings: ' . . . remember one thing – there
standing before you is a living human being, so while you are alive
you are in a position to do something that will do him and you good
[*blago*] and will fulfill the will of God, of the one who sent you into the
world; you are in a position to bind yourself to this person by means
of love.'

Next day, however, a narcissistic 'devil' assails Tolstoy, and love for
his fellow-humans goes out of the window: ' . . . the devil fell upon
me, fell upon me primarily in the form of a self-loving fervor
[*samoliubivogo zadora*], a desire that everybody right here and now
share my opinions . . . '. Tolstoy is referring to arguments he is having
with A. M. Novikov, his children's teacher at the time. He is also upset
that he is masturbating again – that is, indulging in another form of
self-love: 'Next day on the morning of the 30th I slept badly. It was so
loathsome, like after a crime.' The following day it happens again:
'Today an even more wicked attack of the devil.'

Further upsetting Tolstoy is an encounter he has with one of his
peasants who wants to chop down more acacia trees in the garden of
his estate. 'What is it to me?', thinks Tolstoy, but then 'the devil' gets to
him, he gets irritated that the peasants seem to be ruining the garden,
spoiling the view: 'I don't understand how I gave myself over to such
a wicked power. It must be because of that same sin [*tem grekhom*, that
is, masturbation]. Physical things – bile, constipation – are an insufficient explanation.' Tolstoy is ashamed of himself, he can no longer
conjure up the feeling of love for people that he had a few days earlier.
But he is satisfied that he can at least suppress the 'dirty' attacks
of hatred.

The next thing to upset him is a visit on the same day to a dying
peasant girl. Her name is Domashka. He had already visited her and
brought her some kefir on 14 November, and had felt shamed and
humiliated by the experience. Yet go he must again:

> I can and must do something, do what I would wish people to do
> for me; I would wish that they not leave me to die like a dog, alone
> with my sorrow at departing from the world, and that they particip-
> ate in my sorrow, explain to me that they know about my situation.
> That's what I have to do. And I went to her. She is sitting there,
> swollen, pitiful, and simply – speaks. Her mother is weaving, her
> father is busy with a little girl, dressing her. I sat for a long time, not
> knowing how to begin, finally I asked whether she was afraid of

death, whether she wanted it. She simply said yes. Her mother, laughing, started saying that the twelve-year-old girl, her sister, says that she is arranging a special candle for when Domashka dies. Why? Her fancy clothes, she says, will be left to me. But I say that I will load you down with work, you will have to work for her. – I'll work for you as much as you like, she says, as long as the clothes are left to me. I started saying that it will be nice for you there, that you don't have to be afraid of death, that God won't do anything bad to us either in life or in death. I spoke badly, coldly, but I couldn't lie or work up any pathos. Her mother is sitting there, weaving, and the father is listening. But I myself know that just now I was angry because the view onto the garden (which I do not consider my own) has been spoiled for me. God of love, help me to be perfect, as you are. Help me or take me away, destroy me, re-make me into something not so unclean, wicked, lying, greedy for everything that is bad, greedy for lust and for praise, a befouled creature – help me or destroy me completely.[808]

These self-lacerations are followed by descriptions of several more unpleasant incidents, including a fight with Sonia over whether a French translation of *The Kreutzer Sonata* should be permitted (Tolstoy curses himself for getting angry with her, even though he honestly disagrees with her). Tolstoy's unhappy day ends with a reminder to himself not to forget that his life is a mission (*poslanie*), and that, otherwise, 'there is no life, only hell'.

Certainly the three days described in the diary have been 'hell' for Tolstoy, as he says. But now he is going to take a little pleasure in grandiosity. The next day's short entry clarifies the nature of his 'mission' which is to save him from a life of 'hell':

I have to remember that, not only am I an envoy [*poslannik*] who is entrusted with something, but also in the sense that I am an envoy who must observe and elevate, improve myself. They are both one and the same thing: to elevate myself is possible only by carrying out His affairs, and elevating and improving myself is to carry out His affairs.[809]

This is again arrogance, of course, but it is not gratuitous arrogance. It is a desperate measure taken to counter the repeated narcissistic injuries which have befallen Tolstoy on the previous few days. By thinking of himself as God's envoy on earth, almost as Jesus Christ,

Tolstoy temporarily puts himself out of reach of the mundane unpleasantness of arguing with Novikov or the peasant, the shameful practice of masturbation, the unpleasant fight with his wife, or the truly disturbing and self-punishing experience of trying to comfort a dying peasant girl who reminded him of his own mortality. In a sense, all of these incidents are equivalent because in each one Tolstoy feels pain over his lack of perfection, that is, he perceives there is something wrong with *himself*. Self-esteem would not have to be repeatedly boosted with manic, grandiose flights if it were not chronically low to begin with.

Objectively there may be nothing wrong at all with what Tolstoy is condemning in himself, or at least different readers would make differing evaluations (for example, a Christian and an atheist might hold different views on whether masturbation is morally wrong). The point is that, in each case which Tolstoy takes the trouble to write up in his diary, he is expressing disapproval of the way he behaves. *He* is at fault, *he* is imperfect. Narcissus does not like the defective self he sees reflected in the water, so he resorts to two basic methods of soothing the pain:

1) Castigating himself repeatedly for his (real or imagined) faults (masochism).
2) Magnifying himself by being God's 'envoy' (grandiosity).

The first method is paradoxical: how can castigating oneself decrease mental pain? It is itself painful. The answer must be: guilt over one's imperfections is washed away (temporarily). The diaries are an ongoing act of contrition, a vociferous *Mea culpa, mea culpa, mea maxima culpa* before God and before himself. The breast-beating seems endless: 'I am weak and disgusting' (9 April); 'I am bad' (15 May); 'I am very bad' (5 June); 'I have sunk to a very low level' (*ochen' opustilsia* – 16 August); 'I feel like dying, I am sinful' (24 October); and so on.[810] In a letter of 13 November to Biriukov he speaks of a 'whole pile' (*kuchu tseluiu*) of sins that he carries around within himself, and declares that 'I cannot be at peace and be happy when I am fighting against sins.'[811] This sinfulness may never end for Tolstoy, but the recognition of it is similarly endless, acting as an ongoing cleanser, as a 'redeeming sacrifice' (*iskupitel' naia zhertva*), as he says in a letter to Chertkov of 26 September.[812]

The badness can never be permanently washed away by the breast-beating because Tolstoy continues to behave, as he thinks, 'badly', that is, narcissistically, to love himself in ways he himself disapprove of: he masturbates, he wants others to hold *his* views, he gets angry when Sonia attacks *his* moral system, and so on. These perfectly natural expressions of self-interest (somewhat exaggerated in Tolstoy because he is so narcissistically fragile to begin with), are declared 'evil' by the hypermoral Tolstoy. As a result, internal conflict is endless, contrition is continually needed.

But, in a masochistic way, this is good. If there are always faults, then there is always room for improvement. And since the process is repetitious, there is at least an appearance of growth or improvement (*uluchshenie zhizni, roshchenie*). The improvement must not be measured internally, however, but in terms of growing closeness to, that is, similarity to God. In a long letter of 26 September to Chertkov, Tolstoy warns against taking comfort in progress already made beyond lower moral levels of the past. One should be oriented not toward the past, but toward the infinitely perfect God who can only be approached, never attained.[813] One's imperfection is an unalterable fact of life (*zakon vsiakoi zhizni*) by virtue of God's unsurpassable perfection. One's imperfection is even a good thing (*blago*), because without it there could be no movement toward God, no life even: 'if it weren't for [a person's] sinfulness, and if he could immediately become that which he wanted to be by means of his understanding, then things would be worse for him – there would be no reason to live, there would be no life at all'; ' . . . without sin you cannot live . . . '.[814]

In effect, do not look for happiness in the accomplishments of your life, even if these accomplishments are spiritual. Indeed, do not even bother with happiness, and always dwell on your current imperfection, your sins. Only this guarantees movement toward perfection, toward God. Always think badly of yourself. Keep your self-esteem down and be a masochist forever. *This* will make you a saint:[815]

> I have often imagined the hero of a story I'd like to write: an educated person, say, in revolutionary circles, at first a revolutionary, then a narodnik, a socialist, an Orthodox, a monk at Mount Athos, then an atheist, a family man, then a Dukhobor. Whatever he starts, he quits without finishing. People laugh at him. He accomplishes nothing and dies in obscurity, in some hospital somewhere. And, dying, he thinks that he has destroyed his life for no reason. But this one – he is a saint.

The hero Tolstoy imagines here does not find happiness, never does arrive at perfection, and never ceases to consider himself a failure.

His very disgust with himself, however, is the penance which re-
deems him in Tolstoy's eyes (the closest Tolstoy ever came to writing
a story of this sort is *Father Sergius*).

As is well known, Tolstoy preached that 'the kingdom of God is
within us'. For Tolstoy this meant: 'the kingdom of God is within me,
and please do as I do' (provide mirroring). It is probably safe to say
that most people find Tolstoy's philosophy of eternal dissatisfaction
unacceptable not only because it was so obviously derived from his
personal self-dissatisfaction, but also because it requests acts of
moral masochism from us, his readers. Tolstoy may have made a virtue, even a transmissible *Weltanschauung* of his problem. But in the
end his problem was not nearly as transmissible, not as 'infectious' in
his moral preachings as it was in his art. The idealistic Pierre Bezukhov
or the self-destructive Anna Karenina provide great pleasure to
readers. Even the self-castigating murderer Pozdnyshev has a certain
appeal, especially if we are not thinking of him as Tolstoy's double.
But Tolstoy the man, insofar as he asks us to flagellate ourselves just
as he flagellates himself, drives us away. It is pleasure most of us seek,
or at most a close call with pain – not pain itself.

By early December Tolstoy returns to intensive rewriting of (the
ninth and last draft of) *The Kreutzer Sonata* for a few days. He says he
is terribly sick of it (*strashno nadoela mne*), and this will of course be understandable to any serious writer, who knows the experience of
multiple rewritings. Tolstoy says he wants to improve the work's artistic quality. He even says he is in a state of 'inspiration' as he writes.
But then, when he receives word on 9 December that the tsarist censor
will not permit publication of the work, he declares: 'This is only
pleasant [*Tol'ko priiatno*].'[816]

Normally a writer would be upset to receive such information.
However by now (an earlier version of) the work was known from
public readings and from the hundreds of copies in circulation, so it
was not as if the censorship could erase the fame which *The Kreutzer
Sonata* had already brought Tolstoy. On the contrary, for the authorities to think the work so important that it now had to be forbidden
was to pay its author a high compliment. The phrase 'This is only
pleasant' thus has more than one meaning. It was 'pleasant' to be
granted the masochistic wish to be punished, but Tolstoy was being
punished for producing a work of high artistic quality and controversial content, so the punishment was also adulation. Both masochism
and grandiose narcissism are thus expressed by Tolstoy in one short,
efficient phrase.

7

The Relationship with Sonia: a Feminist Note

Sofia Andreevna Tolstaia *née* Bers (1844–1919) was the most important woman in Lev Tolstoy's adult life. Sonia, as he called her, was Lev's major selfobject and his primary maternal icon. But because of his problematical attitude toward his mother, there was by definition a problem in his attitude toward Sonia as well. This is what made the relationship with Sonia so difficult. Sonia herself was close to normal, at least in her younger days. Subsequent problems, in particular her 'hysteria', were reactive. They developed as a result of the peculiar attitudes and expectations her husband brought to the marriage, and which intensified during the course of the marriage.

For most of the duration of their marriage Lev and Sonia had an access to each other's thoughts which went beyond the bounds of ordinary marital conversation, for the two regularly read each other's diaries. This was more than the quaint and harmless practice followed by some among the Russian upper classes. Rather, it became, as Francine du Plessix Gray puts it, a 'morbid habit'.[817] Tolstoy's diaries, in the tradition of Rousseau's *Confessions*, were brutally honest about sexual matters and full of the pain of shame and guilt which an ordinary Russian landowner would hardly have been capable of expressing. Sonia, in response, searched the depths of her own soul, which was neither as deep nor as disturbed as her husband's. The result, as Gray insightfully observes: 'Over the years, this transgression of marital civility – this invasion of the other's innermost thoughts – grew into a pact of mutual punishment and wounding, a sadomasochistic *folie à deux*.'[818]

Sonia had been the object of Tolstoy's sexual desire over the quarter century of their marriage which preceded work on *The Kreutzer Sonata*. If the numerous children seem inadequate evidence of his sexual attraction to his wife, then various diary entries for the year 1889 testify to Tolstoy's ongoing sexual interaction with Sonia, even as he was penning his literary repudiation of sex. On 6 August he notes: 'I ... thought: what if another child is born? How ashamed I will be, especially

189

before the children. They will figure out when it took place, and they will read what I write. And I felt shame and sadness. And I thought: one should be afraid not before people, but before God.' On 19 August he declares that a lecher, like a drunkard, falls at the first weakening of attention, and adds: 'I am a lecher [*bludnik*].'[819]

Sonia likewise perceived the contrast between what Lev was now advocating and what he was doing. When their older children's tutor Vasilii Ivanovich Alekseev visited her in 1890, she remarked: 'It's fine for Lev Nikolaevich to write and advise others to be abstinent, yet he himself . . .', whereupon she nodded in the direction of her little child Vania.[820] In December of 1890 Sonia wrote: 'It would be terrible to get pregnant, everybody would find out this shame and would gleefully repeat the joke now going around in Moscow society: *Voilà le véritable* 'Afterword' *de la Sonate de Kreutzer.*'[821] This last quotation is censored from the 1978 Soviet edition of Sonia's diaries, and consequently is missing from the English edition translated by Cathy Porter as well.[822]

Tolstoy was ready to admit to others (not only write in his diary) that he failed to practise what he preached. Late in 1890, not long after the afterword of the novella was finished, he spoke of his sexuality to Dr E. J. Dillon, saying: 'Yes, I am a sinful man. I know and bewail it. All I can say by way of excuse is that I came into the world with an ardent temperament which I cannot master. It is a case of the spirit being willing and the flesh weak.'[823]

How could Tolstoy's ongoing experience of sporadic sexual intercourse with his wife not have anything to do with his repudiation of marital sexuality in *The Kreutzer Sonata*? How could his characterization of wives in that work as 'long-term prostitutes' not reflect his attitude toward his own wife? Louise Smoluchowski is certainly right to say that the novella was 'insulting' to Sonia, and Martine de Courcel quite correctly perceives the work as 'a moral stab to the heart'. As V. A. Zhdanov observes, the new attitude toward sexuality which Tolstoy developed during the period of writing the novella 'deeply offended' Sonia.[824] Tolstoy was not only rejecting his own sexuality in the work – a purely private matter had he not been married or not living with his wife. Nor was he merely offering a new philosophy of sexuality to the world. He was denigrating the sexual needs of his wife as well.[825] Psychoanalytically speaking, his new puritanical morality had a sadistic component aimed at his wife[826] – this sadism quite apart from any sadism he might have felt, he was indulging in simply by having sex with her.

Of course Tolstoy had been periodically hostile to Sonia's sexuality (and to sexuality in general) ever since he married her. Indeed, from adolescence onward Tolstoy's attitude toward sexuality was ambivalent at best. This may be easily ascertained from the fact that he cried on the occasion of losing his virginity, that he called sexual union 'something terrible and blasphemous' in 1870, that Sonia sometimes reported his being 'cold' toward her in the diaries, and so on. So the thematic content of the novella was nothing new to Sonia. What was new was that, in *The Kreutzer Sonata*, Lev was going public with his peculiar views on sex. Everyone could now judge for themselves the way in which the great Tolstoy was treating his wife. For Sonia, this was adding public insult to private injury. Tolstoy's novella was, among other things, a public sadistic attack on his wife.

Sonia should have left her husband, but as it turns out, she could be as masochistic as he was (even if she could not accept his particular kind of masochism). Sonia even went so far as to obtain a personal audience with the Tsar in order to gain permission for publication of *The Kreutzer Sonata* in the thirteenth volume of an edition of her husband's collected works that she was bringing out.[827] At the time, however, the novella was already widely known in Russia, despite the official ban on it. The damage to Sonia had already been done. Apparently she also believed that her efforts would encourage her husband to continue writing fiction and wrote less time on social and moral tracts. Finally, there was the additional income the thirteenth volume would bring her.

At times Sonia pretended to be unfazed by the tendentious content of the work, but deep down she was mortified. In a diary entry of 12 February 1891 she admits: 'I . . . know in my heart that this story is directed against me, and that it has done me a great wrong, humiliated me in the eyes of the world and destroyed the last vestiges of love between us.'[828] By the following year she was so angry about the novella that she wrote her own retaliatory story, entitled *Who Is to Blame?* In it a chaste, idealistic girl named Anna marries an aging womanizer by the name of Prince Prozorskii. The prince pretends to be interested in Anna's artistic abilities, but only wants her body, deflowering her in a particularly cold and inconsiderate manner. The story ends tragically years later, with Prozorskii killing his wife in a fit of jealousy. The parallels with *The Kreutzer Sonata* are clear, and Prozorskii looks even more evil than Pozdnyshev. Prozorskii's resemblance to Tolstoy is also obvious. For example, he is a writer, and the female narrator makes fun of his belief that he is writing profound moral-philosophical treatises, when in fact he is only skilfully combining hackneyed ideas from other thinkers. Occasionally Sonia would read aloud to visitors this 'report from the conjugal battlefield', as Peter Møller calls it. But she never published it, nor has anyone seen fit to publish it in the more than three-quarters of a century since her death.[829]

Tolstoy's view of the 'conjugal battlefield' is described in painful detail in the 1889 diaries, while he is writing his novella. There is constant friction with his wife:

> 2 March. 'It is difficult with the wife.'
> 3 March. 'Yes, the reign of women is a misfortune. No one but women (like her [Sonia] with her daughters) can make stupidities and vile things clean, even nice, and be completely satisfied.'
> 26 May. 'Sonia is upset. I am withstanding it better.'
> 2 June. 'Again I was oppressed by what seems to me to be Sonia's horribly senseless talk. . . '.
> 15 July. 'Sonia . . . attacked me, tormenting my exhausted heart. It was very painful.'
> 5 August. 'Sonia is in a bad mood.'
> 13 September. 'With difficulty I fought the devil, putting down his temptation to make me angry at Sonia, who is in a mood of hostile suffering.'
> 28 September. 'Sonia is aggrieved that I am hiding my diary from her. . . '.[830]

Once in a rare while Lev will write that Sonia is 'in good spirits' (29 July). But most of the time she is an unhappy woman (although not only because of her husband). Naturally, this distresses him, and sometimes he actually expresses pity for her, for example, on 30 October: 'Vanichka is ailing. I feel very sorry for Sonia.' Very often, however, Lev cannot bring himself to sympathize with Sonia, as on 24 November: 'At dinner Sonia got irritated – again I was not able to feel sorry for her and wish her the best.'[831]

According to his diary, Lev rarely becomes overtly angry at Sonia during the writing of *The Kreutzer Sonata* (or when he does, he apologizes afterwards, for example, 23 June). But anger is often evident below the surface, and he is always having to quash this 'devil':

> 2 June (after listening to Sonia's 'horribly senseless talk'). 'I thank God I do not commit the sin of malicious anger.'

6 October. 'Sonia is in a bad mood. I behaved in such a way as to destroy the vexation in my soul.'

25 October. 'I almost got into a fight with Sonia about arithmetic.'[832]

One tactic for avoiding anger at Sonia is just to think about her loving her children (as long as she doesn't love them *too* much, that is, as long as she loves them in a self-sacrificing, non-sensuous way). In such a situation it becomes possible for Lev even to love his wife: 'I remembered Sonia's concern for Leva, for all of the children, an external concern, but still one which she alone is capable of understanding, and I started to feel love for her' (3 June).[833]

In similar fashion Pozdnyshev too can minimize hostile feelings when his wife is busy looking after her children, especially when she is breast-feeding them (although he cannot really love her). Obviously Pozdnyshev does not get as far as Tolstoy does in quelling anger, for he eventually kills his wife and only then begins to think of the possibility of his own guilt.

In a variant Pozdnyshev even realizes the projective nature of his suspicion of his wife's infidelity: 'I was guilty in my animalistic and inhuman relationship with my wife. I felt this guilt of mine in the depths of my soul, but in order not to recognize my guilt, I needed her guilt.'[834] Having accomplished this projection (but not knowing that it was projection, that is, unconscious of it), Pozdnyshev felt free to unleash great anger at his wife.

Tolstoy worked hard at avoiding just this kind of projection with Sonia. One tactic was to remember his own sins, to feel his own guilt. Tolstoy explains this rather clever psychological manoeuvre in a letter to Chertkov on 26 September:

> In order to stop being angry at a person, in order to make peace, to forgive – if there is something to forgive – even to feel sorry for or to start loving the person, what should one do? The best thing is to recall your own sin against this person, the same as his. This is a special kind of happiness, followed by an instant healing.[835]

If in 'Notes of a Madman' Tolstoy showed how masochism could be used to palliate depression, here he gives a theoretical account of how masochism (in this case searching for an excuse to feel guilty) can be pressed into the service of neutralizing anger. 'If you do this sincerely', he continues to Chertkov, 'if you seriously and vividly recall your own vileness, you will forgive, you will make peace and, God willing, you will feel sorry and start to love'. In order to accomplish this, however, you must not have forgiven yourself for your previous sins: 'Do not forgive yourself, then you will forgive others.'[836]

It is difficult to imagine a worse kind of psychotherapy (one of the aims of most forms of psychotherapy in the West today is self-for-giveness). In any case, as a concrete example of this Tolstoyan approach to the neutralization of anger, we may consider an incident from 2 September: 'In the evening during a most innocent conversation Sonia suddenly lost her temper. I was very sorry for her and I am glad that I see only my guilt. We went to bed late.'[837] Here Lev is quick to see *only* his own 'guilt' – so quick, indeed, that his anger is not even mentioned (while Sonia's is). His anger must, by his own theory, have been neutralized. Sonia, meantime, looks rather bad, for her anger is still there.

The more Lev tries to counteract angry feelings toward Sonia, the more obvious it should be that he *is* hostile. Similarly, it is difficult for him to hide his anger at Pozdnyshev's wife. For example, on 24 July he is trying to counteract the 'negative, malicious' elements in *The Kreutzer Sonata*: 'I worked on Kr. Son. Finished a rough draft. Now I understand that it's necessary to reorganize everything, introducing love and sympathy for her.'[838] The 'her' is unspecified here, and seems to refer to Pozdnyshev's wife, but could it be Sonia as well? He wrote, after all, that he worked on 'Kr. *Son*'. An unconscious pun, perhaps: the cross, the 'Kreuz' of *Son*ia, which he bore all his life.

Another way Lev deals with his feelings about Sonia is to try to block her out completely. Here the narcissism becomes especially evident. Lev has a great need to be *alone with himself* during the writing of his novella, to be out of Sonia's reach and control. He even starts hiding his diary from Sonia (years later this issue would escalate). He also masturbates a lot, which is to say that he needs to keep his sexuality disentangled from Sonia's own considerable sexual needs.[839] On 30 August he writes:

> We were walking home, it was a wonderful moonlit night. I thought little – it's impossible when with others. I much prefer to be alone. But I am not alone when Sonia is with me. We went to bed late, I wanted to sleep badly.[840]

In other words, Lev wants to masturbate but can not do so in Sonia's presence. It is not really 'sex' that he wants here (that he presumably could have had with her). It is himself he wants, it is his separate, independent, narcissistic sexuality he wants to celebrate (and then punish himself for with guilt, of course; masturbation was another handy outlet for masochistic needs).

During the writing of *The Kreutzer Sonata* Sonia is a threat to Lev's narcissistic core. Paradoxically, however, she is a threat because she *is* so close. Lev is forever deflecting his attention inward, toward himself, because he cannot help but respond to Sonia's existence outside of himself. He often feels sorry for her, or is angry with her, as we have seen. After one of their fights Lev writes of Sonia's anger with him: 'She is suffering and she hurts me, like a tooth. . . '.[841] Her suffering is practically contagious, he is so close to her. At first glance this looks like a healthy empathy, but it is not. The focus is on his suffering, not hers. Lev's attention usually veers defensively back toward himself in such cases, he asks himself (or God – roughly the same thing) why *he* is guilty, how *he* can be of assistance, rather than trying to understand first what *she* is feeling. Often his inappropriate blametaking insulates him from any real awareness of what she is feeling. On 24 September, for example, Lev again gratuitously changes the subject to his own 'sinfulness':

> At dinner Sonia was talking about how, when looking at an approaching train, she felt like throwing herself under it. And she became very pitiful to me. The main thing, I know, is that I am at fault. It suffices just to remember my disgusting lust [*pokhot'*] after Sasha [was born]. Yes, one must remember one's sins.[842]

Just as Pozdnyshev feels (after the fact) that he 'murders' his wife with his sexuality, Tolstoy feels that it is his sinful sexuality that makes his wife suicidal. After this, the diary entry launches into a long rigmarole about sin, forgiveness, and repentance (it is the usual quasi-theological drivel). Meantime, what has become of poor Sonia? *She* expressed a suicidal thought, almost a threat, and this ought to have been cause for serious concern. But instead Lev is talking about the topic of *his* sexual desire and guilt over that desire. This is simply not a response to *Sonia*, however sorry he may feel for her initially (and in any case the pity was probably only the usual anger-cancelling kind). Lev needs first to lambaste himself for his 'sins', and this masochistic need comes before Sonia's evident depression.

On 4 July a similar but more complicated and interesting displacement occurs:

This morning and yesterday evening I thought long and clearly about *The Kreutzer Sonata*. Sonia is copying it out, it is disturbing her, and last night she spoke of the young woman's disillusionment, of the sensuality of men, so alien at first, and of their lack of sympathy for children. She is unjust, because she wants to justify herself, while in order to understand and tell the truth, one must repent. The whole drama of the tale, which has never once gone out of my mind during all this time, is now clear in my mind. He has cultivated her sensuality. The doctors have forbidden her to give birth. She is fed to satiety, dressed in chic clothes, and there are all the temptations of art. How could she fail to fall? He must feel that he himself has led her to this, that he really murdered her when he conceived his hatred for her, that he sought out a pretext for murdering her and was glad of it. Yes, yesterday the muzhiks confirmed that *klikushestvo* occurs only in married women, never unmarried girls. So it must be that the phenomenon is caused by sexual excess.[843]

Again Lev is not responding to Sonia's concerns, even if one of those concerns is *his* sexuality (which had indeed initially been 'alien' to her – a reference to her early anorgasmia). Lev shows no sign of dealing with Sonia's obvious misery at having to copy a work that demeans her. She is supposed to 'repent' of her own sexual desires (as he repeatedly does). But she does not 'repent', she does not provide the requested mirroring, and so he goes back off on his narcissistic way. Meantime, Sonia's frustration and anguish continue to be ignored.

Both Sonia and Lev see the similarity of their marital situation to what is depicted in the novella, and both blame Pozdnyshev/Tolstoy. But whereas Sonia is blaming someone else in this process (her husband), Tolstoy is blaming both someone else (his wife) and himself. Also, he is mistaken in blaming sexuality, when he should be looking into the peculiar way he feels about sexuality. But he is incapable of thinking deeply about his aberrant attitude toward sexuality, for then he would have to confront the unacceptable psychological reality of his abandoning, sexually active mother. Tolstoy is much more complicated than his wife, more defended and more disturbed.

The blindness to Sonia's needs is particularly evident in the *non sequitur* at the end of the above quotation. For hysterical *klikushestvo* to occur only in married women (*tol'ko u bab* – the same phrase occurs in *The Kreutzer Sonata*) is hardly evidence of 'sexual excess'. Indeed, it could be evidence of just the opposite – insufficient sexual stimulation, or inappropriate sexual interaction which provides no sexual stimulation for the woman. For example, alcoholism was common among the peasantry in the late nineteenth century. Many husbands took it into their heads to have sexual intercourse precisely when they were too drunk to accomplish the sexual act.[844] Or, *klikushestvo* could have resulted from sexual incompatibility, especially in view of the prevalence of arranged marriages among the peasantry. An entry in the standard Brockhaus-Efron encyclopedia, published just five years after Tolstoy's novella was completed, states: '*Klikushestvo* is most frequently elicited by unhappy love [*neschastnoi liubov'iu*], forced marriage, and generally by woman's sad fate.'[845] In a recent article Julie Vail Brown zeroes in on very early marriage as the cause of the phenomenon in question, citing several Russian psychiatrists who gave a central place to 'early marriage and premature introduction to sexual life'.[846] It is indeed easy to imagine that a woman prematurely introduced to sexual intercourse (essentially child abuse) would experience lingering sexual frustration. Dr N. V. Krainskii tells of two cases where onset of *klikushestvo* could be traced to marriage to a sexually inept husband.[847]

Tolstoy is right at least to relate hysteria to sexuality. Here he demonstrates a vague awareness of views commonly held among Western Europeans and educated Russians in the late nineteenth century. He is even right to attribute the problem to the way *men* behave in sexual interaction with women, as when he writes to Chertkov: 'The husband . . . hates her [the wife] for her irritability, her hysteria which he himself has caused and continues to cause.'[848]

The trouble is, Tolstoy gets things backwards, thinking that the sexual stimulation itself causes hysteria, when instead it is either lack of sexual stimulation, or inadequate or inappropriate sexual stimulation by the man which is the problem. Despite Tolstoy's reference in his novella to the well-known Paris neurologist Jean-Martin Charcot,[849] he missed the then widespread idea that 'hysteria derived from frustrated sexual desires' – to quote an authoritative history of psychiatry.[850] And the reason he missed this idea is that it would have forced him to confront the idea that women – for example, his wife, his daughters, his mother, peasant women – have sexual interests of their own, not just the ones 'taught' them by their husbands on their wedding nights. Certainly there are passages in Lev's diary where Sonia expresses her own sexual needs, for example, on 21 July: 'After dinner Sonia was explaining that she has been faithful and that she is lonely.' This cry for sex and affection is greeted with 'one has to be quiet, humble [krotkim], and attentive. I was unable to say anything else. And I am sorry'[851] – but not sorry enough to take the necessary steps.

It has been said, and with good reason, that Sonia developed symptoms of hysteria as her relations with her husband worsened. Cynthia Asquith refers to Sonia's 'nervous instability, in ailing old age to become hysteria'.[852] Vladimir Zhdanov says that '... hysteria, something Sofia Andreevna had always been predisposed to, became rather pronounced starting precisely in this period [that is, the period when *The Kreutzer Sonata* was being written] ... '.[853] Shirer also speaks of the 'mounting hysteria' in Sonia after the completion of the novella.[854] Not only Tolstoy scholars, but people personally acquainted with Sofia Andreevna spoke of her 'hysterical' behaviour.[855]

As evidence, Zhdanov refers to Sonia's angry story *Who Is to Blame?*, and her agitated readings of this story to random acquaintances who would visit her at Yasnaya Polyana. Zhdanov also mentions one of Sonia's suicide threats, and brings up the emotional diary entry of 20 November 1890:

> I used to copy out everything he wrote, and loved doing so. Now he carefully conceals everything from me and gives it to his daughters instead. He is very systematically destroying me by driving me out of his life in this way, and it is unbearably painful. There are times in this useless life of mine when I am overwhelmed with violent despair. I want to kill myself, run away somewhere, fall in love with someone – anything not to have to live with this man whom for some reason I have always loved, despite everything, although I now see just how I have idealised him, how I have long refused to realise that there is nothing in him but sensuality. Now my eyes have been opened, and I see that my life is destroyed. I so envy people like those Nagornovs, for they are *together*, and have things in common besides the physical bond. And plenty of other people live like them. As for us – my God, he is always so unfriendly, so querulous and so artificial when he speaks to me! How can he treat me like this when I am so open and cheerful with him, so eager for his affection!
>
> I love the peace and leisure of the countryside and am happy to be living here – if only *someone* were slightly sympathetic to me! Days, weeks, months pass when we say not so much as a word to one another. I was so used to running up to him with whatever was on my mind – about the children, some book I was reading or some new

idea. But now he merely snubs me with a look of grim surprise, as if to say: 'So you are still hoping and come crawling up to me with your silly ideas!'

Can there be any spiritual intimacy left between us, or has it died? I think that if only I could go up to him as I used to, go through his papers, read his diaries and discuss it all with him, he would help me go on living; how splendid it would be if he would just speak plainly to me, and everything would be as it was before. But now, even though I am innocent, and have always loved him, and have never done him any harm, I am desperately afraid of him and feel like a criminal. I am afraid of his silent disapproval, sullen, severe, indifferent and unloving, which is far more painful than any words or blows. He is incapable of loving, *he never learnt to* when he was young.[856]

In this desperate cry for love and affection (not just sex) Sonia is perhaps a little too harsh on her husband, a little too emotional, and therefore 'hysterical' in the broad sense of the (Russian or English) word.[857] Certainly this outburst is due, in part, to Lev's intermittent sexual rejection of Sonia. More importantly, it is also due to his emotional rejection of her, or outright disregard of her needs. Sonia sensed that her husband was holding back emotionally – he *had* to be if he condemned his most intimate activity with her. In her autobiography Sonia says that she even came to fear the periods of his sexual passion because they tended to be followed by coldness. She wanted someone to love her 'not passionately, but affectionately' (*ne strastno, a laskovo*[858] – recall Pozdnyshev's deranged belief that these two cannot be combined).

Sonia should never have become so entangled in her husband's innermost thought processes in the first place. Indeed she should never have married a man whose idea of courtship was to shove a stack of sexually explicit diaries under the nose of a sheltered 18-year-old girl (this act is repeated by the characters Levin and Pozdnyshev with their respective future wives). But, after nearly thirty years of marriage to such a man (and his diaries), it would have been very difficult to just back off, so hysteria was inevitable when *he* backed off, and was further aggravated when he kept changing his mind about whether he was backing off or not (ambivalence).

In any case, Lev himself could not really handle Sonia's outbursts, because he was preoccupied with himself and with his hatred of sexuality at the time. At best he noticed the existence of Sonia's outbursts and (both in his novella and in his diary) attributed them to what was on *his* mind, so they ended up being caused by what *he* hated, that is, *his* 'sexual excess'. This, as I observed above, was exactly the reverse of received opinion. Had Tolstoy been able to comprehend the idea that hysteria was thought to be a result of *frustrated female* sexuality, he would have been forced to recognize what he was actually doing to Sonia with his on-again, off-again abstinence. He would have understood that his behaviour now was just as sadistic as it was when he forced her to read his diaries the first time. And this sadism was just as important as the masochism, the 'cross' he bore in remaining with his sexually attractive and increasingly difficult wife.

On one occasion during the writing of *The Kreutzer Sonata* Tolstoy seems to have come perilously close to recognizing the etiological truth of hysteria. In a diary entry for 20 September he reports having a conversation with his acquaintance the peasant writer Ivan Zhuravov (1862–1919), who had come to visit him in Yasnaya Polyana. Zhuravov had written a story about a *klikusha*. Tolstoy read the story and liked it, sending it off on the 21st to Chertkov for publication in *Posrednik*.[859] The night after reading the story Tolstoy describes having a nightmare on the subject: 'At night I had a nightmare: a crazy woman, raving mad, who is being held from behind.' Tolstoy seems to feel sorry for this madwoman, and then suddenly he declares: 'I have made a definitive decision to rework [the novella], the murder is unnecessary.'[860] As I pointed out above, this decision was only temporary, and the murder was reinstated. But why the sudden change of heart, and why specifically in the context of a dream about female insanity?

I would like to suggest that the woman's physical position in Tolstoy's dream offers an answer: she is being held from behind (*szadi*), that is, she is being held in a way that resembles the sexual position traditional among the Russian peasantry, *a tergo, more ferarum*.[861] For most women, this position is not sexually satisfying, for it does not normally stimulate orgasm and leaves a woman frustrated.[862] But sexual frustration was precisely the widespread explanation for hysteria at the time Tolstoy was writing *The Kreutzer Sonata*. In the dream he seems to recognize a probable cause of hysteria among the peasants, but in waking reality he is blind to it (instead hysteria is caused by 'sexual excess'). By remembering the dream while awake, however, Tolstoy is momentarily confronted with the truth, if only at a symbolic level. He is shaken by the experience of his 'nightmare', so shaken that he is moved to radically alter the plot of his story. There may have been a flicker of *appropriate* guilt (instead of guilt over sex). Why have a man murder a woman, after all, if the man's sexual behaviour is already capable of driving her crazy, making her hysterical? A man's sexual inconsiderateness is sufficiently sadistic by itself.

The insight was only temporary, however. It had no place in *The Kreutzer Sonata*, as it undermined the whole antisexual theory behind the work. More importantly, the insight, applied in Tolstoy's own case, would have led him to reconsider his irrational hatred of sexuality, and to question the narcissism of thinking that everyone else should hate it too. The insight would also have led Tolstoy to become conscious of how sadistically he was treating his wife, and consequently to experience massive guilt. But sadistic treatment of the wife did not accord at all with his supposedly Christian world view, while his (equally real) masochism (Sonia as his 'cross') did accord with Christian teaching. So the murder was reinstated. Certainly no one could accuse Tolstoy of *actually* murdering his wife (although the thought did occasionally enter his mind, as we saw earlier from the conversation with Rusanov). At worst, as he wrote to Chertkov, he made Sonia a bit hysterical by having sex with her.

It would be interesting to learn more about Sonia's attitude toward her husband, and to psychoanalyse her. A psychobiography of Sofia Tolstaia has yet to be written. What is truly astonishing, however, is the fact that only selected passages from the autobiography of Tolstoy's wife, entitled *My Life*, have ever been published.[863] Nor has her own 1892–93 novella, entitled *Who Is to Blame? A Woman's Story (On the Occasion of Lev Tolstoj's Kreutzer Sonata)* ever been published, although it has been paraphrased by Peter Møller in his excellent book on *The Kreutzer Sonata*.[864] A full and unexpurgated edition of Sofia Andreevna's diaries also needs to be published. When one considers the vast literature on Tolstoy that has in fact been published – including unreadable volumes by Soviet hack critics, and half-literate memoirs by peasants who had some marginal contact with Tolstoy – it is difficult to understand why much that was written by Tolstoy's own wife has been excluded from publication.

Recently feminist thinkers have paid some attention to the connection between hysteria and the sociocultural oppression of women. If Sonia's symptoms are thought of as 'hysteria' in a broad sense, then feminist thinking on this subject certainly applies to the Tolstoy marriage. In an influential volume on Freud's famous case of Dora, Claire Kahane says: '. . . contemporary feminists are reclaiming hysteria as the dis-ease of women in patriarchal culture'.[865] In Sonia's case, the relevant patriarchal culture is upper-class Russia at the end of the nineteenth century, and the specific patriarch in question is Lev Tolstoy. His intense ambivalence about heterosexual interaction (re-inforced by other factors such as the secretive relationship with Chertkov and the conflicts over property) made Sonia 'hysterical'. I see no other way to explain the relative mildness of Sonia's symptoms before she married Tolstoy, and again after he died. Sonia may have driven Tolstoy out of Yasnaya Polyana with her histrionics in those fateful last days of 1910, but he drove her crazy first. If her symptoms (or his symptoms) are even more embarrassingly evident in her unpublished works than in those writings the Russian archival custodians have deigned to publish, that does not diminish their value. More than a century after the creation of *The Kreutzer Sonata*, it is high time to publish everything that was written by the novella's chief victim.

Notes

1. One illegitimate child was Tolstoy's son Andrei's stableman, Timofei Ermilovich Bazykin (57:218; S. M. Tolstoi, 1994, 182). The child's mother was Aksin'ia Aleksandrovna Bazykina, wife of a peasant in one of Tolstoy's villages (Gusev, 1957, 301–2, 363; Ivanova, 1971, 46–53). Another (somewhat less solidly documented) illegitimate child was named Mariia (Matrena), daughter of another local peasant woman named Mariia Kraineva (Murygin, 1995).
2. Gor'kii, 1949–55, vol 14, 262. The obscenity is deleted in Gorky's text, but the context ('using a salty peasant word') makes it clear that the word is *ebyr'* (thanks to Yuri Druzhnikov for assistance here).
3. Rancour-Laferriere, 1993a, viii.
4. See Aldanov, 1969 (1923), with its insightful introduction by Thomas Winner, and Timkovskii, 1913 (p. 6).
5. Dillon, 1934, 269.
6. Berlin, 1979, 22–81.
7. Aldanov, 1969 (1923), 75–6.
8. Gustafson, 1986.
9. Benson, 1973.
10. 53:208.
11. For example: Gor'kii, 1949–55, vol. 14, 261–2, 291–2; Boborykin, 1978 (1909), vol. I, 272.
12. Grigorovich, 1978, 77. Cf. p. 525 of the same volume for corroboration of this incident by both Nekrasov and Turgenev.
13. Peterson, 1978 (1909), 122.
14. As translated from the memoir of Aleksandr Gol'denveizer (1959, 51) by Ruth Crego Benson (1973, 4).
15. I have slightly modified Ruth Crego Benson's translation (1973, 9) of an 1847 diary entry (46:32–3).
16. 50:42.
17. As translated from a diary entry of 1899 (53:231) by Ruth Crego Benson (1973, 13).
18. Gusev, 1973 (1911), 90; cf. Gol'denveizer, 1959, 78.
19. Gusev, 1973, 141.
20. As quoted from P. A. Sergeenko by Dmitrii Merezhkovskii, 1995 (1900), 27.
21. Diary entry for 24 Aug. 1898 (53:209).
22. As quoted by Andrei Gavriilovich Rusanov in Rusanov and Rusanov, 1972, 186.
23. Diary entry for 4 July 1890 (51:58).
24. Gor'kii, 1949–55, vol. 14, 265.
25. Rusanov and Rusanov, 1972, 190; Gol'denveizer, 1959, 386.
26. Cf. Benson, 1973, 107; Sémon, 1984, 470ff.; Armstrong, 1988, 136; Mandelker, 1993, 40.
27. Gor'kii, 1949–55, vol. 14, 263.
28. Møller, 1988; Engelstein, 1992; cf. also Gornaia, 1988.

29. For example: Berman, 1990; Rogers, 1991; Rancour-Laferriere, 1993a; Schapiro, 1994.
30. Rancour-Laferriere, 1996.
31. Cf. Meyers, 1988, 251.
32. For example, not included are works by the ardent Tolstoyan Isaak Borisovich Fainerman, who published much on Tolstoy under the name of I. Teneromo.
33. Elms, 1994, 22.
34. The transliteration of Tolstoy's title is correct as given. Tolstoy did not follow the convention of writing *sumasshedshii*, according to Boris Eikhenbaum's commentary in the Jubilee edition (26: 853).
35. A few final changes were added in proof in October, after Tolstoy returned from his journey.
36. See Gusev, 1957, 680–84 for the most reliable and detailed account. The distance calculation is mine.
37. Tolstaia, 1978a, vol. I, 495.
38. See Arbuzov, 1904, 44. The Arbuzov memoir has to be used with caution, as it is full of factual errors (for example, Arbuzov has the trip taking place in 1870 instead of 1869).
39. 83: 163–4; 168.
40. For example: 83:139–40, 142, 144. See also the memoir by Stepan Andreevich Bers, Tolstoy's brother-in-law, who says Tolstoy did not like being away from the family even for a short time(Bers, 1978 [1894], vol. 1, 179).
41. 83: 166–7.
42. Cf. Arbuzov, 1904, 46.
43. 83: 167–8.
44. Psychoanalyst Nikolai Osipov (Ossipow, 1923, 149) views the episode as a manifestation of 'strongly pronounced anxiety neurosis'. The notion of anxiety neurosis (Osipov utilizes Freud's term*Angstneurose*) is now somewhat antiquated. Moscow neurologist Aleksandr Vein, borrowing from American medical terminology, calls the episode a 'panic attack' (*panicheskuiu ataku*–Vein, 1995, 11). In modern diagnostic terms (but still speaking very broadly), the episode manifests some features of both an anxiety disorder (*DSM III*, 230 ff.; *DSM IV*, 393 ff.) and depression (*DSM III*, 210 ff.; *DSM IV*, 320 ff.). The anxiety seems predominant in this particular instance, however, for there is an energetic effort to escape from the source of anxious and depressive feelings. A severely depressed person – one whose primary problem is depression – would probably not have the energy to jump up and leave the way Tolstoy does here (I wish to thank Dr Kathryn Jaeger for pointing this out). On some of the technical difficulties of distinguishing anxiety from depression, see the volume edited by Kendall and Watson (1989, esp. 3–26).

 Psychiatrist A. M. Evlakhov refers to the quoted passage as an example of Tolstoy's 'impulsivity', for the departure from Arzamas was indeed sudden (1930, 63). But the anxiety and depression which precipitated it are not analysed, most likely because they do not fit too well with Evlakhov's overall diagnosis of Tolstoy as an epileptic.

45. I use the expression 'depressive anxiety' here (and later) as a convenient shorthand for referring to anxiety with associated depression, not necessarily as an affirmation of a Kleinian view of the origin of anxiety (cf: Bowlby, 1973, 384–7; Klein, 1977 [1935], 262–89). Cf. also the proposed new diagnostic category of 'mixed anxiety-depressive disorder' in *DSM IV*, 723–5.
46. Ozhegov, 1968, 792.
47. Tolstaia, 1978c, 47.
48. The word in this context has been translated variously as 'despair' (Parthé, 1885a; Wilson, 1988, 250; Christian, 1978, vol. I, 222), 'anxiety' (Gustafson, 1986, 192), 'misery' (Spence, 1967, 46), and 'melancholy' (Orwin, 1993, 164). For an excellent analysis of the multiple meanings of the word *toska* in a story by Chekhov, see: Siemens, 1994.
49. For example, 48:62. On Tolstoy's reaction to his brother Nikolai's death, see: McLean, 1989, 150 ff. The periodic depressive moods during the writing of *War and Peace* are especially clear from the memoir of Tat'iana Kuzminskaia (1986).
50. See the memoir of Tolstoy's eldest son Sergei L'vovich Tolstoi (1956, 20, 38) who characterizes the attacks as *boleznennyi pripadok* in each case. Cf. also Gusev, 1957, 683; Gor'kii, 1949–55, vol. 14, 280; Opul'skaia, 1979, 100.
51. Tolstoy sometimes reacts in this superstitious fashion when he has a bad dream about someone, as if the dream were an indicator of something that has happened to the person in objective reality. For example, in a letter of 23 Dec. 1851 to his brother Sergei he writes about their brother Dmitrii: 'What's with Mitin'ka? I had a very bad dream about him on 22 December. Has something happened to him [*Ne sluchilos' li s nim chego nibud'*]?' (59:132).
52. 83:168; 164.
53. Gustafson, 1988, 193; cf. de Courcel, 1988 (1980), 108.
54. Smith and Allred, 1989.
55. 83:168.
56. 83:168, emphasis added.
57. 83:168.
58. 83:168.
59. 83:167.
60. Winnicott, 1972, 36.
61. *SE*, vol XX, 169–70; cf. 137–8.
62. For example: Bowlby, 1960; 1973; 1980; *DSM III*, 50–53; *DSM IV*, 110–13; Greenberg and Mitchell, 1983, 184–7; Thorpe and Burns, 1983, 54; Routh and Bernholtz, 1991; Lipsitz *et al.*, 1994; Deltito and Hahn, 1993; Quinodoz, 1993 (1991).
63. Cf. *DSM IV*, 396. It is possible to take note of the obvious conceptual connection between adult separation anxiety and adult agoraphobia without resolving the question of whether childhood separation anxiety predisposes one to agoraphobia in adulthood (cf. Thyer, 1993).
64. For example, Eikhenbaum in the Jubilee edition, 26:853; Gusev, 1957, 683; Zhdanov, 1993 (1928), 94; Gustafson, 1986, 192–3.
    It should be mentioned that 'Notes of a Madman' has several predecessors which Tolstoy may have had in mind while writing, most

obviously Nikolai Gogol's own story entitled 'Notes of a Madman' (1835). Petr Chaadaev's ironic essay *Apology of a Madman* (1837) is another candidate. Aleksandr Pushkin's poem 'Wanderer' (*Strannik*, 1835), which describes an episode of severe depression, may also be included here (I wish to thank Thomas Newlin for bringing this last work to my attention). Comparative study of Tolstoy's text with its various subtexts or intertexts would no doubt be rewarding, but my primary concern here is Tolstoy's psyche.

65. Shestov, 1967 (1929), 162.
66. Shestov, 1967 (1929), 162, 159, 158.
67. Spence, 1967, 48.
68. Tolstaia, 1978, vol. I, 498, emphasis added.
69. 49:75–6; 77. Compare Osipov (1913, 144) who believes that the narrator of 'Notes of a Madman' is obsessed with the idea of madness.
70. See: I. L. Tolstoi, 1914, 105–12 (= 25:519).
71. Diary entry of 18 November 1889 (50:180). A similar sentiment is expressed by the narrator at the end of *The Devil*.
72. 38:417. For photographs of Tolstoy visiting with patients in two different psychiatric hospitals in 1910, see: Loginova *et al.*, 1995, 508–9.
73. See: Aldanov, 1969 (1923), 8–9, 16–17; Ossipow, 1929; Schefski, 1978.
74. See Parthé, 1985, 80.
75. 26:853; cf. 34:373.
76. 26:475.
77. 26:466.
78. Gusev, 1954, 65.
79. I owe this idea to Barbara Milman.
80. 26:467.
81. 26:853.
82. 26:467.
83. Gusev, 1954, 88–9. Tolstoy's sister reports that, when the brothers would offend little Levochka as a child, he would run away from them and cry. Asked why he was crying, he would reply: 'They are hurting my feelings' (*Menia obizhaiut* – ibid., 88).
84. 23:306.
85. Using terminology which is now somewhat antiquated, Osipov (1913, 146) refers to the child's outbursts as 'hysterical attacks'. With some hesitation he also pronounces the narrator of 'Notes of a Madman' ill with 'anxiety hysteria' (150, 158), i.e., Freud's *Angsthysterie*.
86. 26:475, emphasis added.
87. Katz, 1990, 226.
88. *SE* XIX, 165–70. For an exploration of the prevalence of moral masochism in Russian culture, see: Rancour-Laferriere, 1995.
89. Blanchard, 1984, 31–43.
90. Blanchard, 1984, 33. Gusev treats these passages as referring to Tolstoy himself (1954, 171).
91. 26:467–8.
92. For example, Professor Engelstein (1992, 227) paraphrases an 1871 pedagogical essay: 'nannies were blamed ... for rubbing the penis of a baby boy to put him to sleep'.

93. *SE* XVII, 179–204; Fenichel, 1945, 357. See also Ferber, 1975 on beating fantasies.
94. Flegon, 1973, 181.
95. As quoted by Engelstein, 1992, 227, n. 40.
96. Thanks again to Barbara Milman for this suggestion.
97. 26:468.
98. Cf. de Courcel, 1988, 111.
99. 26:469.
100. In an early paper on 'Notes of a Madman' Osipov speaks of 'panic attacks' (*pristupy boiazni*) as the 'chief symptom' in the work (1913, 150). I disagree. For some reason Osipov plays down the narrator's intense *toska*. He also writes in a rather rambling and incoherent manner, and this makes it difficult to understand what he is getting at. Other early Russian psychoanalysts – e.g., Ermakov, Shpielrein – had the same stylistic problem.
101. On depression as an avenue to a deeper understanding of death than is otherwise available, see: Jamison, 1993, 119. The thoughts of death enable the 'mad' narrator to raise serious moral-philosophical questions about the meaning of *his* life. But, in contrast to Tolstoy's *Confession*, these questions are not raised with respect to humanity generally (cf. Flew, 1963, 112). Perhaps Tolstoy did not publish 'Notes of a Madman' because of this rather narcissistic focus. On the other hand, the narcissistic character Pierre Bezukhov in *War and Peace* arrives at some broad philosophical insights as a result of *his* private bouts of depression (Rancour-Laferriere, 1993a, 98–101). But Pierre is an attractive and thoroughly-developed character in his own right, while the 'madman' is too obviously raw Tolstoy, grinding his new-found religious axe. Pierre is occasionally masochistic, for example, while the 'madman' is excessively masochistic.
102. 23:12; Tolstoy, 1987, 30. Kay Redfield Jamison quotes this passage in *Confession* in her book on manic-depressive illness and art, and lists Tolstoy among other writers 'with probable cyclothymia, major depression, or manic-depressive illness' (1993, 44, 269). Bert Kaplan (1964, 405–11) includes an excerpt from *Confession* in his collection of first-person accounts of mental illness, and refers to Tolstoy's 'depression' (405). David B. Cohen(1994, 100) also quotes Tolstoy, including him among 'those depressed, philosophically gifted people teetering between realism and despair'.

    The clinicians are not alone in pointing to Tolstoy's depressive tendencies. Some Slavic scholars have also noticed the problem. For example, R. F. Christian (1969, 212) describes Tolstoy as a 'victim of growing moodiness and depression' during the period immediately preceding *Confession*. Richard F. Gustafson (1986, 161) refers to the 'depression' manifested in that work, and James L. Rice (1994, 84) draws attention to the 'depressive devaluation' and 'self-destructive urge' of the work. Louise Smoluchowski, in her very sensible and illuminating study of the Tolstoy marriage (1988, 118), speaks of Tolstoy's 'severe depression' in the years 1881–84. Generally speaking, both clinicians and Slavists, while recognizing Tolstoy's great

creative ability, agree that he displayed symptoms of depression at
various periods in his life.

103. 49:81.
104. 26:470.
105. See also the photograph and description of the family crypt in: Puzin,
1988, frontispiece, 11. I was not permitted to examine the inside of the
padlocked burial vault, but according to Puzin the inside as well as
the outside is whitewashed or size painted.

    In 1904, according to Puzin, Tolstoy frequented the Kochaki cem-
etery and took an interest in repairs that were being made on the family crypt there (29, n. 15). At this time also, as we know, he was working
on his *Reminiscences*.
106. See 34:386–7. More specifically, references to the 'green stick' start
appearing in 1905 (Gusev, 1960, 496, 508, 516).
107. 26:469.
108. Parthé, 1985a, 83. See also: Parthé, 1982; 1985b; Burgin, 1987, notes 2,
10, 16; and Rancour-Laferriere, 1993, 161 on nouns of death in
Tolstoy's writing.
109. 26:469.
110. 26:470.
111. 26:470.
112. Cf. Eikhenbaum's commentary, 26:853.
113. 26:472.
114. 26:472.
115. 26:473.
116. 26:474.
117. 26:476.
118. 26:474.
119. 26:474.
120. Osipov, 1913, 150, cf. 158.
121. Plekhanov, 1923, 9.
122. Spence, 1967, 79, 98. Late in his life Tolstoy developed a sentimental longing for death, or at times an apparently peaceful readiness
for death (e. g., Gusev, 1973, 100, 147, 173, 194–5, 198, 234). Such attitudes were not always (at least overtly) linked to anxiety or depression, as in the Arzamas attack, and would bear further psychoanalytic
study.

    In an interesting article Andrej Kodjak has studied the literary de-
velopment and semantic structure of Tolstoy's 'personal myth of immortality'. One component of this myth includes 'a self-sacrificing and
defenseless way of existence' which helps one overcome 'the power of
death' (1985, 193). Although Kodjak is not overtly concerned with
psychological issues, this component is quite similar to the therapeutic moral masochism I have been discussing here.
123. Clinical studies have demonstrated a connection between depression
and masochism. For example, in experimental tests conducted on 20
normal and 20 depressed subjects, it was found that 'depressives have
a higher preference for self-punitive behavior than normals' (Forrest
and Hokanson, 1975, 346; cf. Cohen, 1994, 159–60).

124. Compare Spence (1967, 102), who says: 'Tolstoy's choice, at the time of his conversion, was between suicide and a life of self-sacrifice.' That is, his choice was between actually acting on his depressive thoughts (killing himself) and acting in masochistic fashion (self-sacrifice). However Spence does not explicitly regard the second choice as psychotherapy for the first.

125. See Donskov (1979) on the evolution of Tolstoy's attitude toward the peasantry in his writings.

126. Gor'kii, 1949–55, vol. 14, 270.

127. See, for example: A. T. Ziabrev, 1915, no. 9–10, column 363; E. T. Ziabrev, 1960 (1908–11), 237–40.

128. See Fodor (1984, 51–2) on the element of identification in Tolstoy's 1908 piece *I Cannot Remain Silent*. For evidence of the aging Tolstoy's repeated (and sincere) desire to be arrested and imprisoned, see: 78:88; Tolstoi, 1914, 235, 238; Gusev, 1973, 122; Gor'kii, 1949–55, vol. 14, 282; Blanchard, 1984, 40.

129. Spence (1967, 108) says: 'The ideal of non-resistance flows from the same source as the ideal of complete celibacy.' Spence does not actually name moral masochism as the 'source', however. McLean (1994a, 120) says that Tolstoy's notion of 'nonresistance to evil' is 'what Freudians would call . . . masochistic'. McLean does not elaborate on this, except to suggest that 'it runs against the grain of ideals of masculinity found in most cultures'.

130. Burgin, 1987, 35, 28.

131. See also Sémon, 1984 (444 ff.) on the womb–tomb equation in Tolstoy.

132. Burgin, 1987, 34.

133. Rancour-Laferriere, 1995, 72–7. Cf. Sémon, 1984, 459–67 on *l'unique rédemptrice: la terre-mère* in Tolstoy.

134. For example: Róheim, 1952; Reik, 1957.

135. 23:470.

136. 56:407.

137. Gusev, 1954, 57, 59. The funeral took place on 7 August.

138. Frank, 1969, 62.

139. Armstrong, 1988, 11.

140. 34:349. Large chunks of the *Reminiscences* appeared in various places at various times, including Pavel Biriukov's biography of Tolstoy (e.g., the edition Biriukov, 1921, vol. I). Here I use the version which appears in the Jubilee Edition of Tolstoy's works.

141. For example, Lewin, 1937, 871; Jacobson, 1965, 200. Tolstoy's idealization of his mother (especially in the early novella *Childhood*) initiated what Andrew Wachtel terms 'the myth of the perfect mother' in Russian gentry autobiography (see Wachtel, 1990, 96–9).

142. See, for example: S. A. Tolstaia, 1978c, 40.

143. 34:354.

144. For example, Il'ia L'vovich Tolstoi (1914, 26).

145. See: Molostvov and Sergeenko, 1909, 64; Gusev, 1954, 60.

146. 56:134; cf. Gusev, 1954, 60.

147. 56:133; cf. Gusev, 1954, 60.

It should be mentioned that Tolstoy also loved and respected his father, who died when he was nine years old. But, as Il'ia L'vovich says: '... I felt that the memory of his mamen'ka, whom he did not know, was more dear to him, and that he loved her much more than he did his father' (1914, 28).

148.   Tolstoy's sentimental *culte* of his mother is reminiscent of his depiction of Napoleon's sentimental reflections on 'ma chère, ma tendre, ma pauvre mère' in *War and Peace*. These come in a passage where, as Aleksandr Zholkovskii has shown (1995, 95–6), Tolstoy represents the city of Moscow as a maternal body which Napoleon wishes to violate. There is also a certain similarity between Napoleon's feelings for an imagined 'Maison de ma Mère' in Moscow and Tolstoy's emotional attachment to the maternal house in which he was born, and which was later moved to the village of Dolgoye.

149.   Ossipow, 1923, 97.

150.   Sergei Tolstoi, 1988, 164.

151.   Gusev, 1954, 43; see also S. L. Tolstoi, 1928a, 52.

152.   Gusev, 1954, 44, n. 12.

153.   Gusev, 1954, opposite p. 49. Cf. the illustration opposite p. 16 in Molostvov and Sergeenko, 1909.

154.   Quoted from Zhdanov, 1968, 158; and 27:306. Cf. 27:321 for similar gushings on the moral perfection of girls.

155.   More than twenty years earlier Tolstoy was making the same error in a draft of *Confession* (23:488; cf. 23:508). Curiously, Tolstoy's mother herself lost *her* mother at the age of two years (S. L. Tolstoi, 1928a, 41).

156.   34:365.

157.   34:349.

158.   Quoted by Molostvov and Sergeenko, 1909, 22. The book in question is *Voyages d'Antenor en Grèce et en Asie avec des notions sur l'Égypte* by Étienne de Lantier (1734–1826), which appeared in Paris in 1798 and was reprinted many times.

159.   As related by Makovitskii, 1979–81, vol. III, 113.

160.   34:352. '*Mon petit Benjamin*' might be translated as 'my pet' – after Benjamin, the youngest and most beloved son of Jacob (*Genesis* 43, 26–34).

161.   Quoted by Gusev, 1954, 641–3. See also Molostvov and Sergeenko, 1909, 20–21.

162.   For example, Molostvov and Sergeenko, 1909, 41–2.

163.   S. L. Tolstoi, 1928a, 44; Gusev, 1954, 46–7. Tolstoy later backed off from the claim that his mother's fiancé was named Lev, ascribing the idea to his *Tetushka* (34:394). Someone must have been making the error long before 1903, for Sonia was already parroting it in her 1876 memoir (Tolstaia, 1978b, 29). Whatever the source of the error, and regardless of whether Tolstoy was correct in blaming his *Tetushka*, it is clear that he gladly accepted the error for quite some time.

164.   In referring to his mother's passionate friendship (*strastnaia druzhba*) with M-elle Hénissienne, which ended in disappointment, Tolstoy may be hinting at his mother's Lesbian inclinations.

165. 34:353.
166. 34:353.
167. See: S. L. Tolstoi, 1928a, 123–52.
168. 34:350. Turgenev's remark is repeated in the same memoir (34:386). Apparently Tolstoy was fond of quoting Turgenev's remark (Ivakin, 1994, 106), but he tended to forget that his brother Nikolai was in fact a published writer (ibid.; S. L. Tolstoi, 1928a, 66).
169. 34:383; 385; 346–7.
170. 34:386.
171. 34:386.
172. Narcissism may simply be defined as concern with the self. Disturbed narcissism is excessive or abnormal concern with the self, as in: delusions of grandeur, obsessive pursuit of self-perfection, impaired ability to empathize with others, rage reactions to slights, unjustified feelings of entitlement, and so on.

    Much has already been written about the role of narcissism in Tolstoy's life and/or works, e.g.: Ossipow, 1923; Rothstein, 1984; Josselson, 1986; Rancour-Laferriere, 1993a; 1993b. Already in 1900 Dmitrii Merezhkovsky, with considerable psychological insight, was referring to Tolstoy as 'an eternal Narcissus' (Merezhkovskii, 1995, 18). For a curious pre-psychoanalytic commentary on 'love for oneself' in Tolstoy, see: Posse, 1918, 53–6. In a very interesting 1929 article D. S. Mirsky discusses Tolstoy's 'gigantic egotism' and 'Narcissism' (1989, 304–6). Porché's (1935) 'psychological portrait' offers occasional insights into Tolstoy's narcissism. For a very useful psychoanalytic study of the role of narcissism in literature generally, see: Berman, 1990.
173. Bers, 1978 [1894], vol. 1, 183.
174. Gor'kii, 1949–55, vol. 14. 284.
175. 64:20.
176. Obolenskii, 1978 (1902), vol. I, 358. The deleted obscenity is probably *govennyi* ('a shit'). Thanks to Yuri Druzhnikov for assistance in deciphering the message.
177. Gusev, 1973, 135.
178. 34:348.
179. Cf. Blanchard (1984, 37) on Tolstoy's inability to be content with fame and his tendency to hate himself for wanting it.
180. For example, in a letter to Ge Senior and Ge Junior of 26 November 1888, where he compares his current 'abstinence' from writing to giving up smoking (64:200–1; cf. 64:235).
181. On persisting low self-esteem after loss of a parent in childhood, see: Tyson, 1983. On Tolstoy's low self-esteem in adulthood, see below.
182. Cf. above, p. 20.
183. Stern, 1965, 187; cf. Pigott, 1992, 57.
184. 56:133, emphasis added.
185. I am not the first to raise these questions. Richard Wortman believes that 'the sentimental tone' in Tolstoy's description of maternal loss in the autobiographical novella *Childhood* 'concealed Tolstoi's rage'. He

adds: 'Tolstoi regarded the bereavement, like most children, as an intentional act' (1985, 164).
186. Bowlby, 1980, 412–39.
187. 86:237.
188. For documentation of the original maternal ownership of Yasnaya Polyana, see: Ivanova, 1971, 11–13.
189. As quoted in: Ivanova, 1971, 35–6.
190. Cf. Newlin, 1994.
191. See: 47:35, 275; 59:280, 299–308; Gusev, 1954, 71–2; Ilya Tolstoi, 1969, 32; Kuzminskaia, 1986, 122.
192. 53:169.
193. 53:485.
194. I. L. Tolstoi, 1914, 26. For the same anecdote, see Ilya's sister Aleksandra Tolstaia, 1989 (1953), 9.
195. I. L. Tolstoi, 1914, opposite p. 24.
196. I. Tolstoi, 1969.
197. Assya Humeska has pointed out to me that Russians do not normally designate the age of small children in months (personal communication, 27 October 1995). Tolstoy wrote, for example, that he was '1½ years old' when his mother died. However, had he written '2 years old' he would have been much closer to the truth, even within the Russian convention of using years rather than months to designate the age of children. And in any case, since we know *precisely* how old he was when his mother died, it makes sense to consult scientific studies of childhood behaviour and attitudes which are based on age in months.
198. Mahler, Pine and Bergman, 1975, 291–2; Mahler, 1994 (1979), vol. 2, 137.
199. For example, in his *Reminiscences* he refers to her as *mamen'ka without* quotation marks (34:379). His son Ilya quotes him as saying: 'Way up there, where the top of that larch tree is, was Mamen'ka's room [*mamen'kina komnata*] . . . ' (I. L. Tolstoi, 1914, 26).
200. For example: Raphael, 1982; Furman, 1974; see Krupnick and Solomon, 1987 for a valuable overview of research on the effects of bereavement during childhood. The findings in these and similar studies contradict Judith Armstrong's conclusion that Tolstoy 'was too young to suffer grief' (1988, 5).
201. Bowlby, 1980, 412–39.
202. Furman, 1974, 113, emphasis added.
203. 55:374, as translated by Gustafson, 1986, 14–15; cf. Gusev, 1954, 60–61.
204. 55:207.
205. Pigott, 1992, 57.
206. Lavrin, 1944, 118.
207. Sémon, 1984, 460.
208. Malia, 1976, 180.
209. de Courcel, 1988, 12–13.
210. Abraham, 1994 (1924), 90.
211. Klein, 1994 (1940), 105. Cf. also Klein (1977 [1935], 267–8), where Klein states that the desire for the maternal object's *perfection* is rooted in the wish to restore damage sadistically inflicted (in fantasy) on the object.

212. Quoted by Makovitskii, 1979–81, vol. II, 494.

213. S. L. Tolstoi, 1928a, 126.

214. 64:277.

215. 34:366–7.

216. Wachtel, 1990, 88–92.

217. 34:369. Ossipow (1923, 102) says Tolstoy is hinting at a 'man-and-wife' relationship with Ergol'skaia here.

218. The woman living with Ergol'skaia was Natal'ia Petrovna Okhotnitskaia, an impoverished gentrywoman. For more on this odd couple, see Tat'iana Kuzminskaia's memoir (1986, 134–5).

219. It is possible that Tolstoy is mistaken in interpreting his auntie's use of *Nicolas* as a reference to the father. Joe Aimone has suggested to me that the auntie could be referring to Tolstoy's brother instead. I have not been able to find specific examples of her being sloppy in distinguishing the five children from one another, however. Also, if the auntie had confused Tolstoy with his brother, I think she would have said 'Nikolen'ka' instead.

220. See: Erikson, 1963, 366–9; Etkind, 1993, 112–14.

221. 34:373–4.

222. 60:247–8 (emphasis added). For other variants, see: 7:117–19. B. I. Berman (1992, 40–80) has written an interesting analysis of 'The Dream', relating it to – among other things – Pierre Bezukhov's famous dream of the liquid sphere, Prince Andrei's ruminations under the open sky of Austerlitz, the ending of the story 'Albert' (1858), and the treatment of the character Mar'iana in *The Cossacks* (1862). Berman recognizes that the woman in 'The Dream' is 'the maternal foundation of nature and of happiness in the soul' (74), although he does not come right out and say that the woman represents Tolstoy's mother. Gusev (1957, 264) gives 'The Dream' an exclusively political reading.

223. Mahler, 1994 (1979), vol. 1, 263 (emphasis added); cf. Hardin, 1985, 610. Hardin's very interesting article deals primarily with clinical cases where the image of the mother and the image of the surrogate mother failed to fuse after loss of the surrogate, leading to psychological difficulties in adult relationships. In Tolstoy's case the mother herself died, and there was more than one surrogate over time.

224. For example: Birtchnell, 1972; Brown, 1982; Bowlby, 1980, 295–310.

225. For example: Roy, 1983; Barnes and Prosen, 1985.

226. Gor'kii, 1949–55, vol. 14, 291.

227. 34:354. The error also occurs many years earlier, in a draft of *Confession* (23:508).

228. See: Gusev, 1954, 57–8; Ogareva, 1914, 113; S. L. Tolstoi, 1928a, 63–4.

229. In the fragment 'My life' Tolstoy seems to suggest that he was weaned no earlier than one year old: 'I don't know, and I never will know whether they were swaddling me when I was still an infant at the breast and was trying to pull my arms out, or they were swaddling me when I was already more than a year old to prevent me from scratching sores . . .'. (23:470).

230.   Karl Stern does suggest that Pozdnyshev's murder of his wife is
        a representation of Tolstoy's hatred aimed at 'the archaic proto-
        type', i.e., at Tolstoy's mother (1965, 186). But Stern does not actually
        do a psychoanalysis of the novella or of the biographical back-
        ground to it.
231.   7:149–51; cf. 27:563. Gusev is inclined to date this fragment earlier,
        around 1870 (1963, 22–3).
232.   Tolstaia, 1978a, vol. I, 137.
233.   The drafts and variants of *The Kreutzer Sonata* and its afterword
        were published in 1933 in vol. 27 of the Jubilee Edition (291–432).
        N. K. Gudzii provides a detailed history of the writing and pub-
        lishing of the work in the same volume (563–646; cf. Gudzii,
        1936, 37–69). See also the articles by Zhdanov (1961; 1968) on the
        manuscripts of the work, as well as Opul'skaia's commentary (1979,
        117 ff.).
234.   As quoted by Al'tman, 1966, 118. On railway trains in the life and
        works of Tolstoy, see: Al'tman, 1966, 110–19; Christian, 1969, 232;
        Jahn, 1981; Benson, 1973, 114, 132.
235.   Isenberg, 1993, 84.
236.   27:10–11, as translated in Tolstoy, 1983, 30.
237.   The *Domostroi* was a sixteenth-century didactic tract on household
        management. Among other things, it admonished men to administer
        corporal punishment to wives and children who were disobedient.
238.   Levin, 1993, 52.
239.   27:390; 397.
240.   In some drafts the distinction between Pozdnyshev and the old man
        does not exist, and Pozdnyshev himself comes out in favour of the
        Domostroi (27:392). In one variant where the two men are distin-
        guished, Pozdnyshev asserts that it is only because of the 'inertia' of
        the '*Domostroi* rules' concerning 'the whip' that there is still some
        semblance of honour and faithfulness in marriage (27:409).
241.   27:14 as translated in Tolstoy, 1983, 34.
242.   27:14; Tolstoy, 1983, 34.
243.   Cf. Aldanov, 1969 (1923), 43.
244.   *SE* XI, 180; cf. Beck, 1898, 41; Ossipow, 1923, 132 ff.; Benson, 1973, 123.
245.   27:14, 398.
246.   46:146.
247.   Tolstaia, 1978, vol. I, 130 as translated in Sophia Tolstoy, 1985, 93.
248.   27:14; Tolstoy, 1983, 34.
249.   27:409. Cf. 27:295.
250.   Cf. Isenberg (1993, 105–6) who compares Pozdnyshev's marriage to
        Pierre's first marriage.
251.   Gor'kii, 1949–55, vol. 14, 262. I have supplied the appropriate English
        translation of the Russian word clearly intended by Gorky's ellipsis,
        i.e., *khui*.
252.   27:409. Cf. 27:296.
253.   *SE* XI, 180.
254.   Cf. Sémon 1984 (405), who conveys this idea without using the psy-
        choanalytic term 'narcissistic'.

255. Møller 1988, 12. Møller derives his term 'unmasking' from Lenin's famous phrase describing Tolstoy's work as *sryvanie vsekh i vsiacheskikh masok* (as quoted by Møller, p. 1).
256. Jackson, 1978; Beck, 1898, 42, 27; Knapp, 1988, 65, 70; Flamant, 1992, 31–2; Golstein, 1996; Calder, 1976, 235; Holthusen, 1974, 193; Sémon, 1984, 404–5; 27:40, 420; 51:12.
257. The peculiar sounds produced by Pozdnyshev are reminiscent of a neurological disorder known as Tourette syndrome, as Isenberg observes (1993, 166, n. 18). It is now known that Tolstoy's brother Dmitrii suffered from this disease (Hurst and Hurst, 1994). For a fuller description of the condition, see: Rancour-Laferriere, 1992 (1985), 226–7.
258. 27:49; Tolstoy, 1983, 81.
259. Botkin, 1893.
260. Baumgart, 1990 (1985), 209.
261. See: Isenberg, 1993, 79–108.
262. Isenberg, 1993, 107.
263. See: Møller, 1988, 37.
264. 27:294.
265. 27:362, 363.
266. In this case it is external monologue rather than the inner monologue so typical of Tolstoy's prose. See: Milykh, 1978. Liza Knapp observes that the novella 'never fully lapses into monologue' because of the interruptions made by the narrator, and argues that the work is best regarded as 'a cross between a confession and a philosophical dialogue' (Knapp, 1991, 25).
267. See especially Holthusen (1974) on this problem.
268. Pozdnyshev's personal confession to the narrator is especially inappropriate in the third draft, where the narrator is an idealistic young man in love with a woman he wants to marry. Cf. Sémon, 1984 (389) on the 'excessively cordial' relations of Pozdnyshev and the narrator in this variant.
269. According to Tolstoy's son Lev, Tolstoy got the idea of telling Pozdnyshev's story as first person monologue from Marmeladov's barroom monologue in Dostoevsky's *Crime and Punishment* (L. Tolstoi, 1923, 72). More importantly, however, Tolstoy's narrative arrangement was influenced by Dostoevsky's *Notes from the Underground*, as Robert Louis Jackson has shown (1978).
270. Aldanov, 1969 (1923), 40–41. Evaluations of the artistic quality of the work vary enormously. For example, A. N. Wilson calls KS a 'masterpiece' (1988, 373), while Louise Smoluchowski says it 'seems absurd today' and 'survives as a curiosity . . . in spite of its improbable plot' (1988, 155).
271. Maude, 1987 (1930), vol. II, 269.
272. See especially Baehr, 1976, 45.
273. Cain, 1977, 149.
274. Dillon, 1934, 174.
275. 86:271, 273. For a draft-by-draft history of the writing of the afterword, see Gudzii's commentary, 27:625–46.

216 Notes

276. Benson, 1973, 136.
277. Quoted in Opul'skaia, 1979, 200.
278. Gusev, 1954, 168–9.
279. For details, see: Gusev, 1963, 13–16. For the influence of Schopenhauer on this letter, see: Eikhenbaum, 1982 (1960), 99–100.
280. Engelstein, 1992, 221, 228.
281. I. L. Tolstoi, 1914, 203.
282. 27:79 as translated in Tolstoy, 1983, 267.
283. 27:80; Tolstoy, 1983, 268. Cf. Tolstoy's 1890 story 'Françoise,' an adaptation of de Maupassant's 'Le port', in which a man realizes that the prostitute he is talking with is his sister (27:251–8). On the prostitute-as-sister topos, see: Zholkovsky, 1994a, 685–6; Zholkovskii, 1994, 338–41. For a detailed study of the overall topos of the prostitute in literature see: Zholkovskii, 1994.
284. 27:18, Tolstoy, 1983, 39–40.
285. 27:81, 90–91, 417; Tolstoy, 1983, 269, 280. It goes without saying that Tolstoy is also opposed to homosexual intercourse and masturbation, so he deletes the references he made to these in a draft of the afterword (27:421).
286. Simmons, 1946, 438; Engelstein, 1992, 221; Mandelker, 1993, 30–31; Stites, 1991, 159; Greenwood, 1975, 140. Compare, however, Vladimir Zhdanov (1968, 62–3), who for some reason tries to gloss over Tolstoy's advocacy of total chastity, and even claims that *The Kreutzer Sonata* is primarily concerned with 'morality in the ordinary sense'.
287. Ossipow, 1923, 144.
288. Møller 1988 (cf. also Gornaia, 1988). There are some indications that women readers in Russia were more likely to accept Tolstoy's idea about complete abstinence than were men. Møller says: 'For some women, at any rate, [Tolstoy's] ideal of chastity appeared to be a way out of their degrading sexual experience and the burdens of all too frequent childbirth' (127; cf. Rusanov and Rusanov, 1972, 113–14, 257–8). For such women to regard the sexual experience as 'degrading', however, was probably an indication of the sexual inconsiderateness or ineptitude of their mates.
289. Ganzen, 1978 (1917), vol. I, 462.
290. Zhirkevich, 1939 (427, 439) as translated (in part) in Møller 1988, 10. In the first (1890) interview with Zhirkevich Tolstoy expresses a negative opinion about his own *Anna Karenina*, and makes hostile remarks about the writings of Lermontov, Turgenev, Pushkin, Fet, Dostoevsky, Zola, de Maupassant. . . .
291. As quoted in Gudzii's commentary, 27:596.
292. 51:11.
293. See 30:65, where the expression is *liudi zarazhaiutsia*.
294. Eguchi, 1996, 420; Golstein, 1996, 457.
295. As translated with some modifications from 23:457–8 by Maude, 1987 (1930), vol. II, 271.
296. Lazarev, 1978 (1935), vol. I, 324–5.
297. 86:139.

298. 86:177; 182. Cf. Tolstoy's letter of 12 October to D. A. Khilkov, where he says people should not indulge lustful feelings (*Vsiakii znaet, chto predavat'sia pokhoti ne dolzhno*), and that it is best to avoid getting married (*ne mogu venchat'sia*: 64:184). Cf. also Møller, 1988, 32–3, and David McDuff's Introduction to Tolstoy 1983, 9.
299. 27:88; Tolstoy, 1983, 277.
300. Maude, 1987 (1930), vol. II, 272.
301. 27:80; Tolstoy, 1983, 269.
302. 27:306–7.
303. 51:132.
304. 27:38; cf. also 27:311.
305. 27:82; Tolstoy, 1983, 271.
306. 27:22–3, Tolstoy, 1983, 45.
307. In the third draft, Pozdnyshev, in a temper tantrum, calls his wife a 'whore' (*bliad'*, euphemized in the Jubilee Edition as 'b . . .' – 27:384).
308. See also Sémon, 1984 (439–47) on the idea of women as prostitutes in Tolstoy.
309. 86:183.
310. Even earlier, in *What, Then, Shall We Do?* (1886) Tolstoy was hinting at a parallel between prostitutes and wives. See: Møller, 1988, 28–9.
311. See, for example: Rancour-Laferriere, 1992 (1985), 152, 158–67, 254 ff.
312. After *The Kreutzer Sonata* and its afterword were completed, Tolstoy continued to favour total sexual abstinence, even though he occasionally 'sinned' with his wife, or sometimes made statements that were inconsistent with his advocacy of chastity (e.g., in 1896 he recommended that those who are not chaste at least be faithful to their partners and not practise perversions – 39:183; in 1905 he expressed the wish that women not 'go on strike' by refusing to have babies – Obolenskaia, 1978 [1928], 407). But overall, chastity remained Tolstoy's ideal. In a diary entry for 3 August 1908 he writes: 'one must strive for chastity' (53:208). To Gusev in the same year he says that marriage is a 'fall' (1973, 159). In a collection of letters written to various people in 1893–1908 he recommends chastity for the most part (Gusev, 1924). In 1910 he is still saying complete chastity is the ideal (89:172).
313. See Meyer, 1977, 92, 97.
314. Engels, 1985 (1884), 102.
315. Rancour-Laferriere, 1992, 254–5.
316. Kollontai, 1977 (1921), 264.
317. See: Mandelker, 1993, 6, 30–31; Heldt, 1987, 38–48. Sémon, rather than viewing the work as feminist, traces the rhythmic spurts of sympathy for women which Tolstoy felt as he wrote successive drafts of his essentially misogynist novella (1984, 388–90). Møller says that '. . . from the beginning *The Kreutzer Sonata* was planned with a polemic intent aimed against the emancipatory ideas of the 1860s' (1988, 22; Møller has in mind especially Nikolai Chernyshevsky's *What Is to Be Done?*, with its relatively progressive view of marriages and divorce). Richard Stites, in his pioneering study of the women's liberation movement in Russia, speaks bluntly of Tolstoy's 'anti-feminism' (1991,

159). Charles Isenberg says: '... Tolstoy's feminism is as much a screen and rationalization for his hostility [toward women] as it is an attempt at sympathetic understanding of the female situation' (1993, 93).

318. Zholkovskii, 1994, 326–34.
319. Dumas, 1888.
320. See Zholkovsky (1994a, 682–4) on Tolstoy's somewhat prudish attitude toward the works of de Maupassant.
321. de Maupassant 1974–79, vol I, 1040–46. Although the work was originally printed under a pseudonym, it was reprinted under de Maupassant's own name in 1886 (ibid., 1598).
322. de Maupassant 1974–79, vol. 1, 297.
323. 30:285.
324. de Maupassant 1975, 887, as translated in de Maupassant, 1979, 85.
325. de Maupassant 1975, 910, as translated in de Maupassant, 1979, 109 (emphasis added).
326. 30:5–6.
327. See: Zholkovskii, 1994, 323.
328. See Gudzii's commentary, 27:602.
329. As quoted by Knapp (1991, 27).
330. Knapp, 1991 (30).
331. Cf. Hugh McLean's comment on Tolstoy's 1882 *Harmonization and Translation of the Four Gospels*: '... Jesus *per se* is not even very important; what is important are the ideas Tolstoy has extracted and edited from the words attributed to him' (McLean, 1994a, 111). Charles Isenberg argues that in *The Kreutzer Sonata* 'Tolstoy is not just quoting Matthew but revising the apostle's meaning' (Isenberg, 1993, 81). Compare Marie Sémon (1984, 404–5), who feels that Tolstoy's concerns in *The Kreutzer Sonata* are not truly religious, and that he substitutes a 'moral hygiene' and a 'cult of chastity' for the sacred.
332. 27:86; Tolstoy, 1983, 275.
333. 27:92; Tolstoy, 1983, 282, emphasis added.
334. See especially Tolstoy's letter of 18 Oct. 1889 to the American Shaker A. G. Hollister (64:319–20).
335. See: Gudzii's 1933 commentary (27:571–4); Stockham, 1888; Møller, 1988, 33–5; Edwards, 1993.
336. Edwards, 1993, 98–100.
337. 64:202.
338. McLaughlin, 1970, 233–8. Cf. Troubetskoy, 1992.
339. 51:40; cf. 27:572–3. Gudzii (1936, 51) believes that Tolstoy exaggerates the influence of the Czech woman on him.
340. 27:81; Tolstoy, 1983, 269. The disapproval of sexual intercourse during pregnancy may also be found in Alice B. Stockham's *Tokology* (1888, 159), although I doubt Stockham's attitude did anything more than reinforce a view Tolstoy already held. As for Tolstoy's disapproval of sexual intercourse during breast-feeding, it resembles the postpartum sex taboo observed in those non-industrial societies where men tend to avoid having sustained, monogamous relationships with women (see Rancour-Laferriere 1992 [1985], 139).

Tolstoy's idea that intercourse harms a pregnant or nursing woman to some extent coincides with his wife's views on the matter.
Sonia writes in a diary entry of 25 January 1891: 'A young woman has
none of this sexual passion, especially a woman who is busy bearing
and nursing children' (Tolstaia, 1978, vol. I, 148). But whereas
from Sonia's viewpoint there is simply a decreased sexual interest
during pregnancy and nursing, from Tolstoy's there is a real sense that
sex *endangers* a woman during this period.

341. 27:34; Tolstoy, 1983, 60.
342. Cf. Baehr, 1976, 40.
343. 27:300.
344. Møller, 1988, 14.
345. Rusanov and Rusanov, 1972, 85.
346. '*Klikushestvo* was primarily a woman's condition characterized by
      howling, cursing, and falling to the ground during the liturgy, in the
      midst of church processions, or in the presence of icons, incense, and
      other religious objects. *Klikushi*, as the victims were called, tended to
      complain of indefinite pains in the groin or heart. Some reports men-
      tion foaming at the mouth or bloating of the stomach' (Ivanits, 1989,
      106).
347. 27:35; Tolstoy, 1983, 61. A similar view was expressed by Tolstoy per-
      sonally in the letter to Chertkov of 6 November 1888 (86:182).
      Note that Tolstoy is under the (roughly correct) impression that
      non-human mammals are for the most part abstinent, copulating
      'only when it is possible for them to produce offspring' (27:36; Tolstoy,
      1983, 62). That is, most mammals copulate only during ovulation sig-
      nalled by oestrus in the female (there are some exceptions, such as
      chimpanzees). Here Tolstoy has been influenced by Alice Stockham's
      Tokology, as Robert Edwards demonstrates (1993, 97, 101). Tolstoy
      cannot take this idea very far, however, for it clashes with his other
      idea of the 'animality' of the 'monkey pastime' of sexual intercourse
      (27:36; Tolstoy, 1983, 62). It also clashes with some of the other animal
      imagery in the novella, e.g., the 'piglike' quality of sex during preg-
      nancy (27:34; Tolstoy, 1983, 60), or the recurring images of human
      marriage as a 'dog wedding' and 'dog's love' in some of the drafts
      (e.g.: 27:355, 356, 359, 378, 410). The obsessively canine images of sex
      in the drafts may have something to do with Tolstoy's strong aversion
      to the barking of dogs (Gol'denveizer, 1959, 307, 376).
348. 27:323.
349. 27:35; Tolstoy, 1983, 61.
350. Ossipow, 1923, 140ff.
351. Cf. Tolstoy's letter to Chertkov of 6 Nov. 1888 (86:181–4).
352. See: Lawrence, 1985, 438–99; Benson and Pernoll, 1994, 144, 274. The
      only restriction today's physician might have placed on Lev and
      Sonia would have been (after several children had already been born)
      to recommend against intercourse after 28 weeks of pregnancy (see
      Benson and Pernoll, 1994, 144).
353. 27:91; Tolstoy, 1983, 280.
354. 86:177; 180–84.

355.   Coetzee, 1985, 198.
356.   27:81; Tolstoy, 1983, 269.
357.   As psychoanalyst Ben Karpman observes, this is 'a distinctly masoch-
       istic reaction tied up with a remarkable sense of guilt' (1938, 45).
358.   27:39; Tolstoy, 1983, 67.
359.   27:47; Tolstoy, 1983, 77, emphasis added.
360.   27:87; Tolstoy, 1983, 276–7, emphasis added. Vl. Vol'fson, whose pur-
       itanical 'scientific' views on 'physiology and hygiene' are remarkably
       similar to Tolstoy's, argues that the best way to continue the human
       species is to bring down high childhood mortality rates, rather than
       encourage people to get married (1910, 89–98).
361.   Konstantin Nikolaevich Ziabrev (1846–95), an impoverished, irre-
       sponsible Yasnaya Polyana peasant and follower of Tolstoy (for more
       on Konstantin, see: A. T. Ziabrev, 1915, 79–80; V. P. Ziabrev, 1960,
       191–6). Tolstoy was quite devoted to Konstantin and his family, as is
       evident from the fact that he ploughed, sowed, and harvested
       Konstantin's fields during the summer that Konstantin ran away
       from his wife and family. Konstantin's paternal grandmother was
       Avdot'ia Nikiforovna Ziabreva, Tolstoy's wet-nurse.
362.   50:96, 207.
363.   See, for example: Kon, 1995, 20: Rancour-Laferriere, 1995, 156–7.
364.   Laplanche and Pontalis, 1973, 335. Isenberg (1993, 79–108) uses the
       term 'primal scene' in connection with Tolstoy's novella, but not in
       its original psychoanalytic sense.
365.   See the new interpretation offered from an appropriately 'Russian'
       viewpoint by Etkind, 1993, 97–129. For the original Wolf Man case,
       see *SE* XVII, 3–122. For a contemporary example of a primal scene ex-
       perience as described by a Russian college student, see: Leibin, 1996,
       136–7.
366.   Gusev, 1973, 151.
367.   Kopper, 1989, 178.
368.   Sergeenko, 1939, 524; cf. Zhdanov, 1968, 63.
369.   27:83.
370.   50:121, 214, emphasis added.
371.   See: Rancour-Laferriere, 1993b.
372.   Gustafson, 1986, 458. See also Rancour-Laferriere, 1993a (137,
       199–201, 209) for specific examples of the feeling of 'uniting' with
       non-self in the life of Pierre Bezukhov.
373.   Rancour-Laferriere, 1995, 202–44, and especially n. 82, p. 286.
374.   27:30; Tolstoy, 1983, 55.
375.   86:184.
376.   27:30.
377.   See, for example: Spence, 1967, 105. There is also an allusion to
       Pushkin in Pozdnyshev's phrase *'esli zhizn' dlia zhizni nam dana,
       nezachem zhit'* (27:29). See: Al'tman, 1966, 45.
378.   27:582. Cf. 50:147.
379.   27:31; Tolstoy, 1983, 55–6. Cf. 27:338, 414.
380.   Although Tolstoy understands that the human species would be
       brought to extinction if total sexual abstinence were practised by

everyone, other aspects of his knowledge of biology are shaky at best.

Thus, to translate into biological terms his fantasy about people 'uniting' instead of having sexual intercourse, Tolstoy is saying that altruism will somehow replace sexual reproduction. But human altruism was only selected for in a context of sexual reproduction. Altruism is evolutionarily unlikely unless *someone's* genetic fitness is being improved as a result of it. Thus, in order for so-called reciprocal altruism to work, the chances for increased representation of the genetic material of both reciprocating participants in the next generation have to be increased, but Tolstoy's plan eliminates the next generation categorically. Or, in the case of what sociobiologists term kin altruism, rendering benefits to related individuals profits one's own genetic material being represented in the offspring of kin. But again, by Tolstoy's plan, kin would not be having offspring. So Tolstoy's advocacy of 'uniting' in Christian love cannot be said to have any Darwinian or sociobiological sophistication (true, evolutionary theory was still pretty primitive in 1889, but the idea of kin selection had already been put forth by Darwin in *On the Origin of Species* in 1859).

The one passage where Tolstoy does refer to sterile organisms to support his point, and where he claims to be expressing the view of an 'evolutionist', turns out to be inadequate evolutionary biology:

In order to defend its interests in its struggle with the other animals, the highest form [*poroda*] of animal life – the human race – has to gather itself into a unity, like a swarm of bees, and not reproduce infinitely; like the bees, it must raise sexless individuals, that's to say it must strive for abstinence, not the excitement of lust.... (27:30–31; Tolstoy, 1983, 55).

Tolstoy is here referring to female worker bees, which are sterile. Tolstoy fails to mention, however, that worker bees are not all bees (there are also male drones and the female queen). The reason bees continue to exist, given the fact that no females other than the queen are able to have offspring, is that the system is evolutionarily stable. The genetic payoff for a female worker to care for other bees (kin altruism) is greater than it would be if she were to have her own offspring (technically, because of the haplodiploid type of sex determination in the Hymenoptera, the degree of relatedness between sisters is 3/4, while between mothers and daughters it is only 1/2; see Wilson, 1975, 416). Meantime, however, the worker bee strategy would not succeed if *some* of the bees were not reproducing sexually. Drones do compete for sexual access to a queen. Sex does exist in bees. Tolstoy would have been better off using corals or sponges as examples, for these organisms have true asexual reproduction in addition to sexual reproduction.

In a variant passage of the afterword Tolstoy laughs a little at those who claim to be worried about the end of the human race: '. . . can anyone honestly say that, in giving in to carnal desire, he is thinking about the continuation of the species [*dumaet o prodolzhenii roda*]?' Tolstoy adds: 'If such a solicitous person exists, then let him rest

assured that nature has taken care of this by putting sexual passion
into people, and that it's impossible to imagine people without it'
(27:429). Here Tolstoy gets his biology right. What is wrong, however,
is the overall idea that 'sexual passion' could somehow be circum-
vented, that significant numbers of people could actually abstain from
sexual intercourse, as he recommends. 'Sexual passion' is much too
hard-wired by genes to be just deleted from the phenotype. As is well
known, for example, Tolstoy himself could never abstain for very
long, for he ended up fathering 13 legitimate children with Sofia
Andreevna, plus at least two illegitimate children with peasant women. His Pozdnyshev is also the father of five children. Pozdnyshev uses
his wife in a reproductively effective manner before killing her. His
genes, like those of his creator, are not outsmarted by stupid moral
theories.

381.   37:84; Tolstoy, 1983, 272–3.
382.   For example: Isenberg, 1993, 92.
383.   Heldt, 1987, 39.
384.   Aquil, 1989, 254.
385.   27:26; Tolstoy, 1983, 49–50.
386.   27:26; Tolstoy, 1983, 50.
387.   Ingersoll, 1890, 292.
388.   Comstock, 1904, 19–20.
389.   27:25; Tolstoy, 1983, 49.
390.   27:37; Tolstoy, 1983, 64.
391.   27:311. In this version Pozdnyshev also views women's higher educa-
       tion as just another device for capturing men (27:313).
392.   Heldt, 1987, 46.
393.   27:45; Tolstoy, 1983, 75.
394.   27:33; Tolstoy, 1983, 59.
395.   In the 1933 commentary Gudzii refers to the *sila samobichevaniia*
       in Pozdnyshev (27:570), and Sémon speaks of *l'autoflagellation de
       Pozdnychev* (1988, 389), while Mondry discusses the 'self-contempt'
       and 'self-mutilation' in Pozdnyshev (1988, 173).
396.   See: Tolstaia, 1978a, vol. I, 39, 40.
397.   27:48; Tolstoy, 1983, 78. In an early variant Pozdnyshev actually
       claims to have been in love with his wife when he married her
       (27:399).
398.   For example, Benson, 1973, 120; Heldt, 1987, 45; Flamant, 1992, 33.
399.   In early drafts Pozdnyshev actually has his little daughter with him on
       the train, and behaves toward her in a very solicitous, even very mater-
       nal fashion (*imenno kak mat'* – 27:370). In later drafts she vanishes. Tolstoy
       must have realized how incongruous Pozdnyshev's maternal
       behaviour toward the child was with his brutal murder of the child's
       mother. On the other hand, Tolstoy was perhaps originally trying
       to show that Pozdnyshev was better at 'mothering' the child than
       was the child's supposedly immoral mother. In any case mother-
       hood was very much on Tolstoy's mind, especially in the third draft,
       where Pozdnyshev treats even the narrator in a motherly fashion ('He
       looked at me the way a mother looks at her favorite child' – 27:373).

400. Karpman, 1938, 24. Cf. Cain (1977, 154) on the 'extraordinary egotism' of Pozdnyshev, and Baumgart (1990, 213–14) on Pozdnyshev's narcissism and inability to love.
401. Contrary to what is suggested by N. K. Gei (1971), Pozdnyshev's intense jealousy does not indicate love. Pozdnyshev's jealousy is not of the benign, Proustian type (Swann actually loves Odette). Rather, it is utterly narcissistic and murderous.
402. Schefski, 1989, 20. See also Tat'iana Kuzminskaia's psychoanalytically insightful remarks on Tolstoy's bouts of jealousy (1986, 278–9).
403. Schefski, 1989, 25.
404. 27:366.
405. 27:315. In this draft the wife as well as the husband has attacks of jealousy.
406. Kon, 1995, 31.
407. 27:38–9; Tolstoy, 1983, 66.
408. Asquith, 1961, 143.
409. 50:204.
410. 27:363.
411. 27:410–11.
412. 27:41; Tolstoy, 1983, 68.
413. 27:41; Tolstoy, 1983, 69–70.
414. Tolstoy's friend Chertkov observed that Pozdnyshev was being a 'male egoist' in this portion of the novella (Gudzii, 1936, 68, n. 1). Robert Ingersoll observes that, in Pozdnyshev, 'Count Tolstoi gives us the feelings of a father incapable of natural affection; of one who hates to have his children sick because the orderly course of his wretched life is disturbed' (1890, 293).
415. 27:41; Tolstoy, 1983, 70.
416. 27:43; Tolstoy, 1983, 72.
417. From the eighth (lithographed) version, 27:320.
418. On somewhat different grounds, psychologist Hildegard Baumgart also recognizes that Pozdnyshev's wife represents his mother for him: 'The desperate desire for an asexual relationship between two people with concurrent total fulfillment of one's needs is basically what is behind this [revulsion against sexuality]. It is the desire for a relationship like that between mother and child in earliest childhood.' (Baumgart 1990, 211).
419. Rancour-Laferriere, 1993a, 54–71.
420. For a review of some of the psychoanalytic literature on this topic from a semiotic perspective, see: Rancour-Laferriere, 1985, 136ff.
421. As quoted in Rancour-Laferriere, 1993a, 54. Cf. Armstrong (1988, 31 ff.) on Kitty as replacement for Levin's lost mother in *Anna Karenina*.
422. Shklovskii, 1963, 7; cf. Il'ia Tolstoi, 1914, 26.
423. Gusev, 1973, 329.
424. 48:56.
425. S. L. Tolstoi, 1956, 13, as translated by Smoluchowski, 1988, 61.
426. See: Sergei L'vovich Tolstoi, 1956, 13; Il'ia L'vovich Tolstoi, 1914, 250; Sergei Mikhailovich Tolstoi, 1994, 70; Gol'denveizer, 1959, 387. Another example: on 28 Aug. 1884 he writes in his diary that 'I am 2 x 28 years old'

(49:119). Tolstoy used to tell his wife that he expected to die in 1882 (Rusanov and Rusanov, 1972, 56), i.e., a year in which the last two digits are the reverse of 28. For more examples, see: Al'tman, 1966, 146–8.

427. Cf. Stern, 1975 (186) who refers to Sonia as a 'stand-in' for Tolstoy's mother, but does not offer much concrete evidence.

428. 59:160, as translated by Christian, 1978, vol. I, 24. Cf. I. L. Tolstoi, 1914, 196.

429. 64:240.

430. 48:111. Tolstoy employs very unusual Russian phrasing (probably Yasnaya Polyana peasant dialect) to describe what happens to the mother's breasts when her child is hungry: *u materi prigrublo moloko*, which might be translated as 'mother's milk started to curdle', or more loosely, 'mother's nipples became erect'. Thanks to Yuri Druzhnikov for help with the Russian here.

431. Christian, 1969, 231; Kopper, 1989, 171.

432. See: Gustafson, 1986, 14–15; Rancour-Laferriere, 1993a, 64–7; McLean, 1994b. Compare Jeffrey Berman's interesting analysis of the narrative evasiveness about dead mothers in Emily Brontë's *Wuthering Heights* (Berman, 1990, 86; Brontë lost her mother at the age of three).

433. See: 27:376, 395; 299.

434. See: Rancour-Laferriere, 1993a, 70, n. 26; McLean, 1994b, 226.

435. 27:41; Tolstoy, 1983, 69.

436. The phrase *egoizm materi* also comes up in the diary and in a notebook entry in July of 1889 (50:102, 212).

437. 27:38; Tolstoy, 1983, 65; cf. 27:400.

438. 27:39; Tolstoy, 1983, 66.

439. 27:40; Tolstoy, 1983, 67–8. Cf. 27:400.

440. Costlow, 1983, 228–9; cf. Pearson, 1984 (17–18) on breast-feeding in this novel. Costlow also points out Tolstoy's condemnation of wet nursing in his 1863 play *The Infected Family*.

441. Rancour-Laferriere, 1993a, 55–8, 233.

442. 32:99, as translated in Tolstoy, 1966, 137.

443. 35:105, as translated in Tolstoy, 1977, 255.

444. 25:121, as translated in Tolstoy, 1993, 139. One work of fiction which Tolstoy planned, but never wrote, was going to deal with a clever wet nurse who manages to substitute her own child for the child she is supposed to wet-nurse for a foundling hospital. The woman even manages to keep her child from the people who think they are the real parents and who try to get the child back from the foundling hospital (Molchanov, 1978 [1890], vol. I, 472).

445. 23:470, emphasis added.

446. Gusev, 1954, 62; cf. A. S. Petrovskii's commentary to the Jubilee edition, 48:433. M. P. Kuleshov (1908, sect. 3, p. 5) gives 'Evdokiia' as the name of the wet-nurse, but his book (or rather, collection of pamphlets) is riddled with factual errors, e.g., Tolstoi's mother is 'Mar'ia Ivanovna', Tolstoi is '3½ years old' when his mother dies, etc.

447. 4:155.

448. As translated by Costlow, 1993, 230–31.

449. There is a remote possibility that this Annushka is Avdot'ia Ziabreva, who might have changed her name to the more respectable Anna upon changing her social station (thanks to Yuri Druzhnikov for this suggestion).
450. 36:66–7.
451. See, for example: S. L. Tolstoi, 1928a, 63; Dunn, 1974, 387; Wachtel, 1990, 105. Professor David L. Ransel of Indiana University writes: 'The few cases of family life among the nobility and the merchant class in Russia that I have looked at closely indicate rather strongly that the mothers were not breastfeeding the children . . .' (letter to the author of 20 February 1995).
452. Including, for example: Costlow, 1993, 228; Simmons, 1946, 253–4, 428–9; Zhdanov, 1993, 75, 89, 200–1; Crankshaw, 1974, 203; Troyat, 1967, 280–81; Smoluchowski, 1988, 63–5; Shirer, 1994, 29–30, 112–15.
453. Tolstaia, 1978a, vol. I, 60; cf. Tolstaia, 1978c, 41.
454. Kuzminskaia, 1986, 230–31.
455. 48:57.
456. 48:57.
457. Kuzminskaia, 1986, 232.
458. Kuzminskaia, 1986, 271 (cf. also 244, 249). See also 86:229, where Tolstoy says his first child was bottle-fed.
459. Quoted by Gusev, 1957, 630.
460. Tolstaia, 1978a, vol. I, 78.
461. As quoted by Zhdanov, 1993 (1928), 75.
462. 27:322 (i.e., the eighth, lithographed version).
463. See Tolstoy's letter to his sister-in-law dated 3 March 1871 (61:250).
464. See, for example: Sergei Mikhailovich Tolstoi, 1994, 224.
465. As quoted by the daughter in question, Aleksandra Tolstaia (1989 [1953], 252).
466. I. L. Tolstoi, 1914, 111; I. L. Tolstoi, 1969, 128.
467. As quoted by Zhdanov, 1993, 200.
468. Zhdanov, 1993, 200.
469. 84:46.
470. 49:47, 49, 50.
471. 49:41, 49, 50, 51.
472. Ziabrev, 1915 (no. 9–10), columns 360–61.
473. 86:108.
474. 86:110. See also Opul'skaia, 1979, 127–9.
475. There were continuing difficulties in feeding the Chertkovs' sick child, as can be seen in Tolstoy's expressions of concern in his letters to the Chertkovs (86:123; 127; 130–31). Apparently the wet nurse could not produce enough milk for both infants, and the Chertkov infant was very colicky, requiring enemas. At one point Tolstoy (not surprisingly) declared that he was 'not a believer in . . . someone else's milk', and simply advised the Chertkovs to 'release their sins, that is, do without a wet nurse and without enemas' (86:130–31). Chertkov was offended at this, and Tolstoy apologized in his next letter (86:132–3), and even found another wet nurse for him (86:136).

What eventually became of the original wet nurse and her child is unknown. The Chertkovs' own child eventually died of dysentery in the summer of 1889. In response Tolstoy wrote the Chertkovs a letter recommending that they try to view the event as a blessing, and advising them to bear their cross (86:246–7).

When another child was born to the Chertkovs in 1889, Tolstoy followed developments in its feeding with interest and concern (86:229, 231–2; 234; 236).

476.   86:112; cf. Opul'skaia, 1979, 128.
477.   Ransel, 1988, 271.
478.   The booklet in question is listed in my bibliography as Pokrovskii, 1890. I have not been able to lay hands on this very rare work, and I go on the authority of the Jubilee Edition (27:689) that it was published in 1890, although some sources list 1889. See the commentary by N. N. Gusev and V. D. Pestova in the Jubilee edition (27:680–89) for a detailed account of Tolstoy's involvement in the writing of Pokrovskii's booklet.
479.   27:265–6. Other insertions and revisions by Tolstoy are quoted by the editors of the Jubilee Edition (27:680–89).
480.   24:219.
481.   27:681.
482.   27:265. The wording is exclusively Tolstoy's beginning 'What is it that destroys these 20 . . . ?'
483.   27:35.
484.   27:399.
485.   27:687. I assume Pokrovskii must have agreed with this restriction on sexual intercourse, or else he would not have permitted Tolstoy to insert it into his book.
486.   27:688.
487.   27:687, emphasis added.
488.   27:38; Tolstoy, 1983, 65.
489.   86:229. By mid-May Tolstoy reports to Biriukov that the Chertkovs are doing without a wet-nurse (64:256).
490.   Ernest J. Simmons suggests that Tolstoy's disapproval of wet nursing may have a literary source: 'Tolstoy had obstinate and unreasonable ideas on this score, perhaps long ago suggested to him by his reading of Rousseau' (Simmons, 1946, 254; see also Troyat, 1967, 280; Courcel, 1988, 85). What these authors have in mind, of course, is the famous opening of *Émile* (Rousseau, 1993 [1762], 12–15) where Rousseau states that it is a mother's 'first duty' to nurse her own child. The fact that Pierre Bezukhov mentions this passage in Rousseau to Natasha in the first epilogue of *War and Peace* indicates that Tolstoy had indeed read and thought about the passage. Yet the intense emotion Tolstoy felt about breast feeding and wet nursing can hardly be explained as a mere imitation of Rousseau's view. Indeed the coincidence of Tolstoy's view with Rousseau's probably has more to do with the fact that both authors were wet-nursed in infancy, and both lost their mothers early (Rousseau's mother died giving birth to him).

Here it may be noted that Tolstoy's mother had herself read *Émile* (Molostvov and Sergeenko, 1909, 22) – and obviously failed to follow Rousseau's advice.

Another French author who deals with the theme of breast-feeding, and toward whom Tolstoy's feelings were considerably more ambivalent, is Guy de Maupassant. In de Maupassant's story 'Idylle' (1884), for example, a hungry young worker gladly sucks milk from the breasts of a wet-nurse who hasn't given milk in a long time. Both are gratified by this act, which takes place on a moving train (de Maupassant, 1974–79, vol. I, 1193–7). One can imagine how much Tolstoy would have disapproved of this lovely little story for both its latent eroticism and its author's failure to condemn the practice of wet-nursing. On Tolstoy's tendency to disapprove of the sexual aspect of de Maupassant, see his 'Introduction to the Works of Guy de Maupassant', written in 1893–94 (30:3–24).

491. Cf. Osipov's comparison of sensuality and nourishment in Tolstoy's description of Pozdnyshev (Ossipow, 1923, 136).
492. 27:37.
493. 27:28; Tolstoy, 1983, 52–3.
494. 27:569, and 50:59, emphasis added.
495. Quoted from manuscript no. 6 by Gudzii in 27:579.
496. 50:123.
497. 50:63.
498. 27:404–5.
499. 27:412.
500. 27:23; Tolstoy, 1983, 46.
501. 27:303. See also Goscilo-Kostin (1984, 493) on the irrationality of Pozdnyshev's connection of sexual desire to excessive eating.
502. 27:82; Tolstoy, 1983, 271.
503. As translated from 12:268 by LeBlanc, 1993, 9.
504. LeBlanc, 1993, 10, 12. See also Goscilo-Kostin 1984 on the association of alimentary and sexual appetites in Tolstoy's works.
505. Translated from 29:73–4 by LeBlanc, 1993, 22.
506. LeBlanc, 1995, p. 5 (ms.). Other useful studies of Tolstoy's attitude toward food include: Christian, 1993; Porudominskii, 1992.
507. See: Friedman, 1975, 400. My interpretation of Tolstoy's vegetarianism is derived from Friedman's essay – the only psychoanalytic study of vegetarianism that I have been able to find.
508. 64:168.
509. 64:260.
510. 64:237.
511. Opul'skaia, 1979, 130.
512. As quoted by Opul'skaia, 1979, 130, italics added.
513. Gor'kii, 1949–55, vol. 14, 298.
514. 27:44; Tolstoy, 1983, 74.
515. Aleksandra Tolstaia, 1989 (1953), 283.
516. Pigott, 1992, 58.
517. 27:381, emphasis added. Cf. 27:324. Cf. also 27:413, where the mouth of the sobbing Pozdnyshev extends across the entire width of his face.

518.   50:102.
519.   Apparently childbirth was avoided by the wife's insistence on
         sexual abstinence during times when she might conceive. Once,
         when she suddenly agrees to have sex at the wrong time, Pozdnyshev
         suspects she is 'Uriah's wife', that is, is seeking to cover over the
         results of her affair with Trukhachevsky (27:58; Tolstoy, 1983, 92; cf.
         27:404, 405).
520.   27:385.
521.   27:327. The figure of Trukhachevsky may be derived from Ippolit
         Nagornov, a distant relative of Tolstoy's and an excellent violinist. See
         the commentary by Gudzii (27:568), based in part on the unpublished
         autobiography of Tolstoy's wife; also I. L. Tolstoi, 1969, 79.
522.   27:382. On Tolstoy's ambivalence toward the Jews, sometimes out-
         right anti-Semitism, see: Schefski, 1982. See also Golstein (1996, 459),
         who goes so far as to assert that Tolstoy is making a scapegoat of Jews
         in the novella.
523.   27:53; Tolstoy, 1983, 85.
524.   27:49; Tolstoy, 1983, 80.
525.   Velikovsky, 1937; Karpman, 1938; *SE* XVIII, 223–32. Cf. also:
         Kiell, 1976, 264–6; Baumgart, 1990 (1985), 211; and Lloyd, 1995,
         99–100. Perhaps the image of the 'Hottentot' is an unconscious
         reminiscence of the explicitly homosexual 'Moor' in Jean-Jacques
         Rousseau's *Confessions* (1954 [1765], 71–3), a work Tolstoy ad-
         mired.
526.   Velikovsky, 1937, 21. Cf. Schefski, 1989 (26) who says that Pozdnyshev
         'perversely spurred his wife on to unfaithfulness', but does not discuss
         what the motive might be. Mondry (1988, 172) also observes that
         'Pozdnyshev deliberately manipulated his wife into playing "The
         Kreutzer Sonata" with his rival', and argues that the subsequent mur-
         der was 'an attempt at self-purification'.
527.   Karpman, 1938, 26.
528.   27:49; Tolstoy, 1983, 80, 81.
529.   27:62; Tolstoy, 1983, 97.
530.   27:28; Tolstoy, 1983, 52.
531.   27:57; Tolstoy, 1983, 91.
532.   48:8. An affair between the married Vasilii Perfil'ev (a distant cousin of
         Tolstoy's) and the unmarried pianist Ekaterina Chikhacheva (later
         Sytina) is corroborated by Sytina, 1939 (406).
533.   27:64; Tolstoy, 1983, 100.
534.   For more on homosexuality in Tolstoy's life and works, see: Karlinsky,
         1976; Rancour-Laferriere, 1993a, 139–54; Shirer, 1994, 293ff.; Wilson,
         1988, 86–91; Fodor, 1989, 146–8; Rothstein, 1984, 225–6. Perhaps the
         most direct indication of Tolstoy's homosexual interests is the famous
         diary entry of 29 November 1851: 'I have never been in love with
         women'; 'I have often fallen in love with men [*V muzhchin ia ochen'
         chasto vliublialsia*]. . .'. Here Tolstoy proceeds to list some nine men
         whom he had 'loved' in his adolescence. Of these, he says that he con-
         tinues to love only Dmitrii Alekseevich D'iakov, and also says of
         D'iakov:

. . . I will never forget the night when, wrapped up underneath a travelling rug, we were coming from P. and I felt like kissing him and crying. There was even a voluptuousness to this feeling, but I can't figure out why this came about, because, as I was saying, my imagination never conjured up lubricious pictures, on the contrary, I have a terrible revulsion. (46:238)

Tolstoy also says in the same entry: 'I used to fall in love with men before I had any idea of the existence of *pederasty*; but even after I found out about it, the thought of the possibility of intercourse never entered my head.'

In the literary works there are quite a few passages which deal with homosexuality. Here I will just mention one which previous scholars have missed. The narrator of 'Posthumous Notes of Elder Fedor Kuzmich' (1905) describes getting into bed with his brother as a child and playing a 'jolly game' of smacking their naked bodies against each other (*shlepat' drug druga po golomu telu* – 36:73).

535. Sergei Tolstoi, 1928b, 299.
536. Gol'denveizer, 1959, 380.
537. Bers, 1978 (1894), vol. 1, 186.
538. For example, L. L. Tolstoi, 1923, 10; S. L. Tolstoi, 1928b, 305.
539. Alekseev, 1978 (1948), vol. I, 258.
540. L. L. Tolstoi, 1923, 59.
541. Alexandra Tolstoy, 1958, 258.
542. See: Emerson, 1996.
543. Gusev, 1986, 168.
544. Bers, 1978 (1894), vol. 1, 186.
545. Sergei Tolstoi, 1928b, 309. Cf. Paliukh and Prokhorova, 1977, 133.
546. Paliukh and Prokhorova, 1977, 124–5.
547. Compare Gudzii's commentary (27:568) with Tolstaia, 1978c (69) and Opul'skaia, 1979 (119–21).
548. L. L. Tolstoi, 1923, 70–71.
549. 27:61, 62; Tolstoy, 1983, 96, 97–8.
550. 27:333; cf. Beck, 1898, 21.
551. Rolland, 1911, 182; Gei, 1971, 129; Green, 1967, 22; Isenberg,1993, 99–101; Emerson, 1996, 442.
552. Gor'kii, 1949–55, vol. 14, 276.
553. Thus right before describing the experience Pozdnyshev says that the opening presto 'had a horrible effect' on him, that it 'could not but be harmful' (27:62). In the third draft Pozdnyshev's ambivalence is quite explicit: 'I used to love music terribly. Now I hate it, not because it is connected with him [Trukhachevskii], but because it is both a delight and an abomination [*i prelest' i merzost'*]' (27:382–3).

On Tolstoy's own ambivalence toward the music of Beethoven, see: Rischin, 1989. Son Sergei L'vovich reports that Tolstoy initially perceived 'sensuality' in the opening presto of Beethoven's *Kreutzer Sonata*, but then changed his mind and said that one could not specify the feeling elicited by the work because music in general cannot elicit any specific, nameable feeling (S. L. Tolstoi, 1928b, 309; Paliukh and Prokhorova, 1977, 135).

Another indicator of Tolstoy's ambivalence is the very title of the work. It is curious that precisely the Beethoven piece which ultimately provokes positive feelings toward the wife should supply the title to a work about 'The Man Who Killed His Wife' (Tolstoy's original title). With good reason Romain Rolland says that the title is 'erroneous' in his cogent discussion of the effect of music on Tolstoy (Rolland, 1911, 178–83).

Marie Sémon views *The Kreutzer Sonata* as a highly conflicted product of Tolstoy's artistic imagination, as 'un oeuvre anti-musicale' which nonetheless, she believes, has its own musical rhythms, melodic lines, and other musical properties (1992; others who have drawn – sometimes elaborate – comparisons between musical structures and the structure of Tolstoy's novella include: De Roeck, 1992; Green, 1967; Eguchi, 1996; Emerson, 1996; Papazian, 1996).

554. Alekseev, 1978 (1948), vol. I, 257.
555. Quoted by Gusev, 1986, 169.
556. Gusev, 1973, 150.
557. Sergeenko, 1939, 536.
558. Gusev, 1986, 175.
559. 27:62; Tolstoy, 1983, 98.
560. 1:31, as translated in Tolstoy, 1964, 40. On the autobiographical bases of Tolstoy's *Childhood*, see: Williams, 1995, 43–9.
561. Moisei Al'tman also notes this remarkable similarity between *Childhood* and *The Kreutzer Sonata*, although not from a psychoanalytic perspective (1966, 70). Cf. also Knapp (1991, 34).
562. 46:239.
563. Kohut, 1957, 406, 407.
564. Mahler, 1994 (1979), vol. 2, 153.
565. Rischin, 1989, 22.
566. Pigott, 1992, 58.
567. 27:62; Tolstoy, 1983, 97.
568. Kohut and Levarie in Kohut, 1978, 143. Compare a diary entry from September of 1892: 'I was speaking about music. Again I say that this enjoyment is only of a slightly higher sort than eating' (52:71).

Psychoanalyst L. Bryce Boyer, describing his interaction with a musically talented patient, found that 'the analysand was unable to achieve psychological separation from his mother and . . . music served predominately the function of retaining a life-supporting connexion with her' (Boyer, 1992, 66).
569. S. L. Tolstoi (1928a, 139; cf. 136). See also S. L. Tolstoi (1928b, 300).
570. Sergeenko, 1939, 528.
571. 56:133.
572. 56:133.
573. Karpman, 1938, 32.
574. 27:50; Tolstoy, 1983, 82.
575. In the third draft Pozdnyshev says to himself: '*akh kaby ona umerla!*' (27:380).

576. 27:59; Tolstoy, 1983, 93.
577. Isenberg, 1993, 105–6. Cf. Rancour-Laferriere, 1993, 79–81.
578. Kuzminskaia, 1986, 448–9.
579. Cf. Al'tman, 1966, 17; Baehr, 1976, 42.
580. Isenberg, 1993, 98–9.
581. 27:50; Tolstoy, 1983, 81.
582. 27:365.
583. 27:64; Tolstoy, 1983, 100.
584. 27:66; Tolstoy, 1983, 103.
585. 27:368. Tolstoy crossed out a passage of the seventh draft which made it clear that the wife was actually unfaithful (see Gudzii's commentary, 27:581). In the eighth and ninth (final) drafts it cannot be shown that the wife was unfaithful.
586. Apart from the wife's explicit sexual infidelity in the first draft, the wife deals a different kind of narcissistic blow to the husband in the third draft: she makes him feel ashamed of the emptiness of his professional activities and his failure to be the social activist he appeared to be before they married (27:286–8).
587. Kohut, 1972; 1977, 116.
588. Baumgart, 1990 (1985), 215.
589. Cf. Golstein, 1996, 460, n. 1.
590. 27:70; Tolstoy, 1983, 109.
591. 27:67; Tolstoy, 1983, 104.
592. Golstein, 1996, 460.
593. Cf. Botkin, 1893, 14. In the first draft there is a three-year-old girl with Pozdnyshev on the train, and he is looking after her 'like a nurse or a mother' (27:353). The Pozdnyshev of the final version would be incapable of such child care.
594. 27:72; Tolstoy, 1983, 111.
595. 27:72–3; Tolstoy, 1983, 111, 113.
596. 27:361.
597. 27:392; cf. 409, n. 1.
598. 27:409.
599. 7:149.
600. 27:361.
601. 27:365.
602. 27:368; cf. 27:405.
603. Klein, 1977 (1930), 219.
604. Klein, 1977 (1937), 308 (italics in the original).
605. 27:72; Tolstoy, 1983, 111 (emphasis added).
606. 27:412.
607. In the final version Pozdnyshev says his wife first follows the doctor's orders not to breast-feed her first child (27:39), but then says she breast-fed her children (27:40). In a variant the wife definitely hires a wet nurse (27:401).
608. 27:295.
609. 27:71; Tolstoy, 1983, 109.
610. 27:364.
611. Cf. Pigott, 1992, 59.

612. 27:72.
613. Klein, 1977 (1933), 253.
614. See: ANSSSR, 1950–65, vol. 10, 1645.
615. 27:362.
616. ANSSSR, 1950–65, vol. 10, 509.
617. 27:367.
618. 27:368.
619. With good reason psychoanalyst Ben Karpman suggests that Pozdnyshev '... may have experienced in his early life some highly traumatic experiences that have to do with [the] breast, feeding, weaning...' (1938, 35–6). Unfortunately, Karpman does not elaborate on the pre-Oedipal aspects of this suggestion, and he mistakenly (I believe) explains Pozdnyshev's aversion to sexuality in Oedipal terms (p. 38).

   Alison Sinclair, in her Kleinian reading of the novella, says that Pozdnyshev 'presents a classic example of the paranoid-schizoid position' (1993, 228). I agree that Pozdnyshev makes numerous paranoid assertions in the course of his monologue, but I do not think he undergoes the internal splittings which the Kleinian infant supposedly experiences in the pre-Oedipal paranoid-schizoid position. Pozdnyshev rejects sexuality, but he does not project it outward so completely as to disown it. On the contrary, he keeps castigating himself for his own sexuality, and he keeps assuming narcissistically that other people are as bad as he is. Similarly he bears his rage and other bad feelings within, rather than projecting them outward. When he finally explodes in murderous rage, he does not falsely imagine that others are enraged at him.

620. 27:34; Tolstoy, 1983, 60.
621. *SE* XV, 154. See also Møller (1988, 13) who reads the knife as phallic without referring to Freud, as do Jackson (1978, 289), Burgin (1987, 32), and Isenberg (1993, 92).
622. Jackson, 1978, 289.
623. Klein, 1977 (1931), 243–4.
624. Klein, 1977 (1937), 315.
625. 27:365.
626. 27:366.
627. 27:401.
628. 27:404.
629. 27:45; Tolstoy, 1983, 74. The translation is slightly modified.
630. Dworkin, 1987, 8.
631. Dworkin, 1987, 143.
632. 27:375; cf. p. 379, where love and hatred are called 'two sides of the same feeling' (*tozhe samoe chuvstvo, tol'ko s raznykh kontsov*).
633. For example: Merezhkovskii, 1995 (1900), 94; Wasiolek, 1978,138; Zholkovsky, 1994b, 82.
634. 18:157–8.
635. Zholkovsky, 1994b, 77.
636. 36:62.
637. 27:87; Tolstoy, 1983, 276.

638. 50:176; cf. 27:626.
639. See: Kutepov, 1900; Steeves, 1983; Etkind, 1995, esp. 136.
640. 86:140.
641. As translated by Møller, 1988, 158.
642. Møller, 1988, 157.
643. As quoted by Aldanov, 1969, 82–3.
644. de Courcel, 1988, 207, emphasis added; Charles Isenberg speaks of the 'symbolic self-castration' suggested by the story (1993, 82). Cf also the symbolic self-castration in *Father Sergius*: Benson (1973, 118) says Sergius cuts off 'the symbolically offending organ, his finger'; Hubbs (1988, 232) refers to Sergius's 'symbolic castration'; Zholkovsky (1994b, 82) speaks of the self-mutilation in that work as 'symbolizing self-castration.'
645. 50:108–9. Without utilizing the term masochism, Timkovskii (1913, 124) demonstrates an understanding of this essential contradiction in Tolstoy's philosophy, that is, Tolstoy's ability to feel joyful about the bad things which happen to him.
646. 64:227.
647. 86:253. Tolstoy continued to think this way until the end of his life. For example, in 1907 he expressed his delight at receiving numerous letters from various people accusing him of hypocrisy (propagandizing poverty but living on a rich estate): 'It's so nice that there's a reason for people to scold me.' Any criticism he regarded as 'a steambath for the soul' (*bania dlia dushi*). See: Gusev, 1973 (1911), 78–9.
648. 50:106, 217. These statements are in line with Tolstoy's overall view of family life in the 1880s as a restraining collar (*khomut*) or harness (*zapriazhka*) that one must bear. See: Zhdanov, 1968, 62–3; cf. Gustafson, 1983, 436.
649. Greenwood, 1975, 140.
650. Novikov, 1994, 328.
651. I. L. Tolstoi, 1969, 184.
652. Makovitskii, 1928, 245.
653. See, for example: Zhdanov, 1993 (1928), 238–54; Simmons, 1946, 553–70.
    In early variants of *The Kreutzer Sonata* Tolstoy raises the possibility of a husband tolerating his wife's infidelity. For example, in a crossed-out section of one variant Pozdnyshev says of an unfaithful wife: 'And then I would give her away for her happiness, and I myself would not marry. And I would live for the sake of her happiness, nearby' (27:359). This idea disappears completely by the final version, however. Similarly, in *Anna Karenina* Aleksei Karenin forgives his wife for her infidelity only when he thinks she is dying, and becomes very hostile toward her again when she recovers, that is, when it again becomes possible for her to cuckold him (see: Rancour Laferriere, 1993b, 36, and Thomas Winner's introduction to Aldanov, 1969, viii).
654. 50:129–30. There are some traces of this holy foolishness in the diaries for late 1888–early 1889 as well. See: Opul'skaia, 1979, 148–9.
655. 50:189. Tolstoy also admits in his November reply to Strakhov's criticism of the work that he is dissatisfied with it (64:334).

656. 27:66; Tolstoy, 1983, 103. Baumgart (1990 [1985], 212) has also noted the masochistic aspect of this passage.
657. 27:411.
658. In Tolstoi, 1991, 11.
659. 50:116.
660. 86:222. The phrase inserted by Tolstoy, '*dobryi molodets*', is an expression customarily utilized to glorify epic folk heroes.
661. See Rancour-Laferriere, 1995 (37, 62, 68–9) on masochistic pride.
662. Bergler, 1949, 5.
663. Novick and Novick, 1987, 360.
664. For an overview, see: Rancour-Laferriere, 1995, ch. 5.
665. See: Rancour-Laferriere, 1995, 116–21.
666. 23:469–70, with assistance from the translation by Gustafson, 1986, 20.
667. Cf. Blanchard, 1984, 32, for some speculations on the nature of this particular early memory.
668. See: Rancour-Laferriere, 1995, 69–77.
669. 50:113.
670. An entry from Sonia's diary: '... Masha, generally speaking, is a cross sent to me by God. Apart from torment, from the day of her birth she has given me nothing' (Tolstaia, 1978a, vol. I, 438). Cf. also Sergei Mikhailovich Tolstoy, 1994, 157 ff.
671. See daughter Tat'iana's diaries for the late 1880s (Sukhotina-Tolstaia, 1987). As for Sonia, she resisted her husband's masochistic goals. For example, on 25 November he writes in his diary that 'Sonia gets mad at me because I do not take care of my health, and she hates me. She does the same thing with the children.' In his opinion, Sonia is supposed to go along with his masochism to the extent that she not complain even when he harms himself: 'the sign of true, i.e., self-sacrificial love is when a person whom I love and for whom I labor does not accept my labors, despises them, and nonetheless I am unable to be angry at him and do not value my labor.' This may indeed be the kind of love Tolstoy had for the peasants he previously attempted to emancipate (they turned him down), or the intelligentsia he tried to educate (they largely rejected him) – but it was not the kind of love a normal, loving wife expresses for her ill husband. She had every reason to be angry at him for punishing himself with his vegetarianism, his sawing wood with the peasants, his hard work in the fields, his psychosomatic symptoms. Sonia was incapable of mirroring Tolstoy the way Masha mirrored him, or the way Tanya tried to mirror him. In fact, however, she behaved rather masochistically herself in accepting some of his sadistic treatment of her.
672. Sergei Mikhailovich Tolstoy, 1994 (1989), 172, 159; cf. I. L. Tolstoi, 1969, 128.
673. 64:213. See also: 64:215, 217. For a long time the intrusive Tolstoy managed to prevent both his daughters Masha and Tanya from getting married (see especially S. M. Tolstoi, 1994, 89–102;160–68). As for Sasha, she never married, possibly because of a homosexual orientation. Tolstoy also tended to interfere in the love life of his sister-in-law Tat'iana (Kuzminskaia, 1986).

When Sonia started expressing her own vehement disapproval of Masha getting married to Biriukov, Tolstoy seemed to move over to the side of the young people (e.g., 64:258–9; 261; 268), or at least to remain neutral (64:309). Basically, however, he did not want Masha or his other daughters ever to get married. Tolstoy also tried to interfere with the sexual lives of his sons. There is much room for further psychoanalytic study here.

674. 50:74; 64:261, 299, 182. According to Tolstoy's son Ilya, Masha was the only person in the family who dared express real tenderness for Tolstoy (she would stroke his hand, caress him, say tender things to him, etc.) – and vice-versa, she was the only one he permitted himself to be tender with: 'It was as if he became another person with her' (1914, 244). See also Aleksandra Tolstaia (1989 [1953], 275–6, 292–3), Sergei Mikhailovich Tolstoi (1994, 157–72), and Khrisanf Abrikosov (1928, 268) on Tolstoy's special attachment to Masha.

675. 50:123, 91.

676. Tolstoy's mother, unlike Tolstoy, did not advocate absolute chastity, however, so identification with the lost mother does not have much explanatory value in the sexual realm. It may have some value elsewhere, though (see below).

677. Romashkevich, 1994. In this connection it is interesting to note that, in Tolstoy's play *The Power of Darkness* (1886), the character Nikita threatens to kill his mother Matrena right after he has killed his illegitimate infant (26:211).

678. 48:111, emphasis added.

679. Cf. Pigott (1992, 60), who compares the description of the waxen corpse in *The Kreutzer Sonata* with the description of the dead mother in *Childhood*.

680. Cf. Pigott (1992, 57), who suggests that Pozdnyshev's periodic rages against his wife reflect Tolstoy's lingering hostility toward his dead mother. Cf. Also Golstein (1996, 460), who says that Pozdnyshev's dying wife is 'reminiscent of a mother giving birth', and that 'the attack on sex and its evil implications is intricately connected with the attack on motherhood'.

681. Gusev, 1954, 58–9.

682. Gusev, 1954, 59.

683. In *Resurrection* the mother of Katiusha Maslova gives birth to *five* children, allowing each one to starve to death in infancy (i.e., not breastfeeding any of the five – much as Tolstoy's mother had not breast-fed any of her five children). Katiusha, the sixth, is by chance saved by a gentry woman.

684. This name is crossed out and replaced by Vasia (27:415, n. 3). Tolstoy writes either 'Nikolen'ka' or 'Nikolin'ka' to refer to his eldest brother, sometimes using both spellings on the same page (e.g., 34:387).

685. 27:413; Zhdanov, 1968, 175.

686. Fasmer, 1986–87, vol. 3, 63.

687. 27:76–7; Tolstoy, 1983, 116–17.

688. 27:369, 406, 413.

689. Gusev, 1963, 27.

690. Anderson *et al.*, 1994, 1302.
691. 61:250.
692. 61:251.
693. As quoted in Gusev, 1963, 26. Cf. Sergei Mkhailovich Tolstoi, 1994, 157–8.
694. 49:97–8. Tolstoy is off by one year, for the events in question occurred 13, not 14 years earlier (cf. Zhdanov, 1993, 106).
695. Tolstaia, 1978, vol. I, 84.
696. 61:253; as modified from translation by Christian, 1978, vol. I, 233.
697. 61:255.
698. Gusev, 1963, 27. Gusev believes Sonia's refusal to have more children dates from even earlier, i.e., about November of 1870.
699. Pozdnyshev also states that his wife started using birth control after an illness, but it is not clear that the illness is connected with the birth of the fifth child. See: 27:46, 380; Tolstoy, 1983, 76.
700. See: 27:379–80.
701. Here are the birthdays of the six Tolstoy children alive in September of 1874: Sergei, 28 June 1863; Tat'iana, 4 October 1864; Il'ia, 22 May 1866; Lev, 20 May 1869; Maria, 12 February 1871; Nikolai, 22 April 1874. See: Gusev, 1958, 291, 300, 324, 362, 378, 420.
702. 27:415.
703. Klein, 1977 (1937), 308.
704. 27:77; Tolstoy, 1983, 117.
705. The topic of forgiveness for sin was enormously important for Tolstoy, perhaps because he had such difficulty forgiving his mother for what she did to him. *Anna Karenina* in particular manifests Tolstoy's preoccupation with forgiveness (or the lack thereof), as Dragan Kujundzic has shown in his interesting essay on 'the pardon-machine' in that novel (Kujundzic, 1993).
706. 27:77; Tolstoy, 1983, 118.
707. 27:338.
708. Aldanov, 1969 (1923), 51. See also Nikolai Strakhov's comments quoted by Gudzii (27:584), as well as Holthusen (1974, 197), Isenberg (1993, 91–2), and Bird (1996, 408).
709. Ovsianiko-Kulikovskii, 1905, 267–8.
710. Bird, 1996, 408.
711. Cf. Baumgart, 1990 (1985), 213.
712. 86:274.
713. See Gudzii's commentary (27:584).
714. Ovsianiko-Kulikovskii, 1905, 267.
715. I hesitate to apply *DSM* in a *systematic* fashion to Tolstoy, even when there are detailed reports of symptoms in his diary, because there are too many relevant cultural differences between late twentieth-century United States and late nineteenth-century Russia. Earlier in this book, for example, I pointed out that there is no accurate English equivalent for Russian *toska*, a word that keeps coming up in Tolstoy's diaries for 1889. Also, Tolstoy often reports on 'weakness' (*slabost'*) as one of his symptoms, but this is not a category in *DSM*, although *DSM IV* (324) mentions that it is a symptom sometimes reported from Chinese and other Asian cultures. Another example is

the high value placed on suffering (including mental suffering) in Russian culture, which I have documented extensively (see Rancour Laferriere, 1995). Yet terms like 'masochism' and 'self-destructive behavior' do not appear in the indexes of *DSM IV*, although they obviously apply to Tolstoy's mental problems in 1889. One of the appendices to *DSM IV* contains a 'Glossary of Culture-Bound Syndromes' (844–9), where Russia is not mentioned at all. The 1989 edition of *The International Classification of Diseases, 9th Revision, Clinical Modification* does list 'personality disorder, masochistic type' (category 301.89 in vol. I, 227, 1108).

716. All quotations from volume 50 of the Jubilee Edition.
717. 64:220; 258.
718. Cf. Schefski, 1978 (569): 'Tolstoi himself, though a man with a strong physical constitution, suffered from many nagging pains such as headaches, toothaches, rheumatism, and indigestion. He charted his medical problems in his diaries and letters. Indeed, one is struck by the almost too frequent admissions of poor health found therein.' I agree, except I would delete the word 'almost' from the last sentence.
719. 50:164.
720. 51:16, 17.
721. For example, 50:130, 164, 178; 51:17.
722. Christian (1985, 384) states that Tolstoy's expression *durno spat'* ('sleep badly') 'clearly seems to imply masturbation', while the more common *plokho spat'* (also translatable as 'sleep badly') does not have this sexual connotation. See also Smoluchowski, 1988, 164. Some scholars have mistakenly understood 'sleep badly' to refer to sexual intercourse with Sonia (Zhdanov, 1993, 205, 208; Simmons, 1946, 444).
723. See *The Confessions* (1954 [1781], 297, 549).
724. 50:223, 184, emphasis added.
725. Gudzii, 1936.
726. Gustafson, 1986, 428.
727. See Rothstein, 1984, who deals with selected characters in Tolstoy's fiction, but not with Tolstoy himself.
728. Ossipow, 1923, 12, 36. Cf. Osipov, 1928.
729. 50:87, 89.
730. For example, 64:277, 297.
731. 50:87–8; cf. some of Tolstoy's correspondence from this period, e.g. 64:287, 290. Cf. also Ossipow, 1923, 2.
732. For a similar denial made in 1906, see: Gustafson, 1986, 429. Cf. also Gusev, 1973 (1911), 91. William Blanchard discusses the tendency for feelings of humility to be associated with feelings of self-aggrandizement in Tolstoy (1984, 36–7).
733. 50:44. Cf. the diary entry for 13 June, where Tolstoy declares that he is composed of a body, reason, and God (50:95).
734. 86:253.
735. Spence, 1967, 82. Cf. also Berdiaev (1978 [1912]) on the absence of a need for the saving grace of God the Son in Tolstoy's theology. So often Tolstoy imagined that he *was* God the Son.

736.   86:173.
737.   On the Russian theological tradition of 'Godmanhood', see: Kozyrev,
        1995; Rancour-Laferriere, 1995, 228–30, 286–7. On the influence of
        the Russian sectarian 'God-humans' (*Bogocheloveki*) on Tolstoy, see:
        Prugavin, 1911, 161–76.
            Tolstoy's developing theology will eventually deepen the confu-
        sion between himself and his God. For example, Tolstoy will claim that
        he (and people generally) have free will, yet he will also claim that ev-
        erything that happens in the universe takes place only according to the
        will of God. The individual is at best 'free' to 'collaborate' (*sodeistvovat'*)
        with the will of God (see: Gustafson, 1986, 445). This logical absurdity
        is a true masochist's idea of freedom, and probably derives from simi-
        larly illogical notions of freedom propounded by the Slavophiles ear-
        lier in the nineteenth century (see: Rancour-Laferriere, 1995, 37–42).
738.   Spence, 1967, 100.
739.   Says his son: '*molilsia doma, kladia zemnye poklony*' (L. L. Tolstoi, 1923, p. 11).
740.   Spence, 1967, 101.
741.   See, for example: Berdiaev, 1978 (1912); Spence, 1967, 79–101;
        Gustafson, 1986, 53–109.
742.   I believe that a psychoanalytic study of Tolstoy's (pseudo-) theology
        might take its cue from Richard Gustafson's insight into the maternal
        nature of Tolstoy's God. To be without God, Gustafson says of Tolstoy,
        is to be 'orphaned'. Gustafson quotes a diary entry of 1894: 'You know
        God not so much by reason or even by the heart, but by the sense of
        total dependency on Him, like the feeling a nursing child has in his
        mother's arms.' Since, however, it is precisely this feeling Tolstoy did
        not know, he immediately adds a sort of disclaimer: 'He knows not
        who holds him, warms him, feeds him, but he does know that there is
        this someone and moreover that this someone loves him' (as trans-
        lated from 52:157 by Gustafson, 1986, 14; cf. Rancour-Laferriere,
        1993a, 221; 1994, 92). Gustafson comments: 'The loving, caring mother
        whom one does not know is the constant model for Tolstoy's God'
        (ibid). This statement, which seems oxymoronic on the surface, is
        nonetheless a true representation of how Tolstoy thought about God,
        for Tolstoy indeed never did 'know' the 'loving, caring mother' he
        wishes he had 'known'.
            On 8 April 1889 Tolstoy writes that Christ should be understood
        as 'God who was capable of being born only from God' (50:64) – with
        no apparent help from any particular female, such as Mary, or
        from the Jewish people. Such an idea has to be understood as a
        kind of couvade, or imitation-mothering. God the father is mother-
        ing God the son. 'I and the Father are one' then *means* 'I and the
        Mother are one.'
            In early June Tolstoy writes in his diary about loving God:

        I read the words: Love God with your whole heart . . . etc, you mar-
        vel at these words, relating them to the idea of God in the same book,
        you make no sense of them: it's impossible to love a punishing God etc.
        But the fact of the matter is that these words make sense for one who

has just elucidated God to oneself, having understood him from one-self [*iz sebia*], *they make sense to one who has still felt the umbilical cord connecting one to God.* (50:89, emphasis added).

Where there is an umbilicus there is a child still 'at one' with its mother, not its father. But who is the mother, and who is the child? It would seem that Tolstoy himself is the mother in this particular case, for he finds God within himself, tied to himself by means of the umbilicus (in a variant in another notebook the umbilicus connects Moses to the beloved God within him, so Tolstoy is identifying with the biblical prophet – 50:205).

Usually Tolstoy is a child rather than a parent with respect to his God, however. In his autobiographical novella *Childhood*, for example, little Nikolai Irten'ev's feelings about God clearly derive from his feelings about his mother: 'Repeating prayers which my childish lips had babbled for the first time in imitation of my mother, my love for her and my love for God somehow fused mysteriously into one feeling' (1:44. Benson [1973, 8] notices this 'identity of the image of mother with God' as well). Recall also the passage in the *Reminiscences* where Tolstoy reports that he prayed to his deceased mother's soul in times of trouble – as if she were God, the one to whom one would normally pray (cf. Posse [1918, 62], who refers to the *molitvennaia liubov' Tolstogo k svoei materi*).

Theological scholars today are paying increased attention to the feminine and maternal properties of God (eg. Joseph Sebastian's remarkable 1995 book *God as Feminine*). So also are contemporary object-relations psychoanalysts. Ana-Marie Rizzuto, in her pioneering 1979 book *The Birth of the Living God*, views an individual's private representation of God as a remnant of the manner in which the mother 'mirrored', that is, admired, accepted and recognized the individual in early (pre-Oedipal) development. At that stage the distinction between the self and surrounding objects (especially the maternal object) is not clear, and any subsequent representation of God may consist of elements of both self and object, that is, may be a Kohutian 'selfobject', may retain traces of the Mahlerian 'symbiosis' with the mother (cf. Tolstoy's fondness for the phrase 'I and the Father are one', which really means 'I and the Mother are one'). Or, to use Winnicottian terminology, God may be a 'transitional object', that is, a special kind of illusory object jointly created by child and mother to assist the child in separating from the mother, such as a security blanket, teddy bear, or other toy. There is much potential here for psychoanalyzing Tolstoy's thinking about God from the perspective of contemporary object-relations theory. On recent object-relations theories of God, see: Rizzuto, 1979; Jones, 1991. To use Nikolai Osipov's more old-fashioned Freudian terminology, Tolstoy's view of God reflects the lack of a difference between 'Ichlibido' and 'Objektlibido' directed toward the mother (Ossipow, 1923, 170).

743.   50:141.

744. Quoted by Gusev, 1954, 94; cf. 23:487.
745. For example, A. A. Tolstaia (1978, 91) refers to *'nekrasivoe ego litso'*, G. A. Rusanov says *'litso ego nekrasivo'* (Rusanov & Rusanov, 1972, 23). Cf. Gusev (1957, 570–71).
746. For example, 46:118, 169. See also: Zhdanov, 1993, 25; Kuzminskaia, 1986, 138.
747. For an account of this prenuptial episode, see: Kuzminskaia, 1986, 147–8. See also Rothstein, 1984 (166) on Levin's sense of worthlessness. On Tolstoy's own 'obsession he had of being unacceptable to the other sex', see: Mirsky, 1989 (1929), 309.
748. Tolstaia, 1978a, vol. 1, 494.
749. 48:41; Gusev, 1957, 573; 48:46; Tolstaia, 1978a, vol. I, 37, 45; 48:49.
750. Tolstaia, 1978a, vol. I, 38.
751. As in the early stages of Pozdnyshev's marriage, or Levin's marriage, the new wife was not fully responsive. See: Feiler, 1981; Smoluchowski, 1988, 156–7; Shirer, 1994, 137; Simmons, 1946, 251–2; Zhdanov, 1993 (1928), 68. The literary trace of Sonia's early anorgasmia is a whimsical letter about Sonia as a 'porcelain doll' which Tolstoy wrote to his sister-in-law Tanya Bers in March of 1863.
    I interpret Sonia's initial lack of orgasmic response in intercourse as a sign of incomplete trust in her husband's devotion, or a symptom of her unconscious awareness of her husband's hostility toward her (cf. Rancour-Laferriere, 1992 [1985], 83 ff.). Sonia loved her husband, but deep down she sensed something was terribly wrong in his attitude toward women (she was right). He, in turn, sensed this mistrust, and was narcissistically injured – more seriously injured than if he had not been so narcissistically vulnerable in the first place.
752. Gusev, 1954, 125, 143, 159. Cf. Blanchard, 1984, 33.
753. 34:381.
754. 34:387. N. Timkovskii (1913, 112ff.) noted this tendency of Tolstoy to observe himself from outside himself. As Richard Gustafson observes, the older Tolstoy worked hard at trying not to think of what other people thought of his acts (Gustafson, 1986, 435).
755. Gor'kii, 1949–55, vol. 14, 282.
756. A. A. Tolstaia, 1978, 91.
757. Wilson, 1988, 88.
758. Novikov, 1928, 214.
759. 50:196.
760. 27:13.
761. 27:58–9; Tolstoy, 1983, 93, emphasis added. Cf. Zhdanov, 1968, 178.
762. 27:73; Tolstoy, 1983, 112.
763. Isenberg, 1993, 105.
764. 27:395.
765. 27:411. Cf. 27:322.
766. The enormous psychoanalytic literature on the child's early (pre-Oedipal) relationship with the mother includes, in addition to some of Freud's later works: Brunswick, 1940; Chodorow, 1978; Mahler, 1994 (1979); Kohut, 1971, 1977; Greenberg & Mitchell, 1983.

I have applied Heinz Kohut's notion of the pre-Oedipal 'selfobject' in an analysis of Tolstoy's Pierre Bezukhov (Rancour-Laferriere, 1993a). Kohut would have predicted Tolstoy's difficulties in self–other differentiation. He wrote: 'The creative individual, whether in art or science, is less psychologically separated from his surroundings than the noncreative one; the 'I–you' barrier is not as clearly defined' (Kohut, 1978–90, vol. I, 447). For an interesting application of Kohutian theory to the contemporary Russian writer Eduard Limonov, see: Simmons, 1993, 93–124.

767. 27:68; Tolstoy, 1983, 105, emphasis added.
768. 27:363.
769. 27:50; Tolstoy, 1983, 82.
770. Pozdnyshev considers killing himself as well as his wife already in the first draft (27:361), as well as in other variants (27:404, 412). Compare Tolstoy's unresolved quandary in writing his tale 'The Devil': one ending has the main character Evgenii shooting himself, the other has him shooting Stepanida, the woman he still desires sexually.
771. 27:385. I wish to thank Yuri Druzhnikov for consultation on the original Russian version of this passage.
772. Hildegard Baumgart, in an insightful chapter dealing with the jealousy experienced both by Pozdnyshev and by Tolstoy himself, asks: 'Where does a jealous individual get the strength or the power to demand total control over the beloved, which can go as far as murder in extreme cases? The answer is, Out of the expectation that you and I should always and in fact (and not only in the brief moments of sexual, erotic, or spiritual merging) be one...'. Pozdnyshev desires, but is unable to 'be as one' with his wife in a 'relationship like that between mother and child in earliest childhood' (Baumgart, 1990 [1985], 216, 211).
773. 19:50, as translated in Tolstoy, 1995, 438.
774. As quoted in Rancour-Laferriere, 1993a, 229.
775. Ibid., 216–19.
776. 48:44–5.
777. Cf. Rothstein, 1984 (167) on Levin's ambivalence toward Kitti.
778. Rusanov and Rusanov, 1972, 63.
779. Zhirkevich, 1939, 432–3.
780. Rancour-Laferriere, 1995, 109–12.
781. I. L. Tolstoi, 1914, 219.
782. 84:272.
783. 64:159–60.
784. 20:338, 599; 62:11, 12. See also: Eikhenbaum, 1982 (1960), 102–3; Gusev, 1963, 286.
785. S. M. Tolstoi, 1993, 120–34.
786. de Proyart, 1980.
787. de Proyart, 1980, 146. Cf. Wachtel, who speaks of 'the link between memories of the mother and those of the unspoiled land' in *Childhood* (1990, 55), and Chester on Tolstoy's replacement of the image of the mother with 'the image of the Russian countryside' in the work (1996, 65).

788.　2:180. Cf.: Sémon (1984, 33–46) on the association of women with land-scape and earth in Tolstoy; Dmitrii Merezhkovskii (1995 [1900], 83–4) on the tendency of some Tolstoyan characters to *be* nature, and Tolstoy's treatment of nature as an extension of himself; N. Tim-kovskii (1913, 136) on Tolstoy's 'hunger to merge with nature [*zhazhda sliianiia s prirodoi*], with the sky, with the unknown Infinity which shines through our earthly limitedness'; Judith Armstrong's ana-lysis of an episode of fantasized union with Mother/Nature in *The Cossacks* (1988, 16–21); and my analysis of Pierre Bezukhov's fantasy of mystical fusion with the universe (1993a, 199–201). On the importance of moon and water imagery in Tolstoy's conception of happiness, see: Berman, 1992, 5–39.

789.　23:471.
790.　ANSSSR, 1950–65, XI, 704–5.
791.　Tolstoy is not alone among Russian thinkers in this cryptic signification of the mother. Others as various as Fedorov,Dostoevsky, Berdiaev, and Grossman do it. See: Rancour-Laferriere 1995, 52–3, 56, 91, 239–44.
792.　*SE* XIV, 249; XVIII, 108–9; Fenichel, 1945, 394.
793.　*SE* XIV, 249.
794.　27:414; cf. Opul'skaia, 1979, 172; Gudzii's commentary in 27:580.
795.　50:130, 133.
796.　50:134.
797.　50:140.
798.　86:257.
799.　50:145, 136.
800.　50:144–5.
801.　50:145.
802.　50:326.
803.　50:146.
804.　50:155, 158.
805.　50:170.
806.　50:172, 174.
807.　50:174.
808.　50:185–7.
809.　50:188. There were some other grandiose outbursts in 1889. For ex-ample, on 25 May Tolstoy writes in a notebook: 'Last night a voice was saying to me that the time has come to reveal the evil of the world' (27:530).
810.　50:64, 82, 91, 123, 161.
811.　64:333.
812.　86:265.
813.　Cf. Gustafson, 1986, 431.
814.　86:264, 265. For similar statements on the necessity of sinfulness made sporadically by Tolstoy from 1899 to 1910, see: Gustafson, 1986, 430–31. Gustafson recognizes that, for Tolstoy, 'the movement and approximation toward perfection is endless and relentless' (ibid., 439). But Gustafson does not consider the masochistic factor in this unending movement. Nor does A. G. Grodetskaia (1995) in her inter-esting paper on Tolstoy's earlier justifications of sinfulness.

815. 86:265; cf. 64:299.
816. 50:189–91. On the treatment of *The Kreutzer Sonata* by the official censorship, see: Møller, 1988, 39–91.
817. Gray, 1994, 77.
818. Gray, 1994, 77. Various other scholars have commented in detail on the problems Lev and Sonia had from the very beginning of their marriage. See, for example: Zhdanov, 1993 (1928); Asquith, 1961; Feiler, 1981; Smoluchowski, 1988; Shirer, 1994.
819. 50:120, 123.
820. As quoted by Zhdanov, 1993 (1928), 208.
821. From Sonia's diary entry of 25 December 1890, as quoted by Zhdanov, 1993 (1928), 209.
822. Tolstaia, 1978a, vol. I, 135. There are several instances of such censorship in the 1978 edition of the diaries. As Alexander Fodor remarks, the 'surreptitious removal of passages from the Countess' diaries is an underhanded business by any standard' (Fodor, 1989, 67).
823. Dillon, 1934, 183.
824. Smoluchowski, 1988, 155; de Courcel, 1988, 201; Zhdanov, 1993 (1928), 206.
825. Smoluchowski, 1988, 156–7.
826. Stern, 1965, 186 (*contra* Mirsky, 1989 [1929], 306). Mirsky is inclined to deny the existence of Tolstoy's sadism – even as he presents interesting examples of it, including *The Kreutzer Sonata*. He does not understand psychoanalytic terminology.
827. For a detailed account, see: Møller, 1988, 69–79.
828. Tolstaia, 1978a, vol. I, 153, as translated in Sophia Tolstoy, 1985, 114.
829. See Møller, 1988, 172–7, for a detailed plot summary.
830. 50:44, 45, 86, 90, 107, 119, 141, 149.
831. 50:115, 170, 184.
832. 50:90, 154, 164.
833. 50:90.
834. 27:415.
835. 86:262.
836. 86:262. There is something of a polemic with Dostoevsky in this. In order to remember one's sins against another person, one has to attribute them to oneself personally, that is, take personal responsibility for specific, discrete sins. Dostoevsky, on the other hand, took a collective approach to sin, arguing that 'all are guilty for all'. For a detailed discussion, see: Rancour-Laferriere, 1995, 234–44.
837. 50:133.
838. 50:111.
839. On Sonia's frustrated sexuality, see: Feiler, 1981, 258; Smoluchowski, 1988, 156–7, 169; Shirer, 1994, 137.
840. 50:130.
841. 50:55.
842. 50:147.
843. 50:103. I have slightly modified the translation of this passage by David McDuff given in Tolstoy, 1983, 15.

Tolstoy is incorrect in his assertion that *klikushestvo* occurs 'only in married women'. Dr N. V. Krainskii, who made a detailed study of the disease and personally observed many cases, states that it occurred in females from 12 years of age and older. Unmarried girls, married women, and widows were all vulnerable (Krainskii, 1900, 217; see also Sémon, 1984, 484, n. 106).

844. See, for example: Semenova-Tian-Shanskaia, 1914, 14.
845. '*Klikushestvo*', 1895, 374.
846. Brown, 1986, 381. According to studies of late nineteenth-century peasant marriage practices cited by Barbara Alpern Engel, 'In Tula province, where the average age of marriage for [peasant] women was 18.7, the lowest in Russia, over 20 per cent of peasant women married before they menstruated' (Engel, 1990, 697).
847. Krainskii, 1900, 229.
848. 86:182.
849. 27:35, 323.
850. Ellenberger, 1970, 143; cf. Gay, 1988, 92. The celebrated *Studies on Hysteria* by Sigmund Freud and Josef Breuer, which offered a different kind of sexual etiology of hysteria, did not appear until a few years after Tolstoy had completed *The KreutzerSonata* (1893–95). For a broad historical study of notions of hysteria in America and Western Europe, see Micale, 1995. Micale speaks of the 'enduring sexual associations' (218) of hysteria in turn-of-the-century European culture.
851. 50:110.
852. Asquith, 1961, 47.
853. Zhdanov, 1993 (1928), 207 (cf. 217); cf. Simmons, 1946, 446.
854. Shirer, 1994, 141.
855. For example: Gol'denveizer 1959, 338.
856. Tolstaia, 1978, vol. I, 124–5, as translated (with some modifications) from Sophia Tolstoy, 1985, 88–9. Cf. Zhdanov, 1993 (1928), 208–9.
857. Cf. Micale (1995, 219) on 'the promiscuous application of the hysteria concept' toward the end of the nineteenth century in America and Western Europe. Today hysteria as a diagnosis is disappearing in the medical literature, largely as a result of reclassification and 'medical dismemberment' (ibid., 293). Sonia did not manifest any of the classical symptoms of what today is sometimes called conversion disorder or conversion hysteria, such as tremors, seizures, partial paralysis, coordination disturbance, aphonia, etc. (see, for example: *DSM III*, 244–7; *DSM IV*, 452–7; Nemiah, 1988, 250–54). Sonia did, however, have clear symptoms of so-called histrionic personality disorder (formerly called hysterical personality), such as: self-dramatization (exaggerated expression of emotions), angry outbursts or tantrums, and manipulative suicide threats and attempts (*DSM III*, 313–15; *DSM IV*, 655–8; Nemiah, 1988, 252; various articles in Horowitz, 1977). These increased in frequency with age, until Tolstoy died. Sleeplessness, anxiety, crying spells, paranoid outbursts, and depressive episodes plagued Sonia sporadically as well, especially when there was friction with her husband. The symptoms became especially grave in the months preceding Tolstoy's exit from Yasnaya Polyana in 1910, and

included multiple suicide threats and attempts. Psychiatrists were called in at one point, and they diagnosed paranoia and hysteria (see especially Shirer, 1994, 276–84).

858.   Tolstaia, 1978c, 62.
859.   The story never appeared in print according to the editors of the Jubilee Edition (50:326).
860.   50:145.
861.   Much obscene folklore is devoted to this coital position, as Emil Draitser has shown (ms 1995, 56–61).
862.   Rancour-Laferriere, 1992 (1985), 37, 69–72.
863.   Sof'ia Andreevna Tolstaia, 1978c. P. S. Popov, one of the editors of the Jubilee edition of Tolstoy's letters to his wife refers disdainfully to the autobiography as 'a framework of facts' and 'an extensive and prejudiced indictment against Tolstoy' (83:8).
864.   Møller, 1988, 172–7.
865.   Kahane, 1990, 31; cf. Smith-Rosenberg, 1972.

Bibliography

Abraham, Karl. 1994 (1924). 'A Short Study of the Development of the Libido, Viewed in the Light of Mental Disorders (Abridged)'. *Essential Papers on Object Loss*, ed. Rita V. Frankiel. New York: New York University Press, 72–93.

Abrikosov, Kh. N. 1928. 'Iz vospominanii o L. N. Tolstom'. *Lev Nikolaevich Tolstoi: Iubileinyi sbornik*, ed. N. N. Gusev. Moscow: Gosudarstvennoe izdatel'stvo, 266–78.

Aksel'rod-Ortodoks, L. I. 1922. *L. N. Tolstoi: sbornik statei*. Moscow: Moskovskoe otdelenie Gosudarstvennogo Izdatel'stva.

Aldanov, Mark. 1969 (1923). *Zagadka Tolstogo*. Providence: Brown University Slavic Reprint VII.

Alekseev, V. I. 1978 (1948). 'Iz "vospominanii"'. *L. N. Tolstoi v vospominaniiakh sovremennikov*, ed. G. V. Krasnov. Moscow: Khudozhestvennaia literatura, vol. I, 253–62.

Al'tman, Moisei Semenovich. 1966. *Chitaia Tolstogo*. Tula: Priokskoe knizhnoe izdatel'stvo.

American Psychiatric Association. 1980. *Diagnostic and Statistical Manual of Mental Disorders* (3rd ed.). Washington, DC: American Psychiatric Association. [= *DSM III*].

American Psychiatric Association. 1994. *Diagnostic and Statistical Manual of Mental Disorders* (4th ed.). Washington, DC: American Psychiatric Association. [= *DSM IV*].

Anderson, Kenneth N., Lois E. Anderson and Walter D. Glanze (eds). 1994. *Mosby's Medical, Nursing, and Allied Health Dictionary*, 4th ed. Saint Louis: Mosby.

ANSSSR. 1950–1965. *Slovar' sovremennogo russkogo literaturnogo iazyka*. Moscow–Leningrad: Nauka, 17 vols.

Aquil, Reshma. 1989. 'The Kreutzer Sonata and the Problem of Women and Marriage'. *Essays on Leo Tolstoy*, ed. T. R. Sharma. Meerut: Shalabh Prakashan, 251–6.

Arbuzov, S. P. 1904. *Gr. L. N. Tolstoi: Vospominaniia*. Moscow: Vladimir Chicherin.

Armstrong, Judith M. 1988. *The Unsaid Anna Karenina*. New York: St. Martin's Press.

Asquith, Cynthia. 1961. *Married to Tolstoy*. Cambridge: Houghton Mifflin.

Baehr, Stephen. 1976. 'Art and The Kreutzer Sonata: A Tolstoian Approach'. *Canadian-American Slavic Studies* 10, 39–46.

Barnes, Gordon E. and Harry Prosen. 1985. 'Parental Death and Depression'. *Journal of Abnormal Psychology* 94, 64–9.

Baumgart, Hildegard. 1990 (1985). *Jealousy: Experiences and Solutions*, tr. Manfred and Evelyn Jacobson. Chicago: University of Chicago Press.

Beck, H. 1898. *Des Grafen Leo Tolstoi Kreutzersonate vom Standpunkte des Irrenarztes*. Leipzig: H. W. Theodor Dieter.

Benson, Ralph C. and Martin L. Pernoll. 1994. *Handbook of Obstetrics and Gynecology*. New York: McGraw-Hill.

Benson, Ruth Crego. 1973. *Women in Tolstoy: The Ideal and the Erotic*. Urbana: University of Illinois Press.

Berdiaev, Nikolai. 1978 (1912). 'Vetkhii i Novyi Zavet v religioznom soznanii L. Tolstogo'. *O religii L'va Tolstogo*. Paris: YMCA-Press, 172–95.

Bergler, Edmund. 1949. *The Basic Neurosis: Oral Regression and Psychic Masochism*. New York: Grune and Stratton.

Berlin, Isaiah. 1979. *Russian Thinkers*. New York: Penguin.

Berman, B. I. 1992. *Sokrovennyi Tolstoi: religioznye videniia i prozreniia khudozhestvennogo tvorchestva L'va Nikolaevicha*. Moscow: Gendal'f.

Berman, Jeffrey. 1990. *Narcissism and the Novel*. New York: New York University Press.

Bers, Stepan Andreevich. 1978 (1894). 'Vospominaniia o grafe L. N. Tolstom'. *L. N. Tolstoi v vospominaniiakh sovremennikov*, ed. G. V. Krasnov. Moscow: Khudozhestvennaia literatura, vol. I, 174–93.

Bird, Robert. 1996. 'The Truth of the Inner Being: *'The Kreutzer Sonata'* as a Tragedy of Forgiveness'. *Russian Literature* 40, 405–10.

Biriukov, P. I. 1921. *L. N. Tolstoi: Biografiia*. Berlin: I. P. Ladyzhnikov, 3 vols.

Birtchnell, J. 1972. 'Early Parent Death and Psychiatric Diagnosis'. *Social Psychiatry* 7, 202–10.

Blanchard, William H. 1984. *Revolutionary Morality: A Psychosexual Analysis of Twelve Revolutionists*. Santa Barbara: ABC-Clio Information Services.

Boborykin, P. D. 1978. 'V Moskve – u Tolstogo'. *L. N. Tolstoi v vospominaniiakh sovremennikov*, ed. G. V. Krasnov. Moscow: Khudozhestvennaia literatura, vol. I, 265–73.

Bollas, Christopher. 1978. 'The Transformational Object'. *International Journal of Psycho-Analysis* 60, 97–107.

Botkin, Ia. A. 1893. *Prestupnyi affekt kak uslovie nevmeniaemosti (Analiz prestuplenii Otello i Pozdnysheva)*. Moscow: A. A. Kartsev.

Bowlby, John. 1960. 'Separation Anxiety'. *International Journal of Psycho-Analysis* 41, 89–113.

Bowlby, John. 1973. *Separation: Anxiety and Anger (= Attachment and Loss, vol. II)*. New York: Basic Books.

Bowlby, John. 1980. *Loss: Sadness and Depression (= Attachment and Loss, vol. III)*. New York: Basic Books.

Boyer, L. Bryce. 1992. 'Roles Played by Music as Revealed During Countertransference Facilitated Transference Regression'. *International Journal of Psycho-Analysis* 73 (Part 1), 55–70.

Brown, George W. 1982. 'Early Loss and Depression'. *The Place of Attachment in Human Behaviour*, ed. Colin Murray Parkes and Joan Stevenson-Hinde. New York: Basic Books, 232–68.

Brown, Julie Vail. 1986. 'Female Sexuality and Madness in Russian Culture: Traditional Values and Psychiatric Theory'. *Social Research* 53, 369–85.

Brunswick, Ruth Mack. 1940. 'The Preoedipal Phase of the Libido Development'. *Psychoanalytic Quarterly* 9, 293–319.

Burgin, Diana. 1987. 'Jungian Dactyls on Death and Tolstoy (Verses Burlesque with Notations in Earnest)'. *New Studies in Russian Language and Literature*, ed. Anna Lisa Crone and Catherine Chvany. Columbus: Slavica Publishers, 27–38.

Cain, T. G. S. 1977. *Tolstoy*. London: Paul Elek.

248   *Bibliography*

Calder, Angus. 1976. *Russia Discovered: Nineteenth-Century Fiction from Pushkin to Chekhov*. London: Heinemann.
Chester, Pamela. 1996. 'The Landscape of Recollection: Tolstoy's *Childhood* and the Feminization of the Countryside'. *Engendering Slavic Literatures*, ed. Pamela Chester and Sibelan Forrester. Bloomington: Indiana University Press, 59–82.
Chodorow, Nancy. 1978. *The Reproduction of Mothering: Psychoanalysis and the Sociology of Gender*. Berkeley: University of California Press.
Christian, R. F. 1969. *Tolstoy: A Critical Introduction*. Cambridge: Cambridge University Press.
Christian, R. F. 1993. 'Tolstoy and the First Step'. *Scottish Slavonic Review* 20, 7–16.
Christian, R. F. (ed), tr. 1978. *Tolstoy's Letters*. New York: Charles Scribner's Sons, 2 vols.
Christian, R. F. (ed.), tr. 1985. *Tolstoy's Diaries*, vol. I. London: Athlone Press.
Coetzee, J. M. 1985. 'Confession and Double Thoughts: Tolstoy, Rousseau, Dostoevsky'. *Comparative Literature* 37, 193–232.
Cohen, David B. 1994. *Out of the Blue: Depression and Human Nature*. New York: W. W. Norton.
Comstock, Adelaide. 1904. *The 'Kreutzer Sonata' Reviewed by a Woman*. New York: Broadway Publishing.
Constant de Rebecque, Henri-Benjamin. 1964 (1816). *Adolphe*, tr. Leonard Tancock. London: Penguin.
Costlow, Jane T. 1993. 'The Pastoral Source: Representations of the Maternal Breast in Nineteenth-Century Russia'. *Sexuality and the Body in Russian Culture*, ed. J. Costlow, S. Sandler, J. Vowles. Stanford: Stanford University Press, 223–36.
de Courcel, Martine. 1988 (1980). *Tolstoy: The Ultimate Reconciliation*, tr. Peter Levi. New York: Charles Scribner's Sons.
Crankshaw, Edward. 1974. *Tolstoy: The Making of a Novelist*. New York: Viking.
Cruise, Edwina Jannie. 1977. 'The Ideal Woman in Tolstoi: *Resurrection*'. *Canadian-American Slavic Studies* 11, 281–6.
Deltito, Joseph A. and Richard Hahn. 1993. 'A Three-Generational Presentation of Separation Anxiety in Childhood with Agoraphobia in Adulthood'. *Psychopharmacology Bulletin* 29, 189–93.
Dillon, E. J. 1934. *Count Leo Tolstoy: A New Portrait*. London: Hutchinson & Co.
Donskov, Andrew. 1979. 'The Peasant in Tolstoi's Thought and Writings'. *Canadian Slavonic Papers* 21, 183–96.
Draitser, Emil. 1995. *Contemporary Russian Sexual Folk Humor*, manuscript.
Dumas, Alexandre. 1888. *Affaire Clémenceau: mémoire de l'accusé*. Paris: Ancienne Maison Michel Lévy Frères.
Dunn, Patrick P. 1974. '"That Enemy Is the Baby": Childhood in Imperial Russia'. *The History of Childhood*, ed. L. deMause. New York: Psychohistory Press, 383–405.
Dworkin, Andrea. 1987. *Intercourse*. New York: The Free Press.
Edwards, Anne. 1981. *Sonya: The Life of Countess Tolstoy*. New York: Simon and Schuster.

Edwards, Robert. 1993. 'Tolstoy and Alice B. Stockham: The Influence of "Tokology" on *The Kreutzer Sonata'*. *Tolstoy Studies Journal* 6, 87–104.

Eguchi, Mahoko. 1996. 'Music and Literature as Related Infections: Beethoven's Kreutzer Sonata Op. 47 and Tolstoj's Novella "The Kreutzer Sonata"'. *Russian Literature* 40, 419–32.

Eikhenbaum, Boris. 1982 (1960). *Tolstoi in the Seventies*, tr. Albert Kaspin. Ann Arbor: Ardis.

Ellenberger, Henri F. 1970. *The Discovery of the Unconscious: The History and Evolution of Dynamic Psychiatry*. New York: Basic Books.

Elms, Alan C. 1994. *Uncovering Lives: The Uneasy Alliance of Biography and Psychology*. New York: Oxford University Press.

Emerson, Caryl. 1996. '*What Is Art?* and the Anxiety of Music'. *Russian Literature* 40, 433–450.

Engel, Barbara Alpern. 1990. 'Peasant Morality and Pre-marital Relations in Late 19th Century Russia'. *Journal of Social History* 23, 693–714.

Engels, Friedrich. 1985 (1884). *The Origin of the Family, Private Property and the State*. New York: Penguin.

Engelstein, Laura. 1992. *The Keys to Happiness: Sex and the Search for Modernity in Fin-de-Siècle Russia*. Ithaca: Cornell University Press.

Erikson, Erik. 1963. *Childhood and Society*. New York: W. W. Norton.

Etkind, Aleksandr. 1993. *Eros nevozmozhnogo: istoriia psikhoanaliza v Rossii*. St. Petersburg: Meduza.

Etkind, Aleksandr. 1995. 'Russkie skoptsy: opyt istorii'. *Zvezda*, no. 4, 131–63.

Evlakhov, A. M. 1930. *Konstitutsional'nye osobennosti psikhiki L. N. Tolstogo*, introd. A. V. Lunacharskii. Moscow–Leningrad: Gosudarstvennoe Izdatel'stvo.

Fasmer, Maks. 1986–87 (1950–58). *Etimologicheskii slovar' russkogo iazyka*, 2nd ed. Moscow: Progress, 4 vols.

Feiler, Lily. 1981. 'The Tolstoi Marriage: Conflict and Illusions'. *Canadian Slavonic Papers* 23, 245–60.

Fenichel, Otto. 1945. *The Psychoanalytic Theory of Neurosis*. New York: W. W. Norton.

Ferber, Leon. 1975. 'Beating Fantasies'. *Masturbation from Infancy to Senescence*, ed. I. M. Marcus and J. J. Francis. New York: International Universities Press, 205–22.

Flamant, Françoise. 1992. 'La Sonate à Kreutzer: Est-elle une oeuvre d'art?' *Cahiers Léon Tolstoï* 6, 29–36.

Flegon, A. 1973. *Za predelami russkikh slovarei*. London: Flegon Press.

Flew, Antony. 1963. 'Tolstoi and the Meaning of Life'. *Ethics* 73, 110–18.

Fodor, Alexander. 1984. *Tolstoy and the Russians: Reflections on a Relationship*. Ann Arbor: Ardis.

Fodor, Alexander. 1989. *A Quest for a Non-Violent Russia: The Partnership of Leo Tolstoy and Vladimir Chertkov*. Lanham: University Press of America.

Forrest, Marvin S. and Jack E. Hokanson. 1975. 'Depression and Autonomic Arousal Reduction Accompanying Self-Punitive Behavior'. *Journal of Abnormal Psychology* 84, 346–57.

Frank, Alvin. 1969. 'The Unrememberable and the Unforgettable: Passive Primal Repression'. *Psychoanalytic Study of the Child* 24, 48–77.

Freud, Sigmund. 1953–65. *Standard Edition of the Complete Psychological Works of Sigmund Freud*, trans under direction of J. Strachey. London: Hogarth Press, 24 vols. [= *SE*].

Friedman, Stanley. 1975. 'On Vegetarianism'. *Journal of the American Psychoanalytic Association* 23, 396–406.

Furman, Erna. 1974. *A Child's Parent Dies: Studies in Childhood Bereavement.* New Haven: Yale University Press.

Ganzen, P. G. 1978 (1917). 'Piat' dnei v Iasnoi Poliane (v aprele 1890 g.)'. *L. N. Tolstoi v vospominaniiakh sovremennikov*, ed. G. V. Krasnov. Moscow: Khudozhestvennaia literatura, vol. I, 451–67.

Gay, Peter. 1988. *Freud: A Life for Our Time.* New York: W. W. Norton.

Gei, N. K. 1971. '"Kreitserova sonata" L. Tolstogo kak khudozhestvennaia mnogomernost". *Stranitsy istorii russkoi literatury*, ed. D. F. Markov. Moscow: Nauka, 121–30.

Gol'denveizer, A. B. 1959. *Vblizi Tolstogo.* Moscow: Gosudarstvennoe izdatel'stvo khudozhestvennoi literatury.

Golstein, Vladimir. 1996. 'Narrating the Murder: The Rhetoric of Evasion in "The Kreutzer Sonata"'. *Russian Literature* 40, 451–62.

Gor'kii, Maksim. 1949–1955. *Sobranie sochinenii.* Moscow: Gosudarstvennoe izdatel'stvo khudozhestvennoi literatury, 30 vols.

Gornaia, V. Z. 1988. '"Kreitserova sonata" v vospriiatii sovremennikov pisatelia'. *Iasnopolianskii sbornik 1988*, ed. K. N. Lomunov. Tula: Priokskoe knizhnoe izdatel'stvo, 105–14.

Goscilo-Kostin, Helena. 1984. 'Tolstoyan Fare: Credo à la Carte'. *Slavonic and East European Review* 62, 481–95.

Gray, Francine du Plessix. 1994. 'Forty-Eight Years, No Secrets'. *New Yorker*, 8 August, 76–81.

Green, Dorothy. 1967. '"The Kreutzer Sonata": Tolstoy and Beethoven'. *Melbourne Slavonic Studies* 1, 11–23.

Greenberg, Jay R. and Stephen A. Mitchell. 1983. *Object Relations in Psychoanalytic Theory.* Cambridge: Harvard University Press.

Greenwood, E. B. 1975. *Tolstoy: The Comprehensive Vision.* London: J. M. Dent and Sons.

Grigorovich, D. V. 1978. "Iz 'literaturnykh vospominanii'". *L. N. Tolstoi v vospominaniiakh sovremennikov*, ed. G. V. Krasnov. Moscow: Khudozhestvennaia literatura, vol. I, 77–8.

Grodetskaia, A. G. 1995. 'Opravdanie grekha u Tolstogo'. Manuscript.

Gudzii, N. 1936. *Kak rabotal L. Tolstoi.* Moscow: Sovetskii pisatel'.

Gurevich, Liubov'. 1978 (1912). 'Iz vospominanii o L. N. Tolstom'. *L. N. Tolstoi v vospominaniiakh sovremennikov*, ed. N. M. Fortunatov. Moscow: Khudozhestvennaia literatura, vol. 2, 41–8.

Gusev, N. N. 1924. 'Pis'ma L. N. Tolstogo o liubvi, brake i semeinoi zhizni'. *Tolstoi i o Tolstom: novye materialy*, ed. N. N. Gusev. Moscow: Tipografiia Tsentrosoiuza, 16–24.

Gusev, N. N. 1954. *Lev Nikolaevich Tolstoi: materialy k biografii c 1828 po 1855 god.* Moscow: Izdatel'stvo Akademii Nauk SSSR.

Gusev, N. N. 1957. *Lev Nikolaevich Tolstoi: materialy k biografii c 1855 po 1869 god.* Moscow: Izdatel'stvo Akademii Nauk SSSR.

Gusev, N. N. 1958. *Letopis' zhizni i tvorchestva L'va Nikolaevicha Tolstogo, 1828–1890*. Moscow: Gosudarstvennoe izdatel'stvo khudozhestvennoi literatury.

Gusev, N. N. 1960. *Letopis' zhizni i tvorchestva L'va Nikolaevicha Tolstogo, 1891–1910*. Moscow: Goslitizdat.

Gusev, N. N. 1963. *Lev Nikolaevich Tolstoi: materialy k biografii c 1870 po 1881 god*. Moscow: Izdatel'stvo Akademii Nauk SSSR.

Gusev, N. N. 1973 (1911). *Dva goda s L. N. Tolstym*. Moscow: Khudozhestvennaia literatura.

Gusev, N. N. 1986. 'L. N. Tolstoi i muzyka (iz arkhiva N. N. Guseva)'. *Iasnopolianskii sbornik 1986*, ed. K. N. Lomunov. Tula: Priokskoe knizhnoe izdatel'stvo, 167–76.

Gustafson, Richard F. 1986. *Leo Tolstoy: Resident and Stranger*. Princeton: Princeton University Press.

Hardin, Harry T. 1985. 'On the Vicissitudes of Early Primary Surrogate Mothering'. *Journal of the American Psychoanalytic Association* 33, 609–29.

Heldt, Barbara. 1987. *Terrible Perfection: Women and Russian Literature*. Bloomington: Indiana University Press.

Hershman, D. Jablow and Julian Lieb. 1988. *The Key to Genius*. Buffalo: Prometheus Books.

Holthusen, Johannes. 1974. 'Das Erzählerproblem in Tolstojs "Kreutzersonate"'. *Mnemozina: Studia litteraria russica in honorem Vsevolod Setchkarev*, ed. J. T. Baer and N. W. Ingham. Munich: Wilhelm Fink Verlag, 193–201.

Horowitz, Mardi J. (ed.). 1977. *Hysterical Personality*. New York: Jason Aronson.

Hubbs, Joanna. 1988. *Mother Russia: The Feminine Myth in Russian Culture*. Bloomington: Indiana University Press.

Hurst, Mary Jane and Daniel L. Hurst. 1994. 'Tolstoy's Description of Tourette Syndrome in *Anna Karenina*'. *Journal of Child Neurology* 9, 366–7.

Ingersoll, Robert G. 1890. 'Tolstoi and "The Kreutzer Sonata"'. *North American Review* 151, 289–99.

International Classification of Diseases, Ninth Revision, Clinical Modification, 3rd ed., 1989. Washington, DC: US Department of Health and Human Services, 3 vols.

Isenberg, Charles. 1993. *Telling Silence: Russian Frame Narratives of Renunciation*. Evanston: Northwestern University Press.

Ivakin, I. M. 1994. 'Iz 'zapisok' I. M. Ivakina'. *Neizvestnyi Tolstoi v arkhivakh Rossii i SSHA*, ed. I. P. Borisova. Moscow: Tekhna-2, 92–120.

Ivanits, Linda J. 1989. *Russian Folk Belief*. Armonk, New York: M. E. Sharpe.

Ivanova, Nina Georgievna. 1971. *Derevnia Iasnaia Poliana*. Tula: Priokskoe knizhnoe izdatel'stvo.

Jackson, Robert Louis. 1978. 'Tolstoj's *Kreutzer Sonata* and Dostoevskij's *Notes From the Underground*'. *American Contributions to the Eighth International Congress of Slavists*, vol. 2, ed. Victor Terras. Columbus: Slavica Publishers, 280–91.

Jacobson, Edith. 1965. 'The Return of the Lost Parent'. *Drives, Affects, Behavior, vol. 2: Essays in Memory of Marie Bonaparte*, ed. Max Schur. New York: International Universities Press, 193–211.

Jahn, Gary R. 1981. 'The Image of the Railroad in *Anna Karenina*'. *Slavic and East European Journal* 25/2, 1–10.

Jamison, Kay Redfield. 1993. *Touched with Fire: Manic-Depressive Illness and the Artistic Temperament*. New York: The Free Press.

Jones, James W. 1991. *Contemporary Psychoanalysis and Religion: Transference and Transcendence*. New Haven: Yale University Press.

Josselson, Ruthellen. 1986. 'Tolstoy, Narcissism, and the Psychology of the Self: A Self-Psychology Approach to Prince Andrei in *War and Peace*'. *Psychoanalytic Review* 73, 77–95.

Kahane, Claire. 1990 (1985). 'Why Dora Now?' In *Dora's Case: Freud – Hysteria – Feminism*, ed. Charles Bernheimer and Claire Kahane. New York: Columbia University Press, 19–32.

Kaplan, Bert. (ed.). 1964. *The Inner World of Mental Illness: A Series of First-Person Accounts of What It Was Like*. New York: Harper and Row.

Karlinsky, Simon. 1976. 'Russia's Gay Literature and History (11th–20th Centuries)', *Gay Sunshine* 29–30, 1–6.

Karpman, Benjamin. 1938. 'The Kreutzer Sonata: A Problem in Latent Homosexuality and Castration'. *Psychoanalytic Review* 25, 20–48.

Katz, Anita Weinreb. 1990. 'Paradoxes of Masochism'. *Psychoanalytic Psychology* 7, 225–41.

Kendall, Philip C. and David Watson (eds.) 1989. *Anxiety and Depression: Distinctive and Overlapping Features*. New York: Academic Press.

Kiell, Norman. 1976. *Varieties of Sexual Experience: Psychosexuality in Literature*. New York: International Universities Press.

Klein, Melanie. 1977. *Love, Guilt and Reparation and Other Works 1921–1945*. New York: Delta.

Klein, Melanie. 1994 (1940). 'Mourning and Its Relation to Manic-Depressive States'. *Essential Papers on Object Loss*, ed. Rita V. Frankiel. New York: NYU Press, 95–122.

'Klikushestvo'. 1895. *Entsiklopedicheskii slovar'*. St. Petersburg: I. A. Efron, vol. XV, 374–5.

Knapp, Bettina L. 1988. *Music, Archetype, and the Writer: A Jungian View*. University Park: Pennsylvania State University Press.

Knapp, Liza. 1991. 'Tolstoy on Musical Mimesis: Platonic Aesthetics and Erotics in "The Kreutzer Sonata"'. *Tolstoy Studies Journal* 4, 25–42.

Kodjak, Andrej. 1985. 'Tolstoy's Personal Myth of Immortality'. *Myth in Literature*, ed. Andrej Kodjak, Krystyna Pomorska, Stephen Rudy. Columbus: Slavica Publishers, 188–207.

Kohut, Heinz. 1957. 'Observations on the Psychological Functions of Music'. *Journal of the American Psychoanalytic Association* 5, 389–407.

Kohut, Heinz. 1971. *The Analysis of the Self*. Madison, CT: International Universities Press.

Kohut, Heinz. 1972. 'Thoughts on Narcissism and Narcissistic Rage'. *Psychoanalytic Study of the Child* 27, 360–400.

Kohut, Heinz. 1977. *The Restoration of the Self*. New York: International Universities Press.

Kohut, Heinz. 1978–1990. *The Search for the Self: Selected Writings of Heinz Kohut, 1950–1978*. New York: International Universities Press, 3 vols.

Kollontai, Alexandra. 1977. *Selected Writings of Alexandra Kollontai*, tr., ed. Alix Holt. New York: W. W. Norton.

Kon, Igor S. 1995. *The Sexual Revolution in Russia, From the Age of the Czars to Today*, tr. James Riordan. New York: The Free Press.

Kopper, John M. 1989. 'Tolstoy and the Narrative of Sex: A Reading of "Father Sergius", "The Devil", and "The Kreutzer Sonata".' *In the Shade of the Giant: Essays on Tolstoy*, ed. Hugh McLean (= *California Slavic Studies* 13). Berkeley: University of California Press, 158–86.

Kozyrev, A. P. 1995. 'Bogochelovechestvo'. *Russkaia filosofiia: slovar'*, ed. M. A. Maslin. Moscow: Respublika, 58–60.

Krainskii, N. V. 1900. *Porcha, klikushi i besnovatye, kak iavleniia russkoi narodnoi zhizni*. Novgorod: Gubernskaia Tipografiia.

Krupnick, Janice L. and Fredric Solomon. 1987. 'Death of a Parent or Sibling During Childhood'. *The Psychology of Separation and Loss*, ed. J. Bloom-Feshbach and S. Bloom-Feshbach. San Francisco: Jossey-Bass, 345–71.

Kujundzic, Dragan. 1993. 'Pardoning Woman in *Anna Karenina*'. *Tolstoy Studies Journal* 6, 65–85.

Kuleshov, M. P. 1908. *Lev Nikolaevich Tolstoi po vospominaniiam krest'ian*. Moscow: Tipografiia L. N. Kholcheva.

Kutepov, Konstantin. 1900. *Sekty khlystov i skoptsov*, 2nd ed. Stavropol': T. M. Timofeev.

Kuzminskaia, Tat'iana Andreevna. 1986. *Moia zhizn' doma i v Iasnoi Poliane: Vospominaniia*. Moscow: Pravda.

Laplanche, J. and J. B. Pontalis. 1973. *The Language of Psychoanalysis*, tr. D. Nicholson-Smith. New York: W. W. Norton.

Lavrin, Janko. 1944. *Tolstoy: An Approach*. London: Methuen & Co.

Lawrence, Ruth A. 1985. *Breastfeeding: A Guide for the Medical Profession*, 2nd ed. St. Louis: C. V. Mosby Co.

Lazarev, E. E. 1978 (1935). 'Znakomstvo s L. N. Tolstym'. *L. N. Tolstoi v vospominaniiakh sovremennikov*, ed. G. V. Krasnov. Moscow: Khudozhestvennaia literatura, vol. I, 320–26.

LeBlanc, Ronald. 1993. 'Unpalatable Pleasures: Tolstoy, Food, and Sex'. *Tolstoy Studies Journal* 6, 1–32.

LeBlanc, Ronald. 1995. 'Tolstoy's Way of No Flesh: Abstinence, Vegetarianism, and Christian Physiology'. *Food in Russian History and Culture*, ed. Joyce Toomre and Musya Glants, to appear.

Leibin, Valerii. 1996. '"Ia i Edipov kompleks"'. *Arkhetip*, no. 1, 136–42.

Lerner, Paul M. 1990. 'The Treatment of Early Object Loss: The Need to Search'. *Psychoanalytic Psychology* 7, 79–90.

Levin, Eve. 1993. 'Sexual Vocabulary in Medieval Russia'. *Sexuality and the Body in Russian Culture*, ed. J. Costlow, S. Sandler, J. Vowles. Stanford: Stanford University Press, 41–52.

Lewin, Bertram D. 1937. 'A Type of Neurotic Hypomanic Reaction'. *Archives of Neurology and Psychiatry* 37, 868–73.

Lipsitz, Joshua D., Lynn Y. Martin, Salvatore Mannuzza, Tim F. Chapman et al. 1994. 'Childhood Separation Anxiety Disorder in Patients with Adult Anxiety Disorders'. *American Journal of Psychiatry* 151, 927–9.

Lloyd, Rosemary. 1995. *Closer and Closer Apart: Jealousy in Literature*. Ithaca: Cornell University Press.

Loginova, M, L. Podsvirova, N. Serebrianaia, I Shcherbakova. 1995. *L. N. Tolstoi: dokumenty, fotografii, rukopisy.* Moscow: Planeta.

Mahler, Margaret. 1994 (1979). *The Selected Papers of Margaret S. Mahler, M.D..* Northvale, NJ: Jason Aronson, 2 vols.

Mahler, Margaret S., Fred Pine and Anni Bergman. 1975. *The Psychological Birth of the Human Infant: Symbiosis and Individuation.* New York: Basic Books.

Makovitskii, D. P. 1928. 'Tolstoi v zhizni'. *Lev Nikolaevich Tolstoi: Iubileinyi sbornik,* ed. N. N. Gusev. Moscow: Gosudarstvennoe izdatel'stvo, 241–55.

Makovitskii, D. P. 1979–81. *U Tolstogo: 'Iasnopolianskie zapiski' D. P. Makovitskogo* (=Literaturnoe nasledstvo, vol. 90). Moscow: Nauka, 4 vols, index vol.

Malia, Martin E. 1976. 'Adulthood Refracted: Russia and Leo Tolstoi'. *Daedalus* 105, 169–83.

Mandelker, Amy. 1993. *Framing Anna Karenina: Tolstoy, the Woman Question, and the Victorian Novel.* Columbus: Ohio State University Press.

Maude, Aylmer. 1987 (1930). *The Life of Tolstoy.* New York: Oxford University Press, 2 vols.

Maupassant, Guy de. 1974–79. *Contes et nouvelles.* Paris: Gallimard, 2 vols.

Maupassant, Guy de. 1975. *Romans.* Paris: Éditions Albin Michel.

Maupassant, Guy de. 1979. *Pierre and Jean,* tr. Leonard Tancock. London: Penguin.

McLaughlin, Sigrid. 1970. 'Some Aspects of Tolstoy's Intellectual Development: Tolstoy and Schopenhauer'. *California Slavic Studies* 5, 187–245.

McLean, Hugh. 1989. 'Truth in Dying'. *In the Shade of the Giant: Essays on Tolstoy,* ed. Hugh McLean (= *California Slavic Studies* 13). Berkeley: University of California Press, 130–57.

McLean, Hugh. 1994a. 'Tolstoy and Jesus'. *Christianity and the Eastern Slavs, Volume II* (= *California Slavic Studies XVII*), ed. Robert P. Hughes and Irina Paperno. Berkeley: University of California Press, 103–23.

McLean, Hugh. 1994b. 'The Case of the Missing Mothers, or When Does a Beginning Begin?' *For SK: In Celebration of the Life and Career of Simon Karlinsky,* ed. Michael S. Flier, Robert P. Hughes. Oakland, CA: Berkeley Slavic Specialties, 223– 32.

Merezhkovskii, Dmitrii. 1995. *L. Tolstoi i Dostoevskii: vechnye sputniki.* Moscow: Respublika.

Meyer, Alfred G. 1977. 'Marxism and the Women's Movement'. *Women in Russia,* ed. D. Atkinson, A. Dallin, G. Warshofsky Lapidus. Stanford: Stanford University Press, 85–112.

Meyers, Jeffrey. 1988. 'Filial Memoirs of Tolstoy'. *Biography* 11, 236–52.

Micale, Mark S. 1995. *Approaching Hysteria: Disease and Its Interpretations.* Princeton, NJ: Princeton University Press.

Milykh, M. K. 1978. 'Monolog, ego struktura v "Kreitserovoi sonate" L. Tolstogo'. *Iazyk i stil' L. N. Tolstogo,* ed. K. P. Orlov. Tula: Tul'skii Gosudarstvennyi Pedagogicheskii Institut im. L. N. Tolstogo, 116–30.

Mirsky, D. S. 1989 (1929). 'Some Remarks on Tolstoy'. *Uncollected Writings on Russian Literature,* ed. G. S. Smith. Berkeley: Berkeley Slavic Specialties, 303–11.

Molchanov, A. N. 1978 (1890). 'V Iasnoi poliane'. *L. N. Tolstoi v vospominaniiakh sovremennikov,* ed. G. V. Krasnov. Moscow: Khudozhestvennaia literatura, vol. I, 468–72.

Møller, Peter Ulf. 1988. *Postlude to the Kreutzer Sonata: Tolstoj and the Debate on Sexual Morality in Russian Literature in the 1890s*. Leiden: E. J. Brill.
Molostvov, N. G. and P. A. Sergeenko. 1909. *L. N. Tolstoi: zhizn' i tvorchestvo, 1828–1908 gg*. St. Petersburg: P. P. Soikin.
Mondry, Henrietta. 1988. 'One or Two "Resurrections" in L. Tolstoy's Writing? (Fedorov and The Kreutzer Sonata)'. *Die Welt der Slaven* 33, 169–82.
Murygin, G. 1995. *O L. N. Tolstom i ego potomkakh*. Novosibirsk.
Naginski, Isabelle. 1982. 'Tolstoy's *Childhood*: Literary Apprenticeship and Autobiographical Obsession'. *Ulbandus Review*, no. 2. 191–208.
Nemiah, John C. 1988. 'Psychoneurotic Disorders'. *The New Harvard Guide to Psychiatry*, ed. A. M. Nicholi, Jr. Cambridge: Harvard University Press, 234–58.
Newlin, Thomas. 1994. 'On the Green Couch: Tolstoj, Pastoral, and the Mother Syndrome'. Paper presented at meeting of American Association of Teachers of Slavic and East European Languages, 28 December 1994, San Diego.
Novick, Kerry Kelly and Jack Novick. 1987. 'The Essence of Masochism'. *Psychoanalytic Study of the Child* 42, 353–84.
Novikov, A. M. 1928. 'Zima 1889–1890 godov v Iasnoi Poliane'. *Lev Nikolaevich Tolstoi: Iubileinyi sbornik*, ed. N. N. Gusev. Moscow: Gosudarstvennoe izdatel'stvo, 202–17.
Novikov, M. P. 1994 (1924). 'Ukhod L. N. Tolstogo'. *Neizvestnyi Tolstoi v arkhivakh Rossii i SSHA*, ed. I. P. Borisova. Moscow: Tekhna-2, 323–34.
Obolenskaia, E. V. 1978 (1928). 'Moia mat' i Lev Nikolaevich'. *L. N. Tolstoi v vospominaniiakh sovremennikov*, ed. G. V. Krasnov. Moscow: Khudozhestvennaia literatura, vol. I, 399–408.
Obolenskii, L. E. 1978 (1902). 'Iz "Literaturnykh vospominanii i kharakteristik"'. *L. N. Tolstoi v vospominaniiakh sovremennikov*, ed. G. V. Krasnov. Moscow: Khudozhestvennaia literatura, vol. I, 356–63.
Ogareva, Iu. M. 1914. 'Vospominaniia Iu. M. Ogarevoi'. *Golos minuvshago*, no. 11 (November), 109–27.
Opul'skaia, L. D. 1979. *Lev Nikolaevich Tolstoi: materialy k biografii s 1886 po 1892 god*. Moscow: Nauka.
Orwin, Donna Tussing. 1993. *Tolstoy's Art and Thought, 1847–1880*. Princeton: Princeton University Press.
Osipov, N. 1913. '"Zapiski sumasshedshego", nezakonchennoe proizvedenie L. N. Tolstogo (k voprosu ob emotsii boiazni)'. *Psikhoterapiia* 3, 141–58.
Osipov, N. 1928. 'Lev Tolstoi'. *Rul'*, 9 September, p. 6.
Ossipow, N. 1923. *Tolstois Kindheitserinnerungen: Ein Beitrag zu Freuds Libidotheorie*. Leipzig: Internationaler psychoanalytischer Verlag.
Ossipow, N. 1929. 'Tolstoj und die Medizin'. *Der russische Gedanke*, 186–93.
Ovsianiko-Kulikovskii, D. N. 1905. *L. N. Tolstoi kak khudozhnik*, 2nd ed. Saint Petersburg: Orion.
Ozhegov, S. I. 1968. *Slovar' russkogo iazyka*. Moscow: Sovetskaia entsiklopediia.
Paliukh, Z. G. and A. V. Prokhorova, (eds). 1977. *Lev Tolstoi i muzyka: khronika, notografiia, bibliografiia*. Moscow: Sovetskii kompozitor.
Papazian, Elizabeth A. 1996. 'Presto and Manifesto: The Kreutzer Sonatas of Tolstoj and Beethoven'. *Russian Literature* 40, 491–516.

Parthé, Kathleen. 1982. 'Death Masks in Tolstoi'. *Slavic Review* 41, 297–305.
Parthé, Kathleen. 1985a. 'Tolstoy and the Geometry of Fear'. *Modern Language Studies* 15, 80–94.
Parthé, Kathleen. 1985b. 'The Metamorphosis of Death in Tolstoy'. *Language and Style* 18, 205–14.
Pearson, Irene. 1984. 'The Social and Moral Roles of Food in *Anna Karenina*'. *Journal of Russian Studies* 48, 10–19.
Peterson, N. P. 1978 (1909). 'Iz zapisok byvshego uchitelia'. *L. N. Tolstoi v vospominaniiakh sovremennikov*, ed. G. V. Krasnov. Moscow: Khudozhestvennaia literatura, vol. I, 122–6.
Pigott, Anne Christine. 1992. 'Regard de la psychanalyse sur *La Sonate à Kreutzer*'. *Cahiers Léon Tolstoï* 6, 53–60.
Plekhanov, G. V. 1923 (?). *Stat'i o L. Tolstom*. Moscow: Gosizdat.
Pokrovskii, E. A. 1890. *Ob ukhode za malymi det'mi*. Moscow: Posrednik.
Porché, François. 1935. *Portrait psychologique de Tolstoi*. Paris: Flammarion.
Porudominskii, V. I. 1992. 'L. N. Tolstoi i etika pitaniia'. *Chelovek*, no. 2, 106–18; no. 3, 127–38.
Posse, V. A. 1918. *Liubov' v tvorchestve L. N. Tolstogo*. Borovichi: Zhizn' dlia vsekh.
de Proyart, Jacqueline. 1980. 'L'homme et la nature dans l'oeuvre littéraire de Léon Tolstoï'. *Tolstoi aujourd'hui*. Paris, Institut d'Études Slaves, 141–71.
Prugavin, A. S. 1911. *O L've Tolstom i o tolstovtsakh*. Moscow: I. D. Sytin.
Puzin, Nikolai Pavlovich. 1988. *Kochakovskii nekropol' (semeinoe kladbishche Tolstykh)*. Tula: Priokskoe knizhnoe izdatel'stvo.
Quinodoz, Jean-Michel. 1993 (1991). *The Taming of Solitude: Separation Anxiety in Psychoanalysis*, tr. P. Slotkin. London: Routledge.
Rancour-Laferriere, Daniel. 1992 (1985). *Signs of the Flesh: An Essay on the Evolution of Hominid Sexuality*. Bloomington: Indiana University Press.
Rancour-Laferriere, Daniel. 1993a. *Tolstoy's Pierre Bezukhov: A Psychoanalytic Study*. London: Bristol Classical Press.
Rancour-Laferriere, Daniel. 1993b. 'Anna's Adultery: Distal Sociobiology vs. Proximate Psychoanalysis'. *Tolstoy Studies Journal* 6, 33–46.
Rancour-Laferriere, Daniel. 1994. 'Listening to Lev Nikolaevich'. *Tolstoy Studies Journal* 7, 89–93.
Rancour-Laferriere, Daniel. 1995. *The Slave Soul of Russia: Moral Masochism and the Cult of Suffering*. New York: New York University Press.
Rancour-Laferriere, Daniel. 1996. 'A Note on Psychoanalysis in Russia Today'. Manuscript.
Ransel, David L. 1988. *Mothers of Misery: Child Abandonment in Russia*. Princeton: Princeton University Press.
Raphael, Beverley. 1982. 'The Young Child and the Death of a Parent'. *The Place of Attachment in Human Behavior*, ed. Colin Murray Parkes, Joan Stevenson-Hinde. New York: Basic Books, 131–50.
Reik, Theodor. 1957 (1949). 'The Three Women in a Man's Life'. *Art and Psychoanalysis*, ed. William Phillips. New York: World, 151–64.
Rice, James L. 1994. 'The Dream Mechanism of Tolstoy's *Confession*'. *Tolstoy Studies Journal* 7, 84–8.
Rischin, Ruth. 1989. 'Allegro Tumultuosissimamente: Beethoven in Tolstoy's Fiction'. *In the Shade of the Giant: Essays on Tolstoy*, ed. Hugh McLean (= *California Slavic Studies* 13). Berkeley: University of California Press, 12–60.

Rizzuto, Ana-Maria. 1979. *The Birth of the Living God: A Psychoanalytic Study*. Chicago: University of Chicago Press.
De Roeck, Galina. 1992. 'Tolstoj's *Krejcerova Sonata*: Music as Its Theme and Structure'. *Russian Language Journal* 46, 111–18.
Rogers, Robert. 1991. *Self and Other: Object Relations in Psychoanalysis and Literature*. New York: New York University Press.
Røheim, Géza. 1952. *The Gates of the Dream*. New York: International Universities Press.
Rolland, Romain. 1911. *Tolstoy*, tr. Bernard Miall. London: T. Fisher Unwin.
Romashkevich, Mikhail. 1994. 'Detoubiistvo i nartsissizm'. *Rossiiskii psikhoanaliticheskii vestnik* 3–4, 39–51.
Rothstein, Arnold. 1984. *The Narcissistic Pursuit of Perfection*. New York: International Universities Press.
Rousseau, Jean–Jacques. 1954 (1781). *The Confessions*, tr. J. M. Cohen. Baltimore: Penguin Books.
Rousseau, Jean-Jacques. 1993 (1762). *Émile*, tr. Barbara Foxley. London: J. M. Dent.
Routh, Donald K. and Jean E. Bernholtz. 1991. 'Attachment, Separation, and Phobias'. *Intersections with Attachment*, ed. Jacob L. Gewirtz and William M. Kurtines. Hillsdale, NJ: Lawrence Erlbaum Associates, 295–309.
Roy, Alec. 1983. 'Early Parental Death and Adult Depression'. *Psychological Medicine* 13, 861–5.
Rusanov, G. A. and A. G. Rusanov. 1972. *Vospominaniia o L've Nikolaeviche Tolstom*. Voronezh: Tsentral'no-chernozemnoe knizhnoe izdatel'stvo.
Schapiro, Barbara. 1994. *Literature and the Relational Self*. New York: New York University Press.
Schefski, Harold K. 1978. 'Tolstoj's Case Against Doctors'. *SEEJ* 22, 569–73.
Schefski, Harold K. 1982. 'Tolstoi and the Jews'. *Russian Review* 41, 1–10.
Schefski, Harold K. 1989. 'Tolstoy and Jealousy'. *Irish Slavonic Studies* 10, 17–29.
Sebastian, Joseph. 1995. *God as Feminine: A Dialogue*. Frankfurt am Main: Peter Lang.
Semenova-Tian-Shanskaia, O. P. 1914. *Zhizn' 'Ivana': Ocherki iz byta krest'ian odnoi iz chernozemnykh gubernii*. St. Petersburg: M. M. Stasiulevich.
Sémon, Marie. 1984. *Les femmes dans l'oeuvre de Léon Tolstoi*. Paris: Institut d'Études Slaves.
Sémon, Marie. 1985. 'La nostalgie de Dieu chez Tolstoi'. *Cahiers Léon Tolstoi* 2, 31–40.
Sémon, Marie. 1992. 'La musique de *La Sonate à Kreutzer*'. *Cahiers Léon Tolstoi* 6, 7–19.
Sergeenko, A. 1939. 'Tolstoi o literature i iskusstve. Zapisi V. G. Chertkova i P. A. Sergeenko'. *Literaturnoe nasledstvo* 37–8, 524–65.
Shestov, Leo. 1967 (1929). 'The Last Judgment: Tolstoy's Last Works'. *Tolstoy: A Collection of Critical Essays*, ed. Ralph E. Matlaw. Englewood Cliffs, NJ: Prentice Hall, 157–72.
Shirer, William L. 1994. *Love and Hatred: The Troubled Marriage of Leo and Sonya Tolstoy*. New York: Simon and Schuster.
Shklovskii, Viktor. 1963. *Lev Tolstoi*. Moscow: Molodaia gvardiia.
Siemens, Elena. 1994. 'Seminar on "Toska"'. *Russian Literature* 35, 261–75.

Simmons, Cynthia. 1993. *Their Fathers' Voice: Vassily Aksyonov, Venedikt Erofeev, Eduard Limonov, and Sasha Sokolov*. New York: Peter Lang.

Simmons, Ernest J. 1946. *Leo Tolstoy*. Boston: Little, Brown and Co.

Sinclair, Alison. 1993. *The Deceived Husband: A Kleinian Approach to the Literature of Infidelity*. Oxford: Clarendon Press.

Smith, Timothy W. and Kenneth D. Allred. 1989. 'Major Life Events in Anxiety and Depression'. *Anxiety and Depression: Distinctive and Overlapping Features*, ed. Philip C. Kendall and David Watson. New York: Academic Press, 205–23.

Smith-Rosenberg, Carroll. 1972. 'The Hysterical Woman: Sex Roles and Role Conflict in 19th-Century America'. *Social Research* 39, 652–78.

Smoluchowski, Louise. 1988. *Lev and Sonya: The Story of the Tolstoy Marriage*. New York: Paragon House.

Spence, G. W. 1967. *Tolstoy the Ascetic*. Edinburgh/London: Oliver and Boyd.

Steeves, Paul D. 1983. 'Skoptsy'. *Modern Encyclopedia of Russian and Soviet History*, ed. J. Wieczynski. Gulf Breeze, FL: Academic International Press, vol. 35, 171–5.

Stern, Karl. 1965. *The Flight From Woman*. New York: Noonday Press.

Stites, Richard. 1991. *The Women's Liberation Movement in Russia: Feminism, Nihilism, and Bolshevism, 1860–1930*. Princeton: Princeton University Press.

Stockham, Alice B. 1888. *Tokology: A Book for Every Woman*. Chicago: Alice B. Stockham & Co.

Sukhotina-Tolstaia, T. L. 1987. *Dnevnik*. Moscow: Pravda.

Sytina (Chikhacheva), E. I. 1939. 'Vospominaniia E. I. Sytinoi (Chikhachevoi)'. *Literaturnoe nasledstvo* 37–8, 401–16.

Thorpe, Geoffrey L. and Laurence E. Burns. 1983. *The Agoraphobic Syndrome: Behavioural Approaches to Evaluation and Treatment*. New York: John Wiley & Sons.

Thyer, Bruce A. 1993. 'Childhood Separation Anxiety Disorder and Adult-Onset Agoraphobia: Review of Evidence'. *Anxiety Across the Lifespan: A Developmental Perspective*, ed. Cynthia G. Last. New York: Springer, 128–47.

Timkovskii, N. 1913. *Dusha L. N. Tolstogo*. Moscow: Knigoizdatel'stvo pisatelei.

Tolstaia, A. A. 1978. 'Vospominaniia'. *L. N. Tolstoi v vospominaniiakh sovremennikov*, ed. G. V. Krasnov. Moscow: Khudozhestvennaia literatura, vol. I, 91–104.

Tolstaia, Aleksandra. 1989 (1953). *Otets: Zhizn' L'va Tolstogo*. Moscow: Kniga.

Tolstaia, Sof'ia Andreevna. 1978a. *Dnevniki*. Moscow: Khudozhestvennaia Literatura, 2 vols.

Tolstaia, Sof'ia Andreevna. 1978b. 'Materialy k biografii L. N. Tolstogo i svedeniia o semeistve Tolstykh i preimushchestvenno gr. L'va Nikolaevicha Tolstogo', *L. N. Tolstoi v vospominaniiakh sovremennikov*, ed. G. V. Krasnov. Moscow: Khudozhestvennaia literatura, vol. I, 29–43.

Tolstaia, Sof'ia Andreevna. 1978c. 'Moia zhizn''. *Novyi mir*, no. 8, 34–134.

Tolstoi, Il'ia L'vovich. 1914. *Moi vospominaniia*. Moscow: Tipografiia T-vo I. D. Sytina.

Tolstoi, Il'ia L'vovich. 1969. *Moi vospominaniia*, ed. S. A. Rozanova, O. A. Golinenko, I. A. Pokrovskaia, B. M. Shumova. Moscow: Khudozhestvennaia literatura.

Tolstoi, Lev L'vovich. 1923. *V Iasnoi Poliane: pravda ob ottse i ego zhizni.* Prague: Plamia.

Tolstoi, Lev Nikolaevich. 1928–1964. *Polnoe sobranie sochinenii*, ed V. G. Chertkov *et al.* Moscow-Leningrad: Gosudarstvennoe Izdatel'stvo Khudozhestvennoi Literatury, 90 vols, index vol.

Tolstoi, Lev Nikolaevich. 1991. *Ispoved'. V chem moia vera?* Leningrad: Khudozhestvennaia literatura.

Tolstoi, Serge (Sergei Mikhailovich). 1980. *Tolstoi et les Tolstoi.* Paris: Hermann.

Tolstoi, Sergei L'vovich. 1928a. *Mat' i ded L. N. Tolstogo.* Moscow: Federatsiia.

Tolstoi, Sergei L'vovich. 1928b. 'Muzyka v zhizni L. N. Tolstogo'. *Lev Nikolaevich Tolstoi: Iubileinyi sbornik*, ed. N. N. Gusev. Moscow: Gosudarstvennoe izdatel'stvo, 299–320.

Tolstoi, Sergei L'vovich. 1956. *Ocherki bylogo*, 2nd edition. Moscow: Gosudarstvennoe Izdatel'stvo Khudozhestvennoi Literatury.

Tolstoi, Sergei L'vovich. 1988. 'Iz vospominanii S. L. Tolstogo ob ottse (Publikatsiia N. P. Puzina)'. *Iasnopolianskii sbornik* 1988, ed. K. N. Lomunov. Tula: Priokskoe knizhnoe izdatel'stvo, 161–9.

Tolstoi, Sergei Mikhailovich. 1994 (1989). *Deti Tolstogo*, tr. A. N. Polosina. Tula: Priokskoe knizhnoe izdatel'stvo.

Tolstoy, Alexandra. 1958. 'Tolstoy and Music'. *Russian Review* 17, 258–62.

Tolstoy, Leo. 1937. *Recollections and Essays*, tr. Aylmer Maude. London: Humphrey Milford / Oxford University Press.

Tolstoy, Leo. 1964. *Childhood, Boyhood, Youth*, tr. Rosemary Edmonds. London: Penguin.

Tolstoy, Leo. 1966. *Resurrection*, tr. Rosemary Edmonds. London: Penguin.

Tolstoy, Leo. 1977. *Master and Man and Other Stories*, tr. Paul Foote. London: Penguin.

Tolstoy, Leo. 1983. *The Kreutzer Sonata and Other Stories*, tr. David McDuff. London: Penguin.

Tolstoy, Leo. 1987. *A Confession and Other Religious Writings.* New York: Penguin.

Tolstoy, Leo. 1993. *How Much Land Does a Man Need? and Other Stories*, tr. Ronald Wilks. London: Penguin.

Tolstoy, Leo. 1995. *Anna Karenina*, tr. Louise and Aylmer Maude, George Gibian. New York: W. W. Norton.

Tolstoy, Sophia. 1985. *The Diaries of Sophia Tolstoy*, tr. Cathy Porter. New York: Random House.

Troubetskoy, Wladimir. 1992. 'Tolstoï, Schopenhauer et la musique dans *la Mort d'Ivan Ilitch* et *la Sonate à Kreutzer*'. *Cahiers Léon Tolstoï* 6, 21–28.

Troyat, Henri. 1967 (1965). *Tolstoy*, tr. Nancy Amphoux. New York: Doubleday.

Tyson, Robert L. 1983. 'Some Narcissistic Consequences of Object Loss: A Developmental View'. *Psychoanalytic Quarterly* 52, 205–24.

Vein, Aleksandr. 1995. 'Nervy, chto li, obozhzheny?' *Literaturnaia gazeta* 12 (22 March), p. 11.

Velikovsky, Immanuel. 1937. 'Tolstoy's Kreutzer Sonata and Unconscious Homosexuality'. *Psychoanalytic Review* 24, 18–25.

Vol'fson, Vl. 1910. *Lev Tolstoi o polovoi zhizni i liubvi.* St. Petersburg: M. P. Bogel'man.

Wachtel, Andrew Baruch. 1990. *The Battle for Childhood: Creation of a Russian Myth.* Stanford: Stanford University Press.

Wasiolek, Edward. 1978. *Tolstoy's Major Fiction.* Chicago: University of Chicago Press.

Williams, Gareth. 1995. *Tolstoy's Childhood.* London: Bristol Classical Press.

Wilson, A. N. 1988. *Tolstoy.* New York: W. W. Norton.

Wilson, Edward O. 1975. *Sociobiology: The New Synthesis.* Cambridge: Harvard University Press.

Winnicott, D. W. 1972. *The Maturational Processes and the Facilitating Environment.* London: Hogarth Press.

Wolfenstein, Martha. 1969. 'Loss, Rage, and Repetition'. *Psychoanalytic Study of the Child* 24, 432–60.

Wortman, Richard. 1985. 'Biography and the Russian Intelligentsia'. *Introspection in Biography: The Biographer's Quest for Self-Awareness,* ed. Samuel H. Baron, Carl Pletsch. Hillsdale, NJ: Analytic Press, 157–71.

Zaborova, R. B. 1960. 'Arkhiv M. N. Tolstoi (novye materialy)'. *Iasnopolianskii sbornik: stat'i i materialy,* ed. A. I. Popovkin. Tula: Tul'skoe knizhnoe izdatel'stvo, 166–84.

Zhdanov, V. A. 1961. 'Iz tvorcheskoi istorii "Kreitserovoi sonaty" '. *Tolstoi – khudozhnik,* ed. D. D. Blagoi *et al.* Moscow: Izdatel'stvo Akademii Nauk SSSR, 260–89.

Zhdanov, V. A. 1968. *Ot 'Anny Kareninoi' k 'Voskreseniiu'.* Moscow: Kniga.

Zhdanov, V. A. 1993 (1928). *Liubov' v zhizni L'va Tolstogo.* Moscow: Planeta.

Zhirkevich, A. V. 1939. 'Vstrechi s Tolstym'. *Literaturnoe nasledstvo* 37–8, 417–42.

Zholkovskii, Aleksandr. 1994. 'Topos prostitutsii v literature'. In Aleksandr Zholkovskii and Mikhail Iampol'skii, *Babel'/Babel.* Moscow: Carte Blanche, 317–68.

Zholkovskii, Aleksandr. 1995. *Inventsii.* Moscow: Gendal'f.

Zholkovsky, Alexander. 1994a. 'How a Russian Maupassant Was Made in Odessa and Yasnaya Polyana: Isaak Babel' and the Tolstoy Legacy'. *Slavic Review* 53, 571–93.

Zholkovsky, Alexander. 1994b. *Text counter Text: Rereadings in Russian Literary History.* Stanford: Stanford University Press.

Ziabrev, A. T. 1915. 'Vospominaniia O L. N. Tolstom Krest'ianina Iasnoi Poliany A. T. Ziabreva'. *Ezhemesiachnyi zhurnal,* nos. 8 (74–81), 9–10 (345–66), 11 (139–58).

Ziabrev, V. P. 1960 (1911). 'Vospominaniia O L. N. Tolstom'. *Vospominaniia iasnopolianskikh krest'ian o L. N. Tolstom,* ed. V. A. Zhdanov. Tula: Tul'skoe knizhnoe izdatel'stvo, 177–97.

Ziabrev, E. T. 1960 (1908–11). 'Vospominaniia O L. N. Tolstom'. *Vospominaniia iasnopolianskikh krest'ian o L. N. Tolstom,* ed. V. A. Zhdanov. Tula: Tul'skoe knizhnoe izdatel'stvo, 213–71.

Zweers, Alexander F. 1971. *Grown-up Narrator and Childlike Hero: An Analysis of the Literary Devices Employed in Tolstoj's Trilogy Childhood, Boyhood and Youth.* The Hague: Mouton.

Index